Straight to POD — set up with Rowe. Can be made live immediately.

D1723908

RETHINKING POWER, INSTITUTIONS AND IDEAS IN WORLD POLITICS

The study of international relations has traditionally been dominated by Western ideas and practices, and marginalized the voice and experiences of the non-Western states and societies. As the world moves to a "post-Western" era, it is imperative that the field of IR acquires a more global meaning and relevance.

Drawing together the work of renowned scholar Amitav Acharya and framed by a new introduction and conclusion written for the volume, this book exposes the narrow meaning currently attached to some of the key concepts and ideas in IR, and calls for alternative and broader understandings of them. The need for recasting the discipline has motivated and undergirded Acharya's own scholarship since his entry into the field over three decades ago. This book reflects his own engagement, quarrels and compromise and concludes with suggestions for new pathways to a Global IR – a forward-looking and inclusive enterprise that is reflective of the multiple and global heritage of IR in a changing and interconnected world.

This is essential reading for anyone who is concerned about the history, development and future of international relations and international relations theory.

Amitav Acharya is the UNESCO Chair in Transnational Challenges and Governance and Chair of the ASEAN Studies Center at the School of International Service, American University, Washington, D.C.

He was Professor of Global Governance at the University of Bristol, Professor of International Relations at York University, Toronto, the Nelson Mandela Visiting Professor of International Relations at Rhodes University, South Africa, Fellow of the Harvard University Asia Center, Fellow of Harvard's John F. Kennedy School of Government, and Christensen Fellow at St Catherine's College, Oxford.

"Amitav Acharya is not only the leading non-Western scholar of IR theory in the United States, he is one of the most innovative scholars working in the field. What makes him stand out among the theoretically oriented scholars in the field is the deductive nature of his theorizing that is informed by his own high quality empirical research. He is one of the very few scholars of IR who are equally comfortable doing empirical research as well as theorizing, indeed who consider both these enterprises as two sides of the same coin."

Mohammed Ayoob, University Distinguished Professor of International Relations, Michigan State University, USA.

"At a time when non-Western states are playing an increasingly prominent role in world affairs, Amitav Acharya asks the timely question: to what extent are traditional international relations approaches capable of transcending cultural boundaries and explaining behavior in non-Western systems? He argues that theories home grown in the Global South are often more adept at tapping into these new realities. His own insightful theoretical contributions provide strong evidence to back up this claim, making this book a necessary read."

Jack Snyder, Robert and Renée Belfer Professor of International Relations, Columbia University, USA.

RETHINKING POWER, INSTITUTIONS AND IDEAS IN WORLD POLITICS

Whose IR?

Amitav Acharya

Routledge
Taylor & Francis Group

LONDON AND NEW YORK

First published 2014
by Routledge
2 Park Square, Milton Park, Abingdon, Oxon OX14 4RN

and by Routledge
711 Third Avenue, New York, NY 10017

Routledge is an imprint of the Taylor & Francis Group, an informa business

© 2014 Amitav Acharya

The right of Amitav Acharya to be identified as author of
this work has been asserted by him in accordance with the
Copyright, Designs and Patent Act 1988.

All rights reserved. No part of this book may be reprinted or reproduced
or utilised in any form or by any electronic, mechanical, or other means,
now known or hereafter invented, including photocopying and recording,
or in any information storage or retrieval system, without permission in
writing from the publishers.

Trademark notice: Product or corporate names may be trademarks or
registered trademarks, and are used only for identification and
explanation without intent to infringe.

British Library Cataloguing in Publication Data
A catalogue record for this book is available from the British Library

Library of Congress Cataloging in Publication Data
Acharya, Amitav
    Rethinking power, institutions and ideas in world politics : whose IR? / Amitav Acharya.
    pages cm
    Includes bibliographical references and index.
    1. International relations.   2. World politics.   I. Title.
    JZ1305.A24 2013
    327.101—dc23
    2013018372

ISBN: 978–0–415–70675–9 (hbk)
ISBN: 978–0–415–70674–2 (pbk)
ISBN: 978–1–315–88534–6 (ebk)

Typeset in Bembo
by Swales & Willis Ltd, Exeter, Devon

CONTENTS

Author's note   vii

Introduction   1

PART I
IR theory and its discontents   **21**

1   International relations theories and Western dominance:
    reassessing the foundations of international order   23

2   Dialogue and discovery: in search of international relations
    theories beyond the West   44

3   Comparative regionalism: a field whose time has come?   74

PART II
Power, intervention and global disorders   **87**

4   The Cold War as "long peace" revisited   89

5   State sovereignty after 9/11: disorganized hypocrisy   116

PART III
Institutions, autonomy and regional orders   **139**

6   Multilateralism: beyond hegemony and without victory   141

7   The contested regional architecture of world politics   159

PART IV
Ideas, agency and normative cultures   **181**

8   How ideas spread: whose norms matter? Norm localization and
    institutional change in Asian regionalism   183

9   Norm subsidiarity and regional orders: sovereignty, regionalism
    and rule-making in the Third World   217

Conclusion: towards a global IR? Pathways and pitfalls   250

Index   255

AUTHOR'S NOTE

With very few exceptions, I have chosen not to update the texts as they were writ-ten at the time of their original presentation or publication, although some of the chapters in this volume are previous, often longer draft versions of the text before they were edited for publication.

I am grateful to Nicola Parkin at Routledge for her strong support for this book idea, Peter Harris at Routledge for his excellent handling of the production of the volume, Tamsin Ballard of Swales & Willis Ltd for her editorial work on the volume, and Allan Layug at for his assistance in proofreading the manuscript.

I thank two reviewers for their invaluable comments and suggestions for improv-ing the volume.

INTRODUCTION[1]

Since its relatively recent and vaguely defined origins,[2] International Relations (IR) has seen endless cycles of debates and compromises. The earlier debates were known as "inter-paradigm," and pitted idealists against realists, traditionalists against behaviouralists ("classical" versus "scientific"), and positivists against post-positivists.[3] More recent debates have been between neorealists and neo-liberals[4] and between rationalists and constructivists, although these have resulted in compromises (the neo-neo and rationalist-constructivist syntheses). Whatever the contribution of these debates to the progress of IR, they have by and large left out the ideas, voices and experiences of the non-Western world. The aim of this book is not to start a new grand debate, and certainly not to make the pitch for a new theory of IR. Rather, the intent here is to underscore the long-term and ethnocentric neglect of the non-Western world in IR theory, the limitations and distortions that this inflicts on our understanding of world politics as a whole, and to make the case for a more inclusive, truly global IR.

I attempt to do so with reference to the dominant understandings of three of the most important concepts in the study of IR: *power, institutions* and *ideas*. Roughly, they correspond with the central tenets of realism, liberalism and constructivism, the three mainstream theories that have dominated the study of international relations in our time. A key purpose of this book, mostly a collection of published and unpublished essays and lectures from the past two decades, is to examine how relevant are these concepts in understanding the positions and roles of actors in the world beyond the West. This leads to the other major goal of this book, to identity and explore alternative understandings that can expand the meanings of power, institutions and ideas in the broader and more inclusive context of world politics.

While the discipline known as international relations offers much to students and scholars from the non-Western world, including me personally, it has been unable to realize its full potential due to a persisting tendency to privilege the West vis-à-vis the rest. While this tendency was untenable before, it is even less so today. This is not just or mainly due to the global power shift or the "rise of the rest," as some would fashionably put it. That claim itself can be contested, and carries its own biases and distortions. More importantly, thanks to the transport and communication revolution, it has become increasingly indefensible for scholars of IR not to be aware of the world out there, and develop at least a healthy curiosity for understanding the predicament and perspectives of those actors who inhabit the world beyond the West. This becomes all the more imperative if one recognizes three other facts: (a) the large majority of the member-states of the international system are "non-Western" and belong to the "post-colonial" category; (b) the large majority of conflicts, both inter-state and intra-state, since World War II have taken place in this post-colonial space even though Western powers have been involved in several of them such as Vietnam and Angola; and (c) the large majority of such conflicts have had their origins, both in terms of causes and beginnings in the domestic sphere — the typical arena of conflicts in early stages of state-making — although several of them have taken on inter-state dimensions as well.[5]

The changing and broader context of the study of world politics has become increasingly evident to IR scholars in recent years. But the need for recasting the discipline has motivated and undergirded my own scholarship from the very beginning of my own entry into the field some three decades ago. To some extent therefore, this book reflects my own engagement, quarrels and compromises, with the discipline that we have called, mistakenly in my view, international relations, or IR.

IR theory and its discontents

Although Stanley Hoffmann once described international relations as an "American social science,"[6] it is better described as a "Western," or at least a Euro-American project, with its theory beholden largely to the power and purpose of the West. This is not to say that Western IR theories have ignored non-Western experience entirely. As Jack Snyder points out, it is one thing to claim that "Western IR theories have underplayed the developing world in the subject matters that shaped the evolution of the core of their theories," and quite another to claim that "Western IR theories are substantively alien to the non-Western experience." The latter is at best "an empirical question."[7] I agree with Snyder and identify mainly with the former claim. But I also believe that the two issues are not unrelated. The former shapes the latter. Because the theories are mainly reflective of Western historical trajectories and intellectual traditions, they tend to analyse and incorporate the non-Western experience, when they are taken into consideration from a mainly ethnocentric prism, combining a tendency to assume the superiority of one's own beliefs and systems over that of others and presume one's own background and experience as the right template for judging others. When undertaken, these endeavours have rarely taken into account the distinctive, varied and contrasting experiences of the non-Western world. Had the latter been factored in, I believe they might have, in many instances including those discussed in the different chapters of this book, rendered the established generalizations of IR theory about power, institutions and ideas less universal than claimed by their proponents.

While IR in general suffers from a dose of Westerncentrism, its theory is of particular concern. A word about the meaning of theory is necessary here. In my earlier work with Buzan, we took note, at the risk of some oversimplification, of the "the dichotomy that obtains between the hard positivist understanding of theory which dominates in the US, and the softer reflectivist understanding of theory found more widely in Europe." Whereas the American tradition demands that theory "sets out and explains the relations between causes and effects" and that "theory should contain – or be able to generate – testable hypotheses of a causal nature," the European understanding takes as theory "anything that organises a field systematically, structures questions and establishes a coherent and rigorous set of interrelated concepts and categories."[8] We also counted as a contribution to theory any work that meets any one of three conditions: (1) acknowledgement by others in the IR community as being theory, (2) self-identification as theory by its creators themselves, and (3) "a systematic attempt to generalize about the subject matter of IR."[9] My own assumption here is that the way theory is understood in most parts of the non-Western world is closer to the European understanding than the American one, although it can be understood in both ways. Thus, Yaqin Qin from China defines theory as "a system of ideas . . . a system of generalizations, able to account for facts and associated with practice," and theoretical investigation as "an attempt to find patterns and group things together into sets and classes . . .,"[10] while Takashi Inoguchi of Japan views theory as, among other things, "a set of assumptions and premises that are empirically verifiable," and "a self-contained research program."[11] He also notes the "relatively weak tradition of positivistic hypothesis testing in social science and the relatively strong tradition of descriptive work" in Japan.[12]

IR theory is of course not a monolith, and that some theorists are more sensitive to the non-Western ideas, voices and experiences than others. Moreover, I am acutely conscious of the fact that the West is not a homogenous construct, nor can one meaningfully speak of a non-Western world,[13] any more than one could speak of the Third World or the Global South. But the diversity of the units and inhabitants of these categories should not blind us to the fact that their histories, experiences, ideas and beliefs have received scant recognition in the literature on international relations. Together, these essays both identify the neglect of non-Western international relations and offer arguments about how this gap can be best addressed, with the help of altered assumptions about agency and structure, a greater focus on comparative regionalism, the emphasis on a social constructivist epistemology, and deductive approaches to theory-building.

With these clarifications and caveats, let me outline the key parts of the books. Chapters 1 to 3 deal with the theoretical perspectives that frame this book. In chapter 1, I elaborate on the dimensions of Western dominance that this book is largely about, including autocentrism, false universalism, disjuncture, and agency denial. It then examines how these dimensions and tendencies have informed the understanding and conceptualization of international order, including sovereignty, great power management, institutions and values. I conclude this chapter with an analysis of the *The Expansion of International Society, the* foundational text of the English School. Although I do not include it as a mainstream theory, and although the English School was to some degree a pioneer in trying to analyse the place of the non-Western world in the evolving international order, it was especially susceptible to the different elements of Western dominance I have identified above. This included ethnocentrism (autocentrism) and false universalism, especially in assuming that the international system is the European states-system writ large. It glossed over the role of imperialism, racism and militarism in this expansion and "universalization" of Europe. It gave scant acknowledgement to the role of non-Western states in the construction of the post-War international order, and to the variations in the diffusion of fundamental institutions such as sovereignty and security caused by that role. While the more recent contributions to the English School have addressed some of these biases, getting a sense of the early views of the English School serves as a powerful reminder of the Western-centric metanarrative that underscores a good deal of the literature on international relations today.

Although scholars of international relations increasingly realize that their discipline, including its theories and methods, often neglect voices and experiences outside of the West, they have as yet paid insufficient attention to how we address this problem and move the discipline forward. While some question whether "Western" and "non-Western" (or "post-Western") are useful labels, there are also other perspectives, including those who believe in the adequacy of existing theories and approaches, those who argue for particular national "schools" of IR, and those who dismiss recent efforts to broaden IR theory as "mimicry" in terms of their epistemological underpinnings. After reviewing these debates, chapter 2 identifies some avenues for further research with a view to bring out the global heritage of IR. These include, among other things, paying greater attention to the genealogy of international systems, the diversity of regionalisms and regional worlds, the integration of area studies with international relations, people-centric approaches to IR, security and development, and the agency role of non-Western ideas and actors in building global order.[14] I also argue in this chapter for broadening the epistemology of international relations theory with the help of non-Western philosophies such as Hinduism and Buddhism. This is necessary not only to end the neglect of religion in IR theory, but also to build different and alternative theories which originate from non-Western contexts and experiences.

Among the most important avenues for redefining, deepening and extending IR theory is regionalism, one of my enduring interests and indeed my original and still among the most important entry point into the theoretical debates in IR. Hence its origins and evolution deserves special reflection. A major argument that informs this book is my belief that comparative studies of regional dynamics and regionalism are a good way to bridge the gap between Westerncentric IR theory and the experience of the non-Western world. Yet, this exercise must also acknowledge the multiple and global heritage of regionalism. Although regionalism had emerged as a distinctive field of study from the 1950s, the indisputable focus of theoretical and empirical work in this area has been Western European regionalism, from the beginning as the European Coal and Steel Community to its culmination as the European Union in the early 1990s. Moreover, the application of the West European and North Atlantic integration model to Third World – be it federalism, functionalism, neo-functionalism or transactionalism – has been deeply problematic, as these theories, derived largely from the West European experience, failed to find institutional footholds in the Third World. This is changing, however, especially with the contribution of the "new regionalism" approach, as discussed in chapter 3, as well as growing interest in the study of regionalism in different parts of the world. As chapter 3 shows, there have emerged a variety of regionalisms and regional institutions outside Europe which call for a more differentiated view of the purposes and contributions of regionalism, thereby making the field of comparative regionalism a much broader and richer field than ever before.

The rest of the book is organized along three main sections corresponding to its three main themes: power, institutions and ideas. The division is not neat, but overlapping, as might be expected in the real world of world politics. The following provides a brief overview of the three sections.

Power, intervention and global disorders

I entered the field of IR when the Cold War was still raging, with its end nowhere in sight, although it would end sooner than any IR theory or theorist had anticipated. Indeed one school of IR thought that was gaining prominence in the 1980s, namely, neorealism (or structural realism) held that bipolarity would go on for a while. The most renowned of the neorealists, Kenneth Waltz, had found causal arguments to support his claim that bipolar systems like the Cold War are more stable than multipolar ones.[15]

This was my first, and in many ways still the most depressing, encounter with IR theory, even though neorealism counts only as only one of its strands, albeit a very influential one. But even before I came to hear of neorealism, I was already uncomfortable with central positioning of power, especially material power defined in terms of military and economic capabilities, in the realist view of international relations.

Like many new entrants to the field in the 1980s, I learnt my first lessons in international relations from Hans Morgenthau's *Politics among Nations*, first published in 1948. Many IR scholars may not realize that in India and other non-Western countries (China would be another one, as I was to find out later) *Politics Among Nations* was not viewed as a realist treatise, to be read along with other *Liberal*, or *Marxist* readings (constructivism did not exist then) but as a general textbook of IR. It was actually the only textbook that I knew during my student days in India. And for me the defining message of that book was the association of international politics with power politics. "The aspiration for power being the distinguishing element of international politics, as of all politics, international politics is of necessity power politics."[16] I felt a fundamental discomfort with the idea that states always define their interests mainly in terms of power, especially if power was defined as the coercive power over others based on superior material capabilities. As a novice to the field, I almost reflexively felt that this assertion could not always be valid. I should stress that there have since been reinterpretations of Morgenthau, and these have pointed to a broader and more nuanced view of power and power politics in Morgenthau's classic text.[17] But this is beside my point here; I am talking of my understanding of the principal message of that book during my very first brush with international relations theory. I am confident that this would have been the same for many other newcomers to international relations theory – such as those in China where Morgenthau's text was also widely used. That impression was reinforced by the second of his six principles of political realism, which reads: "The main signpost that helps political realism to find its way through the landscape of international politics is the concept of interest defined in terms of power."[18] Even now when I am more familiar and comfortable with the subtleties in Morgenthau's theory, or realism more generally, and realize that the position of Morgenthau and other realists is subject to different interpretations,[19] the idea that all international politics is at its most basic power politics seems unconvincing to me. While some states may define interest as power and seek power over others some of the time, surely not all states do it all the time. This reaction might partly stem from my own upbringing. To someone growing up in an India that was still under the spell of the Nehruvian worldview that firmly rejected power politics and Cold War alliances in favour of a *moralpolitik* (to be discussed further in chapter 9) Morgenthau's dictum appeared incredible to say the least. I have never fully overcome that sense of discomfort, even though I (as well as much of the Indian elite opinion) have moved past our earlier enchantment with the Nehruvian worldview. This rejection would shape my theoretical stance for the future: including my attraction to liberal internationalism at first and constructivism later. More importantly, I learnt never to trust assertions which its proponent claimed to be "universally valid." The fundamental lesson here is the limits of a particular set of assertions about world politics that is held by one proponent in one time and space to be sensible and universally valid, but which would seem to another person in a different time and space, to be parochial and dangerously self-fulfilling.

But Morgenthau was and is not a total loss for me. I readily agree with, and strongly endorse, his principle number five: "Political realism refuses to identify the moral aspirations of a particular nation with the moral laws that govern the universe."[20] To me this is indeed the most "universally valid" message in Morgenthau's theory of international relations, and in classical realism to the extent it identifies with him. I came to like it even more as I got more familiar with the excesses of US foreign policy in subsequent years, from the Cold War to the War on Terror, justified on ethical and moral grounds, a major instance of which, the War on Terror, is discussed in chapter 5.

My most serious quarrel with realism turned out to be not with Morgenthau's classical realism, but with Waltz's structural (or neo-) realism that became prominent after the publication in 1979 of his *Theory of International Politics*. Unlike classical realists, neorealism holds that international politics is shaped not by human nature but by the distribution of power, e.g. bipolarity and multipolarity. And even before the publication of his 1979 book, Waltz had advanced a claim that bipolar systems had properties that would make them more stable than multipolar ones, like Europe before World War II.[21]

Yet, the major features of the Cold War international system were not only the bipolar distribution of power, but also the frequency and pervasiveness of superpower intervention, especially in the Third World. To anyone familiar with security issues in the Third World (discussed in chapter 4), the two were closely linked. Competitive superpower intervention was a primary contributing factor, if not always the cause, behind a good number of regional conflicts worldwide. So it was really beyond me how any theory could equate the bipolarity with stability or peace.

IR theory, including its realist and liberal strands, is at best ambiguous about the necessity and morality of great power intervention in the Third World. To be sure, intervention is not a new issue in world politics, and there had already been a long tradition of thinking about intervention in political thought so that "no serious student of the subject can fail to feel that intervention is sometimes justifiable."[22] But the Cold War was a period of intervention so pervasive that Hedley Bull described "the interventionary behaviour of the two superpowers" as an "endemic and 'structural'" feature of the post-War international system.[23] Neorealist theory appeared to take this logic much further, representing it as a mechanism of stability. Thus it would view the Cold War as a period of "long peace."[24] Yet, as chapter 4 discusses, the Cold War was also a period of rampant superpower intervention, which led to plenty of violence and bloodshed, thereby negating neorealist thought that associates superpower interventionism with stability and order.

The end of the Cold War was not immediately followed by multipolarity, as was generally anticipated, but by a "unipolar moment," with the United States as the world's sole superpower. While chapter 4 deals with the core issue of power and intervention under bipolarity, chapter 5 focuses on the central issue of power and intervention under the unipolar moment: the War on Terror. While in chapter 4, I take on the neorealist view of the polarity–stability nexus, in chapter 5, I question the most well-known realist perspective on state sovereignty. While the former was a narrow and ethnocentric view of stability during the Cold War, at issue in the latter chapter is the self-serving view of sovereignty adopted by the US in the War on Terror.

The 9/11 tragedy marked a critical and curious turning point in the evolving debate over the meaning of sovereignty and the purposes of intervention. In response, the George W. Bush administration proposed a strategic doctrine of "selective sovereignty" that would legitimize intervention in states that are accused of supporting terrorism or acquiring weapons of mass destruction, or both (as Saddam Hussein's Iraq was accused of). This new rationale for intervention was paradoxically justified as a means of ensuring a "well-ordered world of sovereign states," which had been imperilled by transnational terrorist networks. Moreover, the Bush administration linked it to the evolving idea of humanitarian intervention, which in its view had already created a justifiable basis for redefining sovereignty. Yet, this rationalization was palpably self-serving. The rationale for intervention for humanitarian reasons had little to do with that for the War on Terror and the two could not be convincingly conflated. The Bush Doctrine and the War on Terror marked a forceful return on the part of the United States, which enjoyed as close to a global preponderance of power as any nation has ever done in history (perhaps with the exception of the Roman Empire at its heyday, to which the US was often compared), to unilateralism and parochially defined self-interest. This might have vindicated Morgenthau's fifth principle, but it was far from clear whether power could trump legitimacy in international relations.

Moreover, the Bush Doctrine posed a frontal and ironic challenge to the preeminent realist interpretation of sovereignty in international relations, advanced by Stephen Krasner in his 1999 book *Sovereignty: Organized Hypocrisy*.[25] For Krasner, sovereignty is a prime example of a fundamental norm that persists despite its frequent violations – i.e. violations that are motivated by considerations of power rather than commitments to some principles, and violations that are often tolerated and accepted by the international community. Yet, this perspective understates the normative appeal of sovereignty in the post-colonial states, discussed in chapter 9, when sovereignty and non-intervention were seen as a bulwark against colonialism and neocolonialism. Moreover, contrary to the "organized hypocrisy" thesis, it would be misleading to describe the international response to the invasion of Iraq as tolerance or acquiescence, given the widespread questioning of the legitimacy of that action. The Bush administration's attempt to justify its war on Iraq, such as protecting the human rights of the Iraqis, were clearly rebuffed by most of the world as a facade masking naked geopolitical and ideological underpinnings of the invasion. Hence, the challenge to sovereignty posed by the War on Terror is better described as a form of "disorganized hypocrisy" because it overlooked the differing degrees of legitimacy involved in principled and multilaterally organized violations that protect human security and violations that are unilateral and aimed at protecting national geopolitical objectives.

The foregoing captures my disagreements with the realist/neorealist perspectives over two of the core concepts of IR theory: power and sovereignty.[26] First, while the distribution of power in its traditional sense matters, claims about its positive ordering function can be narrowly conceptualized and overstated. Viewed in the non-Western context, bipolarity was not a period of global order, and the Cold War was no "long peace." They permitted and even encouraged a great deal of regional disorder. Second, material power is by itself not a sufficient determinant of stability and order. Its impact is mediated by, and subject to, the legitimation functions of institutions and norms. The War on Terror launched by the US after 9/11, especially the invasion of Iraq, aroused worldwide misgivings, including from the allies of the US, and was militarily and politically costly to the US because it did not have the authority from the UN Security Council, and was seen as a violation of both the existing (non-intervention) and emerging (R2P) international norms. Hence, the combination of raw power and intervention that marked not only the Cold War bipolarity, but also the immediate post-Cold War unipolar moment in the form of the War on Terror, contributed not to order, but to global disorders. Associating them with stability not only raises disturbing normative questions about the functions of IR theory, but also about IR theory's dissociation with, and its contribution to the marginalization of, the non-Western world.

Institutions, autonomy and regional orders

The debate among neorealists and neoliberals concerning the role of international institutions in world politics that raged in the 1980s was a remarkably parochial affair. The institution-building and dynamics in the Third World, the rationale and functions of Third World regional institutions, and the role of Third World states to the making of the global institutional order, found little mention in the literature on regime theory and neoliberal institutionalism. In general, I have had little trouble accepting the liberalism view that institutions matter in world politics and are a major force for cooperation and peace. But the major, unanswered question would be: whose institutions matter?

A distinctive aspect of the theoretical literature on the institution of multilateralism has been its close association with power, especially hegemonic power. This has led to a remarkably top-down conception of their creation and contribution. The conceptualization of post-war global multilateralism suffered from a robust and persisting Americanocentrism, as evident in the conceptualization of multilateralism as the product of *American* hegemony, rather than American *hegemony*, made popular by Ruggie's important edited volume *Multilateralism Matters*. This to me seriously obscured the role of inclusive and cooperative regional institutions in the Third World that operated either independent of, or in resistance to, American power but still contributed to multilateral principles and institutions.

The traditional conceptualization of multilateralism by liberal institutionalist theory has been under challenge. That version was too beholden to the state, American power and purpose, Western leadership, and the global level of interactions. What is coming in their place is as yet indeterminate, but I propose one possible direction, *post-hegemonic multilateralism*. Chapter 6 begins by examining the dominant version in the post-World War II period, which I call hegemonic multilateralism. It continues by analysing three principal challenges: civil society, emerging powers, and regionalism. Despite their limitations, they could redefine the residual elements of the multilateral order developed under American hegemony. While some liberal protagonists hope and foresee that the old multilateralism might outlive US power, I argue that the challenges are strong enough to make the prospects for change greater than commonly thought. Moreover, these challenges could also form the basis for a new post-hegemonic multilateralism in international relations.

I have also been disappointed with the tendency in the international relations theoretical literature to study institutional dynamics mainly in terms of global multilateral institutions or regional institutions in or dealing with European affairs, such as the Concert of Europe, the EU at various stages of its evolution, and NATO. While the conceptualization of multilateralism has been Americanocentric, regionalism, as I have argued in chapter 3, has been shaped by a heavy dose of Eurocentrism. But another feature of the literature on regionalism is its emphasis on the role of structural power. In keeping with a central theme of the previous chapters, chapter 7 – a review essay featuring two of the most important books of regional orders to be published in recent years[27] – takes issue with the perspectives that privilege power in the creation and maintenance of regional institutions. While power does matter, resistance to power may matter even more in the construction of regional orders. While the study of regionalism can be advanced by challenging the static and materialist conception of regions, and by offering – as the two books do – coherent frameworks for the comparative studies of regions, the relationship between regions and hegemons remain under-theorized and unclear, leading them to neglect the issue of the relative autonomy of regions. This chapter suggests some avenues for further research to address these gaps. One concerns variations in the design of regional institutions especially between European and non-European institutions, and their effect on cooperation. It also suggests that scholars of regions and regional security should pay attention to the indigenous construction of regions, rather than simply viewing them as byproducts of external geopolitical currents or great power interactions.

My overall argument with liberal and neoliberal institutionalism concerns the disjuncture that exists between its universalist claims and the regional realities in the non-Western world. First, an important part of the role that international institutions and multilateralism play in world politics comes from regionalism. Hence, regional institution-building should not be relegated to being the poor cousin of global-level multilateralism. The juxtaposition between regionalism and multilateralism can be overstated. The former can be a building bloc of the latter.

Second, there is no one or standard model for regional institutionalization. The purposes and modalities of the institutions of multilateralism and regionalism vary, e.g. regime security in the developing world versus national security in the West. Institutions can vary widely in terms of the degree of formalization and legalization; regional bodies in the non-Western world such as ASEAN have been less legalistic or bureaucratized than those in Europe or the transatlantic arena. Yet, they cannot be dismissed as inconsequential because they had exercised a strong normative influence. Moreover, institutionalist theory should not assume that a shared liberal-democratic politics is a precondition for effective institutionalization and peace among states. Peaceful change, including creation of pluralistic security communities can grow out of shared vulnerabilities and goals other than those associated with liberal democracy, such as a common commitment to development and stability.[28] Hence, despite a widespread tendency to use the West European integration experience and record as the quintessential benchmark for successful regionalism, regionalism has a multiple and global heritage and there are plenty of differences between the EU approach to regional integration and the catalysts and patterns of regional cooperation in the non-Western world. The former cannot serve as a model for the latter.

Third, institutions do not always reflect great power interests or leadership but may have been created with a view to challenge or socialize it. Institutions, especially at the regional level, can resist and redefine liberal claims about power and values that reflect a largely Western understanding and experience. Some institutions may seek an autonomous space from great power influence. Even in cases where when a great power gets involved, it is not always as the creator but also as a follower, not as the pre-eminent socializer, but as the socializee. In Asia, a host of institutions built around ASEAN have evolved contrary to the hegemonic institutionalism model, in the sense that while having multiple great powers, including the US, in their membership, they are "led" by the region's weaker states. Hence, while power matters, resistance to and the socialization of power may matter even more in the institutional dynamics of world politics. Examples of such resistance and socialization dynamics can be found in chapter 7.

Hence, the dominant narrative of multilateralism as a unique product of *American* hegemony, and created *after victory*, on terms essentially laid down by the hegemonic power, might seem valid in a certain time and context, but it does not capture the wide varieties of multilateralism and cooperative institution-building out there or that can be made possible. And that narrative needs a significant dose of updating in view of the changed and changing landscape of actors and issues in world politics. Multilateralism can be created, modified and reinvented "without victory" or "beyond hegemony." To enhance its explanatory power and universalist aspirations, institutionalist theories must broaden their scope on investigation, and pay more attention to the variations in the purposes, patterns and outcomes of regionalism and multilateralism, particularly the varieties of multilateralism and regionalism in the non-Western world.

Ideas, agency and normative cultures

In the 1990s, the debate between rationalism and constructivism replaced the neo-realist–neoliberal debate as the major point of contention in international relations theory.[29] When I first encountered it, I saw in constructivism a clear potential to secure greater recognition for the agency of non-Western actors. Lacking in material power, weak states often resort to normative action and agency to realize a measure of autonomy and reshape power politics. I was reminded of Donald Puchala's argument that for "Third World countries, ideas and ideologies are far more important" than power or wealth, because their powerlessness amidst "unequal distribution of the world's wealth" are "constants."[30] Constructivism also allows the possibility of cooperation in the absence of strong formalistic and legalistic institutions. Its main causal mechanisms, ideas and norms, can be diffused and shared with or without formal organizations with large, permanent bureaucracies, like the European Union.[31]

Indeed, my own work using constructivism has focused on demonstrating that normative purpose may lead to the emergence and endurance of institutions without great power sponsorship but through the leadership of weak states. But its challenge to the rationalism of neorealism and neoliberalism notwithstanding, constructivism could not completely rise above their penchant for ignoring the agency of non-Western actors. I have been especially uncomfortable with the theory's tendency to privilege the moral cosmopolitanism of Western transnational actors in explaining norm diffusion in world politics. It is as if all the big ideas come from the West, transmitted mainly by Western transnational movements, with the non-Western actors as passive recipients. Both the chapters in this section deal with the diffusion of ideas and norms in world politics, but depart significantly from the standard early approaches of constructivism to the study of norm dynamics and bring into sharp focus the agency of local, less powerful actors in the non-Western world. The focus of these chapters is not whether ideas matter, which has hitherto preoccupied the rationalist-constructivist "debate," but *whose ideas matter.*

Early constructivist scholarship on norm dynamics was dominated by "hard" cases of moral transformation in which "good" global norms prevailed over the "bad" local beliefs and practices. But many local beliefs are themselves part of a legitimate normative order, which offers feedback and conditions the acceptance of foreign norms. Going beyond the static notion of congruence, chapter 8 proposes a model of normative change which describes how local actors, even when faced with opportunities for enhancing their authority and legitimacy through the borrowing of universal norms, reconstruct the latter to ensure a proper fit with their cognitive priors and identities. Congruence building thus becomes the key to compliance, and localization, and not just wholesale acceptance or rejection, settles normative contestation. Comparing two cases of normative contestation in Asia, cooperative security and humanitarian intervention, this chapter shows that the variation in their degree of acceptance could be explained by the relative scope for local choice and constitutive localization.

While chapter 8 is concerned with offering an agency oriented explanation of how global norms are diffused to the local level, chapter 9 does the reverse, by offering a similar framework for studying the diffusion of locally constructed norms to the transnational and global level. I illustrate this with the help of the diffusion of sovereignty norms. I look at why and how Third World states and regions create rules to regulate relationships among them and with the outside world. It develops and tests a new conceptual tool, norm subsidiarity, which concerns the process whereby local actors create rules with a view to preserving their autonomy from dominance, neglect, violation, or abuse by more powerful central actors. After a theoretical discussion of the definition, motivations and effects of norm subsidiarity, the chapter offers a case study of normative action against Cold War alliances (especially South East Asia Treaty Organization) by a group of Third World leaders led by India's Jawaharlal Nehru at the Bandung Asia–Africa Conference in 1955. It then offers examples from Latin America, the Middle East and Africa to highlight the practice of norm subsidiarity. The theory and practice of norm subsidiarity shed more light on the agency role of Third World countries in world politics.[32]

Both localization and subsidiarity stress the agency of local actors, the importance of cognitive priors, and the need to build congruence between existing and emerging norms. Both recognize that normative change in most cases is evolutionary, not a one-step transformation, i.e. shaming should be pursued alongside saving face, and should not be an end in itself. The idea of norm subsidiarity fills a void in IR theory about norm creation and propagation from the Third World or the Global South.

Overall, chapters 8 and 9 advance my view that normative change in world politics is not a one-way street in which good global norms promoted mainly by Western transnational norm entrepreneurs displace bad local ideas, norms and practices in the non-Western world. This discursive undercurrent in earlier constructivist theories of norm dynamics, which also mirrors earlier assumptions of the English School and liberalism, need to be replaced with a broader perspective that views norms constructed at different locations and by varieties of agents in terms of a dynamic process of contestation, congruence-building and circulation. The circulation can be understood as a process of continuous feedback: global–local, North–South, East–West. I also argue that constructivism needs to acknowledge the multiple and global heritage of norms, and respect the diversity of *normative cultures*[33] in world politics and different forms and sites of agency involved in the spread of ideas and the construction of political and security communities.[34]

Conclusions, clarifications and confessions

I do not pretend here to present a theory of world politics. Most of the chapters in this book, and my other writings related to these chapters (and listed in the references), were written on different occasions and came about independently of each other. But I do believe that they reflect an underlying common set of thematic interests and approaches, and it is possible to draw from them some generalizations about world politics. Below I offer seven of them.

1. Material power matters but resistance to power also matters in shaping regional and world order (chapters 6 and 7). Acceptance of hegemony or great power primacy is not a natural or *voluntary* response to the absence of world government.
2. The distribution of material power is by itself not a sufficient condition of stability and order. Its impact is subject to the de/legitimizing role of institutions, values and norms, including those of less materially powerful actors (chapters 4 and 5).
3   Institutions are an important factor in peace and order-building in world politics, but institutional dynamics is not always or necessarily the prerogative of a hegemon or a group of great powers. Institution-building and multilateralism at the regional level occurs frequently and around the world and can shape the role and effectiveness of global multilateralism (chapters 6 and 7).

4   There is no single model of institution-building in world politics; significant variations exist between Europe and other regions, and among the non-European forms (chapters 3 and 7).

5   International politics is shaped by both material and ideational forces. But ideas and norms are seldom adopted wholesale. Localization, rather than replication is a more common mode of the spread of ideas and norms in world politics (chapter 8).

6   A great deal of international politics occurs at the regional level. But regional theatres and actors are not passive recipients of outside ideas and norms but active agents who resist, select, contextulize and modify them to fit the local context and need. Regional and local actors may also create and export norms to compensate for the neglect, abuse, and hypocrisy of global level actors (chapters 8 and 9). This process of norm circulation shapes normative change in world politics.

7   The dominant conception of the universal in IR theory, in the sense of one model of government, institutionalization and norm diffusion applying to all, is neither possible, nor necessarily desirable. True universality lies in recognizing the diversity of actors and agents in world politics and finding common ground among them.

These propositions neither derive from nor address the deficiencies of any single theory. Rather they straddle the traditional theoretical divides. Together, they address the central concerns of three of the most widely shared theoretical approaches to IR: realism (power), liberalism (institutions) and constructivism (ideas). Although this book has much to say about the non-Western world and its place in IR theory, these above positions are not meant to apply only to the behaviour of non-Western actors, but to world politics more generally. They are central to my concern, increasingly shared by many scholars, for a genuinely global field of IR or global IR, which I shall discuss further in the conclusion to this volume.

Some clarifications and qualifications are in order. First, my critique of the exclusions and limitations of the major theories of IR that are discussed in this book and that form the basis of my "rethinking power, institutions and ideas in world politics" are by no means unique or exhaustive. Many other scholars have offered their own critiques (and some of these contributions are discussed in chapter 2). My main reason for identifying and discussing these and not others in this book are two-fold. The first is that in my own work as an IR scholar, I am more familiar with them, because I had to deal with them more often than others. This book is a retrospective work, and hence reflects my personal evolution, predisposition and preoccupations as an IR scholar.

Second, several of the key concepts employed here and in my other works to describe and analyze the international relations of the non-Western world are borrowed from the existing, and admittedly Westerncentric, IR literature. These include concepts such as sovereignty, non-intervention, multilateralism, security communities, etc., which have been central to my theoretical work in this book or elsewhere. Productive dialogue sometimes requires that one uses a common set of concepts. In advancing such a dialogue between traditional IR theory and the emerging voices from the non-Western world, this book attempts to contextualize these concepts, critically examines the validity of the former in the non-Western world and, where possible, suggests ways of broadening or redefining them.

I use these cases and examples mainly as a way of making a case of encouraging the discipline to define, or even relaunch itself. I will discuss this issue of relaunching in the concluding chapter of this book after the intervening sections and chapters have given the reader a fuller sense of what is being challenged and on what grounds. But I hope even these limited numbers of examples of exclusions and limitations as could be found in these chapters should build a large and strong enough basis to convince us all of the need to acknowledge the ethnocentrism of our discipline and to identify pathways for moving it forward.

I acknowledge that the features and tendencies of the theories of the discipline that I critique in this book may seem pretty normal or even permissible to others. But I do know, through my long association with scholars from the developing world (and many from the developed world), that these gaps are important. They do hurt the progress of the discipline in acquiring a more global following and content, the importance of which is increasingly being recognized. Aside from highlighting this fact in discussing the limitations of existing theoretical approaches in the context of real world issues, this book also offers alternative perspectives on the three central concerns of mainstream IR theory: power, institutions and ideas, and the empirics such as sovereignty, security, intervention, the War on Terror, regionalism and multilateralism.

At the same time, I also acknowledge the limitations of this book. The book is mainly concerned with political–security aspects of international relations, and neglects the political economic dynamics.[35] And a good many of the examples that I offer to make my theoretical points through the chapters are drawn from Asia, the region I am most familiar with, while other regions get less attention. More importantly, I do not devote as much space as I would like to in this book in discussing the role of non-state actors. I do discuss the role of non-state actors: radical Islamic groups in chapter 5 and of civil society actors in multilateralism in chapter 6. Some other work where I deal with non-state actors (and increasingly find that my own conceptual contributions are applicable as much to the non-state actors as to states) are not included in this volume and I direct the readers' attention to these.[36] But in general I have been more state-centric in my work than I am comfortable with. And I do think that my discussion of the "philosophy of science" issue in chapter 2 does not do justice to the subject. Addressing the marginalization of the non-Western experience has to be done more vigorously at the epistemological level.

A further limitation, as already hinted, is that I do not discuss non-mainstream (or "critical") theories and approaches, although I do acknowledge that some of them, especially feminism and post-colonialism, are more sensitive to the non-Western milieu (indeed many of its leading contributors are from there) than others, and hence my own concerns and convictions overlap with theirs.[37] Although my concerns overlap with the "emancipatory" claims of some of the critical approaches, (especially those of post-colonialism), I am not sufficiently familiar with them and do not sufficiently identify with the methodological stance of some of them. I also do not agree with those who offer a categorical and almost total rejection of Western ideas and approaches to international order. This is in keeping with my own reading of the positions and attitudes of the non-Western world towards the evolving world order. I find the role of the majority of non-Western world – whether collectively or as regional and national entities – to have been adaptive and reformative, rather than rejectionist and revisionist.[38] Their goal has been one of relative autonomy and due recognition, rather than total independence from that system.

Despite these limitations, it is my hope that this book will serve to highlight the exclusions and limitations of the discipline as it stands now. If it stimulates further awareness of and rethinking about what IR fundamentally represents in today's changing world, and about possible pathways to broaden and redefine the discipline towards greater inclusiveness, then this modest volume would have achieved its most important purpose.

Notes

1 I thank Mohammed Ayoob and Jack Snyder for their comments on an earlier draft of the introduction. This chapter incorporates the theoretical ideas and passages from my lecture: "The Limitations of Mainstream International Relations Theories for Under-standing the Politics of Forced Migration," which was delivered at the Centre for International Studies, Oxford University, 27 October 2008. It also draws upon Amitav Acharya "Ethnocentrism and Emancipatory IR Theory," in *Displacing Security*, eds., Samantha Arnold and J. Marshall Bier, Proceedings of the YCISS Annual Conference, 1999 (Toronto: Centre for International and Security Studies, York University, 2000).

2 In an essay published in 1996, Professor Ken Booth from the University of Wales, Aberystwyth, invoked the "foundational myth" ("part fictions/part truths") that "inter-national politics" was "founded" at his university in 1919 with an endowment from David Davies, "a wealthy Liberal MP in Wales." Note that he was not using the term "international relations," which has a wider meaning, although his essay was a chapter in a volume entitled "International Theory." Ken Booth, "75 Years On: Rewriting the Subject's Past – Reinventing its Future," in *International Theory: Positivism and Beyond*, eds., Steve Smith, Ken Booth, and Marysia Zalewski (Cambridge: Cambridge University Press, 1996), 328, 330. It is not clear that other scholars, especially in the US, even recognize, much less care, about the pre-war British and European foundations of the field. And lost in all this is any sense that the field of international relations/politics might have had a multiple, global heritage in the ideas and practices of other societies and cultures, even if it was not so-named there. What seems clear, however, is that the field can claim a limited pre-Second World War British lineage, which was substantially overlaid and modified by a distinctively post-Second World War American imprint, albeit drawing largely upon European diplomatic history. Everything else was basically ignored.

3 Michael Banks, "The Inter-Paradigm Debate," in *International Relations: A Handbook of Current Theory*, eds., Margot Light and A.J.R. Groom (London: Frances Pinter, 1985), 7–26; Yosef Lapid, "The Third Debate: On the Prospects of International Theory in a Post-Positivist Era," *International Studies Quarterly* 33, no. 3 (1989): 235–254; K. J. Holsti, *The Dividing Discipline. Hegemony and Diversity in International Theory* (Boston: Allen & Unwin, 1985); Richard Ashley, "The Geopolitics of Geopolitical Space: Toward a Critical Social Theory of International Politics," *Alternatives: Global, Local, Political*

12, no. 4 (1987): 403–434; James Der Derian and Michael Shapiro, eds., *International/Intertextual Relations: Postmodern Readings of World Politics* (Lexington, Mass.: Lexington Books, 1989); and Ole Wæver, "The Rise and Fall of the Inter-Paradigm Debate," in *International Theory: Positivism and Beyond*, eds., Steve Smith, Ken Booth, and Marysia Zalewski (Cambridge: Cambridge University Press, 1996).

4 Joseph S. Nye, Jr., "Neorealism and Neoliberalism," *World Politics* 40, no. 2 (1988): 235–251; David Baldwin, ed., *Neorealism and Neoinstitutionalism* (New York: Columbia University Press, 1993); and Peter J. Katzenstein, Robert O. Keohane, Stephen D. Krasner, eds., *Exploration and Contestation in the Study of World Politics* (Cambridge: The MIT Press, 1999).

5 Mohammed Ayoob, "Inequality and Theorizing in International Relations: The Case for Subaltern Realism," *International Studies Review* 4, no. 3 (2002): 27–48.

6 Stanley Hoffmann, "An American Social Science: International Relations," *Daedalus* 106, no. 3 (1977): 41–60.

7 Correspondence with Jack Snyder, 13 February 2013. Snyder accepts that ". . . Western IR theories have underplayed the developing world in the subject matters that shaped the evolution of the core of their theories, especially the European balance of power, the causes of great power war, the conditions permitting the emergence of cooperation international economic relations, and the institutions needed to sustain rule-governed relations among the major states. There is a little in the canon of IR theory on empire, peripheral competition, and colonization, but it is mainly handled as a side effect of central system processes involving the great powers. Just as the older historians would sometimes talk about theories of empire that focused on processes in the periphery, so too did IR theorists such as Steve Walt sometimes focus on the strategic behavior of peripheral states in key theoretical works, but this was rare." This is pretty similar to my own view, except that I see the above as the root cause of an ethnocentric and distorted view of the experience of the non-Western experience. The reference to Walt is to his book that draws substantially from Middle Eastern cases, Stephen M. Walt, *The Origin of Alliances* (Ithaca: Cornell University Press, 1987).

8 Amitav Acharya and Barry Buzan, "Why Is There No Non-Western International Relations Theory: An Introduction," *International Relations of the Asia-Pacific* (Special Issue edited by Amitav Acharya and Barry Buzan), 7, no. 3 (2007): 287–312. The exact wordings in the quotes here are taken from a draft version of the article/chapter written in 2006. Ole Wæver, "Insecurity, Security, and Asecurity in the West European Non-War Community," in *Security Communities*, eds., Emanuel Adler and Michael Barnett (Cambridge: Cambridge University Press, 1998). The softer understanding is more consistent with the "classical" approach, as articulated by Hedley Bull, "The theory of international relations should undoubtedly attempt to be scientific in the sense of being a coherent, precise, and orderly body of knowledge, and in the sense of being consistent with the philosophical foundations of modern science." Hedley Bull, "International Theory: The Case for a Classical Approach," *World Politics* 18, no. 3 (1966): 361–377. Among the most well-known articulations of the American approach are: Morton A. Kaplan, "The New Great Debate: Traditionalism *vs.* Science in International Relations," *World Politics* 19, no. 1 (1966): 1–20; and Kenneth N. Waltz, *Theory of International Politics* (New York: Random House, 1979).

9 Amitav Acharya and Barry Buzan, "Why Is There No Non-Western International Relations Theory: An Introduction," in *Non-Western International Relations Theory: Perspectives on and Beyond Asia*, eds., Amitav Acharya and Barry Buzan (London and New York: Routledge, 2010), 3, 6. The book is an expanded version of the 2007 special issue of the *International Relations of the Asia-Pacific*, but some of the original articles in the journal have been revised for the book and hence may not be reproduced in their exact original form. Hence I give both references.

10 Qin Yaqin, "Why Is There No Chinese International Relations Theory," in *Non-Western International Relations Theory: Perspectives on and Beyond Asia*, eds., Amitav Acharya and Barry Buzan (London and New York: Routledge, 2010), 26.

11 Takashi Inoguchi, "Are There Any Theories of International Relations in Japan?" *International Relations of the Asia-Pacific*, (Special Issue edited by Acharya and Buzan), 7, no. 3 (2007): 369–390, 369.

12 Takashi Inoguchi, "Why Are There No Non-Western Theories of International Relations: The Case of Japan," in *Non-Western International Relations Theory: Perspectives on and Beyond Asia*, eds., Amitav Acharya and Barry Buzan (London and New York: Routledge, 2010), 51.

13 By "non-Western," I mean the members of what used to be called, and is still recognized by many as such, the "Third World," albeit acknowledging it as a more differentiated and regionalized entity today than the conventional understanding of the term implied. There could be legitimate grounds for doubt and debate about whether there is any such thing as a non-West. I discuss these reasons in chapter 2.

14 By agency, I do not limit myself to the standard version of the "agent-structure debate," where agency is defined in terms of individuals and states whereas structure is understood in terms of norms and institutions. See "Glossary," in Tim Dunne, Milja Kurki, and Steve Smith, eds., *International Relations Theories: Discipline and* Diversity, 3rd edition (Oxford: Oxford University Press, 2013), 351. Agency includes purposive action and influence of any actors, including states, non-state actors, and *institutions as actors.* Moreover, as discussed later in this chapter, agency can be material as well as ideational; the latter sometimes being more important in the case of states and institutions lacking significant material powers, as in the non-Western world.

15 See chapter 4 for a discussion of this view and its critics.

16 The quote is from the 4th edition published in 1967. Hans J. Morgenthau, *Politics Among Nations: The Struggle for Power and Peace*, 4th edition (New York: Alfred A. Knopf, 1967), 29.

17 See especially, Michael C. Williams, *Realism Reconsidered: The Legacy of Hans Morgenthau in International Relations* (New York: Oxford University Press, 2007). The new interpretation holds, among other things, that Morgenthau took a broad view of power. "Power may comprise anything that establishes and maintains the power of man over man. Thus power covers all social relationships which serve that end, from physical violence to the most subtle psychological ties by which one mind controls another." Morgenthau, *Politics Among Nations*, 4th edition, 9. He also accounts for non-material aspects of power, including the character of a nation and its quality of governance of a country, well before the notion of "soft power" or "normative power" became vogue. Arash Heydarian Pashakhanlou, "Comparing and Contrasting Classical Realism and Neorealism: A Re-examination of Hans Morgenthau's and Kenneth Waltz's Theories of International Relations," e-International Relations, 23 July 2009, http://www.e-ir.info/2009/07/23/comparing-and-contrasting-classical-realism-and-neo-realism/.

18 Morgenthau, *Politics Among Nations*, 4th edition, 5.

19 There is also room to debate Morgenthau's position on these aspects. The fourth edition of the book presents his third principle as: "Realism does not endow its key concept of interest defined as power with a meaning that is fixed once and for all." Morgenthau, *Politics Among Nations*, 4th edition, 8. But the fifth edition of the book presents the same third principle in a somewhat and for me crucially different way: "Realism assumes that its key concept of interest defined as power is an objective category which is universally valid, but it does not endow that concept with a meaning that is fixed once and for all." Hans J. Morgenthau, *Politics Among Nations: The Struggle for Power and Peace*, 5th Edition (New York: Alfred A. Knopf, 1978), https://www.mtholyoke.edu/acad/intrel/morg6.htm. The appearance of "objective category which is universally valid" undercuts the interpretative flexibility of the third principle found in the 4th edition which would be closer to my own position.

20 Morgenthau, *Politics Among Nations*, 4th edition, 10.

21 Kenneth N. Waltz, "The Stability of a Bipolar World," *Daedalus* 93, no. 3 (1964): 881–909. The persistence of this belief in the post-Cold War period can be seen in John Mearsheimer, "Back to the Future: Instability in Europe After the Cold War,"

International Security 15, no. 1 (1990): 5–55. More recently, Layne has drawn upon Waltz's neorealism to argue not only that unipolarity would not last (or be durable), but also that the subsequent multipolarity would be conflict-prone. Christopher Layne, "The Unipolar Illusion: Why New Great Powers Will Rise," *International Security* 17, no. 4 (1993): 5–51. This view ignores the possibility that the emerging and future world order may be too complex (including possibility of regionalization) to be defined and analysed in terms of the conventional understanding of polarity and stability.

22 Hedley Bull, "Introduction," in *Intervention in World Politics*, ed., Hedley Bull (Oxford: Clarendon Press, 1984), 2.

23 Ibid., 5.

24 To be fair, this remarkable, and to me incredible, turn of phrase came not from an international relations scholar, but from a historian. But Gaddis was not unfamiliar with international relations theory; indeed he contributed to it. John Lewis Gaddis, "International Relations Theory and the End of the Cold War," *International Security* 17, no. 3 (1992–1993): 5–58; and John Lewis Gaddis, "The Long Peace: Elements of Stability in the Post-War International System," *International Security* 10, no. 4 (1986): 92–142.

25 Stephen Krasner, *Sovereignty: Organized Hypocrisy* (Princeton: Princeton University Press, 1999).

26 I have developed these disagreements with the logic and necessity of the power politics from the Cold War era to the War on Terror in several other essays, especially: "The New World Order and International Security After the Gulf War: An Assessment," *India Quarterly* 48, no. 3 (1992): 1–14; "State-Society Relations: Asian and World Order after September 11," in *World's in Collision: Terror and the Future of Global Order*, eds., Ken Booth and Tim Dunne (London: Palgrave, 2002), 194–204; "Rethinking International Order After September 11: Some Preliminary Observations," paper presented to The 4th Southeast Asian Conflict Studies Network (SEACSN) Regional Workshop, Universiti Sains Malaysia, Penang, Malaysia; *The Age of Fear: Power Versus Principle in the War on Terror* (Singapore: Marshall Cavendish, and New Delhi: Rupa & Co, 2004); and "The Bush Doctrine and Asian Regional Order: the Perils and Pitfalls of Preemption," in *Confronting the Bush Doctrine: Critical Views from the Asia-Pacific*, eds., Mel Gurtov and Peter Van Ness (London: RoutledgeCurzon, 2005).

27 Barry Buzan and Ole Waever, *Regions and Powers: The Structure of International Security* (Cambridge: Cambridge University Press, 2003); and Peter J. Katzenstein, *A World of Regions: Asia and Europe in the American Imperium* (Ithaca: Cornell University Press, 2005).

28 This argument is elaborated in Amitav Acharya, "Collective Identity and Conflict Management in Southeast Asia," in *Security Communities*, eds., Emmanuel Adler and Michael Barnett (Cambridge: Cambridge University Press, 1998), 198–227; and Amitav Acharya, *Constructing a Security Community in Southeast Asia: ASEAN and the Problem of Regional Order*.

29 Peter Katzenstein, Robert Keohane, and Stephen Krasner, eds., *Exploration and Contestation in the Study of World Politics* (Cambridge: MIT Press, 1999).

30 Donald J. Puchala, "Third World Thinking and Contemporary Relations," in *International Relations Theory and the Third World*, ed., Stephanie Newman (New York: St Martin's Press 1995), 151.

31 Acharya, *Constructing a Security Community in Southeast Asia*; and Acharya, *Whose Ideas Matter? Agency and Power in Asian Regionalism*.

32 Aside from the case studies of normative agency discussed in chapters 8 and 9, one could point to the idea of human development and human security, largely a contribution of Pakistani economist Mahbub ul Haq and Indian economist Amartya Sen. See Amitav Acharya, "Human Security: East Versus West," *International Journal* 56, no. 3 (2001): 442–460. Another example is the idea of "responsible sovereignty," the basis of the Responsibility to Protect (R2P) norm, credited to Sudanese diplomat Francis Deng. See his, "Idealism and Realism: Negotiating Sovereignty in Divided Nations," The 2010 Dag Hammarskjöld Lecture, http://www.un.org/en/preventgenocide/adviser/pdf/DH_Lecture_2010.pdf.

33 The idea of normative culture is different from cultural norms. The latter locates the sources of norms within the existing culture of a country or region, while the former suggests that norms can be borrowed or diffused from outside, albeit modified or localized on the basis of some preexisting norms or cognitive priors, to constitute a distinctive national or regional culture, which can then be projected outward. On cultural norms, see, Peter J. Katzenstein, *Cultural Norms and National Security: Police and Military in Postwar Japan* (Ithaca: Cornell University Press, 1998). My work on normative culture is represented in the two chapters (9 and 10) in this section.

34 I have advanced these arguments about the diffusion of norms and ideas and the creation of security communities through a number of other essays and books. See: "A Regional Security Community in Southeast Asia?" *Journal of Strategic Studies* 18, no. 3 (1995): 175–200; "Collective Identity and Conflict Management in Southeast Asia"; "Do Norms and Identity Matter? Community and Power in Southeast Asia's Regional Order," *Pacific Review* 18, no. 1 (2005): 95–118; *Constructing a Security Community in Southeast Asia: ASEAN and the Problem of Regional Order; Whose Ideas Matter? Agency and Power in Asian Regionalism*; "Ideas, Norms and Regional Orders," in *International Relations Theory and Regional Transformation*, ed., T.V. Paul (Cambridge: Cambridge University Press, 2012), 183–209; and *Civilizations in Embrace: The Spread of Ideas and the Transformation of Power* (Singapore: Institute of Southeast Asian Studies, 2012).

35 I should note, however, that relative unfamiliarity with a particular subfield of IR has not prevented other scholars from advancing theoretical proposition and claims about world politics as a whole. Examples Robert Keohane's neoliberal institutionalism, which were drawn largely from an international political economy base. Robert O. Keohane, *International Institutions and State Power: Essays in International Relations Theory* (Boulder, Colo.: Westview Press, 1989).

36 Some examples of my own work dealing with non-state actors in international relations include, Amitav Acharya, "Democratisation and the Prospects for Participatory Regionalism in Southeast Asia," *Third World Quarterly* 24, no. 2 (2003): 375–390; Amitav Acharya, "Regionalism: The Meso Public Domain in Latin America and South-East Asia," in *The Market or the Public Domain: Global Governance and the Asymmetry of Power*, ed., Daniel Drache (London and New York: Routledge, 2001), 296–318; Amitav Acharya, "Local and Transnational Civil Society as Agents of Norm Diffusion," paper presented to the Global Governance Workshop, Department of International Development, Oxford University; and Amitav Acharya, *Contesting Freedom: Human Rights, Democracy and Participatory Regionalism in Southeast Asia* (Chiangmai, Thailand: Silkworm Books, forthcoming).

37 See Acharya "Ethnocentrism and Emancipatory IR Theory".

38 This point is made convincingly by Mohammed Ayoob, perhaps the best scholar of the international relations of the Third World, in his seminal article "The Third World in the System of States: Acute Schizophrenia or Growing Pains?," *International Studies Quarterly* 33, no. 1 (1989): 67–79.

PART I
IR theory and its discontents

1

INTERNATIONAL RELATIONS THEORIES AND WESTERN DOMINANCE: REASSESSING THE FOUNDATIONS OF INTERNATIONAL ORDER[1]

In the field of international relations, there is now a growing recognition that what passes for "theory" has been, and continues to be, shaped mainly by the Western ideas, experiences, and practices. Stanley Hoffmann once famously described the field of international relations as an "American social science."[2] If this is true of the entire field, it is even more so of its theory, although the latter is more accurately characterized as "Western," rather than merely "American," despite the latter's greater claim to "social scientifism." International relations as a field of study is no longer the exclusive preserve of either American or Western universities. Some of the fastest growth in the discipline are taking place in non-Western countries, especially China, India and even Indonesia. In China, for example, some four dozen universities are now conferring bachelor degree in international studies. Yet, IR theory remains stubbornly Western, incorporating relatively few insights and voices from the non-West.

Why this is the case? One rare investigation into this question, by a project led by myself and Barry Buzan, addressing the question "Why Is There No Non-Western IR Theory?" came up with a number of possible explanations. These explanations range from the hegemonic status of Western scholars, publications and institutions in IR, to a realization that Western IRT has discovered the right path to understanding IR, or the right answers to the puzzles and problems of the day, to a serious lack of institutional resources, the problem of language, and the close nexus between IR academics and the government which discourages theoretical work. We also found an uncritical acceptance of Western theory, a lack of confidence to take on Western theorists, blind deference to scholars from prestigious Western institutions, and too much political and policy engagement for IR scholars in universities in the developing world. In this situation, what passes for theory here is mostly theory-testing, scholars looking at Western thinking, and applying to the local context, rather than injecting indigenous ideas and insights from local practices to the main body of IR theory.

Of these, the hegemonic status of Western IRT is of particular importance. To elaborate, the question of Western dominance in IR theory is:

> . . . not about whether Western IRT has found all the right paths to truth. It is about whether, because Western IRT has been carried by the dominance of Western power over the last few centuries, it has acquired a Gramscian hegemonic status that operates largely unconsciously in the minds of others, and regardless of whether the theory is correct or not. Here one would need to take into account the intellectual impact of Western imperialism and the success of the powerful in imprinting their own understandings onto the minds and practices of the non-Western world . . . the process of decolonisation left in its wake a world remodeled, sometimes badly, on the lines of the European state and its 'anarchical society' form of international relations. The price of independence was that local elites accept this structure, and a good case can be made that they not only did so under duress, but absorbed and made their own a whole set of key Western ideas about the practice of political economy, including most conspicuously and most universally, sovereignty, territoriality and nationalism.[3]

But if we assume some form of Western dominance in IR theory exists, can we come to some agreement as to what it actually means, or how is it manifested? Is Western dominance merely an intellectual question, i.e. establishing the "non-universality" of IR theory, or a normative one, extending to an examination of whether and how IRT has legitimized the West's dominant position in the international system? And finally, how is Western dominance reflected in some of the principal approaches to international order?

I should note here that it is not my aim to start a new "debate," as happened in the past between idealists and realists, or traditionalists and behaviouralists, or rationalists and post-positivists. This would amount to taking an extreme position for and against something or someone. I do not dismiss, much less denounce, the contribution of IR theory in spreading the discipline of international relations in the non-West. I also acknowledge that IR theory is not a monolith, and that some theories are more sensitive to non-Western experience and hence more cognizant of the dominance of the West over the non-West than others. These include post-colonialism, feminism, and even some versions of what may be called "subaltern constructivism," i.e. social constructivism that recognizes the two-way diffusion of ideas and norms and examines the patterns of socialization leading to community-building in the non-Western world. I also do not consider the problem of Western dominance as a grand conspiracy by Western intellectual elites and their leaders to keep the rest of the world down and out. Instead, I view Western dominance as inevitable, perhaps even necessary, deriving from the West's recent historical position. Instead of being a grand conspiracy, I see it as a series of loosely connected intellectual discourses, which have excluded the non-West, due as much to the intellectual conditioning associated with Western power and influence as to the ignorance or laziness of the theorist, or his/her proclivity for generating testable hypotheses by keeping the relevant samples relatively small and familiar, and thus Western.

Despite these caveats, I think we do have a problem in IR theory's claim to universality that is worthy of serious intellectual investigation. But before setting out to do so, let me offer some clarifications about the key terms that I will use and my definition of the problem to be investigated.

Western dominance and international order

I first turn to the notion of Western dominance. This is a difficult task. Normally, dominance means physical subjugation of the weak by the strong. But there can be other, softer forms of dominance. The Gramscian notion of hegemony offers a useful framework for capturing the essence of dominance. First, dominance, like the Gramscian notion of hegemony is both material and ideational. Since IR theory is essentially a set of ideas, it is a natural arena where Western dominance would be clearly manifested. Second, drawing upon the well-known formulation of Robert Cox that "Theory is always *for* someone and *for* some purpose,"[4] IR theory can be generally understood as serving the purpose of the dominant Western actors. Last but not the least, dominance, like hegemony, is both sustained by coercion and consent, but consent may be the more important element. It is therefore not surprising to see many scholars in the non-West accepting and using IR theory without much hesitance, at least initially, and that the field of international relations has progressed in the non-West despite having been rooted in Western historiography and foreign policy experience.

Dominance can take many different forms: exclusion, ethnocentrism, marginalization, oppression, contempt, ignorance, etc. In this chapter, I will define Western dominance in terms of four dimensions: (1) auto-centrism (2) universalism, (3) disjuncture, and (4) agency denial. Together, they have contributed to four essential tendencies in IR theorizing.

1. Auto-centrism refers to the tendency of theorizing about key principles of mechanisms of international order from mainly Western ideas, culture, politics, historical experiences and contemporary praxis. Conversely, it is reflected in the disregard, exclusion and marginalization of non-Western ideas, culture, politics, historical experiences and contemporary praxis. Part of this auto-centrism can be attributed to a sense of superiority of the Western pattern over non-Western one.[5]

2. False universalism refers to the tendency to view or present Western ideas and practices as the universal standard, while non-Western principles and practices are viewed as particularisms, aberrations or inferiorities. As Steve Walt noted

in justifying his selection of Middle East case studies to develop a theory about the origin of alliances, "international relations scholars have long relied on historical cases and quantitative data drawn from European diplomatic history without being accused of a narrow geographic, temporal, or cultural focus."[6] Much of what passes for IR theory might be similarly construed as European diplomatic history and contemporary American foreign policy management.

3. Disjuncture refers to the lack of fit between what passes for IR theory and the experience of the non-Western world, although Western scholars seldom see this as an obstacle to theory-building. We have serious problems when applying theories of conflict, cooperation, institution-building, norm diffusion dynamics that dominate the literature of IR to the non-West.

4. Agency denial refers to the lack of acknowledgment of the agency of non-Western states, regional institutions, civil society actors in contributing to world order, through additions and extensions to the principles and mechanisms which were devised by the West and by creating new ones. Non-Western actors are seen as consumers rather than producers, or as passive recipients rather than active borrowers of theoretical knowledge claims.

I should stress here that these four dimensions are not mutually exclusive, but inter-related and run parallel with each other. But the scope of my analysis of Western dominance does not stop with an investigation of these four dimensions. This is not just a question about investigating how the development of IR theory has mainly been a Western enterprise and contribution. I have framed the title of this chapter in a deliberately ambiguous manner. My argument is that these above four tendencies in IR theory, which reflect the dominant position of the West in the international system, have also legitimized Western dominance of the international system. Most academic studies of IR theory's lack of universality focus mainly on the issue of Western intellectual hegemony. But no consideration of Western dominance in the formulation of IR theory can be complete without looking at the other part of equation: how IR theory, while itself being a product of Western dominance, has also legitimized Western dominance. This interactive relationship between IR theory and Western dominance is at the core of my investigation. Simply put, the development of IR theory is reflective of the dominant position of the West in the international system. And conversely, IR theory has helped to legitimize that dominance.

While international relations theory has a broad and complex domain, let me look specifically at the ordering principles and mechanisms in world politics. This is based on the assumption, contestably so perhaps, that issues and mechanisms of international order dominate the theories of international relations and constitute the core of the theory of the discipline. IR theory is in many ways about investigating the sources, mechanisms and limitations of international order-building. In this project, I look specifically at four ordering elements:

1. Sovereignty: The organizing principle of international order
2. Powers: Great Power relationships

3. Institutions: International and regional institutions
4. Values and norms: Norm dynamics and normative change.

There are other mechanisms which could be added to the above list: international law, balance of power, democracy, etc. One might include the discussion of international law in sovereignty and institutions, and of balance of power in the discussion of great powers, and democracy can be looked at within the context of institutions (democratic peace as the basis of liberal international order).

Although my analysis does not specify a historical timeframe, it is very much concerned with exploring continuities between Western dominance in the classical notions and practices of international order and those in the contemporary setting. Ideas change, so do theories of international order. Contributions to IR theory which reflected primarily Western ideas and sanctioned Western dominance from the seventeenth to twentieth centuries may have lost some of their relevance or appeal today. Yet, some elements of Western dominance that marked the origins of these ideas may still persist. The study of international relations is changing in major ways, but an important question is whether Western dominance of it persists, in terms of the four dimensions identified earlier, and whether the lack of non-Western voices and weak representation of non-Western experiences in IR theory today can be partly explained by the foundational principles and practices of international order in earlier junctures. This is a major intellectual puzzle and challenge for IR scholars.

Sovereignty and its discontents

That theoretical writings on the origins and impact of sovereignty derive mainly from the European experience and exclude the ideas, voices and historical experiences of the non-Western world is not difficult to prove. For example, IR theory has also seldom considered outcomes other than the sovereign state-system out of the struggle between centralization and decentralization. But as Victoria Hui argues, the tendency among Western IR theorists to regard empire (the Chinese experience after the Warring States period) as aberration and decentralization (the Westphalia model) as the norm of international order-building is misleading.[7] The outcome of the Warring States period in China leading to the establishment of the Qin Empire should join the peace of Westphalia as an authentic, rather than aberrant, prospect for IR theorists. David Kang has argued that the tendency among international relations theorists to dismiss hierarchy as an organizing principle of international order is similarly misplaced. For Kang, in East Asia, the hierarchical Chinese tributary system had been a stabilizing force, and may explain today why Asian states are not balancing China to the extent consistent with realist theory.[8]

But theoretical writings on sovereignty are a vivid reminder of how IR theory reflects Western dominance and has served to legitimize it. The natural law conceptions of sovereignty, identified with writers like Hugo Grotius, did not exclude non-Western states. This changed with the rising power of European nations and the consolidation of their colonial empires. European superiority in science, technology, warfare, among other areas, and European subjugation of non-Western territory required a new justification that could not be found under natural law conceptions of sovereignty under which the non-Western states could be considered to have sovereignty. Hence emerged a new body of international law, the positive international law regime, which would specify that sovereign statehood required a "delimited territory, a stable population, and most importantly, a reliable government with the will and capacity to carry out international obligations."[9] Non-Western states were seen as not having been in possession of these, presumably because they were, in the words of English Legal Positivist writer W.E. Hall, "differently civilised."[10] The constitutive recognition principle that resulted from this was both a reflection of rising Western power as well as an "instrument of Western dominance" used to exclude not just colonies but also independent entities such as China.[11]

With decolonization, the Westphalian model was assumed to have become the universal model of the sovereign state-system. As Daniel Philpott puts it, "The history of sovereignty is the history of Westphalia's geographic extension."[12] And Chris Clapham adds: "The Third World states took to Westphalian sovereignty like duckling to water."[13]

Yet, the assumption that the non-West is incapable of playing the positive international law "sovereignty game" did not quite disappear after decolonization. Confronted with serious disjunctures between Westphalian sovereignty and the realities of state-building in the Third World, writers on sovereignty came up with a distinction between juridical and empirical statehood, and the idea of "negative sovereignty," focusing mainly on the non-intervention principle. Jackson's idea of negative sovereignty (see note 9) makes two assumptions: (1) the Third World States are mostly incapable of exercising positive sovereignty, (2) the principle of non-intervention is an instrument of state survival and regime security of Third World states, rather than the pursuit of positive and normative concerns.

These assumptions can be questioned. If positive sovereignty meant an ability to engage in the high politics of international affairs, i.e. questions of order, stability and justice, as well as power politics, then there can be many examples of Third World states playing the sovereignty game. India and China and the Colombo power in the 1950s, played such roles; while many of them suffered from contested boundaries, they did have "a stable population, and most importantly, a reliable government with the will and capacity to carry out international obligations." Moral concerns, such as decolonization and resistance to superpower intervention, rather than narrowly conceived regime survival, played an important part in their concern with sovereignty. Hence, it would be wrong to assert that the sovereignty game in the non-Western world was primarily one of negative sovereignty. Perhaps it was sufficiently distinctive to form a category of its own, combining both non-intervention and playing a part in the positive construction of international order mechanisms, such as peace-keeping.

Yet, the contributions of the non-West to the global sovereignty regime have not been captured in theoretical writings on the subject. While there is some literature on the contribution of Latin America to the non-intervention norm, Asia's has been ignored. For example, some European writers of sovereignty such as Vattel have considered intervention for the sake of protecting the balance of power as a legitimate prerogative of great powers, rather than as a threat to international order. But such exceptions would be unthinkable in the non-Western world, including post-war Asia, especially in the wake of the 1955 Bandung Conference, which was attended by more non-Western nations (total of 29) than the United Nations Conference on International Organization (UNCIO), which drafted the UN charter in 1945. While Latin America's response to the Monroe Doctrine extended the European principle geographically, the Asian construction of non-intervention extended the Westphalian principle beyond its original meaning by delegitimizing participation in Cold War military pacts (which was seen as a form of intervention). The global sovereignty regime has developed with contributions from Europe, Latin America, Asia and Africa, and hence cannot simply be referred to as a unilinear and uncontested spread of European/Westphalian sovereignty.[14]

A final point about the sovereignty debate, which has entered a new stage since the end of the Cold War, may be noted here. The right of absolute sovereignty is now being seriously challenged, where states have abused the rights of their citizens, and where they have failed to protect these rights because of weakness or collapse. Notwithstanding its justifications to its non-Western critics, the doctrine of humanitarian intervention at its core assumes the inability of the non-Western countries to fulfill their obligations as *civilized sovereign* nations. Moreover, to some of these critics, humanitarian intervention is not as universal a principle as its Western proponents make it out to be because the problems that justify such intervention are not problems for the West. To quote a Chinese scholar: "For stronger, more developed countries largely free of international intervention in their own internal affairs, legitimizing international intervention would not involve loss of independence, sovereignty, or people's welfare. However, in the case of weaker, developing countries, legitimizing international intervention entails loss of, damage to, independence, sovereignty, political stability, and people's welfare."[15]

Great power management

The primacy or "special responsibility" of great powers in the management of international order was well-recognized in classical European writings on the balance of power. But it was the European Concert which formalized the principle in a multilateral context. The fact that the Concert was also known for marginalizing the weaker states, even to the point of sanctioning their territorial dismemberment or even disappearance, has rarely been seen as an issue for scholars who have used it in the twentieth century as the ideal type of "security regimes,"[16] a term developed by Robert Jervis, that may come to operate for the management of international order, or those who have advocated regional concerts such as Kupchan and

Kupchan's "concert-based collective security system" in post-Cold War Europe,[17] or the idea of an Asia–Pacific Concert of Powers.[18]

Obviously then, the idea of great power centrality in the management of international order did not disappear with the breakdown of the Concert system or the discrediting of the balance of power system after World War I. Instead, it was enshrined in the League of Nations and its successor the UN, as seen in the institutionalization of the veto system. Of course, great power status was no longer limited to Western nations. But the inclusion of China in the permanent membership of the UN Security Council did not dispel Western dominance in the system of great power management.

The principle of great power management did come under attack during the formative years of the post-war order. Writing in British prison in 1944, India's nationalist leader and future prime minister Jawaharlal Nehru wrote a scathing critique, under the title "Realism and Geopolitics: World Conquest or World Association?," of an idea proposed by Nicholas Spykman and Walter Lippmann (also backed by Winston Churchill). This was the idea that post-war world order be organized around regional security systems under great power "orbits." Nehru attacked this form of great power sphere of influence as "a continuation of power politics on a vaster scale . . . it is difficult to see how he [Lippmann] can see world peace or co-operation emerging out of it."[19] As an alternative, Nehru proposed the idea of a "commonwealth of states," or a "world association" based on the principle of equality of states. Yet, we have no reference to Nehru's critique in IR texts dealing with the idealist–realist debate or the realist–liberal debate.

As the Cold War progressed, the world saw the legitimization of the principle of great power leadership and management of international order, this time from a neo-realist perspective. Its founder, Kenneth Waltz accepted the primacy of great powers in world politics. But he went a step further than the classical balance of power theorists by holding that the stability of the international system depended on the number of great powers in the system. Hence his predictive premise that bipolarity would be more stable than multipolarity. For Waltz, stability meant not just the ability of the system (bipolarity) to endure, but also the reduced propensity of the system to produce conflict and violence. Yet, this was in disregard of the widespread prevalence of conflict in the Third World under bipolarity, so much so that it led some non-Western theorists to perceive a causal link between systemic order and regional disorders. Mohammed Ayoob, following another Indian scholar Sisir Gupta, argued that because of the costs involved in any direct superpower confrontation in the central theatre under mutual assured destruction, superpower intervention in the Third World served as a safety valve for the release of superpower tensions.[20] In other words, under Cold War bipolarity, Third World conflicts were more permissible. For this reason, as will be discussed in chapter 4, as far as the non-West was concerned, the Cold War was hardly a "long peace."

If so, then great power management could be implicated in a great deal of international disorder. At the same time, IR theory, whether neo-realist or neoliberal, failed to recognize the management of regional international orders by weak non-Western states, such as the role of the Association of Southeast Asian Nations, the Gulf Cooperation Council and the MERCOSUR group. Instead, we see a remarkable continuity in thinking about international order in terms of great power primacy, and anxieties about the collapse of international order if weak powers or middle powers were to assume such responsibility. During the Cold War, much of the criticism of the Non-Aligned Movement was inspired by such fears. After the end of the Cold War, the Waltzian view that multipolarity is less stable than bipolarity inspired Mearsheimer's "back to the future" thesis concerning instability in Europe. In the Third World, it underpinned widespread Western concerns about a possible "decompression effect" due to the rise of regional powers who are supposed to be less inclined and able to preserve and manage international order.

Institutions and cooperation

While realists see great power-managed balance of power as key to managing international order, liberals accord a similar place to international institutions. One foundation of liberal institutionalism is the Kantian notion of ever-widening pacific unions. Kant believed that peace depended on both the existence of republican constitutions within states and a pacific union among liberal states. While he recognized the right of liberal states to act belligerently towards non-liberal states, Kant denounced European conquest and subjugation of non-European societies. The cosmopolitan right mentioned in Kant's third definitive article, which is to operate in conjunction with the pacific union among liberal states, is a right of hospitality. This is "the right of a stranger not to be treated in a hostile manner by another upon his arrival on the other's territory."[21] This right "does not extend beyond the conditions of the possibility of attempting interaction with the old inhabitants." It certainly did not permit European colonial powers to engage in conquest and oppression. In a revealing paragraph, Kant contrasts the cosmopolitan right of hospitality with the behaviour of colonial powers, whom he accuses of engaging in *inhospitable* behaviour, and showing "injustice . . . when *visiting* foreign lands and peoples (which to them is one and the same as *conquering* those lands and peoples").[22] Apart from "America, the Negro countries, the Spice Islands, the Cape," he mentions *Hindoostan*, where the European powers "brought in foreign troops under the pretext of merely intending to establish trading posts. But with these they introduced the oppression of the native inhabitants, the incitement of the different states involved to expansive wars, famine, unrest, faithlessness, and the whole litany of evils that weigh upon the human species."[23] Kant also defended the action of China and Japan in limiting the role of European trading companies in their territories. He believed that the actions of the traders were both futile, it brought no profit (a mistaken or premature assessment) to them, the only benefit being in some cases (e.g. the Sugar Islands) the training of sailors who could then engage in warfare in Europe.

But some questions about and contradictions in Kantian universalism remain. Did Kant recognize the right of non-European societies to choose their own political systems? He certainly took liberal polity as both necessary for peace and perhaps even inevitable (conforming to his teleological view of history). The fact that Kant denounced colonialism does not mean he allowed for peaceful long-lasting association between liberal and non-liberal states. On the contrary, as noted, he allowed for liberal states engaging in what Hume called "imprudent vehemence" against nonliberal states. Similarly, could there be peaceful association between non-liberal states in the Kantian world? This was clearly outside the purview of his theory. He imagined that a pacific union would be ever expanding, and would gradually bring in non-Western states, but only if they had become liberal.

These aspects of the Kantian approach continue to haunt contemporary neo-Kantian theories of international institutions. Consider the theory of regional integration, the main body of liberal theory in the post-war period, which comprised the neo-functionalism of Ernst Haas and the transactionalism (security community theory) of Karl Detusch. Neo-functionalism was founded on the assumptions of liberal-pluralist politics the absence of which opened a serious gap between what Haas called the "European and the Universal Processes" of regional integration.[24] Joseph Nye drew attention to the absence of democratic politics in the Third World as one of the principal reasons why West European regional integration could not take place there.[25] Deutsch's theory of security communities did speak about convergent political values as a condition of their emergence, but recent Western writers on the subject, as could be found in the Adler and Barnett book, insist that this convergence must be strictly about Western liberal democratic values. From this perspective, the non-Western world would be unsuitable for the development of security communities. Yet the experience of Southeast Asia and the Southern cone of Latin America shows their progress towards a durable peace.[26]

Moreover, there is a serious disjuncture between Euro-Atlantic based regional integration theories and regionalism in the non-Atlantic world over the fundamental motivating force behind regionalism. While European regionalism sought to move regional international politics beyond the nation-state, non-Western sought the creation and consolidation of nation-states, however artificially-conceived. Hence, unlike the European Union, the Organization of African Unity (OAU; now the African Union) and the Arab League during their initial years functioned more as "the instrument of national independence rather than of regional integration."[27] Moreover, instead of adopting EU-style supranationalism, non-Western regional institutions embraced an expanded version of non-intervention, which even disallowed legalistic bureaucracies and dispute-settlement mechanisms.

The disjuncture between European integration theory and Third World cooperation survives to this day. While in the earlier era it led to comparisons between European and Third World regionalism in terms of their capacity for supranationalism, today, it is manifested in the literature on comparative institutional design.

Hence, the "widespread assumption . . . that in order to be 'proper' regionalism, a degree of EU-style institutionalism should be in place."[28] What Peter Katzenstein sees as the persistent tendency in the literature on regionalism "to compare European 'success' with Asian 'failure'" persists despite the fact that "Theories based on Western, and especially West European experience, have been of little use in making sense of Asian regionalism."[29]

Values and norms

International relations theorists have increasingly recognized the importance of values and norms in shaping international order. Some see cultural values as the basis of the relative prosperity and progress of nations, hence important determinants of their ability to shape international order. Values and norms also act as sources of conflict and cooperation, which are directly relevant to prospects for international order. One does not have to take the cultural fault line argument to its Huntingtonian extreme to accept that value differences can cause international disorder. Conversely, the diffusion of values, norms and persuasion mechanisms can seriously affect prospects for community building in international relations – for example the development of security communities. Hence, the constructivist theory of norm diffusion offers an important window to order-building in international relations.

Let me turn to one of the pathways through which values shape international order by affecting a nation's prosperity and progress. John Stuart Mill considered liberty as a fundamental basis for differentiating between states, and their progress (hence status) in international relations. His views on China are especially relevant. Mill praised China as "– a nation of much talent, and, in some respects, even wisdom, owing to the rare good fortune of having been provided at an early period with a particularly good set of customs. . . ." Yet China was not to be imitated because it suppressed "individuality." If that happened, warned Mill, "Europe, notwithstanding its noble antecedents and its professed Christianity, will tend to become another China."[30] Mill was assuming that China could not go very far in the ladder of progress with its traditional Confucian system of values that rendered its "people all alike, all governing their thoughts and conduct by the same maxims and rules."

How ironic then, that in the 1980s and early 1990s at least, there emerged an "Asian values" claim, arguing precisely the opposite: that Confucian values which placed society above the self were the basis of East Asia's economic miracle? Much has of course been written about this so-called Asian values debate, but few have debated claims about "Western values in international relations." Yet in a 1966 essay, under precisely that title, Martin Wight had asserted "persistent and recurrent" Western ideas that lie at the core of international relations, such as conceptions of international society, the maintenance of order, intervention and international morality.[31] Wisely, however, he started the essay with a few caveats: first, the claim about Western values is contextual because it is bound up with the Cold

War; second, there was a huge diversity among the beliefs of Westerners ("Western men were perhaps more various in their range of beliefs than men of any other culture"); and third, Western values are not the same as Western practice, or put differently, "there is no simple way of deducing Western values from Western practice."[32]

Compare this with the Asian values debate. Unlike Wight, who was Dean of the School of European Studies and Professor of History at the University of Sussex when he wrote his Western values essay, contemporary claims about Asian values were first made by a group of policy-intellectuals and policy-makers in Asia. Whereas Wight identified as the core of Western values the Whig or constitutional tradition in diplomacy associated with Grotius, Locke, Halifax, Montesquieu, Burke, Castlereagh, Tocqueville, Lincoln, Gladstone, and Churchill, among others, the idea of Asian values were associated mainly with contemporary Asian leaders like Lee Kuan Yew, Mahathir Mohamad, Suharto, and Jiang Zemin. The proponents of Asian values did not make qualifications to their claims. They invited widespread criticism. Critics pointed to the diversity among Asian societies and states which made any notion of a homogenous set of shared values questionable. More importantly, the critics targeted the evident correlation between Asian values and the authoritarian or semi-authoritarian political systems presided over by their proponents.

This may seem well-deserved criticism. But underlying the criticism of Asian values was an assumption about the moral superiority of the Western individualism over Eastern communitarianism, not too far from the line Mill had taken. Moreover, it placed the Western norms of human rights and democratic governance as universal values in terms of which the Asian values construct must be judged. The attack on Asian values, while understandable, was in some respects one-sided. First, not all who have spoken about Asian values are from non-liberal states. The first Asian leader to speak of Asian values and identity, it is often forgotten, was India's Jawaharlal Nehru – nobody's idea of a tin-pot dictator. Furthermore, it obscured the existence of "good" Asian values and "bad" Western ones, and the possibility of some Asian values having a more universal applicability. For example, the principle of consensus and informalism, values that are often associated with Asian institutions and contrasted with the hard legalism of Western institutions, is commonplace in other non-Western regional bodies. The outright dismissal of Asian values because of the identity and political styles of its advocates was perhaps to some degree an instinctive reaction that is symptomatic of Western dominance of the kind this chapter has already identified.

Another part of my investigation into the role of ideational forces in international order as a way of illustrating Western dominance has to do with the theory of norm diffusion. This is integral to the social constructivist theory of IR. While constructivism is sympathetic to questions about culture and identity in international relations, it has unfortunately not risen above the problems of Western dominance by not recognizing the diffusion of non-Western norms and ideas and the role of non-Western norm entrepreneurs. These problems are especially evident in what I have termed the "moral cosmopolitanism" bias in the constructivist literature on norm diffusion.[33] With little reflection it will be easy to realize that moral cosmopolitanism fits right into the dimensions of Western dominance that I have identified at the outset. The literature on human rights has essentially been about good global norms championed by the West replacing bad local practices mostly, if not exclusively in the non-Western world, even though human rights principles and traditions do exist in the non-Western world. For "moral cosmopolitanists," norms that make a universalistic claim about what is good are considered more desirable and more likely to prevail than norms that are localized or particularistic. This position stems from a well-known Western dislike of cultural relativism (unless it is Western culture), which is seen, often rightly, as a pretext for Third World dictators to abuse human rights. But not all local (Third World) social norms legitimize human rights abuses; and not all who resist the Western human rights conceptions and campaigns are authoritarian regimes. For example, democratic countries such as India and the Philippines defended relativism in the human rights debate in the early 1990s and professed Western double standards. Moreover, the moral cosmopolitanism approach also ignores the global or regional diffusion of non-Western norms, such as the regional diffusion of the cultural norms of Japan as discussed by Katzenstein, or the norms of consensus in ASEAN which have diffused to the wider Asia Pacific multilateral institutions.[34] Nor does moral cosmopolitanism look at the functions of resistance, localization, and feedback by non-Western norm takers and entrepreneurs. In other words, the moral cosmopolitanism framework exhibits all the four features – auto-centrism, universalism, disjuncture, and agency denial – which constitute my indicators of Western dominance.

"The Expansion of International Society"

Among the more well-known theoretical traditions in IR, few have examined the place of non-Western countries in the international system more systematically than the English School.[35] Yet, no other school of IR has rendered the idea of Western dominance more integral to its theoretical worldview. Hence, a closer look at *The Expansion of International Society*, the major *foundational* text of the English School, is helpful for illustrating my own arguments about Western dominance and the problematic nature of the universalistic claims of IR theory.[36]

The narrative of *The Expansion* is, in a nutshell, based on a claim that the universal international society of today is founded upon the expansion of the European-derived international society. That expansion was physical as well as normative and institutional. By the First World War, the European-derived international system had become "universal in the sense that it covered all the world and included states from Asia, Africa, and the Americas as well as Europe." Moreover, in this society, the "dominance of the European or Western powers at the turn of the century was expressed not only in their superior economic and military power and in their commanding intellectual and cultural authority but also in the rules and institutions of international society . . ."[37]

The founders of the English School, such as Hedley Bull, Adam Watson, Martin Wight, and Herbert Butterfield, were not entirely oblivious to the charge of Eurocentrism levelled against their project. Their project contained an acknowledgement of the existence of other historical state-systems, and the growing importance of the non-Western states in international relations, yet their approach remained Eurocentric. In a 1978 concept paper for the Committee's project which led to *The Expansion of International Society*, Bull noted that:

> Today, non-Western states form the overwhelming majority, the society of states is proclaimed to be universal or global; the rules of international law have been modified so as to take account of the interests and attitudes of the non-Western majority . . . In terms of economic and military strength the Western minority of states and peoples are still in the ascendancy, but a shift in the distribution of power towards the non-Western states and peoples has taken place.[38]

Moreover, Bull and Watson did concede that the universal international system of the early twentieth century was based upon European hegemony, and posited the possibility of a universal international system – a "genuinely universal and non-hegemonial structure of rules and institutions,"[39] which is not based on European hegemony. But they rejected the view that their perspective might seem Eurocentric by blaming it on the fact of history, because "it was in fact Europe and not America, Asia, or Africa that first dominated and, in so doing, unified the world, it is not our perspective but the historical record itself that can be called Eurocentric."[40] If this may not seem disingenuous enough, there is the impression that their entire *Expansion* project was conceived on the very positioning of Europe as the "ideal type" of international society/civilization.[41] One gets the sense from the organizing framework of *The Expansion* that the non-Western states basically inherited the European model without much resistance and perhaps even with some passion. Moreover, the conceptual framework of *The Expansion*, bearing Bull's imprint, seems to suggest that in order to be a "proper" international society, or indeed to qualify as one, a group of states must look and act like the European international society. At its base, Bull's idea of a universal international society is mostly an extension of the European model. But if we take the meaning of universalism beyond the sense of one set of ideas and practices "applying to all," as discussed in the conclusion of this book, then the European order hardly qualifies as the basis of something truly universal.

Then there is the deafening silence over the role of force in the expansion of international society. Bull argued that European-led international society was made possible because at that juncture, "the capacity of Asian and African powers to enter into relationships on a reciprocal basis with European states was less than in earlier times."[42] One might presume that the emphasis here is on "reciprocity" in diplomatic relations, but does it have anything to do with superior military force? In his chapter in *The Expansion*, Michael Howard concluded that "superior military technology was . . . not in itself a sufficient explanation for the European conquest of the world during the centuries of imperial power."[43] Yet it would be patently absurd, going by historical experience, to downplay the role of force in the spread of European colonialism, which is the original and fundamental driver in the creation and expansion of universal international society. Ultimately, "the standard of civilization" criteria, which the Europeans used normatively to exclude most non-European states from their conception of international society, was contingent on the ability of the European colonial powers to enforce it through their superior military might. This was an important reason why Japan focused so much on expanding its military capabilities (to enter the international society and keep its place there).[44]

The Expansion stressed the role of voluntary acceptance of European rules, institutions and practices by non-Western states as a reason for the expansion of European international society. Asian and African states found utility in incorporating European rules, institutions and standards for instituting their own domestic reforms and their adoption of these standards eventually led to the end of the extraterritoriality regimes and European privileges by narrowing the gap between themselves and European states.[45] Yet the explicit assumption that non-Western states were willing and even keen to enter into a European-conceived and managed international society understates the coercive nature of the assimilation of non-Europeans into the European/Universal international society.

In other words, before we consider whether non-Western states were *unable* to forge reciprocal relationships with the Europeans, one must consider whether they were *willing* to do so. There is no question that some non-Western rulers, for reasons of enhancing their prestige and power, willingly accepted the rules and institutions of European international society. However, this was true only of some states in the non-Western world, especially those that were large and powerful and harboured their own imperial ambitions. Japan's case fits well. But did many others, including large and important civilizational entities such as China and India crave entry into European international society? Hardly. This was especially so in the early stages of European expansion, when the benefits of entry into the European international society were not clear to non-Western societies[46] and, more importantly, when entry might have even been seen as dangerous and harmful from their vantage-point, and when reciprocity mainly meant offering trade and political concessions to the Europeans.

In this context, the very idea of "reciprocity" that Bull spoke of is problematic. Going by Bull's formulation of "the capacity of Asian and African powers to enter into relationships on a reciprocal basis with European states," the Europeans were demanding from non-Western societies an ability "to provide domestic law and order, administrative integrity, protection of the rights of foreign citizens, or the fulfilment of contracts."[47] In reality, the European demand for reciprocity was intended to secure for themselves trade opportunities and privileges (everything else, including spreading the gospel, was secondary), which had been gained sometimes through consent, sometimes through use of force. The benefits to non–Western states in these arrangements were unclear. Many non–Western states recognized that they would be entering into a relationship that would be one-sided in the favour of the Europeans. The demand for reciprocity in this sense could be construed as an excuse for exploitation. By viewing the expansion of European international society as a matter of Europeans seeking reciprocity, the early English School obscures the fact that colonialism was a fundamentally a non–reciprocal institution.

This brings us to the "standard of civilization" criteria employed by the Europeans to marginalize and exclude non–Western states from the purportedly universal international society. Bull and Watson acknowledge that standard of civilization reflected European arrogance, and that it was highly self-serving. They also acknowledged important variations among the European states and societies themselves regarding the values and capabilities to meet the standard of civilization. Some Europeans had low capacities similar to many in the non–West. Moreover, European states did not always adhere to their very own *European values*. They also accepted variations among the non–Western states and societies regarding values and interaction capacities. Some had more of these than others. Yet, Bull and Watson continued to insist that the standard of civilization was based on the realities of international life.[48] Bull himself was somewhat ambiguous and self-contradictory in his critique of the standard of civilization. He defends the standard of civilization criteria: "It could hardly have been expected that European states could have extended the full benefits of membership of the society of states to political entities that were in no position to enter into relationships on a basis of reciprocity. . . ."[49]

The Expansion accorded little agency to non–Western states and societies in the construction of international order. Bull asserted that the critique of the commonly accepted view of the standard of civilization thesis "neglects the influence of Asian international practices on the evolution of European ones."[50] But he did not specify what these influences were and how they had shaped European practices. He spoke of a "revolt against the West,"[51] but this revolt was cast as one against European colonialism, rather than against Western dominance of international order per se. In general, the early English School is highly deferential to the role of the great powers. The five mechanisms of order management that Bull identifies in his major personal work, *The Anarchical Society*,[52] namely, diplomacy, international law, war, balance of power and great powers, not only exclude norms (although one might say its discussion was subsumed under diplomacy, institutions and international law), they are also great-power centric; they lend themselves to be captured and dominated by the great powers themselves, with the possible exception of the first one: diplomacy. Non-great powers, especially from the non–Western world, may support these mechanisms to make them stronger, but can they really challenge them or significantly modify them?

Some of the problems and biases of the early English School have since been recognized and to some extent addressed by more recent scholarship from that

School. The revisionist English School pays much greater attention to world history.[53] Thus Adam Watson, though belonging to the original English School, came up with a more complete historical work that answers some of the deficiencies of the early English School.[54] Barry Buzan and Richard Little, latter-day stalwarts of the English School, have challenged the early English School's Eurocentrism.[55] As they put it, "the English School . . . made a serious attempt to work from a world history perspective . . . However, when we look at the English School's account of the expansion of international society the analysis once again becomes resolutely Eurocentric."[56] They offer an expanded notion of the international system that recognizes the non-European antecedents of the contemporary international system. Hence, "one can only explore the origins and significance of the idea of international system by comprehending its non-European dimension."[57] Another scholar from the English School who has contributed to the broadening of the English School's enquiry is Andrew Hurrell with his more agency oriented work on regionalism and regional orders.[58]

Conclusion

I have concentrated on identifying some dimensions of Western dominance with respect to four major instruments of international order. I should end by issuing a note of caution about the limitations of drawing too sharp a distinction between the West and the non-West. As Martin Wight noted in his analysis of Western values, neither West nor the non-West are categories that could be regarded as homogenous. The West is no longer one, if it ever was. Nor can there be any certainty about the shape and identity of the entity that has been excluded from IR theory. Is there a Third World, or Global South? The concept of the Third World has fallen into serious disuse since the end of the Cold War. But Global South is not entirely uncontroversial either.

I do not assume that only non-Western scholars are taking up the issue of Western dominance in IR theory. Many Western scholars are also uncomfortable with the status quo. This has led some to object that this distinction between West and non-West has become increasingly unsustainable and should be subsumed under a single global conversation about the nature and purpose of IR theory. While a global conversation is what we should really aim for, just because "West" and "non-West" are not homogenous categories does not mean that there is no problem of Western dominance in IR theory, both historically and in contemporary times. Like global warming, the problem of IR theory and Western dominance can no longer be wished away. But unlike global warming, it may be desirable here to let the temperature rise a bit for a much overdue debate, which unlike the grand inter-paradigm debates before, might actually end in rendering IR less of an American or Western "social science": a more "uniting" rather than "dividing discipline."[59]

Notes

1 This chapter is primarily based on a lecture bearing the same title in the "Reenvisioning Global Justice/Global Order" Seminar Series, Centre for International Studies, Oxford University, delivered on 22 February 2007, when I was the Politics Group Visitor at Nuffiled College. This section on the "Expansion of International Society Revisited," is based on my farewell lecture to the Department of Politics and International Relations, University of Bristol, on 9 December 2008.

2 Stanley Hoffmann, "An American Social Science: International Relations," *Daedalus* 106, no. 3 (1977): 41–60.

3 Amitav Acharya and Barry Buzan, "Why Is There No Non-Western International Relations Theory? An Introduction," *International Relations of Asia Pacific* (Special Issue edited by Amitav Acharya and Barry Buzan) 7, no. 3 (2007), 294.

4 Robert W. Cox, "Social Forces, States and World Orders: Beyond International Relations Theory," *Millennium – Journal of International Studies* 10, no. 2 (1981): 126–155.

5 Amitav Acharya, "Ethnocentrism and Emancipatory IR Theory," in *Displacing Security,* eds., Samantha Arnold and J. Marshall Bier (Toronto: Centre for International and Security Studies, York University, 2000).

6 Stephen M. Walt, *The Origin of Alliances* (Ithaca: Cornell University Press, 1987), 14–15.

7 Victoria Tin-bor Hui, "Toward a Dynamic Theory of International Politics: Insights from Comparing Ancient China and Early Modern Europe," *International Organization* 58, no. 1 (2004), 175–205.

8 David Kang, "Getting Asia Wrong: The Need for New Analytical Frameworks," *International Security* 27, no. 4 (2003): 57–85.

9 Robert H. Jackson, *Quasi-States: Sovereignty, International Relations and the Third World* (Cambridge: Cambridge University Press, 1991), 61.

10 Cited in Jackson, Ibid., 61.

11 Hedley Bull, cited in Jackson, Ibid., 61.

12 Daniel Philpott, "Westphalia, Authority and International Society", in *Sovereignty at the Millennium*, ed., Robert Jackson (Oxford: Blackwell, 1999), 160.

13 Christopher Clapham, "Sovereignty and the Third World State," in *Sovereignty at the Millennium*, ed., Robert Jackson (Oxford: Blackwell, 1999), 101.

14 To be discussed in chapter 9.

15 Jia Qingguo, "China," in *Humanitarian Intervention: The Evolving Asian Debate* (Tokyo: Japan Centre for International Exchange, 2003), 30.

16 Robert Jervis, "Security Regimes," *International Organization* 36, no. 2 (1982): 357–378.

17 Charles A. Kupchan and Clifford A. Kupchan, "Concerts, Collective Security, and the Future of Europe," *International Security* 16, no. 1 (1991): 114–161.

18 Susan Shirk, "Asia Pacific Regional Security: Balance of Power or Concert of Powers?", in *Regional Orders: Building Security in a New World*, eds., David A. Lake and Patrick Morgan (University Park, PA: The Pennsylvania State University Press, 1997): 245–270.

19 Jawaharlal Nehru, *The Discovery of India*, 23rd Impression (New Delhi: Oxford University Press, 2003), 539.

20 Mohammed Ayoob, "Security in the Third World: The Worm about to Turn?," *International Affairs* 60, no. 1 (1983–1984): 41–51.

21 Immanuel Kant, "Toward Perpetual Peace: A Philosophical Sketch," in *Toward Perpetual Peace and Other Writings on Politics, Peace and History*, ed., Pauline Kleingeld (Translated by David L. Coclasure) (New Haven, CT: Yale University Press, 2006), 82.

22 Ibid.

23 Ibid., 83.

24 Ernst B. Haas, "International Integration: The European and the Universal Process," *International Organization* 15, no. 3 (1961): 366–392. Chapter 5 discusses the limits of regional integration theories in the non–Western world.

25 Joseph S. Nye, "Central American Regional Integration," *International Regionalism*, ed., Joseph S. Nye (Boston, MA: Little, Brown, 1968), 381–382.

26 Amitav Acharya, *Constructing a Security Community in Southeast Asia: ASEAN and the Problem of Regional Order* (London: Routledge, 2001).

27 Lynn H. Miller, "The Prospect for Order Through Regional Security", in *Regional Politics and World Order*, eds., Richard A. Falk and Saul H. Mendlovitz (San Francisco, CA: W.H. Freeman and Company, 1973), 58.

28 Shaun Breslin, Richard Higgott and Ben Rosamond, "Regions in Comparative Perspective," in *New Regionalisms in the Global Political Economy*, eds., Shaun Breslin, et al. (London: Routledge, 2002), 13.

29 Peter J. Katzenstein, "Introduction: Asian Regionalism in Comparative Perspective," in *Network Power: Japan and Asia*, eds., Peter J. Katzenstein and Takashi Shiraishi (Ithaca, NY: Cornell University Press, 1997), 5.

30 John Stuart Mill, *On Liberty, 4th Edition* (London: Longman, Roberts & Green, 1869). http://www.bartleby.com/130/1.html.

31 Martin Wight, "Western values in international relations," in *Diplomatic Investigations*, eds., Herbert Butterfield and Martin Wight (London: Allen & Unwin, 1966), 96 and 4.

32 Ibid., 89.

33 Amitav Acharya, "How Ideas Spread: Whose Norms Matter: Norm Localization and Institutional Change in Asian Regionalism," *International Organization* 58, no. 2 (2004): 239–275. This article appears as chapter 8 of this book.

34 Peter Katzenstein, *A World of Regions: Asia and Europe* in the *American Imperium* (Ithaca, NY: Cornell University Press, 2005); Amitav Acharya, "Ideas, Identity, and Institution-Building: From the 'ASEAN Way' to the 'Asia Pacific Way,'" *Pacific Review* 10, no. 2 (1997): 319–346.

35 The only exception to this claim would be post-colonialism, whose following though growing, is yet to rival the influence of the English School.

36 *The Expansion of International Society* has been called as "the most complete achievement" of the English School by an important intellectual history of the School. Brunello Vigezzi, *The British Committee on the Theory of International Politics 1954–1985: The Rediscovery of History* (Milan, Italy: Edizioni Unicopli, 2005), 289. I do not imply here that the English School is monolithic or unchanging. Notable subsequent contributions to the core theoretical literature of the English School include Tim Dunne, *Inventing International Society* (London: St. Martin Press, 1998); Barry Buzan, *From International to World Society? English School Theory and the Social Structure of Globalisation* (Cambridge: Cambridge University Press, 2004); Andrew Linklater and Hidemi Suganami, *The English School of International Relations: A Contemporary Reassessment* (Cambridge: Cambridge University Press, 2006); and Andrew Hurrell, *On Global Order: Power, Values, and the Constitution of International Society* (Oxford: Oxford University Press, 2007). A contribution that took particular account of the non-Western world, see: Adam Watson, *The Evolution of International Society: A Comparative Historical Analysis* (London: Routledge, 1992, Reissued in 2009 with a new introduction by Barry Buzan and Richard Little). Also important in relating the English School to the colonial order, hence especially relevant to my critique, is Edward Keene, *Beyond the Anarchical Society: Grotius, Colonialism and Order in World Politics* (Cambridge: Cambridge University Press, 2002).

37 Hedley Bull, "The Revolt against the West," in *The Expansion of International Society*, eds., Hedley Bull and Adam Watson (Oxford: Clarendon Press, 1984), 217.

38 Hedley Bull, "The Revolt Against Western Dominance: From a European to a Global International Order," in Vigezzi, *The British Committee on the Theory of International Politics*, 425.

39 Hedley Bull and Adam Watson, "Introduction," in *The Expansion of International Society*, eds., Hedley Bull and Adam Watson (Oxford: Clarendon Press, 1984), 8.

40 Ibid., 2.

41 Buzan and Little argue that: "in their individual and joint contributions to *The Expansion of International Society*, Bull and Watson (1984), central figures in the first generation of the English School, demonstrate a clear awareness of the need to consider the question of global connections in their attempt to establish a "grand narrative" from an international relations and world historical perspective. They work, however, from an essentially Eurocentric perspective and argue that the basic features of the contemporary international political structure have been inherited from Europe." Barry Buzan and Richard Little, "World History and the Development of Non-Western International Relations Theory," in *Non-Western International Relations Theory: Perspectives On and Beyond Asia*, eds., Amitav Acharya and Barry Buzan (New York: Routledge, 2010).

42 Bull, "The Emergence of a Universal International Society," 125. In their revisionist work on the English School, Buzan and Little speak of "interaction capacity" by which they mean "adequate transportation and communication capabilities, in order to bring all actors into close enough contact that would allow them, at least in principle, to make war or alliance." Barry Buzan and Richard Little, "Why International Relations Has Failed as an Intellectual Project and What to do About it," *Millennium – Journal of International Studies* 30 no. 19 (2001): 19–39, 26. See also, Barry Buzan and Richard Little, *International Systems in World History: Remaking the Study of International Relations* (Oxford: Oxford University Press, 2000). It is not clear whether the original English School scholars understood "the capacity of Asian and African powers to enter into relationships on a reciprocal basis" in a similar broad sense, but it would be reasonable to assume that superior military capacity would be one of the elements, albeit an understated one in their overall explanation of the causes of the initial expansion of the European international society.

43 Michael Howard, "The Military Factor in European Expansion," in *The Expansion of International Society*, eds. Hedley Bull and Adam Watson (Oxford: Clarendon Press, 1984), 41.

44 Hidemi Suganami brings this out clearly in "Japan's Entry into *International* Society," in *The Expansion of International Society*, Hedley Bull and Adam Watson, eds. (Oxford: Clarendon Press, 1984), 185–199.

45 Hedley Bull and Adam Watson, "Conclusion," in *The Expansion of International Society*, eds., Hedley Bull and Adam Watson (Oxford: Clarendon Press, 1984), 437.

46 The best example of this attitude was of course Qing emperor Qian Long's letter to the British King George III in 1793, ". . . our Celestial Empire possesses all things in prolific abundance and lacks no product within its own borders. There was therefore no need to import the manufactures of outside barbarians in exchange for our own produce." E. Backhouse and J.O.P. Bland, *Annals and Memoirs of the Court of Peking: From the 16th to the 20th Century* (Boston, MA: Houghton Mifflin, 1914), 326.

47 Bull and Watson, "Conclusion," 427.

48 Ibid.

49 Ibid., 122.

50 Ibid., 123.

51 Hedley Bull, "The Revolt against the West," in *The Expansion of International Society*, eds., Hedley Bull and Adam Watson (Oxford: Clarendon Press, 1984), 217–228.

52 Hedley Bull, *The Anarchical Society: A Study of Order in World Politics* (New York: Columbia University Press, 1977).

53 Buzan and Little, *International Systems in World History*.

54 Watson, *The Evolution of International Society*.

55 Barry Buzan and Richard Little, "The Idea of 'International System': Theory Meets History," *International Political Science Review* 15 no. 3 (1994): 231–255. See also: Buzan and Little, "The Historical Expansion of International Society," in *The International Studies Encyclopedia*, V, ed., Robert A. Denemark (Chichester, UK: Wiley-Blackwell for the International Studies Association, 2010).

56 Barry Buzan and Richard Little, "World History and the Development of International Relations Theory," in *Non-Western International Relations Theory: Perspectives on and Beyond Asia*, eds., Amitav Acharya and Barry Buzan (London: Routledge, 2010), 199.

57 Buzan and Little, "The Idea of 'International System'," 235.

58 Andrew Hurrell, "One World? Many Worlds? The Place of Regions in the Study of International Society," *International Affairs* 83 no. 1 (2007): 127–146. Buzan has encouraged regional adaptations of the ES framework. Barry Buzan and Ana Gonzalez-Pelaez, eds., *International Society and the Middle East: English School Theory at the Regional Level* (Bassingstoke, UK: Palgrave Macmillan, 2009).

59 Kalevi. J. Holsti, *The Dividing Discipline: Hegemony and Diversity in International Theory* (Winchester, MA: Allen & Unwin, 1985).

2

DIALOGUE AND DISCOVERY: IN SEARCH OF INTERNATIONAL RELATIONS THEORIES BEYOND THE WEST[1]

That the study of International Relations (IR) – the main theories, the dominant centres of teaching and research, the leading publications – neglects or marginalizes the world beyond the West is no longer a novel argument that requires proving or elaboration.[2] What is more challenging is to find some agreement on how to redress this problem and move forward. Some of the ideas and avenues suggested towards a genuinely international field of IR have themselves been criticized and provoked controversy. This includes questions about what to study, how to study, where to study IR. Resolving all these controversies and finding common ground may not be possible, or even desirable, but having a dialogue about them seems timely and essential to the original cause that everyone agrees on: that the current parochialism and ethnocentrism of "International Relations" as a field of study, especially its dominant theoretical approaches, are unacceptable and perhaps untenable. As a further contribution to the ongoing debate and reflection on this question, my goals in this chapter are two-fold. First, I highlight some of these issues that have aroused controversy and should be subjected to further dialogue. Then I offer some thoughts on how to move forward in this effort, while keeping the debate and dialogue alive and well, in the voyage of discovery of approaches that may contribute towards a genuinely global discipline of international relations.

Dissent to dialogue

Efforts to address the "problem of Western dominance" in international relations theories (IRT) by developing "non-Western" or "post-Western" approaches (my own preference is for the former, although the exact naming is a key point of disagreement to be discussed later) have provoked debates over four main questions:

1. Whether existing IR theories are already adequate to account for non-Western experiences and voices, and those which have not been are already expanding their analytic scope and reach to issues and concerns of the world as a whole. These include not only critical theories, but also the mainstream theories such as realism, liberalism and constructivism.
2. Whether attempts to develop indigenous concepts and theories end up simply mimicking Western theories.
3. Whether the "West," "non-Western," and "post-Western" are useful categories, or whether one should approach the problem as a single global dialogue on the limitations and exclusions of IR theory.
4. Whether one should engage in developing IRT through national or regional or institutional "schools."

In the sections below, I briefly deal with each of these questions.

The adequacy of existing IRT

A special issue of the journal *International Relations of the Asia-Pacific* entitled "Why Is There No Non-Western International Relations Theory"[3] explored the question: have existing IR theories found the right answers to all the main questions of interest to international relations scholars? Its finding, drawing on the various case studies in the volume, was that it had not. But this remains an important point of objection to non-Western IRT (NWIRT) from mainstream theorists (who are uncomfortable with the notion, even though they have not seriously objected to it, perhaps because it is too new and feeble to pose a challenge to Western dominance). Again, no one denies that existing IRT is too narrow – that is, that is leaves out non-Western voices and the distinctive features of non-Western relationships. But there is a sense that existing IRT can address this distinctiveness (which can be overstated in an era of globalization). Thus, G. John Ikenberry and Michael Mastanduno argue that while international dynamics in Asia might have had some distinctive features historically, this distinctiveness had been diluted by the progressive integration of the region into the modern international system. The international relations of Asia has acquired the behavioral norms and attributes associated with the modern inter-state system which originated from Europe and still retains much of the features of the Westphalian model. Hence, the core concepts of IRT such as hegemony, the distribution of power, international institutions, and political identity, are as relevant in the Asian context as anywhere else.[4]

Unlike Ikenberry and Mastanduno, Jack Snyder accepts China's claim to a distinctive strategic culture. But in offering some sensible points of caution (to be discussed later) against the development of a "distinctively Chinese approach to international relations theory," Snyder argues that China's undeniably distinctive situation does not have to be analyzed by the use of a distinctive theory." Instead, this distinctiveness can be the basis for "gaining deeper insight into more general theories that can be applied across a broad range of contexts."[5] In other words,

Snyder asks that existing IRT be applied to China in order to be broadened and deepened on the basis of findings about their fit or lack thereof. This is akin to Alagappa's position in the context of Asia that "Asia is fertile ground to debate, test, and develop many of these [Western] concepts and competing theories, and to counteract the ethnocentric bias."[6]

Snyder's preference for using Chinese distinctiveness to test and broaden the standard Western-dominated IRT, as opposed to using a distinctively Chinese philosophy and historical context to unseat the latter, is revealing. For him, the "main difference" between existing theories such as realism and liberalism, and Confucianism (which Snyder assumes as the main philosophical basis for a Chinese school) is that "realism and liberalism present themselves as universally applicable paradigms, whereas Confucianism is formulated a (sic) specific to Chinese or East Asian civilization."[7] Yet one might ask: are realism and liberalism genuinely universal, even though they present themselves as such? One hardly needs to be reminded of the Western historical and philosophical roots of both. To give just one example, one of the most influential strands of liberal institutionalism, i.e. neofunctionalism, conceded that the European model of integration did not work in other parts of the world, and hence a distinction should be made between the "European" and the "universal" process of international integration.[8] But there is a larger point here. To say that IRT should be inclusive of non-Western voices and realities is not to say that Western-derived theories are irrelevant, especially when they apply to relationships within the West and between Western and the non-Western actors. Indeed, there is hardly any agreement on the need to reject or dismiss the entire corpus of Western IRT. Contending that one cannot dismiss "the entire cannon [of IR theory] as flawed when it comes to the Third World," Sondhi argues: "Rather than dismissing IR theory outright for its shortcomings in explaining the problems of countries such as in South Asia, we may be better advised to look toward peripheral regions for what they can contribute to testing, revising, and advancing our theories of international politics."[9] In many countries around the world, there is a good deal of acceptance of the very largely Western-derived IRT. To be sure, IRT shows major gaps when it comes to explaining the political, economic and security relationships in the non-Western world.[10] But dismissing Western theories simply because they are Western can be a slippery slope to the relativist trap.

It is important to bear in mind that the so-called mainstream IRT is not monolithic and unchanging. William Brown argues that IRT has been made more relevant to the non-Western world with the help of extensions and "advances."[11] There is also the "constructivist turn" (one might say onslaught or even dominance, but certainly it is now considered "mainstream") in international relations theory. One suspects that constructivism, despite its distinctly Western origin, has helped to foster a growing body of theoretical work on Africa, Asia, Latin America, and Islam.[12] This could be due to its sensitivity to questions of identity and culture, identified by Arlene Tickner as one of the major sources of non-Western theorizing.[13] This is not necessarily to say that constructivism has encouraged *scholars from those regions* to take a greater interest in IRT in general. But in the words of a Malaysian scholar, "Thinking in the constructivist vein has been about the best gift made available to scholars and leaders in the [Asian] region."[14] One might also see post-colonialism, feminism and other strands of critical IRT – all of which have significant Western pedigree – for having played a similar role in broadening the relevance and appeal of theory generally. In short, the evolution and growing diversity of Western IR is one reason why it may be wrong to reject IRT as it exists today as irrelevant to the non-Western world. Some IRT are less static and ethnocentric than others. Examples include constructivism's attention to culture, institutionalism's insights into conflict and cooperation in the non-Western context, and realism's insights into why state sovereignty and inequality persist in the South.[15] And critical IRT itself, although born in the West, if not in the USA, has offered many valuable insights into studying non-Western IR. The challenge is to infuse and enrich these with more voices, perspectives, philosophical positions and arguments from the non-Western world, including approaches that pose radical alternatives to the ontological, epistemological and methodological positions of the dominant IRT.

Nonetheless, it is clear that the call for bridging the North–South gap in IRT by testing, extending and revising the existing Western IRT like realism, liberalism, and constructivism would not address the need and demand for change. Such extensions would not sufficiently dampen the dominance of Western IRT.[16] What is needed is "proposals for alternative theories about the functioning of international relations that have their origin in the South."[17] This leads to the question of what constitutes authentic NWIRT and whether some of the non-Western formulations on IRT are simple mimicry of the Western or are "genuinely" post-Western, a subject to which I shall turn to now.

Mimicry[18] *or demolition?*

In an earlier survey of the field of IR, William Olson and Nicholas Onuf hoped to see "the ideal of a cosmopolitan discipline in which adepts from many cultures enrich the discourse of International Relations with all the world's ways of seeing and knowing." But they also warned that the globalization of IR may well indicate "the successful diffusion of the Anglo-American cognitive style and professional stance rather than the absorption of alien modes of thought."[19] To some, this is precisely what is happening to a good deal of the recent efforts to explore the possibility of non-Western IR theories. Are these efforts then mere "mimicry" or "local variations" of Western theories and debates?[20]

One issue here is that it is not entirely clear whether those why cry mimicry are seeking a "sequel" or a "reboot." Part of the answer to the mimicry issue needs to be considered in conjunction with the question previously discussed: do all existing theories lack (or lack to the same degree) meaning or relevance when analysing the non-Western world? Are we to summarily reject IRT just because they are Western or put a stop to making any references to them? What are the alternative pathways being suggested that would qualify as genuinely non-Western or post-Western? An obvious alternative would be the critical theories of international relations, but these, as noted, are not divorced from Western influence either. Should we start from an indigenous base and then link up with available Western theories, if and where it helps a better understanding of the problem at hand? This would require lesser reliance on deductive theorizing aimed at "testing" theories. Instead, a good pathway to developing IRT beyond the West would be to rely on "induction" or "abduction" in generalizing from a local experience on its own terms, or "using a dialectical combination of theory and empirical findings, moving back and forth between the two to produce an appropriate account."[21] These questions require much more careful debate and dialogue, without which we run the risk of trivializing the whole idea of developing a genuinely universal discipline of IR.

For example, one may be tempted to view some of the recent efforts to develop non-Western or post-Western approaches in terms of a desire to extend and universalize the English School or constructivism or securitization theories because of the declared or perceived prior theoretical positions of their key proponents (i.e. Buzan, Acharya, and Weaver respectively). But this would be wrong. One does not necessarily find in these efforts a conscious effort to privilege any particular theory. This is certainly true of the Acharya–Buzan efforts,[22] which highlight a certain ethnocentrism and Western bias in all of them, and whose main focus and urging has been against Western theory testing and for theory building – the latter being conceived as thinking theoretically about a region or a country on its own terms, that is, to look precisely for "alternative theories about the functioning of international relations that have their origin in the South."[23]

More work of this nature could certainly help. For example, the central position of the state in IRT is being challenged as African IR debates would suggest.[24] The next step would be to develop alternative theories of statehood "out of Africa" that would displace the influential "out of North America" perspective around "juridical" versus "empirical" statehood.[25] Moreover, the search for IRT beyond the West should not be wedded to the epistemology of current theories, whether mainstream or critical. A search for alternative knowledge should question dominant claims about knowledge production and offer alternative pathways, as will be discussed later.[26]

West versus the rest

Neither Western nor non-Western is a homogenous concept. Contestations over IRT occurs within as much as between them. Non-Western is to some extent useful as a term of convenience to interrogate the idea of "Western" that has been so dominant and pervasive in the mainstream IRT, and as a point of reference to engage theorists such as the founders of the English School who used these concepts "Western" and "European" to lay out their own beliefs about the foundations and evolution of international relations.[27] This is certainly a far cry from the "West versus the rest" formulations that one finds in some recent policy discourses,[28] for which I see little justification in the debate over the universality of IRT.

There are good arguments against using a dichotomous view. If the West is not one, much less so is the non-West in terms of positions, perspectives and aspirations with respect to theory. Some argue that Africa is more marginalized in IRT compared to Asia and Latin America,[29] although I am not sure everyone will agree. Yet while the controversy over whether West and non-West are useful remains, one suspects alternative categories such as "Third World," "Global South," "subaltern," "post-colonial," "post-Western"[30] will each prove to be unsatisfactory. Moreover, many who question the utility of the term non-West seem to have relatively less issue with the idea and phrase "West." Is the West a more cohesive and meaningful term? If so, what then does one make of the differences between the American, Continental European, and English School versions of, and approaches to, IR?

It may be argued that while the term non-Western may have some utility when we designate physical spaces, cultural contexts and identities of scholars, it is less satisfying as the basis of articulating coherent, autonomous ideas and theories of IR. Perhaps it is in this former sense that Chan and Mandaville speak of "bodies of non-Western knowledge," and Tickner and Waever refer to "non-Western and 'Third World' contexts," and "non-Western scholars."[31] Why not then non-Western IRT?

Yet, even this limited sense still leaves room for contestation. Is there a singular non-Western context? In writing theoretically, IR scholars naturally tend to dwell on local and regional contexts and concerns of their time; theory is thus effectively regionalized. For Asia, for example, it's growth (and now "rise"); for Africa, it is marginalization and structural adjustment (in the 1980s and 1990s at least); for Latin America, it is dependence, hegemony, and defence of democracy, etc. Just as the meaning of "theory" varies between the US and Europe,[32] the study of IR means different things in different regions.[33] And then there is the question of who is a non-Western scholar? How does one define a scholar born in Jamaica (with or without dual citizenship) but working in Canada?

But the issue of what one might call it should not be used to delegitimize work which in different pathways contributes to the goal of moving IRT past Western-centrism. Writing from a postcolonial perspective, Pinar Bilgin notes that the idea of a "non-Western" in IR scholarship does not imply passive submission to IR knowledge generated by the West. What may be regarded as "non-Western" does not necessarily originate within "teleological Westernisation," and those that do not appear to be radically different but appear to be framed within the categories and concepts of Western IRT cannot be dismissed as "the robotic 'Stepford Wife' to 'Western IR'." Such a stance, as Bilgin concludes, "denies agency to 'non-Western' scholars and represents them as unthinking emulators."[34] I agree wholeheartedly.

At the same time, as noted above, one should recognize that dialogues about the limitations of IRT are occurring within, as well as between the West and the non-West. On the one hand, many Western scholars are uncomfortable with the earlier parochialism of the field. Thus, Buzan and Little challenge and seek to "reformulate" Bull and Watson's *The Expansion of International Society*.[35] On the other hand, some non-Western scholars continue to believe in the centrality of existing Western IRT and do not want it replaced. Others question the way a NWIRT is being developed.

The pathways to a universal discipline of IR need not and will not be identical, a diversity that should be welcomed. There remain important differences between the structural conditions for the study of IR in the South and those in the West, which should be recognized. But at the same time, both the West and the rest are increasingly diverse within themselves, and there are cross-cutting cleavages and identities as well. Not only do non-Western scholars draw from their Western counterparts, the so-called Western IRT may also have roots in the non-Western spheres.[36] Iranian scholar Homeira Moshirzadeh notes that, "studies done from a Third World perspective have similarities to and differences from those done by Western scholars." This underscores the "importance of understanding the contexts within which non-Western IRs are developed."[37]

None of what has been mentioned above should preclude the need for and possibility of a single global dialogue that accommodates diversity. But as Jorgensen notes, in moving the discipline forward, one should "acknowledge the actually existing global diversity of practicing the discipline," although "diversity should probably not be cherished for its own sake." The challenge is to "take the steam out of several claims about universal validity but will also raise the important issue of the relative merits of the different ways of knowing the 'international.'"[38]

Let a "Thousand Flowers" bloom?

If one is to question the integrity of the idea of a NWIRT as a homogenous and overarching project, shouldn't the natural next step be to open it to national and regional voices? Is organizing IRT into national or regional schools necessary or desirable? For those who are involved in such enterprise, there are several obvious advantages: it is easier to make a statement about a particular approach, propagate viewpoints, mobilize interest and resources, and attract attention and even prestige. One looks no further than the establishment of an English School section in the International Studies Association to get a sense of this.

It is of course not always the case that such schools are internally homogenous or externally exclusive. To cite again the example of the English School (which also goes by the name of the "international society" perspective), it has had Hedley Bull, an Australian, Robert Jackson a Canadian, and more contentiously Charles Manning, a South African, and the Chinese-born but UK-trained Yongjin Zhang (now at Bristol). And within the School itself, there have been divisions over leadership and naming.[39] But there are also important downsides to the national or regional schools. They can become intellectual and methodological (if not ideological) straightjackets, creating barriers to pluralization and cross-national/regional discourse. And they can and do become exceptionalist, self-serving, and even repressive. They can seem, fairly or unfairly, to be rationalizations of a country's (or rather power's) shifting fortunes, decline or rise. The Singapore School of the 1990s, more a policy discourse than an academic project, was widely seen as an intellectual justification for Lee Kuan Yew's brand of soft authoritarianism. One probably would not hear much about a Chinese School of IR if China was not a "rising" power. Reading a fascinating history of the emergence of the English School through the deliberations of the British Committee on the Theory of International Relations,[40] it is hard to escape the feeling that these might have been the ruminations and rationalizations of the intellectual elite of a decaying power. At the risk of oversimplification, can one think of the founders of the English School as a group of British scholars, their country sidelined by the centrality of the US–Soviet rivalry and the development of a European Community in which Britain was a late and skeptical participant, who would nostalgically ruminate (with the help of an American grant) over a European-dominated global past in which Britain was once *the* dominant actor? Even though it no longer dominated the world, it had left a substantial legacy that is being voluntarily emulated by everyone else on the planet. If we are to accept the view that IRT often reflects a particular national context and grows out of a specific national experience, might one then be justified in viewing the early English School as a way of understanding and perhaps taking comfort in the decline of Europe, if not of Britain alone?[41]

Hence the question that one must confront here is whether the development of non-Western IR theories is the exclusive preserve of a strong nation or power, e.g. China, Japan, India, Iran, etc. This, of course, would be hardly unusual, given the historically close nexus between power (Britain, Europe, and USA) and production of IR knowledge. But then in attempting to broaden IRT beyond one set of parochialisms, we would end up replacing one set of parochialisms with another or a combination of them.[42]

One can illustrate some of these problems with reference to current efforts to develop a Chinese School of IRT. Although claims to distinctiveness in the international system are not a Chinese monopoly,[43] nowhere is the attempt to develop a national school of IRT on the basis of national cultural identity more pronounced than in today's China. Since the reform era began, there has been a debate within China over "whether an IR theory (or a set of theories) with Chinese characteristics should and could be established."[44] The early advocates of such theories were referring to themes such as the "Five Principles of Peaceful Co-Existence," "anti-hegemonism," and China's "independent foreign policy." But this invited skepticism from others within China's IR community who saw it as a way of legitimizing Chinese official interpretation of world affairs. In the end, few successful attempts could be made about drawing from the classical Chinese tradition of thought and diplomacy.[45] This has changed now. In recent years, attempts to construct a Chinese School of IRT revolves around providing a theoretical basis for China's "peaceful rise" (although shades of the earlier focus on foreign policy concerns such as anti-hegemonism, five principles, etc. remain). Moreover, such efforts have been accompanied by a revival of selected historical ideas and

institutions including but not limited to Confucianism. Qin argues that social theory must have a "theoretical hard core" centred on a "big idea" or a "big problematic." For China, it is the idea of *Datong* or "Universal Great Harmony," key
elements of which are the tributary system and the "all under heaven" worldview
(*Tainxia*) (he does not include Confucianism, although others do).[46]

Jack Snyder has warned against this development in no uncertain terms: ". . .
a monolithic Chinese School could produce a stultifying uniformity, intellectual
cheerleading for government policies, and an ideological justification for a blink-
ered Chinese nationalism that hinders rather than expands understanding."[47] Moreover, everyone, not least the key proponents of a Chinese School of IRT, presents
Confucianism (and to a lesser extent the earlier Zhou dynasty vintage concept
of Tianxia or "all under heaven") as the main basis of a Chinese School, thereby
lending themselves to the charge of ethnocentrism when a more transnational, pan-
Asian and thus universal strand of thinking within China, especially Buddhism (to
be discussed later), could be taken.

A similar caution has been sounded about India, the other emerging power from
Asia. Compared to China, there is much less interest and success in India in developing an Indian School.[48] This is notwithstanding the fact that IR has a longer history
here than in China, and Indian scholars bemoan the advances in IR teaching and
research in China while India, once Asia's leader in this, is left further behind.[49] A
recent report on the state of IR in India has argued that one of the goals of improv-
ing the sorry state of international studies in India should be to "ensure that Indian
IS [international studies] scholarship contributes to increasing the knowledge base
on India's role as a responsible power fostering peace, security, good governance,
economic development, and resolution of a wide range of problems in its immediate
region and the world."[50] This is not a call for developing an "Indian school of IRT"
in the way the case for a Chinese school of IRT has been made. But it underscores
the potential for self-centrism in any such enterprise, a danger that was recognized by
Bajpai before anyone took note of India's rise when he warned that there is a danger
inherent in efforts to develop an IRT out of India – that of "lapsing into uncritical
nativism or seeking some essentialist 'Indian' vision."[51]

There are other dangers associated with such schools. It revives the question: is
IRT the preserve of great powers? Does progress in IR require pitting American
and European ethnocentrism against Chinese and Indian ethnocentrism? Are we
to substitute Western (American, British) hegemony and parochialism for another.
And, if not global, then a regional hegemony? It is interesting to note in this context that that there are fewer demands for an African school. Peter Vale, a respected
African voice notes: "There is almost nothing in the IR canon on Africa. Each time
there is an encounter between IR and Africa the discipline and its cult figures resort
to their individual default position – Realism, Liberalism, Critique and Social Construction. Each of these lenses are carefully grounded in western epistemology and
most, of course, are at great distance from Africa and its ways." But when addressing the question, "Should there be a fully African IR?" he answers, "Of course not.
But, plainly, there should be a greater sensitivity to African ways of knowing the

international."[52] Another danger concerns the lack of freedom of expression. This would stifle the development of any kind of theory, but the danger is especially inherent in monolithic national or transnational schools. Iran is a case in point. In Iran, Islam has emerged as a major basis for theorizing about IR, but "younger scholars have been cautious not to transcend what is traditionally regarded theologically acceptable by major religious authorities."[53]

Discourse to discovery

Despite my disagreement with some of the criticisms levelled against the emerging literature on NWIRT, I welcome these criticisms and debates as they point to productive avenues for further research. They have served to clarify numerous ways in which Western IRT dominates and excludes. But we also need to move beyond discourses to research and scholarship in order to identify potentially complementary and alternative sources of theorizing that includes the non-Western states and societies.

Genealogy of international systems

Rethinking IR should also involve revisiting the prevailing genealogy of supposedly Western concepts which have claimed universality. And a good starting point is Westphalia, and our "Westphalic"[54] view of international systems, or the view that the modern international system is Westphalia "writ large." As Buzan and Little put it, "Westphalia-based IR theory is not only incapable of understanding premodern international systems, but also . . . its lack of historical perspective makes it unable to answer, in many instances address, the most important questions about the modern international system."[55]

Early English School theorists led by Bull and Watson took the view that the contemporary international system resulted from a world-wide acceptance and incorporation by non-Western societies of the rules and norms of European international society, leading to what might be called Westphalia writ large. For Bull, this process of expansion of European international society resulted from the failure of non-Western rulers to conduct themselves on the basis of equality and reciprocity (whether the failure might have been the result of the use of coercion or force is sidestepped).[56] Buzan and Little, drawing upon C.H. Alexandrowicz's painstakingly detailed analysis of the treaties between European East India companies (as representatives of European sovereigns in whose name they were contracted) and the Asian rulers, question the view that the Europeans always regarded the non-Western societies as unequal and dealt with them on the basis of the "standards of civilization" thesis to dismiss their claim to sovereignty and exclude them from the society of states. Alexandrowicz's research shows that the encounter between the "two worlds took place on a footing of equality and the ensuing commercial and political transactions, far from being in a legal vacuum, were governed by the law of nations as adjusted to local inter-state custom." This was a far cry from the principle of *terra nullius* (though it might have been originally intended).[57]

But much more work needs to be done on non-Western international systems. First, the existing literature on pre-Westphalian international systems or international order shows not only a Western bias, but also a power bias or a bias towards dominant powers, or "structure of the dominant units."[58] Hence, the idea of an international system implies close or intense interactions, often around a central power or hegemon, or a balance of power system featuring two or more great powers. It fails to capture systems where relations among units are neither hegemonic, nor of a balance of power type. Interactions anchored on trade, ideas (including political ideas) and culture, where empire, hegemony or explicit and continuous power balancing is absent, are ignored. This leaves out large parts of the world. For example, the Indian Ocean, with a long history of commerce and flow of ideas (sans direct conquest or hegemony) is not considered to be an international system, while the Mediterranean is (thanks to *pax Romana*).

Our explorations into pre-Westphalian international systems need to be expanded. First, international systems do not have to resemble Westphalian type of relationships that resemble or approximate anarchy, e.g. the Greek city-states or the Warring States of China to qualify for the term. Second, international systems are not just built around political–military interactions, but also economic and social ones.[59] Third, international systems could develop out of ideational interactions as much as material ones such as trade and conquest. These elements often come together, although one can find examples where the flow of trade, migration and ideas can occur without the backing of military force. A case in point would be what historians refer to as the "Indianisation of Southeast Asia."[60] Moreover, while one would not go so far as to suggest that international systems could be purely ideational, or "ideas all the way down," one should not ignore their importance either, and one might – following Wendt – look for their ideational structure (the distribution of ideas) first before turning to the materialist structure (distribution of power), rather than the other way around.[61]

Moreover, we should recognize that the dominant Western source of thinking about international relations concepts and theories is not just Westphalia, but also the classical Mediterranean. A good deal of the ideas that we use in IRT today come directly or indirectly from the world that Greece and Rome made, but not from the Phoenicians, Egyptians, or Persians. This refers not only to established theories, but also more recent variations and formulations. Realists have long traced their lineage to Thucydides, but Reus-Smit has written a fascinating work on the constitutive principles of international society from the Greek city-states, Daniel Deudney has challenged both realism and liberalism with a republican security theory originating from the Roman Republic, and Ned Lebow has derived a "cultural theory of international relations" from the Greek concept of honour.[62] We are yet to see such grand theorizing from the Sumerian,[63] Egyptian, Chinese or Indian pasts, stuck as we are with the idea of Kautilya being an Indian Machiavelli, rather than Machiavelli being an Italian (or Mediterranean) Kautilya.

Agency

The issue of genealogy is closely linked to the question of agency. In developing IRT beyond the West, Tickner asks that our focus should be "less on the developing world as an *object* of IR study, but rather as an *agent* of IR knowledge."[64] When the positivist notion of standards of civilization replaced natural law which had recognized the status of all nations under international law, it denied the agency of non-Western polities and societies in regulating international affairs. The latter could not play the positive game of sovereignty,[65] including the all-important game of power balancing. Yet, especially if we define agency as having material and ideational dimensions, then non-Western societies have much to claim, even in the modern era of Western dominance. A case in point, discussed in Alexandrowicz, is Grotius's concept of *Mare Liberum*. Widely credited as the founder of the doctrine, Grotius is now believed to have been deeply informed and influenced by the "outstanding precedent for maritime freedom offered by the regime in the Indian Ocean in contrast to maritime practice in Europe" [*mare clausum*].[66]

Until now, the role of non-Western countries or the Third World in the international system has been conceptualized and presented as that of dissent and rebellion in terms of Bull's classic formulation of a "revolt against the West." But as Ayoob notes, the Third World has also served a conformist role.[67] One could extend the argument further, and claim that the so-called Third World has been a maker of international rules and norms.[68] This is constitutive *rule making, not just rule mimicking*. It can be seen from two types of diffusion of fundamental norms of international relations – constitutive localization and subsidiarity, including those of sovereignty and non-intervention. The idea of constitutive localization suggests significant modification and adaptation of foreign norms (including Western norms that are prominent at the global level) on the basis of indigenous, pre-existing beliefs and practices. The idea of subsidiarity refers to the creation of new rules and exporting them to the wider regional and global level to influence and shape relations within the Third World and between the Third World and the West. This normative agency of non-Western actors compensates for their lack of structural power, and is a rich site for theory building. Examples include norms of Arabism from the Middle East, Latin American and African norms of inviolability of postcolonial boundaries, Latin America's strengthening and institutionalization of non-intervention, and the Asian construction and modification of the same norm to delegitimize great power alliances and power balancing. Although some of these norms are of Western origin, their creative adaptation and repatriation are important examples of agency that cannot be denied a place in IRT.

Humanizing IRT

One of the key issues in recent debates about IRT, especially the post-positivist challenge to the neorealist–neoliberal synthesis, is the centrality of the state in mainstream IRT (whether realism, liberalism or Wendtian constructivism). Hence, a concept that puts the individual at the centre of IRT is richly appealing in thinking about alternative IRT. The emergence and growing prominence of approaches to various sub-fields of IR with the human prefix, such as human development, human security, humanitarian intervention and humane globalization, along with the earlier and ongoing study of human rights, is therefore a development of fundamental importance.

These concepts and understandings capture many of the key challenges that have been excluded from mainstream IRT. The referent object in human development/security is not necessarily the individual person (hence making it seem like a liberal innovation), but *people* (more plural and more inclusively societal). While critical IR theory, including post-modern, post-structural, feminism, Marxist, share some of the same concerns as these human-oriented approaches, as Chenoy and Tadjabaksh argue, they can be conceptualized outside of the standard critical theories.[69] Indeed, the ideas of human security and human development were developed by people like Mahbub-ul Haq of Pakistan and Amartya Sen from India, even though it was appropriated by Western governments like Canada and Norway.[70] Hence a human perspective on IRT is a natural and indispensable companion to any meaningful search for non-Western IRT.

But much more work needs to be done here. There are unresolved debates over these human-prefixed concepts, especially with regard to what they mean, whose agenda they serve, how are they to be advanced, and whether they are (especially human security) too broad to be analytically meaningful and too idealistic to serve any policy purpose. These questions mirror questions about the current IRT posed by critical approaches. But the linkages between various human-prefixed concepts are not sufficiently understood or often contested. For example, how is human development (freedom from want) related to human security (freedom from fear)? This is especially interesting from the perspective of non-Western IRT since it evokes a North–South divide, although there is now a growing acceptance that human security is both freedom from fear and freedom from want.[71] Moreover, the human-prefixed concepts, while attracting growing interest, have not been advanced to the point of challenging the centrality of the state or the international institutions controlled by states in any of the mainstream theories. How many college textbooks in IR include a chapter on human security?

Ontology and epistemology

Can there be anything about the epistemology of IR which is genuinely non-Western? If there is, can it get past the disciplinary gatekeepers? Patrick Thaddeus Jackson contends that "to be genuinely non-Western, we need ways of generating theory that is not prone to King, Keohane, and Verba type of generating theory."[72] What is then important is not just the content of IR, but the ways of doing IR.

But content is important too. And the two, ontology and epistemology, are not unrelated. The tendency towards presentism that plagues a good deal of IRT straddles both. As Peter Vale notes, "there is no way forward in the discipline without addressing three events which IR, with its penchant for presentism, has never seen – Slavery, Colonialism and Empire."[73] Part of the answer lies in broadening our conception of what philosophy of science actually means, as Jackson in a recent contribution has so admirably done. Jackson makes a powerful case for pluralism in IR, particularly in so far as our understanding of what constitutes "science" is concerned.[74] In so doing, he strikes a powerful blow to the IR orthodoxy, especially in America, which has been responsible for a large measure of gate-keeping against non-Western experiences and voices, either by dismissing them as the stuff of area studies or as "unscientific." But Jackson also insists that "putting the 'science question' to rest certainly does not mean that we enter a realm where anything goes."[75] Scientific knowledge for him has three indispensable "constituent components": it must be systematic, it must be capable of taking (and one presumes tackling successfully) public criticism, and "it must be intended to produce worldly knowledge."[76]

It is the third element that is problematic for those looking for new IR knowledge from sources outside of Western history and philosophy. A good deal of what one might bring into IRT from there is indeed "worldly knowledge," but some things are not. They might be other-worldly, or be perceived as such, or they may lie at some intersection between science and spirituality. Of course, our conception of what is this-worldly and what is not might be shaped by our limited understanding of other cultures or our prejudices about them. One is reminded of Max Weber, whose definition of science is the starting point and glue of Jackson's book. Weber's work linked the rationalism of the Calvinist ethic with the development of capitalism, and against that backdrop explained why the world's cultures lacking such an ethic, such as Hinduism and Confucianism, had not found it possible to develop industrially and economically to a similar extent. Whether his understanding of Indian and Chinese cultures showed ignorance or prejudice, or both, is a matter of debate. Nonetheless, it was certainly erroneous. There is plenty in both Indian and Chinese cultures which is rationalistic and conducive to economic development; and to assert that economic development would not be possible in cultural and economic settings other than one's own smacks of the kind of ethnocentrism that permeates contemporary IRT. Similarly, some of the non-Western IR knowledge that comes from religious and philosophical sources, may not be strictly "this-worldly," or may combine the material with the spiritual. For example, Shani argues that one should look at the world's religions such as the Sikh Khalsa Panth or Islamic Ummah as sources of post-Western IRT because these concepts offer "an alternative conception of universality – and a potentially more "solidarist" conception of international society – than that offered by western Westphalian IR."[77]

Another example may be found in the world's oldest religion – Hinduism. The Hindu epic *Mahabharata*, which describes a fratricidal conflict between the Kauravas and the Pandavas, should be a rewarding source to look for concepts and theories of IR; it is after all a meta-narrative of just and unjust war, alliances and betrayals, self-interest and morality, and good and bad governance.[78] The *Bhagabad Gita*, Hinduism's most sacred text, is a component of Mahabharata. Its opening describes Arjuna, the Pandava camp's most celebrated warrior, halting at the edge of the battlefield, overcome with remorse at the prospect of slaying his own relatives who are arrayed on the opposite side. Lord Krishna, Arjuna's god-charioteer, counsels him to fight on because the death only destroys the mortal body, while the soul (*atman*) is permanent. "Our bodies are known to end, but the embodied self is enduring, indestructible and immeasurable, therefore, Arjuna, fight the battle."[79] Lord Krishna also gives Arjuna several other reasons for not abstaining from war – just cause, personal honour, shame from enemies, and the opportunity to rule. The following passages from *Gita* are especially noteworthy: "If you refuse to fight this righteous war, then, [you would be] shirking your duty and losing your reputation";[80] "the warrior chiefs who thought highly of you, will now despise you, thinking that it was fear which drove you from battle."[81] "Die, and you will win heaven; conquer, and you will enjoy sovereignty of the earth; therefore stand up, Arjuna, determined (sic) to fight."[82] In other words, Lord Krishna's pleadings with the warrior Arjuna not to abstain from war resonate with the logic of righteous action which is both "this-worldly" (honour, shame, power) and "other worldly" (the indestructibility of the soul or the *atman*).

The question that now arises is: whether and how can we bring this into IR knowledge if we insist on a conduct of enquiry that applies Jackson's admittedly pluralist conception of science, but still insist on a strict separation between this and other worldliness, and between the material and the transcendental or spiritual? If we are concerned with broadening the conduct of enquiry in IR, then something more than science is involved or should be involved no matter how broadly we define what constitutes scientific knowledge. We could of course self-consciously include elements such as ethics or scriptural knowledge which may not easily pass the test of this-worldliness, and call it the non-scientific elements of IRT, but then again we would be deliberately consigning it to second-class status since, as Jackson points out, the labelling of "scientific" carries much prestige and disciplining impact in IRT. Our insistence on science risks further marginalizing a good deal of the sources of IR knowledge which are wholly or partially unscientific, or whose affinity with science cannot be clearly established.

To illustrate the complexities and dilemmas involved in drawing IR knowledge from non-Western philosophies, I will give one important example from Buddhist philosophy which has received practically no attention from scholars of international relations.[83] I choose this because it is a transnational religion, having spread from India to China, Japan, Korea and Southeast Asia. Its pan-Asian nature is not unimportant in our present quest for NWIRT or post-Western IRT, since Asia is supposedly the continent of the future, and IRT is always subservient to power shifts.

In a fascinating study, the present Dalai Lama explores the relationship between science and Buddhist philosophy. Buddhist philosophy accepts and employs the empiricism of science, especially "direct observation" and "reasoned inference" (i.e. knowledge "can be phenomenally given or it can be inferred"), but *may* part company with science when it comes to a third way, "reliable authority." (I say *may* because the Dalai Lama qualifies his assertion by comparing reliable authority with the scientific practice of accepting "results published by experimenters in peer-reviewed journals without . . . repeating these experiments.") Buddhist philosophy believes in a "further level of reality, which may remain obscure to the unenlightened mind." These include "law of karma," "scripture cited as a particularly correct source of authority," or the teaching of Buddha which for Buddhists "has proven to be reliable in the examination of the nature of existence and path to liberation." Hence, while on two domains – the application of empirical experience and reason – there is a great methodological convergence" between Buddhism and science, science does not accept scriptural authority.[84] And certain methods of scientific enquiry, like Popper's falsification thesis, would render the gap wider. Although Popper's falsification "resonates with" Tibetan Buddhism's "principle of the scope of negation," which underscores the difference between "which is 'not found' and that which is 'found not to exist'," the emphasis on falsification would mean that "many questions that pertain to our human existence" such as ethics and spirituality would be excluded.[85]

A few implications of this argument for IRT may be noted. First, it is not difficult to see that the "further level of reality" may well apply to most other religious doctrines, such as the Islamic Sunnah and Hadith or Christian theology. Second, while the Dalai Lama argues that though science excludes questions of metaphysics and ethics,[86] IRT in general (although some versions more so than others) does not – which justifies keeping some distance between them (i.e. science and IR). Third, Popper's falsification thesis deserves to be noted for what it really is – a narrow and particular view of scientific conduct in IR, we need to expand the meaning of what constitutes scientific conduct in IR (as Jackson has done).

In comparing science enquiry with Buddhist philosophy, the Dalai Lama brings particularly to attention the doctrine of emptiness, or *sunyata*, originating from the Indian Buddhist philosopher Nagarjuna (second century), which is the source of the Buddhist schools of Madhymika (Middle Way) and Yogacara. The core argument of *Sunyata* is the "fundamental disparity between the way we perceive the world, including our own experience in it, and the way things actually are." Sunyata rejects the tendency to perceive the world, including "all things and events, whether material, mental or even abstract concepts like time," as if they "possess self-enclosed, definable, discrete, and enduring reality," or as if they are "an essential core to our being, which characterizes our individuality and identity as a discreet ego, independent of the physical and mental elements that constitute our existence." Instead,

> . . . any belief in an objective reality grounded in the assumption of intrinsic, independent existence is simply untenable . . . To intrinsically possess such independent existence . . . would mean that nothing has the capacity to

interact with or exert influence on any other phenomena . . . In the theory of emptiness, everything is argued as merely being composed of dependently related events; of continuously interacting phenomena with no fixed, immutable essence, which are themselves in dynamic and constantly changing relations. Thus, things and events are 'empty' in that they can never possess any immutable essence, intrinsic reality or absolute 'being' that affords independence.[87]

The doctrine of emptiness thus revolves around the distinction between "self nature" and "dependent origination." "Self nature" (*svabhava*) refers to the "inherent essence of a thing," or to "what exists in and of itself," or to "absolute existence," or "to a substantive being, unchanging and immovable." The opposite of this is "dependent origination" (*pratitya-samutpada*), which implies "the relative and conditional status regarding all existing things."[88] Following from this, "causation implies contingency and dependence, while anything that inherently existed would be immutable and self-enclosed."[89] Moreover, change is the order of things, "nothing can possess unchanging essence, nothing ever *is*, for all is subject to change and is in the process of becoming which never becomes. Importantly, the self, too, is ultimately of the same changeable, non-permanent nature."[90]

The Dalai Lama finds "an unmistakable resonance" between these Buddhist ideas of "emptiness and interdependence," and the new quantum physics of relativity. The latter challenged the old Newtonian physics with its "mechanistic worldview in which certain universal physical laws, including gravity and the laws of mechanics, effectively determined the pattern of natural actions," and claimed matter "to be less solid and definable than it appears."[91] For the Dalai Lama, both quantum physics and the idea of emptiness tell us "that reality is not what appears to be."[92]

Some may be tempted to compare the above tenets of Buddhist philosophy with some of the core ideas of constructivism (and to some extent post-modernism). Constructivism claims that: (1) interests and identities (self and the other) are never permanent or fixed, but constantly changing and evolving through interactions (dynamic relationships), (2) agents and structures are always in process, and that, (3) it "seizes the middle ground" between the extremes of materialism and "ideas-all-the-way down." Buddhism, it may be pointed out here, is not a purely ideational doctrine – it rejects the idea of an "essential core to . . . our individuality and identity that is independent of the physical and mental elements that constitute our existence."[93] Constructivism holds that interests and identities are not preordained or immutable. The Nagarjuna-inspired *Yogacara* philosophy contains the idea of "store consciousness": "we don't get ideas just from our five senses; we get them also from the seeds and traces that have been deposited in our store consciousness, a sort of natural, preexisting characteristics of the mind and the one that gives us the illusion that we exist. We are not tabula rasa, in other words, blank slates upon which our experience writes a sort of fresh text."[94] Also interesting in this context are post-modern IR theorists who disavow any "belief in an objective reality grounded in the assumption of intrinsic, independent existence,"[95] and Foucault's notion of the "regime of truth" in disciplines and sciences which constitutes "conventional truth" and whose deconstruction is central to the post-modern method of knowledge production.

But to simply apply labels like constructivism to the doctrine of "dependent origination" would seem as a teleological sin to some, i.e. projecting a modern concept backwards to classical wisdom. But IR theorists have not shied away from attaching labels like realism and liberalism to the writings of classical theological writers like Thucydides, St Thomas Aquinas, Machiavelli, Hobbes, and Kant. Can we dismiss the doctrine of emptiness and ideas like "self nature," "dependent origination," and "store consciousness" as too unscientific to deserve a place in the source of non-Western IR knowledge, or as potentially valuable ways of exploring an alternative theory of knowledge that could enrich the study of international relations? Moreover, these concepts blur the distinction between scientific conduct (including Jackson's broader rendering of it) and knowledge that cannot be called either wholly scientific or wholly unscientific, either fully "this worldly" or wholly "other worldly," since they appear to combine both elements. Can we then reject them outright or condemn them to marginalized space by labelling them unscientific by using Jackson's "worldliness" criteria?

In my view, such knowledge should have its place in IRT, and is an important source of NWIRT. In this respect, Jackson's last words in the book are of special importance: "The issues we study and the problems with which we grapple are too important for us to countenance the categorical dismissal of alien ways of producing knowledge simply because they do not 'world' in the way that we are used to worlding, are not systematic in the way that we are used to being systematic, and do not engage in the kind of public criticism with which we are comfortable."[96] In my view, we know that there are lots of alien ways of producing knowledge out there, including the wisdoms of other civilizations and classical and modern international and regional systems which are wonderfully and creatively unscientific. IR can ignore them at its peril, especially in its moment of liberation from the disciplining hands of an American social science that is now being resisted from within.

Bringing area studies back in

There was a time not so long ago when in most parts of the non-Western world, IR began and ended with area specialization. One interesting feature, and potential danger of the recent conversations about IRT beyond the West, is that most of them occur without reference to, or serious engagement with, the area studies tradition. Although area studies, or "international studies," lurk beneath these conversations, there seems to be a zealous effort and undue haste to move beyond area studies and differentiate it from IR. Somehow, area studies seem outdated, unfashionable. To some extent, the a-theoretical nature of area studies generates the need to distinguish IR from it, especially those who focus on theory. Another reason is a perception (unjustified) that the whole idea of area studies is becoming obsolete, whether because of globalization, or the lack of demand from policy-makers which is crucial to funding and sustenance. This view, while popular in the 1990s, is ever more questionable today. It will be ironic if non-Western scholars move away from area studies, within which IR had been traditionally anchored (as in India) at a time when in the West, there is growing confirmation of the need to bring area studies back in.

There is no doubt that what we used to call area studies is itself changing. Until recently, it was fashionable to draw a sharp contrast between the two. Discipline-based scholars aspire to be social scientists who "do not seek to master the literature on a region, but rather to master the literature of a discipline."[97] Area specialists scoff at their lack of grounding in the local contexts. Katzenstein laments the "superficial and speculative" connections that strictly disciplinary perspectives make "to the vari-egated experiences of various parts of the world."[98] Discipline scholars on the other hand, attack area specialists for being little more than "'real estate agents' with a stake in a plot of land rather than an intellectual theory." Their work has been described variously as "a-theoretical," "journalistic," and "mushy." They are faulted for not knowing statistics, for "offering resistance to rigorous methods for evaluating argu-ments," for not generating "scientific knowledge" and for being "cameras," rather than "thinkers."[99] In contrast, disciplinary social science was seen, in the words of the former President of the Social Science Research Council David Featherman, as being more "universally applicable and globally useful."[100]

But this divide can be and is being bridged. I have pointed to the emergence of two such approaches.[101] The first is "disciplinary area studies" combining two orientations. This includes scholars who may be termed "regionally-oriented disci-plinarists (or social scientists, to use an American term)," and "discipline-oriented regionalists." The former's main specialization is theory (usually drawn from Europe and the US global role), but they have been attracted to the world's regions for a variety of reasons, such as economic rise (as with Asia) and the growing importance of regional powers, China, India, Brazil, South Africa and regional institutions in different parts of the non-Western world. This is in contrast to the earlier atten-tion to non-Western regions from international relations scholars, which owed largely to their status as Cold War flashpoints. The latter category, "discipline-oriented regionalists," includes scholars whose initial primary focus might have been on regional affairs, but who have now increasingly embraced theory, not least because of the entry of the "regionally-oriented disciplinarians" whose contribu-tion has been to inspire younger scholars from the region to undertake theory-guided research.

A second category of hybrid scholarship may be called "transnational area studies," whose practitioners may be called "transnational regionalists." While acknowledging that "exclusive specialization in a particular area . . . misses the connections between developments in different parts of the world," Katzenstein argues that area studies is important for analyzing transnational relations, as the basis for "contingent generalizations that go beyond specific locales."[102] These scholars are primarily trained in regional affairs, but they are also increasingly interested and involved in comparative research on trans-regional phenomena, without the help of the theory of a particular discipline or having any disciplinary grounding (thus unlike discipline-oriented area specialists, although the two may overlap) especially those linked to the effects of globalization. These two approaches are not mutually exclusive. Unlike disciplinary area studies scholars, transnational regionalists are not necessarily theory-guided, but are interested in looking beyond their respective areas and hence in comparative studies of issues which are transnational in scope, such as AIDS, terrorism, etc.

Contemporary regional worlds

It is often forgotten that theorizing about IR has a fundamental local/regional context. Stephen Walt, who reformulated balance of power theory by relying principally on Middle Eastern diplomatic history, thus defended his approach: "The argument that the Middle East is *sui generis* applies with equal force to any other region. Yet, international relations scholars have long relied on historical cases and quantitative data drawn from European diplomatic history without being accused of a narrow geographic, temporal, or cultural focus."[103] His point is clear and persuasive: since Europe is the source of so much of IRT and no one complains about it, why not the Middle East, Asia, Africa or Latin America?

The growing worldwide interest in the comparative study of regionalism and regional orders offers a rich source of IRT, although its potential is yet to be fully realized. Let me note three areas of contributions that are by no means exhaustive. One key direction here is the disjuncture between the more universalistic claims of Western IRT and the reality of the politics and security of regions and regional orders. Africa as a region is perhaps the most challenging to conventional IRT. As noted, Africa's place in IRT has been famously framed as a matter of "juridical" versus "empirical" sovereignty, but the real challenge Africa poses to IRT is something else. As Kevin Dunn points out, the African experience challenges neorealism's (Waltz's) anarchy–hierarchy divide, given that there is no hierarchy within states that are too weak to police themselves. It also interrogates more generally IR's domestic/international divide, given the prominent role of international actors in keeping Africa's fragile states going. Africa for them challenges the centrality of state in IRT, because the state here has given way to, or at least competes with, multiple other forms of authority. Since ". . . many African countries are better conceived of as stateless configurations: societies operating within a complex web of patronage, primordial and various other forms of attachment and identification," to view them from a Westphalian prism obscures reality and "perpetuates 'juridical' states." Dunn argues that the development of warlordism in some African states should not be viewed as "temporary aberrations," but as "alternative structures and practices to the dominant Westphalian state systems."[104] If so, then theorizing about these alternate forms assumes urgency and importance in any meaningful quest for an IRT for Africa.

Latin American shows that regional political and economic resistance to hegemony can be a fruitful basis of developing theory. Haluani identifies several theories with strong Latin American roots, beyond the Calvo and Drago doctrines, including dependency theory, populism, liberation theology, and Cepalism. Cepalism, Comision Economica para America Latin (CEPAL), the UN's economic commission for Latin America, challenged the IMF–World Bank's development and reform strategy with something that came to be known as *Cepalismo* which "sought to work on indigenous models, based on local capabilities and priorities."[105] Raul Prebisch criticized what he saw as "socially and culturally insensitive" IMF–World Bank technocraticism, and argued that globalization and the free market benefitted mainly Western countries.[106] At the same time, Cepalism also has equivalents in other regions, including Africa and Asia, thereby creating a more universal base.

Finally, Asia is at the heart of our growing interest in understanding why regional institutions differ, and the implications of these differences for world order. I have already referred to the distinctive contribution of regions to the global sovereignty regime: for example, Latin America's norm of non-intervention which permitted a collective defence system involving the USA, and Asia's Nehru Doctrine which did not. In recent years, the difference between European regionalism and those in other parts of the world, especially Asia, has emerged as a major area of contention that has been a driving force behind the comparative study of regionalism and regional institutions. Traditionally, theories of regionalism have been heavily drawn from the European experience. Europe also provided the benchmark for judging the success and failure of regionalism elsewhere. "[There] is a widespread assumption . . . that in order to be 'proper' regionalism, a degree of EU-style institutionalism should be in place."[107] But this is, happily, no longer the case. Theoretical challenges from other parts of the world, particularly Asia, have undermined the hitherto "paradigmatic status" of European regionalism.[108] Differences between Asian and European institutions, such as the former's soft, informal, networked-type regionalism versus the latter's heavily institutionalized and legalized variety, no longer automatically leads one to consider the former as a more desirable universal model.[109] Theorizing about Asian regionalism on its own terms, with or without the help of Western IRT, has advanced sufficiently to ensure that European regionalism acts as an inspiration perhaps, but not a model. More work on the distinctiveness of different regions and differences in the design and performance of regional institutions is important in adding diversity to IRT and allows us to focus on the local construction of global order – a necessary counter to the hyper-globalization perspective. It also adds richness and diversity to the idea of NWIRTs.

Conclusion

Few doubt that IR as a discipline and IRT as they are understood today are insufficiently international, but there remain important disagreements as to how to move forward. The idea of "non-Western IRT," no matter how problematic, has helped to capture the dimensions of IR's false universalism and to foster debate and open up the discipline further. Dissent and debate occur within as much as between Western and non-Western categories. Just as some of the debates over historic international systems and the idea of the expansion of international society have occurred within the English School, some of the best criticisms of the idea of a NWIRT come from those who want a greater, stronger voice for the non-Western societies.

But it is time to move further and forward. A dialogue to sort out differences over what constitutes progress, what is to be challenged and what is to be added, and how to conduct our enquiry is of course essential, but such dialogue should not aspire to another type of false universalism that obscures or wishes away the differences that obviously exist between the Western and the non-Western narratives and theories of IR and those within each. Moreover, discourse is no substitute for discovery. We need much more vigorous and open-ended excursions to the sources of IR knowledge which lie all around us. In conclusion, let me respond briefly to some of the reservations and criticisms that could be, and have been, directed at my approach – most admirably by Professor Kimberly Hutchings in her essay in this issue of *Millennium*.[110]

In her discussion of two powerful traditions of dialogue, Socratic and Habermasian, Professor Hutchings exposes how the concept of "'West' in relation to dialogue is not, and has never been a neutral descriptive term." Since Western political philosophy is one major source of contemporary IRT, her discussion helps us to better understand one of the more powerful reasons behind Westerncentrism in IR studies.

One of the key challenges facing IR is our collective failure to understand and foster its development as a two-way dialogue. Power structures and intellectual predispositions, shaped by history and identity, stand in the way of acknowledging the agency and contribution of other voices even when one knows it to be out there. For example, Professor Hutchings says that the "identification of the thought and practice of Ancient Greece with the 'west' is, of course, highly contested. Ancient Greek thought did not emerge in a vacuum, but was shaped by, as well as influencing, traditions of African and Asian thought. It is no more 'western' than 'non-western'." Yet, how many scholars, including those in the IR community, recognize that the first element of the proposition, i.e. that Greek thought might indeed have been shaped by African and Asian thought? Otherwise, our textbooks would have been written very differently. As with Greek thought, the development of IRT has been closely equated with European history and practices of statecraft in which Europe (and later the United States) have had the dominant influence. It has rarely been seen as a two-way process with the infusion of the ideas and experiences of other societies and peoples. And indeed, addressing this ethnocentrism is precisely what lies behind the whole project of NWIRT.

Let me add one more point to what has been already said in clarifying and qualifying the term "non-Western." In her discussion of Habbermasian communicative dialogue, Professor Hutchings points to challenges it faces from those who seek to emphasize "issues of concrete identity" and those who "take account of the complexity and power-relations involved in real-life dialogic exchanges." To some extent, the persistence of terms which we consider problematic, such as Western and non-Western, reflect and take into account identities – real or imagined (or constructed) – and power relations in international affairs. They cannot simply be wished away precisely because of "the complexity and power-relations involved in real-life dialogic exchanges" that goes on everyday international politics.

Some scholars may be uncomfortable with my call for giving more space to the study of regions, regionalisms, and regional orders as a pathway for advancing IR studies beyond the West. To clarify, I am not asking for "regionalizing" the discipline at the expense of universalism. This would be going too far. The concept of what constitutes a "region" remains contested, although there seems to be greater agreement that regions are socially constructed, rather than geographically or culturally preordained.[111] I have also pointed out the dangers of parochialism and exceptionalism inherent in "provincializing" IR (e.g., Chinese School or Indian School), although I support it under certain conditions. But the study of regions, and regional perspectives on IR, are extremely important for the development of the discipline. This view is confirmed – and I am sure many others will have the same experience – by my encounters with the expectations of fellow IR scholars from all around the world. The study of regions brings greater richness and diversity to the discipline. It also offers a useful pathway for integrating area studies and IR to the benefit of both. Regional perspectives are not antithetical to universalism, as the "regional world" approach developed at the University of Chicago attests.[112]

Perhaps in seeking a common ground, I could invoke Amartya Sen's point about the heritage of dialogue and democracy in India which goes into the heart of our dialogue over the state of IRT today and what to do about it. In a radio interview about his book, *The Argumentative Indian*,[113] Sen first points out that the Indian practice of democracy is not just about elections but also about civil discourse, including a "willingness to listen to different points of view." This upholds the "long and written-up argumentative tradition" in India. To illustrate his point, Sen actually invokes the argument in *Bhagbad Gita* between Lord Krishna and the warrior Arjuna about the necessity and morality of war (which I have already discussed in this chapter, before I actually heard Sen's interview). But Sen also points out that this tradition of dialogue is not unique to India, but "actually a global heritage." To quote his own words, "There is a global tradition here, the whole idea that it is all Western is quite mistaken." He rejects the underlying assumption that this tradition "somehow belongs to the West and then it is for [the][W]est to decide whether to impose it or not impose it, rather than recognizing the global background."[114]

Yet, IRT has been written and presented as if it springs almost entirely from an exclusively Western heritage. Only by uncovering the assumptions and power structures that obscures IRT's global heritage can we move from dissent to dialogue and then from dialogue to discovery. This indeed is the central point of this chapter.

Notes

1 This chapter is based on the author's remarks in the "opening dialogue" of the Millennium Annual Conference of the London School of Economics, 16–17 October 2011. It is the initial longer version of the article that appeared in the *Millennium: Journal of International Studies* 39, no. 3 (2011): 619–637.

2 Amitav Acharya, "Ethnocentrism and Emancipatory IR Theory," in *Displacing Security*, eds., Samantha Arnold and J. Marshall Bier (Toronto: Centre for International and Security Studies, York University, 2000); Arlene Tickner, "Seeing IR Differently: Notes from the Third World," *Millennium: Journal of International Studies* 32, no. 2 (2003): 295–324; Amitav Acharya and Barry Buzan, eds., "Why Is There No Non-Western International Relations Theory? Reflections on and from Asia," Special Issue of *International Relations of Asia Pacific* 7, no. 3 (2007): 285–286; Arlene Tickner and Ole Waever, eds., *International Relations Scholarship Around the World* (London and New York: Routledge, 2009); and Amitav Acharya and Barry Buzan, eds., *Non-Western International Relations Theory: Perspectives on and Beyond Asia* (London and New York: Routledge, 2010).

3 Acharya and Buzan, eds., "Why Is There No Non-Western International Relations Theory?"

4 G. John Ikenberry and Michael Mastanduno, "The United States and Stability in East Asia," in *International Relations Theory and the Asia-Pacific*, ed., G. John Ikenberry and Michael Mastanduno (New York: Columbia University Press, 2003), 421–422.

5 Jack Snyder, "Some Good and Bad Reasons for a Distinctively Chinese Approach to International Relations Theory," paper presented at the annual meeting of the APSA 2008 Annual Meeting, Hynes Convention Center, Boston, Massachusetts, 28 August 2008, 9.

6 Muthia Alagappa, ed., *Asian Security Practice: Material and Ideational Perspectives* (Stanford: Stanford University Press, 1998), 9.

7 Snyder, "Some Good and Bad Reasons for a Distinctively Chinese Approach to International Relations Theory," 10.

8 Ernst B. Haas, "International Integration: The European and the Universal Process," *International Organization* 15, no. 3 (1961): 366–392.

9 Sunil Sondhi, "South Asia in International Relations Theory," paper prepared for the 47th Annual Convention of the International Studies Association, San Diego, 22–25 March 2006, 15–17.

10 Stephanie G. Neuman, *International Relations Theory and the Third World* (New York: St Martin's Press, 1998).

11 William Brown, "Africa and International Relations: A Comment on IR Theory, Anarchy and Statehood," *Review of International Studies* 32, no. 1 (2006): 119–143.

12 "Constructivism's theoretical reach extends past the West and into the Third World." Michael Barnett, "Radical Chic? Subaltern Realism: A Rejoinder," *International Studies Review* 4, no. 3 (2002): 49–62, 52; Tadjbakhsh attests to the usefulness of constructivism in analyzing Islamic sources of IRT. Shahrbanou Tadjbakhsh, "International Relations Theory and the Islamic Worldview," in *Non-Western International Relations Theory*, eds., Amitav Acharya and Barry Buzan (London and New York: Routledge, 2010).

13 Tickner, "Seeing IR Differently: Notes from the Third World."

14 Azhari Karim, "ASEAN: Association to Community: Constructed in the Image of Malaysia's Global Diplomacy," in *Malaysia's Foreign Policy: Continuity and Change*, ed., Abdul Razak Baginda (Singapore: Marshal Cavendish Editions, 2007), 113.

15 One important example is Ayoob's Subaltern Realism. See Mohammed Ayoob, "Inequality and Theorizing in International Relations: The Case for Subaltern Realism," *International Studies Review* 4, no. 3 (2002): 27–48.

16 Caroline Thomas and Peter Wilkin, "Still Waiting after all these Years: 'The Third World' on the Periphery of International Relations," *The British Journal of Politics & International Relations* 6, no. 2 (2004): 241–258.

17 Karen Smith, "Can it be Home-Grown: Challenges to Developing IR Theory in the

Global South," paper presented to the 47th Annual Convention of the International Studies Association, San Diego, 22–25 March 2006, 2.

18 "Mimicry" is a term attributed to postcolonial scholar Homi Bhaba, (See Pinar Bilgin, "Thinking Past 'Western IR,'" *Third World Quarterly* 29, no. 1 (2008): 5–23, 14) but this would exaggerate Bhaba's relevance and contribution to IRT. I use it in the literal sense of emulation, or imitation, which has a constructivist pedigree.

19 William Olson and Nicholas Onuf, "The Growth of a Discipline," in *International Relations: British and American Perspectives*, ed., Steve Smith (New York: Blackwell, 1985), 18.

20 Giorgio Shani, "Toward a Post-Western IR: The *Umma, Khalsa Panth*, and Critical International Relations Theory," *International Studies Review* 10, no. 4 (2008): 722–734; 723. See also: Ching-Chang Chen, "The Absence of Non-western IR Theory in Asia Reconsidered," *International Relations of the Asia-Pacific* 11, no. 1 (2011): 1–23.

21 Hiroyuki Hoshiro, "Book Reviews: Whose Ideas Matter? Agency and Power in Asian Regionalism," *Pacific Affairs* 83, no. 3 (2010): 547–548.

22 Acharya, "Ethnocentrism and Emancipatory IR Theory." The Acharya–Buzan effort *does not* privilege any particular Western theory – including constructivism and the English School – as the answer to our search for non-Western IR theories. Acharya and Buzan, *Non-Western International Relations Theory: Perspectives on and Beyond Asia.*

23 Smith, "Can it be Home-Grown: Challenges to Developing IR Theory in the Global South," 2.

24 Kevin Dunn, "Tales from the Dark Side: Africa's Challenge to International Relations Theory," *Journal of Third World Studies* 17, no. 1 (2000): 61–90; Kevin C. Dunn and Timothy M. Shaw, eds., *Africa's Challenge to International Relations Theory* (New York: Palgrave, 2001); Peter Vale, "IR and the Global South: Final Confessions of a Schizophrenic Teacher," 30 October 2009. Available at: http://www.e-ir.info/?p=2644 (accessed 15 January 2011).

25 Robert Jackson and Carl Rosberg, "Why Africa's Weak States Persist: The Empirical and the Juridical in Statehood," *World Politics* 35, no. 1 (1982): 1–24.

26 An example how scholars have begun to rethink the question of epistemology could be found in Qin Yaqin, "Why Is There No Chinese International Relations Theory?" in *Non-Western International Relations Theory: Perspectives on and Beyond Asia*, eds., Amitav Acharya and Barry Buzan (London and New York: Routledge, 2010), 26–50. Qin sees the absence of dualism in Chinese philosophy as an obstacle to Chinese engagement with mainstream Western theories but also an opportunity to do something different, by constructing an epistemology of international relations theory on the basis of non-dualistic thought. See also Ronald Bleiker, "East-West Stories of War and Peace: Neorealist Claims in Light of Ancient Chinese Philosophy," in *The Zen of International Relations: IR Theory from East to West*, eds., Stephen Chan, Peter G. Mandaville, and Roland Bleiker (Basingstoke, U.K.: Palgrave, 2001): 177–201.

27 This was the main logic behind the use of the term "non-Western" in the Acharya–Buzan project. For the usage of these terms in the early English School literature, see: Hedley Bull and Adam Watson, eds., *The Expansion of International Society* (Oxford: Clarendon Press, 1984), including the introduction and conclusion by Bull and Watson and Bull's chapter, "The Revolt against the West." See also Martin Wight, "Western Values in International Relations," in *Diplomatic Investigations: Essays in the Theory of International Politics*, eds., Herbert Butterfield and Martin Wight (London: Allen and Unwin, 1966), 89–131. But in general, *The Expansion of International Society* employs other terms "European" and "Third World."

28 See, for example, Kishore Mahbubani, *Can Asians Think: Understanding the Divide Between East and West*, 3rd edition (Singapore: Times Editions, 2004) and Kishore Mahbubani, *The New Asian Hemisphere: The Irresistible Shift of Global Power to the East* (New York: PublicAffairs, 2008).

29 See Dunn's opening paragraph in his "Tales from the Dark Side: Africa's Challenge to International Relations Theory."

30 Stephanie Newman, *International Relations Theory and the Third World*; Karen Smith, "Can it be Done? Challenges to Developing IR Theory in the Global South," paper presented to the 47th ISA Convention, 22–25 March 2006; Mohammed Ayoob, "Inequality and Theorizing in International Relations: The Case for Subaltern Realism." Shani, "Toward a Post-Western IR."

31 Stephen Chan and Peter Mandaville, "Introduction: Within International Relations Itself, a New Culture Rises Up," in *The Zen of International Relations*, eds., Stephen Chan, Peter Mandaville and Roland Bleiker (Basingstoke, U.K.: Palgrave Macmillan, 2001), 8; Arlene Tickner and Ole Waever, "Introduction: Geocultural Epistemologies," 3, and "Conclusion: Worlding Where the West Once Was," 332, in *International Relations Scholarship Around the World*, eds., Tickner and Waever (London and New York: Routledge, 2009).

32 Acharya and Buzan, "Why Is There No Non-Western International Relations Theory: An Introduction," in *Non-Western International Relations Theory*.

33 ". . . one of the difficulties of making sense of IR around the world is its ambivalent meaning in different places. In Southeast Asia and East Asia, for instance, American IR is a global standard that some scholars and junior intellectual cohorts want to aspire to, . . . in Israel and Iran, it is a means to overcoming the isolation of an embattled intellectual community . . . in China, it is a symptom of American power, which Chinese IR may one day replace . . .; and in other cases it is simply irrelevant to local concerns and interests." Itty Abraham, "Book Review: *International Relations Scholarship Around the World*, eds., Arlene Tickner and Ole Waever," *International Studies Review* 12, no. 3 (2010): 470–472, 471.

34 Bilgin, "Thinking Past 'Western IR,'" 13.

35 Buzan and Little, *International Systems and World History Remaking the Study of International Relations* (Oxford: Oxford University Press, 2000).

36 Surveying realism in South America, two scholars argue: "It seems to us that the conversations that take place shape not only the recipients of theory transference but also the context from whence the idea/theory originated. The dialogue that occurs – if and when it occurs – shapes and reflects back to all participants, disturbing and blurring disciplinary borders. Ideas do not emerge in a vacuum and we cannot guarantee that they are solely the product of a specific geographical or institutional setting as opposed to the product of a dialogue from other sources and influences." Helen Louise Turton and Lucas G. Freire, "Hybridity under Hegemonic Influence in IR Scholarship: Realism in South America," paper presented to the ISA/ABRI Conference on Diversity and Inequality in World Politics, Rio de Janeiro, Brazil, 22–24 July 2009, 26.

37 Homeira Moshirzadeh, "A 'Hegemonic Discipline' in an 'Anti-Hegemonic' Country," *International Political Sociology* 3, no. 3 (2009): 342–346, 342.

38 Knud Erik Jorgensen, "The World(s) of IR: Continental Perspectives," 28 April 2010, http://www.e-ir.info/?p=3991.

39 Manning's position within the English School remains contentious. See Tim Dunne, "A British School of International Relations," in *The British Study of Politics in the Twentieth Century*, eds., Jack Hayward, Brian Barry and Archie Brown (Oxford: Oxford University Press, 1999), 398; Tim Dunne, *Inventing International Society: A History of the English School* (Basingstoke, U.K.: Palgrave Macmillan, 1998); Andrew Linklater and Hidemi Suganami, *The English School of International Relations: A Contemporary Reassessment* (Cambridge: Cambridge University Press, 2006).

40 Brunello Vigezzi, *The British Committee on the Theory of International Politics (1954–1985): The Rediscovery of History* (Milano, Italy: Edizioni Unicopli, 2005).

41 I make this point, despite being aware that while the theme of European decline features centrally in one of Bull's initial papers for the British Committee and forms the rationale for *The Expansion of International Society*, Bull was referring to Western, rather than European decline. Vigezzi, *The British Committee on the Theory of International Politics*, 298. Vigezzi draws this conclusion from a reading of a paper written by Bull for the British Committee entitled: "The European International Order."

42 Is it better to avoid organizing and naming schools after countries or regions (or cities and universities, e.g. Frankfurt School or Stanford School) and instead base them on themes, methods or broad concerns and perspectives? In my view, while such an approach might make them seem more inclusive, the problems will not disappear, since they have to be centrally located somewhere, as well as helped by someone's resources and organized around a group of like-minded intellectuals).

43 On the other side of the power shift, Africa's uniqueness, albeit as a marginalized place, is discussed in Dunn, "Tales from the Dark Side: Africa's Challenge to International Relations Theory,"1; Mueller, Review of Dunn and Shaw, 2001, 67.

44 Wang Jisi, "International Relations Studies in China Today: Achievements, Trends and Conditions," in *International Relations Studies in China: A Review of Ford Foundation Past Grantmaking and Future Choices* (Beijing, China: Ford Foundation China Representative Office, 2003), 114. See also, Song Xinning, "Building International Relations Theory with Chinese Characteristics," *Journal of Contemporary China* 10, no. 26 (2001): 61–74; Yongjin Zhang, "International Relations Theory in China Today: The State of the Field," *The China Journal*, no. 47 (2002): 101–108.

45 Jisi, "International Relations Studies in China Today: Achievements, Trends and Conditions," 115.

46 Qin, "Why Is There No Chinese International Relations Theory." Qin identifies International Society as the big idea for the English School, and more questionably, Democratic Peace for American IRT. On *Tianxia*, see, William A. Callahan, "Chinese Visions of World Order: Post-hegemonic or a New Hegemony?" *International Studies Review* 10, no. 4 (2008): 749–761.

47 Snyder, "Some Good and Bad Reasons for a Distinctively Chinese Approach to International Relations Theory."

48 Navnita Chaddha Behera, "Reimagining IR in India," in *Non-Western International Relations Theory*, eds., Amitav Acharya and Barry Buzan (London and New York: Routledge, 2010), 92–116.

49 For recent discussions on the state of IRT in India, see: Amitabh Mattoo, "Upgrading the Study of International Relations," *Hindu*, 21 April 2009, http://www.hinduonnet.com/thehindu/thscrip/print.pl?file=2009042156680800.htm&date=2009/04/21/&prd=th&; Amitabh Mattoo, "The State of International Studies in India," *International Studies* 46, no. 1–2 (2009): 37–48; and Kanti Bajpai, "Obstacles to Good Work in Indian International Relations," *International Studies* 46, no. 1–2 (2009): 109–128.

50 "Report of the Workshop on International Studies in India," (Singapore: Lee Kuan Yew School of Public Policy, National University of Singapore, 2009), 12.

51 Kanti Bajpai, "International Relations in India: Bringing Theory (Back) Home," in *International Relations in India: Bringing Theory Back Home*, eds., Kanti Bajpai and Siddharth Mallavarapu (New Delhi, India: Orient Longman, 2001), 31.

52 Vale, "IR and the Global South: Final Confessions of a Schizophrenic Teacher."

53 Moshirzadeh, "A 'Hegemonic Discipline' in an 'Anti-Hegemonic' Country."

54 Bajpai, "International Relations in India: Bringing Theory (Back) Home," 32.

55 Buzan and Little, *International Systems in World History*, 3.

56 While conceding that the prevailing European view of the emergence of a universal internal society – anchored on the "standards of civilization" thesis – had been rightly criticized because Europeans of the past, such as the natural law theorists St Thomas Aquinas did have a global conception of international society even though it had an inner European, Christian core, Bull nonetheless argued: 'it could hardly have been expected that European states could have extended the full benefits of membership of the society of states to political entities that were in no position to enter into relationships on a basis of reciprocity . . .' Hedley Bull, "The Emergence of a Universal International Society," Bull and Watson, eds., *The Expansion of International Society*, 122. In the conclusion to the volume, Bull and Watson note: "The standards of international conduct which the European powers observed in relation to one another could not in fact be met by those Asian and African states that were unable to provide

domestic law and order, administrative integrity, protection of rights of foreign citizens, or the fulfillment of contracts." Bull and Watson, "Conclusion," in *The Expansion of International Society*, 427.

57 C.H. Alexandrowicz, *An Introduction to the History of the Law of Nations in the East Indies* (Oxford: Clarendon Press, 1967), 225. Alexandrowicz's work, based on far more detailed empirical research than Bull could ever undertake, concludes:

> Though the Europeans had sailed to the East Indies since the end of the fifteenth century equipped with legal titles of a unilateral character and though they had at first intended to discover and to occupy lands, and where necessary, to estab-lish their territorial possessions by conquest, they had in practice to fall back on negotiation and treaty making in preference to resorting to war. In fact they found themselves in the middle of a network of States and inter-State relations based on traditions which were more ancient than their own and in no way inferior to notions of European civilization. (224)

58 Buzan and Little, *International Systems in World History*, 7.

59 Wallerstein and other World Systems theorists make this point, although somewhat extremely. Wallerstein's work has been criticized for regarding political–security inter-actions as epiphenomenal, for focusing only on the post-1500 period, and for leaving out many parts of the world.

60 Paul Wheatley, "Presidential Address: India Beyond the Ganges – Desultory Reflections on the Origins of Civilization in Southeast Asia," *Journal of Asian Stud-ies* 42, no. 1 (1982): 13–28; Ian W. Mabbett, "The 'Indianization' of Southeast Asia: Reflections on the Historical Sources," *Journal of Southeast Asian Studies* 8, no. 2 (1976): 143–161.

61 For Wendt, while one should not dismiss power and interest entirely from one's ana-lytic framework, as done by some "radical constructivists," instead of "turn[ing] first to material forces, defined as power and interest, and bring[ing] in ideas only to mop up unexplained residual variance," we should "begin our theorizing about interna-tional politics with the distribution of ideas, and especially culture, in the system, and then bring in material forces, rather than the other way around." Alexander Wendt, *Social Theory of International Politics* (Cambridge: Cambridge University Press, 1999), 370–371.

62 Christian Reus-Smit, *The Moral Purpose of the State: Culture, Social Identity, and Institu-tional Rationality in International Relations* (Princeton: Princeton University Press, 2001); Daniel Deudney, *Bounding Power: Republican Security Theory from the Polis to the Global Village* (Princeton: Princeton University Press, 2007); and Richard Ned Lebow, *A Cul-tural Theory of International Relations* (Cambridge: Cambridge University Press, 2008).

63 An important effort is Raymond Cohen and Raymond Westbrook, *Amarna Diplomacy: The Beginnings of International Relations* (Baltimore, MD.: Johns Hopkins University Press, 2002), although the book suffers from trying to interpret historical interactions by using modern IR concepts and theories.

64 Tickner, "Seeing IR Differently: Notes from the Third World," 300.

65 Robert H. Jackson, *Quasi-States: Sovereignty, International Relations and The Third World* (Cambridge: Cambridge University Press, 1990).

66 Alexandrowicz, *An Introduction to the History of the Law of Nations in the East Indies*, 65.

67 Mohammed Ayoob, "The Third World in the System of States: Acute Schizophrenia or Growing Pains?" *International Studies Quarterly* 33, no. 1 (1989): 67–79.

68 Amitav Acharya, "Norm Subsidiarity and Regional Orders: Sovereignty, Regionalism and Rule-Making in the Third World," *International Studies Quarterly* 55, no. 1 (2011): 95–123.

69 Shahrbanou Tadjkbhash and Anuradha Chenoy, *Human Security, Concept and Principles* (London: Routledge, 2007).

70 Amitav Acharya, "Human Security: East Versus West," *International Journal* 56, no. 3 (2001): 442–460.

71 Amitav Acharya, "Human Security," in *The Globalisation of World Politics*, 5th edition, eds., John Baylis, Steve Smith and Patricia Owens (Oxford: Oxford University Press, 2010).

72 Comments at the Seminar, "Why IR is Decreasingly an American Social Science," (the Launch of *Non-Western International Relations Theory*, by Amitav Acharya and Barry Buzan), American University, Washington, D.C. 3 May 2010. The reference was to: Gary King, Robert O. Keohane, & Sidney Verba, *Designing Social Inquiry: Scientific Inference in Qualitative Research* (Princeton: Princeton University Press, 1994).

73 Vale, "IR and the Global South: Final Confessions of a Schizophrenic Teacher."

74 Patrick Thaddeus Jackson, *The Conduct of Inquiry in International Relations: Philosophy of Science and Its Implications for the Study of World Politics* (Oxford: Routledge, 2010).

75 Ibid., 196.

76 Ibid., 193.

77 Shani, "Toward a *Post-Western* IR," Abstract.

78 One might also look at Raymond Westbrook and Raymond Cohen, *Isaiah's Vision Of Peace In Biblical And Modern International Relations: Swords Into Plowshares* (Houndmills, U.K.: Palgrave Macmillan, 2008).

79 *The Bhagavad-Gita*, Chapter 2, passage 18, translated by Barbara Stoler Miller (New York: Bantam Dell, 1986), 34.

80 *The Bhagavad-Gita*, Chapter 2, passage 33.

81 *The Bhagavad-Gita*, Chapter 2, passage 35.

82 *Srimad Bhagavad Gita*, edited by Ashok Kaushik, English translation by Janak Datta, 7th edition (New Delhi: Star Publications, 2007), 55–57; *The Bhagavad-Gita*, Chapter 2, passage 37.

83 With the admirable exception of *The Zen of International Relations*.

84 Dalai Lama, *The Universe in a Single Atom: The Convergence of Science and Spirituality* (New York: Morgan Road Books, 2005), 28–29.

85 Dalai Lama, *The Universe in a Single Atom: The Convergence of Science and Spirituality*, 35.

86 Ibid.

87 *The Universe in a Single Atom: The Convergence of Science and Spirituality*, 46–47.

88 Gajin M. Nagao, *Mādhyamika and Yogācāra: A Study of Mahāyāna Philosophies: Collected Papers*. Translated by Leslie S. Kawamura (Albany, NY: State University of New York Press, 1991), 174–175.

89 Dalai Lama, *The Universe in a Single Atom: The Convergence of Science and Spirituality*, 47. The concepts of self nature and dependent origination also correspond to the ideas of "absolute" truth (*paramārtha satya*) which denotes "everyday world of experience . . . a pluralistic world of things and events with distinct identities and causation" and "relative" (or ultimate) truth (*samvrti satya*), or "things and events do not possess discreet, independent realities" (Ibid., 66–67).

90 Merv Fowler, *Buddhism: Religious Practices and Beliefs* (New Delhi, India: Adarsh Books, 2000), 85.

91 Dalai Lama, *The Universe in a Single Atom: The Convergence of Science and Spirituality*, 50.

92 Ibid., 50.

93 Ibid., 46.

94 Richard Bernstein, *The Ultimate Journey* (New York: Knopf, 2001), 176.

95 Dalai Lama, *The Universe in a Single Atom: The Convergence of Science and Spirituality*.

96 Jackson, *The Conduct of Inquiry in International Relations: Philosophy of Science and Its Implications for the Study of World Politics*, 212.

97 Robert H. Bates, "Area Studies and the Discipline: A Useful Controversy?" *PS: Political Science and Politics* 30, no. 2 (1997): 166–169, 166.

98 Peter J. Katzenstein, *A World of Regions: Asia and Europe in the American Imperium* (Ithaca: Cornell University Press, 2005), x–xi.

99 Christopher Shea, "Political Scientists Clash Over Value of Area Studies," *Chronicle of Higher Education* (January 1997), A12–A13.
100 Cited in David Ludden, "Area Studies in the Age of Globalization," University of Pennsylvania, 1998, http://www.sas.upenn.edu/~dludden/areast2.htm, 2.
101 Amitav Acharya, "International Relations and Area Studies: Towards A New Synthesis," Singapore: Institute of Defense and Strategic Studies, 2005, http://www.rsis.edu.sg/publications/SSIS/SSIS002.pdf.
102 Katzenstein, *A World of Regions*, x–xi.
103 Stephen Walt, *The Origins of Alliances* (Ithaca: Cornell University Press, 1987), 14–15.
104 Dunn, "Tales from the Dark Side."
105 Makram Haluani, "How? International? are Theories in International Relations?: The View from Latin America" Paper presented at the Annual Meeting of the International Studies Association, San Diego, California, 22 March 2006, 8.
106 Ibid., 8–9.
107 Shaun Breslin, Richard Higgott and Ben Rosamond, "Regions in Comparative Perspective," in *New Regionalisms in the Global Political Economy*, eds., Shaun Breslin, et al. (London: Routledge, 2002), 13.
108 Richard Higgott, "The Theory and Practice of Region," in *Regional Integration in East Asia and Europe: Convergence or Divergence*, eds., Bertrand Fort and Douglas (London: Routledge, 2006), 23.
109 Katzenstein, *A World of Regions*; Amitav Acharya, *Whose Ideas Matter: Agency and Power in Asian Regionalism* (Ithaca: Cornell University Press, 2009).
110 Kimberly Hutchings, "Dialogue Between Whom? The Role of the West/ Non-West Distinction in Promoting Global Dialogue in IR," *Millennium: Journal of International Studies* 39, no. 3 (2011): 639–647. All subsequent quotes from her are from the same article. Professor Hutchings was my interlocutor in the "Opening Dialogue" of the Millennium Annual Conference at the London School of Economics, 16–17 October 2011.
111 Amitav Acharya, "Review Essay: The Emerging Regional Architecture of World Politics," *World Politics* 59, no. 4 (2007): 629–652.
112 Sita Ranchod-Nilsson, "Regional Worlds: Transforming Pedagogy in Area Studies and International Studies," http://regionalworlds.uchicago.edu/transformingpedagogy.pdf; and Arjun Appadurai, *Modernity at Large: Cultural Dimensions of Globalization* (Minneapolis: University of Minnesota Press, 1996).
113 Amartya Sen, *The Argumentative Indian: Writings On Indian History, Culture and Identity* (New York: Farrar, Straus and Giroux, 2005).
114 These quotes are from Sen's interview with National Public Radio in the United States. Amartya Sen, 'The Argumentative Indian,' aired 13 October 2005, http://www.npr.org/templates/story/story.php?storyId=4957424.

3

COMPARATIVE REGIONALISM: A FIELD WHOSE TIME HAS COME?[1]

The multiple and global heritage of regionalism[2]

In 1948, one of the first books on regionalism in English language to be published in the non-Western world appeared under the editorship of K.M. Panikkar, an Indian scholar–diplomat who was once India's ambassador to China.[3] In the volume, which bore the title *Regionalism and World Security*,[4] Panikkar traced the origins of the idea of regional organization (which he equated with the term regionalism) to the Armed Neutrality of Northern Powers in the Napoleonic War, the US Monroe Doctrine, the concept of Mettleeuropa advocated by Frederich Neuman for the Danubian regions, and the exclusive economic and political blocs developed by Nazi Germany in Europe and Imperial Japan in East Asia. What is interesting about this genealogy is that all these, with the exception of the Japanese Greater East Asia Co-prosperity Sphere, were Western and all, with the exception of the first one (Armed Neutrality of Northern Powers), assumed the "establishment of the paramountcy of a Great Power in a defined geographical region." Hence, "so far, regional organization has meant nothing more than a polite phraseology for *lebensraum*."[5]

Against this hegemonic concept, Pannikar advanced what might be seen as an alternative conception of regionalism:

> The conditions of different regions in the world differ so much that the promotion of higher standards of living, for example, has a different meaning in relation to the people of South-east Asia to what it has in European countries. The programme of any action to give effect to this object has to be worked out in terms of particular regions. Similar is the case with conditions of social progress . . . Besides, from the point of view of standards of living, social and economic progress, and the observance of human rights and

fundamental freedoms, it is the regions further away from Europe and America that require urgent attention.[6]

Panikkar's statement contains three important messages for the students of regionalism today. First, it shows that scholars and policy-makers (he was both) in regions other than Europe and America were thinking of regionalism as a way of addressing the most pressing challenges that these societies faced.

Second, he saw regionalism not as the prerogative of the great powers in extending their influence over their weaker counterparts, but as a means for all regions – especially the regions "further away from Europe and America" including those which would be subsequently known as the "Third World" – to address their social, economic and political (including human rights) needs and challenges. As will be seen shortly, the Latin American countries were also exponents of regionalism – not the Monroe Doctrine variety, but as instruments of managing conflict and achieving peace in the hemisphere on the basis of equality and non-intervention. It is also worth noting that Panikkar's concept of regionalism was cast in broader terms – social, political and developmental – than just political or security issues, as was the case with the European and American approaches.

Third and most important, the statement underscores the sheer diversity of regions in terms of economic, social and political conditions, with the clear implication that no single institution, formula, or approach can apply to all of them. Although Panikkar was referring to the practical problems that regionalism might address, given the diversity of regions, can any single theory or model explain the prospects and outcome of regionalism in all parts of the world?

In short, Panikkar presented regionalism as a universal aspiration rather than a European formula or an American doctrine (one chapter of the book was about Europe, the rest covered the Arab League, the Inter-American System, South-East Asia, the Indian Ocean and the Pacific), and challenged the hitherto conflation of regionalism and regional organization with regional power blocs or spheres of influence. Hegemonic regionalism – or the idea that world order should be managed by a number of regional groups each under their respective local great powers – had also been challenged by Latin American countries in the form of the Calvo Doctrine (1868) and the Drago Doctrine (1902) which stressed the importance of local autonomy and disapproved intervention by great powers like the United States in Latin American affairs. Decades later, India's first Prime Minister Nehru, who also was one of the most influential voices of the newly independent countries, vigorously criticized the idea of regional power blocs as the "continuation of power politics on a vaster scale" and thus detrimental to "world peace and cooperation."[7] These alternative forms of regionalism would also underpin the political and security role of more contemporary regional organizations, such as the Organization of American States (OAS), the Arab League, the Organization of African Unity (OAU, later African Union, or AU), and the Association of Southeast Asian Nations (ASEAN).

Another heritage of regionalism that is often forgotten by contemporary scholars was the various regionalist ideologies and movements that emerged in the nineteenth and twentieth centuries. These ideas, including pan-Americanism, pan-Africanism, pan-Arabism and pan-Asianism, were founded on shared conceptions of history and culture (sometimes imagined), and a common project for the advancement of decolonization. They were multi-dimensional, encompassing racial, social, economic and political unity, rather than reflecting a purely political or strategic purpose. Although these ideologies were later taken up and pursued by formal intergovernmental regional institutions like the OAS, the Arab League, and the OAU, they are best seen as a form of inter-societal, rather than inter-governmental, regionalism. While some aspired to the creation of nation-states out of colonial structures, others like Nkrumah of Africa, Nasser of the Arab world, and Aung San of Southeast Asia and Nehru of wider Asia, openly envisioned federations or at least supranational entities.

Moreover, these movements were led not just by political elites who would later become the leaders of individual countries, but also by intellectuals, poets (such as the ardent pan-Asianist and the Nobel literature prize winner Rabindranath Tagore of India), and art-lovers (such as Okakura Tenshin of Japan who famously coined the phrase "Asia is One"). Pan Africanism was championed by people from diverse backgrounds, including the Trinidadian lawyer and writer Henry Sylvester Williams (1869–1911) who organized the First Pan-African Conference in London in 1900, Americo-Liberian educator and politician Edward Wilmot Blyden, and the American W.E.B. Du Bois.[8]

On the inter-governmental front, the Latin American countries emerged as the strongest proponents of regionalism as a mechanism for the pacific settlement of disputes and maintenance of order during the drafting of the UN Charter. This occurred within the context of the so-called universalism–regionalism debate that took place around the founding of the UN and the drafting of the UN charter at the San Francisco conference in 1945. The universalists, led by the US President Franklin Roosevelt, argued for investing all authority for peace and security in the hands of one overarching organization – the UN Security Council – while regionalists, mainly from Latin America but also from the newly formed Arab League, supported sharing that authority with regional groupings. Such regionalist doctrines of peace, as they came to be known, were based on the claim that geographic neighbours had a better understanding of local problems and were better placed and able to provide help than a distant UN. Their efforts led to a compromise, whereby regional groups were given a role in maintaining international peace and security. The Latin American states pointed to their own experience in developing regional norms and mechanisms, such as non-intervention and pacific settlement of disputes, to make their case. As a delegate to the San Francisco Conference put it, "inserting the inter-American system into the [UN] Charter . . . was a question of safeguarding a whole tradition which was dear to our continent . . . and a very active one" and would "contribute . . . to world peace and security."[9] The Charter's recognition of the role of regional organizations in conflict control and pacific settlement of disputes (Article 33/1, Chapter VI and Article 52/2, Chapter VIII) would be described by US Senator Arthur Vandenberg as an achievement that "infinitely strengthened the world Organization" by incorporating "these regional king-links into the global chain."[10]

Thus, whether in the economic, social, political and security realm, regionalism in practice had always had a multiple, global heritage. Yet from the 1960s onwards, a very narrow theoretical tool kit and approach developed by a group of European and American scholars came to dominate international relations scholars' idea of what regionalism means and how to study its origins, evolution and effectiveness. This paradigm of regionalism emerged with the establishment of the European Coal and Steel Community (ECSC) in 1951 and evolved through the creation and progress of the European Economic Community (EEC). Although commonly known as regional integration theory, it would be more accurate, following Wiener and Diez, to call this body of work, including its main variants, federalism, neo-functionalism and transactionalism (also known as communications theory), as "European integration theory."[11]

The intellectual history of this body of work is too well-known to require elaboration here.[12] But it is necessary to stress here that none of these theories performed well when applied to non-Western areas and their efforts at regionalism. In one of the most important articles on regionalism published in 1961, the neo-functionalist guru Ernst Haas compared the Western hemisphere, the Arab region and the European members of the Soviet Bloc, and concluded that the conditions required for integration in the EEC area, such as an industrial economy and liberal politics, did not obtain elsewhere. He thus concluded that "Whatever assurance may be warranted in our discussion of European integration is not readily transferable to other regional contexts."[13] Haas did not imply that regional integration in other parts of the world, driven by "different functional pursuits" than that in Western Europe, and "responding to a different set of converging interests," would not succeed. On the contrary, other regions will have their own functional objectives and approaches to integration, or "impulses peculiar to them." These different purposes and trajectories, Haas concluded meant that there could be no "universal 'law of integration' deduced from the European example."[14]

Haas's prescient warning seemed to have been ignored by those latter-day advocates of the "European example," who tended to judge, explicitly or implicitly, the performance of non-European regional institutions on the basis of the European benchmark. To quote Richard Higgott, the European project acquired a "paradigmatic status . . . against which all other regional projects are judged."[15]

By the mid-1970s, European integration theory was being overwhelmed by the forces of international interdependence – a precursor to globalization, which thus required new theoretical tools, such as the theory of power and interdependence and international regimes. Since then, our understanding of regionalism, regions, and theories of regionalism have changed considerably. Regional integration theories not only became obsolescent, as Haas acknowledged in 1975,[16] although some of their insights were transferred into theories of international interdependence, or claimed persisting relevance in some modified form.[17] The varieties of subsequent theoretical frameworks that appeared for studying comparative regionalism include regime theory, neoliberal institutionalism, the new regionalism approach, and constructivism. If one includes the critical approaches to regionalism, less prominent but conceptually significant (partly because they tend to be subsumed under the new regionalism literature), then the situation today becomes far more plural and thus a far cry from the heyday of European integration theories, which were basically three (or really two, since federalism did not make the grade to a comparable extent in the post-World War II period). Moreover, these newer theories have helped to redefine and broaden the study of regionalism and regional integration. Above all, they have seriously challenged, if not yet displaced, the dominance of European models. How has this happened?

From Eurocentrism to Euro-exceptionalism?

Some credit for this must be given to what became fashionably known since the 1990s as "new regionalism."[18] New regionalism does not represent a theory, much less a coherent theory, at least not in the sense that we regard neofunctionalism or neoliberal institutionalism as theories. It is better seen as an intellectual movement to broaden the scope of regionalism studies, taking into consideration the impact of globalization. The major impetus for new regionalism seems to have been disillusionment with the narrow focus of existing approaches which stressed formal structures and inter-governmental interactions to the exclusion of non-state actors and informal linkages and processes of interaction. It was also a natural response to globalization, especially the challenge posed by transnational actors and challenges to the nation-state, such as migration, refugees, environmental degradation, transnational crime, and financial volatility. Existing formal regional institutions seemed ill-equipped to address such challenges at first, and even as some of them (including the EU) were adapting to such challenges, ad hoc, bottom-up and informal networks and responses were emerging around these issue areas, which the literature on regionalism needed to account for.

But not all of new regionalism is really new. The idea that regionalism can be a bottom-up process, organized and driven by the concerns and identities of weaker actors, rather than top down or dictated by the great powers, was intrinsic to some of the regionalist ideas we have already examined, including the pan-regionalist movements. The distinctive aspect of the new regionalism movement was its effort to bring non-state actors and informal processes into the purview of regionalism studies. Although the initial support for the new regionalism project came from the United Nations University (UNU), rather than the EU, a good deal of the new regionalism literature is European, and its conceptualization was led by European scholars. Subsequent EU-funded projects, such as those undertaken by GARNET,[19] have also embraced the insights and approaches of the new regionalism movement, although comparisons with the EU have been a central element of such projects. This said, the new regionalism movement helped European and non-European experts to interact, socialize and understand each other's regionalisms to an extent unimaginable under the previous scholarship on regionalism in Europe and the US inspired by the integration theories.

The other major development[20] that broadened the scope of regionalism studies was the advent of constructivism. While the new regionalism literature was inspired by a critique of formal regionalism, the constructivist approach to regionalism (which was not wholly distinct from, but overlapping with, new regionalism) was motivated by a desire to counter the rationalist and materialist assumptions of previous theories, such as neo-functionalism and neo-liberal institutionalism. The so-called constructivist turn in IR theory, especially after the end of the Cold War, brought in ideational and normative elements to the study of regionalism and introduced the notion of socialization in marked contrast to the neofunctionalist emphasis on "the instrumental motives of actors," which takes "self-interest for granted and relies on it for delineating actor perceptions."[21]

Constructivists see ideas, norms, and identity playing a crucial role in regionalism. These elements shape expectations and facilitate cooperation through shared understandings of goals and outcomes. They act as "cognitive priors" that condition how new approaches to economic, political and security management are received. They also provide a yardstick for measuring the outcome of regionalism; the success or failure of regional institutions can be judged normatively rather than just on the basis of their material indicators like free trade. Constructivists not only hold that identities matter,[22] but also that regional identities, much like regions themselves, are not a given or a constant. Moreover, national and regional identities can co-exist and even complement each other, instead of being mutually exclusive.[23]

The turn to constructivism in the study of regionalism, at least in Europe, could also be seen as a natural response among scholars to the state of West European regionalism, especially the advent of the European Union with a single market, a common currency, and political-security initiatives that would lead some to label the Union as a "normative power." Another factor was the post-Cold War expansion of the EU to take in new members from East and Central Europe in search of a new sense of "European identity," which would soon prove to have been exaggerated.

Nonetheless, by positing that regionalism could be driven by inter-subjective forces rather than purely rationalist ones and judged in terms of normative outcomes rather than purely material ones, constructivism has not only transformed the study of European regionalism. It has also encouraged new ways of studying regionalism in the non-Western world, such as Southeast Asian, Latin American, Arab and African regionalisms, where culture and identity could be defining issues, and whose contributions could be mainly in the normative domain while their formal regional institutions are not integrative in the neofunctionalist sense.[24]

There have also been important shifts in the practice of regionalism. In particular, a host of new regional institutions have emerged. Asia, during the Cold War, could boast of only one viable regional grouping – ASEAN. ASEAN has now been joined by the Asia Pacific Economic Cooperation (APEC), ASEAN Regional

Forum (ARF), ASEAN Plus Three (APT), Shanghai Cooperation Organization (SCO), Asia–Europe Meeting (ASEM – an interregional body) and the East Asia Summit (EAS). As noted, the OAU has become the African Union (AU). The new name notwithstanding, it is doubtful whether it aspires to be EU-like. Latin America has come up with institutional mechanisms for the defence of democracy like the Inter-American Democratic Charter.

Moreover, the ongoing global power shift with the rise of China, India, Brazil, and others creates the potential to redefine the purpose of regionalism and the role of regional institutions, either by strengthening or undermining them. For example, some of these powers may engage in "leapfrogging," i.e. ignoring the neighbourhood in favour of the global perch like the G-20, as India and China appear to be doing, while others, like South Africa, may claim to represent their regions and seek to use regional platforms to legitimize and enhance their global role. There is also the danger that the emerging powers of the world will develop their own "Monroe Doctrines," thereby rendering regionalism closer to the kind that Panikkar and Nehru disapproved of (although I see the danger of this to be rather slight).

On the positive side, regionalism everywhere is acquiring new meanings and regional institutions are taking on whole sets of new missions and covering new issue areas, including transnational challenges like climate change, financial volatility, pandemics, natural disasters. which were not within their purview before. But the importance of these issue areas and approaches to them varies. For example, Asia's regionalism has yet to embrace the doctrine of humanitarian intervention in the way Africa's regionalism has done it, at least at a declaratory level. Latin American regionalism has developed a much greater interest, normatively and institutionally, in defending democracy than other non-Western regions, although its record on this score is far from perfect. Asia is moving faster in organizing regional financial stability mechanisms than Africa, Latin America or the Middle East. These variations need to be recognized and respected, studied and explained, rather than ignored or lamented. This is one of the pre-eminent challenges for the students of regionalism.

While cooperation and integration are different, some regions other than Europe are also integrating, economically at least, but not through the European pathway. East Asia has pursued a market-led rather than organization-driven integration. Regional institutions in Africa, Asia, and Latin America have all made their contributions to peace and security consistent with their own set goals or objectives. Latin America's contribution to non-intervention, Africa's contribution to the norm of inviolability of postcolonial boundaries, and Asia's contribution to the non-alignment norm are some of the examples of what I have called "norm subsidiarity." We find increasing evidence of such norm creation and propagation by all the regions of the world, some of them for local application only, while others have diffused across regions and globally.[25]

Although it is clearly premature to reach any firm conclusion, the present crisis in the EU has the potential to render the study of regionalism less Eurocentric. If the crisis leads to the weakening, if not unravelling of the European project, then its legitimacy as a model for the rest of the world would not be left unscathed. If, on the other hand, the crisis ends up in promoting greater EU integration, for example, with a move towards fiscal union to supplement the monetary union, then the European model would become even more distinctive, perhaps too distinctive to be emulated by others. In short, we could move from Eurocentrism to Euro-exceptionalism in the field of regionalism studies and comparative regionalism. To those seeking difference and diversity in the discipline of comparative regionalism, this may be a blessing in disguise.

Conclusion: what's in a name?

In the past two decades, there have been some important shifts, one might even say "advances" (although not everyone would agree), in the study of regionalism. Most scholars of regionalism today would have little problem in accepting that regionalism is not the monopoly of states but also encompasses interactions among non-state actors and between states and non-state actors within a given area. We have also come a long way from the days when regionalism was defined largely in terms of formal intergovernmental organizations with a charter and a bureaucracy. It is well understood now that regionalism is different from regionalization in the sense that the latter could be market-driven, less political than the former. Another shift, particularly advanced by constructivism, is that regions are not a geographic given, but socially constructed – made and remade through interactions. There is also a fairly common acceptance among scholars and policy-makers that domestic and transnational factors play a significant role in shaping the emergence and purposes of regionalism and regional institutions.

More importantly, the Eurocentricism of the theoretical apparatus of the field is being seriously questioned, although not yet fully reversed, not the least because of the genuine interest and commitment of many European and Europe-based scholars to work closely with their counterparts from the non-Western world to redefine and broaden the scope and tools of enquiry. Against this backdrop, there is even less reason to invoke old biases by insisting that the field of study be termed as comparative regional integration studies (which features in the very title of this EU-funded conference). My own preferred term is comparative regionalism, which speaks, to borrow the useful distinction drawn by Professor Schmitter earlier at this conference, to the idea of regional cooperation, rather than that of regional integration.

To me, there are two major differences between the two. First, integration by definition implies loss of sovereignty, voluntary or through pressure. Regionalism does not. This does not make regionalism less important, as some suggest, but what it means is that we need different concepts and approaches to study the phenomena. This leads to a second difference. Integration studies have always been heavily influenced by the EU's history and experience. The founding theories of integration studies, especially neo-functionalism and transactionalism, were heavily drawn from the early life of what we call the EU today.

By contrast, my main point in this chapter has been to argue that regionalism or comparative regionalism has a much more diverse beginning and a global heritage than regional integration and comparative regional integration studies. Regional integration is a distinctively Western European idea and is rather limited in scope. The ideas and literature that constitute comparative regionalism came from and were enriched by contributions from many regions, including Latin America, Asia, US, Middle East, Africa and, of course, Europe. It is this multiple and global heritage of comparative regionalism that I address in the pages below.

In keeping with the rapid growth and development of regionalism and institutions in the non-Western world, including in regions which were relatively late starters (e.g. Asia), there have emerged new ways of looking at regional cooperation, and claims about distinctive approaches (e.g. "the ASEAN Way") that are different from the EU. Whether these approaches are more appropriate and thus more "workable" for non-Western settings than the EU model remains a matter of contestation. But they do warrant Sbragia's following observation: "the field of comparative regionalism reflects a process that is so complex and geographically expansive that it can fruitfully accommodate a wide variety of theoretical and methodological approaches. Most interestingly, non-Western scholars will undoubtedly help shape its future evolution."[26]

But herein lays a set of crucial challenges, which those seeking to develop the "new" field of comparative regionalism must address. Let me identify five of them, although the list is far from exhaustive.

1. Given the diversity of regions, and the proliferation of theoretical approaches, can we have agreement over a set of theories and concepts that can be meaningfully employed across regions for systematic comparisons and coherent explanations? Or should we leave the field of comparative regionalism to be eternally contested and contestable?

2. In theorizing comparative regionalism, should we err on the side of induction, rather than deduction? This means that instead of having a set of general theoretical propositions and hypotheses (which tend to derive from the EU experience) to test in different regions, should we analyse each region on its own merit and then cumulatively generalize what is common and what is different?

3. Should we have an agreed performance criteria for regionalisms (when we can tell a particular region or type of regionalism has been successful) or should we leave it open and evolving, and region-specific?[27]

4. Should the fundamental question to be addressed by the field move beyond the success or efficacy of institutions – or "do regional institutions and regionalisms matter?" – to the question "how do they matter?" The wider institutionalist literature has moved in that direction.

5. How do we conceptualize the relative autonomy of regions? If regions are simply reflections of the global distribution of power, and are deemed to lack autonomy, that is, an ability to organize their economic, political and social processes independent of outside forces and global processes, then can we say

that the field of comparative regionalism has any value and is worth pursuing? How do we theorize regions in an era of globalization: as building blocks, as sites of resistance, or both? It is important not to neglect the latter, i.e. regionalism of resistance, in favour of the former, i.e. regionalism of absorption (into the globalization process). Relatedly, it is important to understand how regions produce and transmit their own ideas and images about other regions and the world at large. Comparative regionalism scholars, if they are to retain a sense of meaningful regional autonomy, must also look at how regions create, borrow, localize and repatriate ideas/norms as well as practices, processes which I have called "constitutive localization" and "norm subsidiarity."[28]

With these and other questions to play with, comparative regionalism, mindful of its diverse and global heritage, and enjoying growing diversity and pluralism, is a cause for celebration.

Notes

1 Keynote address to the Conference on Regional Integration in Europe and Africa: Models, Policies, and Comparative Perspectives, University of Pretoria, South Africa, 16–18 February 2011. It was published under the same title in *International Spectator* 47, no. 1 (2012): 3–15.
2 I define "regionalism" as purposive interaction, formal or informal, among state and non-state actors of a given area in pursuit of shared external, domestic and transnational goals. While the concept of regionalism can be very broad, the main referent of this chapter is regional international institutions and the transnational dynamics around them, as understood among comparative regionalism scholars, rather than the processes of sub-state mobilization and cooperation as understood by scholars of comparative federalism, territorial politics or devolution in the EU area. The examples of the latter would be the German Lander, the Spanish autonomous communities, the Italian regioni, the devolved nations in the UK, Flanders and Wallonia in Belgium. I am grateful to an annonymous reviewer for this volume for pointing our the need for this clarification.
3 Kavalam M. Panikkar was one of the most prolific and influential writers on Asian history and international relations of his time, most well-known for his formulation "Vasco Da Gama age," in a classic work entitled *Asia and Western Dominance: A Survey of the Vasco Da Gama Epoch of Asian History, 1498–1945* (London: George Allen and Unwin, 1953).
4 Kavalam M. Panikkar, "Regionalism and World Security," in *Regionalism and Security*, by K. M. Panikkar et al. (New Delhi, India: Indian Council of World Affairs, 1948).
5 Panikkar, "Regionalism and World Security," 1.
6 Panikkar, "Regionalism and World Security," 5–6.
7 Jawaharlal Nehru, *The Discovery of India* (New Delhi, India: Oxford, 1946), 539.
8 An important aspect here is that many of the champions of pan-Africanism were not from Africa itself, attesting to the possibility of an outside-in or sympathetic regionalism.
9 UNCIO, *Documents of the United Nations Conference on International Organization (UNCIO), San Francisco, 1945* (London and New York: United Nations Information Organizations, 1945), VI, 9.
10 Ibid., 5.
11 Antje Weiner and Thomas Diez, eds., *European Integration Theory* (Oxford: Oxford University Press, 2004).
12 For an excellent overview, see, Ibid.

13 Ernst B. Haas, "International Integration: The European and the Universal Process," *International Organization* 15, no. 3 (1961): 366–392, 378.

14 Ibid., 289.

15 Richard Higgott, "The Theory and Practice of Region," in *Regional Integration in East Asia and Europe: Convergence or Divergence*, eds., Bertrand Fort and Douglas Webber (London: Routledge, 2006), 23.

16 Ernst B. Haas, *The Obsolescence of Regional Integration Theory* (Berkeley: University of California, Institute of International Studies, Research Series no. 25, 1975); and Ernst B. Haas, "Does Constructivism Subsume Neofunctionalism?" in *The Social Construction of Europe*, eds., Thomas Christiansen, Knud Erik Jørgensen and Antje Wiener (London: Sage, 2001), 22–31.

17 Donald J. Puchala, "The Integration Theorists and the Study of International Relations," *International Organization* 55, no. 3 (2001): 553–588; and Philippe B. Schmitter, "Neo-Neofunctionalism," in *European Integration Theory*, eds., Antje Weiner and Thomas Diez (Oxford: Oxford University Press, 2004), 45–74. The transactionalist approach of Karl Deutsch and his associates, especially the idea of security communities, have been resurrected, albeit modified with a heavy infusion of constructivist concepts, such as ideas, norms and socialization which were only implicit in the original theory. See, Emanuel Adler and Michael Barnett, eds., *Security Communities* (Cambridge: Cambridge University Press, 1998); Amitav Acharya, *Constructing a Security Community in Southeast Asia: ASEAN and the Problem of Regional Order* (London and New York: Routledge, 2001 and 2009).

18 The first volume of the UNU-Wider (World Institute for Development Economic Research) sponsored project was Björn Hettne, András Inotai and Osvaldo Sunkel, *Globalism and the New Regionalism* (Basingstoke, U.K.: Palgrave Macmillan, 1999). See also: Mario Telò, *European Union and New Regionalism: Regional Actors and Global Governance in a Post-Hegemonic Era* (London: Ashgate, 2007).

19 GARNET stands for Network of Excellence on *Global Governance, Regionalisation and Regulation: The Role of the EU*. It was funded under the European Commission's 6th Framework Programme and comprised 42 leading research centres and universities. I participated in several of its activities. See for example, Amitav Acharya, "Regional Worlds in a Post-Hegemonic Era," Keynote Speech at the GARNET Annual Conference on "Mapping Integration and Regionalism in a Global World" in Bordeaux, France, 17–18 September, 2008, http://www.spirit.sciencespobordeaux.fr/Cahiers%20de%20SPIRIT/Cahiers%20de%20SPIRIT_1_Acharya.pdf.

20 I have not dealt with critical perspectives, but these accentuated the emphasis of new regionalism on informal sectors and provided a powerful critique of EU type neoliberalism.

21 Ernst B. Haas, "The Study of Regional Integration: Reflections on the Joys and Anguish of Pretheorising," in *Regional Politics and World Order*, eds., Richard A. Falk and Saul H. Mendlovitz (San Francisco: Institute of Contemporary Studies, 1972), 117.

22 Here, I have a fundamental disagreement with the other keynote speaker at the conference, Professor Philippe Schmitter, himself a pioneer of European Integration Theory, who argued forcefully that "regionalism is about interest and not identity." This echoes his perspective from an earlier essay that "integration is basically (but not exclusively) a rational process whereby actors calculate anticipated returns from various alternative strategies of participation in joint decision-making structures," and that while "'[i]rrational' postures or strategies – whether for dogmatic/ideological or personal/emotive reasons – are never absent from social action, even at the international level, but they are from this theory." P.C. Schmitter, "Neo-Neofunctionalism," in *European Integration Theory*, eds., A. Weiner and R. Diez (Oxford: Oxford University Press, 2004), 45–74, 55. For me identity, including that based on ideological or emotive forces, matters in Europe as much as elsewhere, although claims about a European identity could be exaggerated. I do not argue that values, culture and identity alone matter in shaping regionalism. But

it is equally fallacious to apply a rationalist straightjacket to the study of comparative regionalism.

23 Peter J. Katzenstein, *A World of Regions: Asia and Europe in the American Imperium* (Ithaca: Cornell University Press, 2005), 76, 81.

24 See for example, Acharya, *Constructing a Security Community in Southeast Asia: ASEAN and the Problem of Regional Order*, and Amitav Acharya, *Whose Ideas Matter: Agency and Power in Asian Regionalism* (Ithaca: Cornell University Press, 2009).

25 Amitav Acharya, "Norm Subsidiarity and Regional Orders: Sovereignty, Regionalism, and Rule-Making in the Third World," *International Studies Quarterly* 55, no. 1 (2011): 95–123.

26 Alberta Sbragia, "Review Article: Comparative Regionalism: What it Might be?" *Journal of Common Market Studies* 46, Issue Supplement s1 (2008): 29–49, 44.

27 This was a key question addressed in the edited volume, *Crafting Cooperation*, and requires further study. See Amitav Acharya and Alastair Iain Johnston, *Crafting Cooperation: Regional International Institutions in Comparative Perspective* (Cambridge: Cambridge University Press, 2007).

28 Amitav Acharya, "How Ideas Spread: Whose Norms Matter: Norm Localization and Institutional Change in Asian Regionalism," *International Organization* 58, no. 2 (2004): 239–275.

PART II

Power, intervention and global disorders

4

THE COLD WAR AS "LONG PEACE" REVISITED[1]

Among international relations scholars, there has been much debate on the consequences of the end of the Cold War for war and peace in the international system. A major contributor to this debate, John Mearsheimer, has argued emphatically that "a Europe without the superpowers . . . would probably be substantially more prone to violence than the past 45 years," despite the continent's growing economic interdependence, the role of political and functional institutions such as the European Union and the Organization of Security and Cooperation in Europe, and the pluralist domestic structure of European nations.[2] As he sees it, "with the end of the Cold War, Europe is reverting to a state system that created powerful incentives for aggression in the past." Because of this, he concludes, "we are likely soon to regret the passing of the Cold War."

Mearsheimer's thesis[3] focuses on the European theatre. Several commentators have nonetheless reached a similar pessimistic conclusion about stability in the post-Cold War Third World. Thus, Jose Cintra argues that the Cold War had suppressed "many potential third-world conflicts"; their geopolitical retrenchment will ensure that "other conflicts will very probably arise from decompression and from a loosening of the controls and self-controls" exercised by the superpowers.[4] Stanley Hoffmann similarly envisages a "New World Disorder in the Third World," a situation far more chaotic than the world of the Cold War, when the superpowers, knowing that they could blow themselves up, restrained themselves and their allies."[5] Testifying before the Senate Armed Services Committee, the Director of the US Defense Intelligence Agency warns of "regional flashpoints" in the Middle East, East Asia and South Asia, which could become serious threats to US security because the end of bipolarity "has removed the tampering mechanism that often kept these situations under control."[6] In a more cautious vein, Robert Jervis argues that while the Cold War might have had a mixed impact on Third World conflicts, "In the net, however, it generally dampened conflict and we can therefore expect more rather than less of it in future."[7]

A more nuanced view of the future has been offered by Goldgeiger and McFaul, who use two different theoretical lenses to analyse and predict the future of what they call the "core" and the "periphery." Structural realist predictions that multipolarity will heighten anarchy, competition, and balancing behaviour will not, in their view, apply to security relations among the Great Powers who constitute the core. Instead, "political democracy, economic interdependence, and nuclear weapons" (all are largely unrelated to polarity or the distribution of power), will help lessen the security dilemma and reduce the risk of armed conflict within the core. But the situation in the periphery, roughly comprising what has been called the "Third World," will be radically different. Lacking the attributes that will bring stability to the core, the periphery will feature fragile regional security systems experiencing heightened conflict and disorder.[8] Stability in the periphery will be undermined by inter-state strife, arms races, and balancing behaviour. In telling the "tale of two worlds of international politics in the post-Cold War era," Goldgeiger and McFaul conclude that while "structural realism is inadequate to explain the behaviour of states in the core . . . [it] is relevant for understanding regional security systems in the periphery."[9]

If such views were to hold true, it would have major ramifications for theorists and practitioners of international relations. The long-standing debate in international relations theory (IRT) on the linkage between polarity and stability has remained unsettled; if the end of the Cold War was to engender greater instability in the greater part of the international system where the vast majority of the world's population lives, then the debate would have to be settled decisively in favour of those who view bipolarity as a more "stable" international order than multipolarity. A more unstable Third World would also legitimize the rampant interventionism of the superpowers in the Third World during the Cold War period and silence critics of Great Power intervention as a tool of global order–maintenance. Academic analysts concerned with the future of war would need to pay more attention to systemic, as opposed to domestic/local, causes of international conflict.

In this chapter, I challenge the dominant view of the stability–instability equation in the Third World. First, I argue that the claim that bipolar international systems are more stable than multipolar ones might have been true of Europe and the central strategic balance during the Cold War, but it is misleading as a theoretical tool for analysing regional stability in the Third World. During the Cold War, the supposedly "stable" system structure permitted a great deal of regional instability in the Third World. On the other hand, a multipolar system structure, in which the balance of power may be more uncertain and the behaviour of states less predictable, may allow stability in regional security systems, at least in some parts of the Third World.

My second argument is that the post-Cold War security outlook for the Third World is too complex to be understood within a neorealist or structural realist framework alone, as suggested by Goldgeiger and McFaul. While one cannot overlook the high incidence of conflict in the Third World today, the perils of strategic uncertainty can be exaggerated. And the blessings of multipolarity can be understated. The end of bipolarity will not have a single or uniform impact on the Third

World. Some of its consequences will be destabilizing, while others may bring about increased stability. Moreover, liberal arguments concerning international stability, such as democracy and interdependence, could also apply to the Third World. As a result, the Third World in the post-Cold War era will not be a single vast theatre of conflict and disorder. The overall picture will vary from region to region, and the determinants of stability–instability will be increasingly localized. The security predicament of the Third World regions will range from localized anarchies to pluralistic security communities of the kind found in the core.

Polarity, stability and anarchy: the Third World and international order

Although the supposition that the Cold War was a period of "stability" in the international system as a whole and, consequently, its end would be highly destabilizing is shared by a number of different analysts, including political scientists, historians, and policy-makers, its main theoretical basis comes from a well-known tenet of neorealism (also known as structural realism). An influential strand of realist theory, neorealism holds that bipolar systems are more stable than multipolar systems, an argument made most forcefully by Kenneth Waltz (although, as John Lewis Gaddis points out, Morton Kaplan also made similar arguments[10]). Writing at the height of the Cold War, Waltz argued that bipolarity "encourage[s] the limitation of violence in the relations of states"[11] primarily by reducing the scope for misunderstanding, misperception and confusion. The fewer the number of actors, the greater the predictability of interaction between them. As Waltz put it, "In a bipolar world uncertainty lessens and calculations are easier to make."[12] Furthermore, bipolarity leads to an overall extension of the sphere of international stability because "with only two world powers, there are no peripheries." The intensity of superpower competition during the Cold War, which Waltz accepted as the chief empirical model of bipolarity, produced reluctance on their part to accept even small territorial losses anywhere in the world. This reduced the possibility of international conflict by extending "the geographic scope of both powers' concern." Waltz contrasted these attributes of bipolarity with the dangers inherent in a multipolar system. In a "multipolar world, who is a danger to whom is often unclear; the incentive to regard all disequilibrating changes with concern and respond to them with whatever effort may be required is consequently weakened."[13] Mearsheimer carries this argument further by pointing out that while "a bipolar system has only one dyad across which war might break out," a "multipolar system is much more fluid and has many such dyads," thereby making war more likely.[14]

A specific virtue of the Cold War bipolarity emphasized by Waltz and Gaddis relates to the restrained and regulatory role of the superpowers in dealing with major international conflicts. According to Waltz, ". . . the pressures of a bipolar world strongly encourage[d] them [the superpowers] to act internationally in ways better than their characters may lead one to expect."[15] Gaddis speaks of the tendency of "self-regulation" in the bipolar relationship. Referring to the willingness and ability of the two superpowers to manage major international crises during the Cold War period, Gaddis concludes that this functioned like "the automatic pilot on an airplane or the governor on a steam engine" in counteracting threats to international stability. The critical elements of these "self-regulating mechanisms" include, among other things, a "fundamental agreement among major states within the system on the objectives they are seeking to uphold by participating in it" as well as "agreed-upon procedures exist for resolving differences among them."[16] Moreover, a bipolar structure is more likely than a multipolar system to ensure the stability of alliances, thereby helping the ability of the leading actors to regulate international conflict.

Neorealists, Waltz in particular, point to historical evidence to support their claim regarding the positive correlation between bipolarity and international stability. Thus, the experience of the US–Soviet rivalry attests to the ability of a bipolar system to manage crises and maintain alliances without resort to war. These attributes of bipolarity compare favourably to the relationship among the pre-1945 Great Powers interacting in a multipolar international environment.

Waltz's arguments concerning the positive linkage between bipolarity and international stability have not gone unchallenged in IRT. Gilpin, himself a realist, rejects Waltz's view that wars are caused by uncertainty and miscalculation that are characteristic features of multipolarity. Instead, "it is the perceived certainty of gain [associated with bipolarity] that most frequently causes nations to go to war."[17] Gilpin further argues that bipolarity creates the "conditions for relatively small causes to lead to disproportionately large effects."[18] Thus, under a bipolar order, minor crises in obscure countries could escalate into serious international confrontation as a result of superpower involvement. A similar argument concerning the conflict-escalating potential of bipolarity has been made by Rosecrance. Referring to the zero-sum nature of bipolar competition, Rosecrance points to the risk that even simple action by one principal actor is likely to provoke hostile countermeasures from the other side. Because a bipolar system ensures that antagonisms will be reciprocated, it "does not reduce motivations for expansion [in the geopolitical conduct of the two principal actors] and may even increase them."[19]

While the above arguments cast doubt on the theoretical position concerning the stability of bipolar systems, other theorists have pointed to the positive effects of multipolarity on international stability. Deutsch and Singer argue that multipolarity, by increasing "the range and flexibility of interactions" among a larger number of powerful actors, inhibits recourse to war and facilitates cooperation. In their view, "as the number of possible exchanges increases, so does the probability that the 'invisible hand' of pluralistic interests will be effective."[20] Furthermore, in multipolarity, "the share of attention that any nation can devote to any other must of necessity diminish"; thus conflicts in peripheral areas will have a limited potential for escalation.[21] Multipolarity is also likely to have a "dampening effect upon arms races."[22]

The theoretical debate on the linkage between polarity and stability has produced no clear winner.[23] But in this chapter, I argue that the debate fails to capture key aspects of the security predicament of the Third World. It takes a virtually undifferentiated view of the international system, ignoring important dissimilarities between the North and the South. The fact that much of this debate took place before problems of conflict and security in the Third World became a subject of attention and serious scholarship among IR theorists further underscores this point. Similarly, the historical evidence used to support the arguments of both sides comes from the historical evolution of the European states system.[24] These generalizations miss out on the consequences of the decolonization process and the emergence of the Third World for the maintenance of international order.

Viewed from the perspective of the Third World, I note two major deficiencies of the polarity–stability debate. The first relates to an excessively narrow view of stability and a tendency to conflate stability and peace. Because of their tendency to generalize from Great Power behaviour, the polarity–stability debate equates stability with the absence of system-threatening war among the Great Powers. For Waltz, stability meant, first and foremost, the capacity of a system to maintain itself, and not necessarily the frequency or intensity of conflicts within or between its constituent units. In other words, the stability of the system does not depend on the stability of all its constituents. Even his critics, including those who view multipolar systems as being more stable, share similar assumptions about the meaning of stability. Deutsch and Singer, for example, define stability as "the probability that the system retains all of its essential characteristics: that no single nation becomes dominant; that most of its members continue to survive; and that *large-scale war* does not occur" (emphasis added). For Gaddis, "the most convincing argument for 'stability' [of the bipolar world] is that so far at least, World War III has not occurred."[25]

If such a narrow view of "stability' is accepted, then a "stable" system should permit any number of limited or small-scale and internal wars, including conflicts in its peripheral areas, so long as such conflicts do not threaten the existence of the system structure. Thus, according to Waltz, the risk of miscalculation inherent in multipolarity is "more likely to permit the unfolding of a series of events that finally threatens a change in the balance and brings the [major] powers to war," while bipolarity "is the lesser evil because it costs only money and *the fighting of limited wars*" (emphasis added).[26] But the category of limited war can be very broad indeed. Under bipolarity, Rosecrance points out, "substantial territorial and/or political changes can take place in international relations without impinging on the overarching stability."[27] Since the notion of system structure refers to the distribution of capabilities among the units, only those units who occupy the upper rungs of the power matrix could affect system structure by virtue of their conflictual or cooperative behaviour. Systemic instability could only result from major power or hegemonic wars. The weaker members of the system, such as the Third World countries, simply do not possess the capabilities needed to affect the system structure. Thus, if one accepts Waltz's theoretical position, the high incidence of Cold War conflicts in the Third World does not challenge the essential stability of bipolar international systems, as long as the central balance and its European strategic core remain war-free.

A second problem with the polarity–stability debate should be noted, as it is especially relevant to the issue of ethnocentrism of IRT. Because of their preoccupation with major power relationships and a consequent tendency to rely on the European states system for evidence, the protagonists in the debate ignored actual trends regarding conflict and order in the Third World. Neither Waltz nor his critics looked at the Third World to seek evidence for their theoretical arguments. In a similar vein, the current pessimistic predictions about post-Cold War instability in the Third World are based on a considerable amount of false alarm and exaggeration. If one examines trends in the Third World carefully, as this chapter does, then a different picture of its stability will emerge.

Moreover, because both bipolarity and multipolarity are systemic structures, to use them as central explanatory variables in assessing the likelihood of international conflict means ignoring the importance of domestic and regional factors in conflict formation. As this chapter argues, it is precisely these factors which are often central to an understanding of the security problematic of the Third World.[28] Furthermore, a system–centric view is likely to ignore the role of regionally based security institutions and regimes, which may significantly affect the probability and scale of conflict in the Third World. Finally, by focusing on the relationship among the Great Powers as the central determinant of international stability and order, the polarity–stability debate has ignored another crucial systemic factor affecting order–maintenance: the relationship between the North and the South.

The above reasons limit the relevance of the polarity–stability debate as a conceptual framework for assessing prospects for Third World stability in the post-Cold War era. To be useful for this purpose, the debate must go beyond its Euro-centric universe and its hitherto preoccupation with Great Power relationships. It must embrace a more differentiated view of the conditions of international order, one that reflects the distinctive security predicament of the Third World. To provide such a view is a key aim of this chapter. But an important point of clarification regarding my conceptual framework needs to be made here. While my assessment is intended to highlight the limitations of the hitherto narrow and somewhat ethnocentric conceptual terrain of both sides of the polarity–stability debate, my critique is directed specifically against the position of Waltz, Mearsheimer and others, who make grand claims about the essential stability of bipolar systems. My findings support the view that multipolarity may be more conducive to stability and peace, but I arrive at this conclusion by examining a broader and more complex range of determinants, with particular emphasis on the linkage between systemic structure and regional stability, on the one hand, and the indigenous sources of conflict and order in the Third World, on the other.

Structural uncertainty and regional order: the Third World in the post-Cold War era

If the structural stability of the Cold War period did not preclude large-scale regional disorder in the Third World, what are the likely implications of structural uncertainty? Neorealist theory argues that the collapse of bipolarity creates acute uncertainty about the balance of power. If, as Waltz put it, "In a bipolar world uncertainty lessens and calculations are easier to make,"[29] then multipolarity increases the scope for misunderstanding, misperception and confusion. In heightened anarchy, the principle of self-help assumes greater importance. States are increasingly likely to resort to balancing behaviour, either by increasing their domestic power through military acquisitions or by forging alliances with other more powerful states. This, in turn, may aggravate the security dilemma in the Third World, producing destabilizing arms races and increasing the risk of armed conflict. Thus, from a structural realist perspective, strategic uncertainty caused by the end of bipolarity is likely to make the Third World a much more dangerous place.

On the surface, developments in the post-Cold War seem to bear out the structural realist prognosis. The Third World today remains a dangerous place, plagued by a large number of ethnic, territorial and political conflicts. But one is not quite sure whether these conflicts can be viewed as a direct consequence of the end of bipolarity. For example, the rise of ethnic and territorial conflicts in the Third World has been blamed on the end of the Cold War. The disintegration of the Soviet Union is said to have exacerbated ethnic tensions by removing "ideological models that ha[d] offered uniting symbols of nation-building in countries that would otherwise be torn apart by ethnic, cultural, religious, or linguistic differences."[30] In a similar vein, Barry Buzan argues that "If the territorial jigsaw can be extensively reshaped in the First and Second Worlds, it will become harder to resist the pressures to try to find more sensible and congenial territorial arrangements in the ex-Third World."[31]

But the fundamental causative factor in both cases seems to be the *collapse of the Soviet Union* and not *the end of bipolarity* per se. It is quite possible that had the end of bipolarity come about in some other way, one that left the Soviet Union intact ideologically and territorially, then it would not have produced any negative demonstration effect on Third World ethnic or territorial relations.

Another reason why neorealist theory cannot use the example of recent Third World ethnic and territorial conflicts to make its point about the destabilizing consequences of multipolarity is that these threats are hardly new. Roberto Garcia Moritan observes:

> Many of the regional problems and or conflicts that were essentially local expressions of the rivalry are now proving soluble. But there are many other conflicts rooted in other sources, among them historical, political, colonial, ethnic, religious, or socio-economic legacies, that continue to produce international tensions. Cutting across these local issues are the major disparities of wealth and opportunity that separate the industrialized nations and the developing world. These have existed for decades. The failure to deal effectively with this gap is a source of additional tension, which itself frustrates long-term efforts to provide wider prosperity. The end of the Cold War has been irrelevant for many such conflicts.[32]

For example, the danger of ethnic conflict predates the end of the Cold War and was an even more serious problem then. Data compiled by the *Minorities at Risk Project* suggests that "ethnopolitical conflicts were relatively common, and increased steadily, throughout the Cold War," with the greatest absolute and proportional increase in number of groups involved in ethnopolitical conflicts occurring between the 1960s and 1970s (from 36 groups to 55). This contrasts with a rate of increase of only 8 (from 62 to 70) from the 1980s to the early 1990s. Thus, as the project's Director, Ted Robert Gurr, concludes, "the 'explosion of' ethnopolitical conflicts since the end of the Cold War is, in fact, a continuation of a trend that began as early as the 1960s." His project's findings also suggest that "ongoing ethnopolitical conflicts that began after 1987 are not appreciably more intense than those that began earlier," although they might "have caused greater dislocation of populations."[33]

Neorealist thinking also exaggerates the dangers of strategic multipolarity. For example, fears that post-colonial boundaries in the Third World are being undermined by the end of the Cold War are, to say the least, premature. The separation of Eritrea from Ethiopia after three decades of struggle makes it the first African state to be created through secession since decolonization. But in many respects, Eritrea is a special case.[34] As the *Economist* put it, while Eritrean independence breaks Africa's secession taboo, its claim for independence is "unusually strong" due to special historical circumstances in the sense that it never formed part of Ethiopia during the colonial era. Even if it encourages other movements, it "need not spell disaster for the continent."[35] Similarly, the likelihood of serious territorial conflicts elsewhere in the Third World could be overstated. Even at the height of the decolonization process during the Cold War, territorial conflicts were not a significant feature of the Third World's security dilemma. As research by Kal Holsti suggests, "The traditional national security problematic of most states in Europe was defined as protecting specific pieces of real estate. This is not the premier security problem for most states in the Third World."[36] There is as yet no concrete proof that we are about to see a major outbreak or escalation of territorial conflicts in the Third World; in fact the trends point in the opposite direction[37]

Another example of overplaying the dangers of strategic multipolarity is the issue of Third World militarization. Using realist logic, Goldgeiger and McFaul hold that the end of superpower rivalry means that "states in the developing world will have to seek means for enhancing security within their own states or regions." In other words, cuts in superpower military assistance programs in the Third World mean their former clients may seek greater military self-reliance, thereby fuelling new regional arms races.[38] Reinforcing the possibility of greater militarism in the Third World is the availability of large quantities of surplus military hardware from the vast arsenals of the major powers at bargain prices. But available evidence points to the fact that multipolarity need not aggravate the security dilemma and produce arms races. Recent data shows that the military build-up in the Third World has substantially declined with the end of the Cold War. (For an overview of trends in Third World defence expenditures and weapons acquisitions, see Box 4.1.) The reasons for this trend may be found in the fact that "The end of the East–West divide has . . . heralded the demise of 'patron support', 'militarization by invitation', and soft financing terms. Only the richest countries are now able to buy weapons on a large scale."[39] Analysing the decline of arms transfers to Africa, Thomas and Mazrui argue that this owes primarily to the end of superpower competition and several of its related effects such as recent successes in settling African civil wars (which were escalated by the Cold War) and the rise of pro-democracy movements (other factors include the end of anti-colonial armed struggles, economic crisis and concerns expressed by the International Monetary Fund (IMF) and the World Bank regarding high levels of military spending in countries undergoing structural adjustment). In the rich nations of East Asia, defence expenditures and arms imports have risen since the end of the Cold War. But this region is hardly a microcosm of the Third World. Arms acquisitions by states in this region do not necessarily constitute an arms race, but are more plausibly a by-product of post-Cold War bargain-hunting and economic affluence.[40] Available evidence seems to bear out Rosecrance's argument that multipolarity has a "dampening effect upon arms races."[41]

What about the proliferation of weapons of mass destruction in the Third World? Do the uncertainties of a multipolar system create greater incentive for states to seek such weapons? While one does not have to be a realist to appreciate the danger posed by the proliferation of weapons of mass destruction, the fact remains that it cannot be attributed to the end of the Cold War. If anything, the Cold War itself had aggravated the problem, especially because both the US and the Soviet Union overlooked and tolerated proliferation efforts by their clients and allies in the Third World. For example, massive US military and economic aid to Pakistan in the aftermath of the Soviet invasion of Afghanistan was meant to discourage the latter's nuclear program by providing it with a conventional alternative. But its net effect was to ease the pressure on Pakistan's nuclear program, which reached a weapon capability during this very period. A number of Soviet allies acquired chemical and nuclear material, ostensibly with Moscow's knowledge and backing. On the other hand, strategic uncertainty associated with multipolarity may actually help multilateral non-proliferation efforts. For example, the fear of "loose-nukes" created by the break-up of the Soviet Union has contributed to a strengthening of global non-proliferation efforts. International consensus against nuclear weapons has never been stronger. While strategic bipolarity legitimized the use of nuclear weapons, now the international community has begun seriously into looking at ways of ensuring their reduction and perhaps eventual elimination. The indefinite extension of the Nuclear Non-Proliferation Treaty and the proliferation of nuclear-weapon free-zones in the Third World, both occurring in the post-Cold War era, attest to this.[42]

Brad Roberts has argued that "States acquiring massively destructive military capabilities will be forced by the power inherent in those weapons to learn to possess them wisely . . . this requires of leaders in the developing world that they act like the rational actors assumed in all deterrence models."[43] This is true of any kind of international system, whether bipolar or multipolar. But the uncertainties of the latter may make states with dangerous weapons even more cautious in choosing their strategic options. If the end of bipolarity "entails merely that the Third World will do more of its own fighting,"[44] then Third World states with weapons of mass destruction are likely to be more careful in weighing the costs and consequences of their possession and use of weapons of mass destruction. Given the demonstrated effect of nuclear weapons in inducing caution in the European theatre (as well as the central strategic balance in general) during the Cold War, there is no reason to believe, short of blind ethnocentrism, that the Third World leaders will behave like "madmen" once in possession of such weapons.

Yet another fear of a multipolar order as seen from a structural realist perspective is the localized hegemony of stronger Third World states. In anarchy what counts most is power. Power in the international system (including its Third World segment) is rather unevenly distributed, hence the ever-present danger of powerful states seeking to dominate weaker ones. The Cold War was marked by a rough global parity of power between the two superpowers. Regional imbalances did not matter much during the Cold War period, when the global superpower balance overwhelmed the aspirations of any would-be Third World regional hegemons.

Will the post-Cold War era see the rise of regional hegemons, as realist theory predicts? There has been widespread concern that superpower retrenchment might encourage countries such as India, Indonesia, Nigeria, Iran and Iraq to step into the resulting geopolitical "vacuum." As US president, George Bush drew attention to "a dangerous combination . . . [of] regimes armed with old and unappeasable animosities and modern weapons of mass destruction."[45] On closer reflection, however, the threat to international order posed by regional hegemons appears to be much more modest. Under bipolarity, regional powers derived a measure of autonomy from the superpower stand-off while securing material assistance from them to further their regional ambitions. The end of the Cold War marks the end of the need for the superpowers to cultivate "regional policemen" (such as Iran under the Nixon Doctrine), or regional proxies (such as Vietnam and Cuba for the Soviet Union) as part of their competitive search for influence. In a multipolar system, potential regional hegemons cannot "count on foreign patrons to support them reflexively, supply them with arms, or salvage for them an honourable peace."[46] Without superpower backing, even the most powerful among Third World states may find it more difficult to sustain military adventures,[47] and may be deterred from seeking to fulfill their external ambitions through military means. The Iraqi experience during the Gulf War is illustrative of the predicament of regional powers deprived of an opportunity to exploit the superpower rivalry.[48]

Are neorealists correct in assuming that multipolarity will drive states towards more competitive balancing behaviour? On the contrary, it is bipolarity that is more conducive to such behaviour. In an overarching global bipolar order, regional security relations reflect, and are shaped by, the competition between the two major powers. Such an order subsumes and dominates cooperative security systems established at the regional level. Bipolar superpower dominance undermines the autonomy of regional security arrangements in ensuring the pacific settlement of regional conflicts. Thus, during the Cold War, the superpowers ignored, bypassed, and manipulated indigenous security arrangements in the Third World geared to pacific settlement of disputes, and encouraged balance-of-power arrangements that often aggravated ideological polarizations within regions. With the end of the Cold War, security relations in the Third World have become more inclusive. The diminished global engagement of the Great Powers provides Third World regional security organizations with an opportunity to assume a greater role in the management of peace and stability issues in their neighbourhood. Furthermore, as the security relationship among the core states develops the attributes of a security community (as suggested by Goldgeiger and McFaul), Third World regional security relations will no longer be influenced by an intensely competitive external dynamic. As a result, the prospects for more cooperative relations within Third World regions will improve.

Neorealist predictions also ignore those consequences of multipolarity that promote greater stability in the Third World stability. Under Cold War bipolarity, minor crises in obscure countries could escalate into serious international confrontation as a result of superpower involvement. As Gilpin noted, bipolarity creates the "conditions for relatively small causes to lead to disproportionately large effects."[49] Transition to multipolarity, on the other hand, reduces the scope for the internationalization, prolongation and escalation of Third World regional conflicts.

While critics of neorealism point to the increasing importance of interdependence and democracy as undercutting the potentially destabilzing effects of the end of the Cold War in Europe, they agree with realist thinking in believing that these factors do not matter much in the Third World. This view is questionable. The Third World has seen a dramatic spread of democracy and increase in economic interdependence, the effects of which should matter in shaping future stability. Throughout the Third World, including Africa itself, many cases of democratization have been remarkably peaceful. Multi-party democratic elections led to the replacement of existing regimes in Zambia, Madagascar and Cape Verde. Internationally monitored elections saw the peaceful return of the governments of Seychelles, Guinea Bissau and Kenya. In the Horn of Africa, the independent state of Eritrea embraced democracy and led to the ending of the revolutionary war in Ethiopia, and the latter itself has seen "a remarkable effort to negotiate the framework of a democratic federation." These developments provide further confirmation that the appeal of violent methods of political change in the Third World may be diminishing. As Richard Falk points out: "The great struggles in the South during the 1980s, ranging from the overthrow of the Marcos regimes [sic] to the heroic challenges directed at oppressive rule in China and Burma, and on behalf of expanded democracy in South Korea, relied on non-violent mass mobilization, explicitly renouncing armed struggle." Even the "intifada," Falk adds, conformed to this trend, resting "upon an inner logic of confronting the military violence of the occupiers with an essential vulnerability of unarmed civilians."[50]

While the downfall of repressive regimes leading to democratic transitions may contribute to increased Third World instability in the short-term, democratization should also create more favourable conditions of stability and order in the long-term.[51] As Brad Roberts contends, democratization will "constrain" Third World anarchy by "compelling a search for common interests with erstwhile competitors."[52] Democratization addresses many causes of internal instability in the Third World. This is not just the view of Western Liberals. A recent report by a panel sponsored by the OAU notes, "despite their apparently diverse causes, complex nature and manifold forms, internal conflicts in Africa were basically the result of denial of basic democratic rights and freedoms, broadly conceived; and that they tended to be triggered-off by acts of injustice, real or imagined, precisely in situations where recourse to democratic redress seemed hopeless."[53] At a time when "the romance seems to have gone out of Third World revolutions,"[54] democratization provides an alternative, and peaceful approach to desired political change. Whether democracies tend to live in peace with each other may be a debatable proposition in the West.[55] But in the Third World, the correlation (spill-over effect) between internal strife and regional instability has always been strong, largely due to the tendency of weak states ruled by insecure regimes to "succumb to the temptation to consolidate their domestic position at the expense of their neighbours by cultivating external frictions or conflicts."[56] Thus, greater internal stability and regime legitimacy in Third World states enhances the prospects for regional security and lessen the scope for unwelcome external meddling in these countries.

Regional interdependence and integration has been slower to develop in the Third World than in Europe and the West. In the past, economic regionalism in the Third World was undermined by the difficulty of ensuring an equitable distribution of benefits. Regional economic integration among developing countries remained hostage to political and security concerns of the participating countries and their prior interest in fuller integration with the global economy through inter-regional trade and investment linkages. But the trends are now firmly towards greater intra-regional and inter-regional interdependence. Witness, for example, ASEAN's decision in 1992 to create a regional free trade area, the OAU's signing of an African Economic Community Treaty in 1991, and the emergence of two new trade groupings in South America (the Mercosur group including Argentina, Brazil, Paraguay and Uruguay, created in 1991, and the Group of Three including Mexico, Venezuela and Colombia, established in 1994).[57] The renewed interest in economic regionalism stemmed partly from doubts about the future of GATT (since dispelled), as well as fears about the emergence of protectionist regional trading blocs in Europe and North America.

Moreover, interdependence between the North and the South has been on the rise.[58] Faster growth rates in the Third World are already providing Northern countries with greater market opportunities. Moreover, greater productivity in the Third World is having beneficial effects for the North's standard of living, while for the latter, "cheaper imports mean lower prices and, hence, higher real incomes."[59] The market-oriented economic reforms (including IMF-induced structural adjustment programs) are lessening the earlier distrust among Third World elites of Western multinationals and investment flows. There has also been a trend toward economic cooperation between the North and the South. New regional economic groupings with a North–South membership include the Asia Pacific Economic Cooperation (APEC) and the North American Free Trade Agreement (NAFTA). The intended southward extension of NAFTA and Malaysia's proposal for an East Asian grouping under Japanese leadership are additional indicators of greater North–South cooperation. Such regional trading groups will expand market opportunities for the participating developing countries and alleviate their fear of protectionism in global markets. The end of the Cold War has already ended the economic isolation of many former socialist economies, such as Vietnam and India. Their progressive integration into the global economy will have a moderating effect on the prospects for North–South economic cooperation in the post-Cold War era and help prevent the escalation of political, cultural and civilizational differences which might otherwise promote new forms of conflict and constrain conflict management.[60]

During the Cold War, the major Third World platform, the Non-Aligned Movement (NAM), spearheaded the South's conscious and collective challenge to the dominant international order. To this end, NAM pursued a broad agenda that included demands for a speedy completion of the decolonization process, superpower non-interference in the Third World, global disarmament and strengthening of global and regional mechanisms for conflict-resolution.[61] NAM's record in realizing these objectives has attracted much criticism, but its achievements cannot be dismissed. Despite the diversity within its membership, NAM was able to provide a collective psychological framework for Third World states to strengthen their independence and to play an active role in international affairs.[62] Membership in NAM provided many Third World states with some room to manoeuver in their relationship with the superpowers and to resist pressures for alliances and alignment.[63] NAM led the global condemnation of apartheid and pursued the liberation of Rhodesia and Namibia with considerable energy and dedication. While NAM had no influence over the superpower arms control process, it did succeed in raising the level of ethical concern against the doctrine of nuclear deterrence. Through the UN Disarmament conferences which it helped to initiate, NAM members highlighted the pernicious effects of the arms race and articulated the linkage between disarmament and development.

Yet, NAM's efforts to reshape the prevailing international order were seriously constrained. The allowance of too much diversity within NAM with respect to external security guarantees (only states which were members of "a multilateral military alliance concluded in the context of Great Power conflicts" were ineligible to join NAM; close bilateral relationships with superpowers were not an impediment) undermined the group's unity. It also made NAM susceptible to intra-mural tensions as evident over Cuba's unsuccessful efforts during the 1979 Havana Summit to gain recognition for the Soviet Union as the "natural ally" of NAM. NAM's credibility suffered further from its poor record in international conflict-resolution. While focusing on the larger issues of global disarmament and superpower rivalry, it was unable to develop institutions and mechanisms for addressing local and regional conflicts such as those in the Gulf, Lebanon, Cambodia, Afghanistan and Southern Africa. According to one observer, "During the last three decades, many non-aligned countries were involved in some kind of conflict, directly or indirectly, either with a fellow non-aligned country, or with great powers, or with some aligned countries. It is not difficult to comprehend the inability of NAM to prevent conflict within the group initially, and later, to resolve it quickly if the conflict had surfaced for one reasons or the other."[64]

With the end of the Cold War, NAM faces distinct risks of further marginalization in global peace and security affairs.[65] The collapse of the bipolar structure has prompted inevitable questions regarding the movement's continued relevance. Despite a growing membership (now at 108), the NAM's post-Cold War direction remains unclear. Some members, such as India (perhaps reflecting its desire for a permanent seat in the UN Security Council), see the "central" role of NAM as that of wanting "to push for democratisation of the UN."[66] Others, especially Malaysia, would like to use NAM to counter "this so-called New World Order propagated by a big power [US]."[67] Indonesia, the current Chair of NAM, seeks to shift the priorities of NAM from the political to the economic arena: "We have to address the new concerns of the world – environment and development, human rights and democratisation, refugees and massive migration."[68] Indonesia has also led efforts to strike a moderate and pragmatic tone for NAM in global North–South negotiations.[69] In Jakarta's view, while the end of the Cold War did not "in any way diminish . . . the relevance and the validity of the basic principles and objectives of the Non-Aligned Movement," it "like everybody else must adapt itself in a dynamic way . . . to the new political and economic realities in the world,"[70] realities which call for a posture of cooperation, rather than confrontation.

Although NAM emerged primarily as a political institution, its agenda was broadened to the economic arena in the 1960s and 1970s. As Tim Shaw points out, while "in its first decade it was a reaction to . . . international bipolarity; in its second decade, it has been a critical reaction to international inequality."[71] The most important example of this is NAM's strong advocacy of the idea of a New International Economic Order (NIEO),[72] first voiced at the Fourth NAM Summit in Algiers in 1973.

The concept of NIEO embraced a number of demands such as the creation of a new structure to regulate world trade in primary commodities, improved conditions for the transfer of Northern technology to the South, better market access for the export of Southern manufactured goods to the North, negotiating codes of conduct for multinational corporations, reform of the international monetary system to ensure greater flow of financial resources (both concessional and non-concessional) and the resolution of the debt problem and promotion of collective self-reliance through South–South cooperation in trade, finance and infrastructure.[73] But the process of North–South negotiations aimed at the realization of these objectives has run its course without producing any significant breakthroughs for the South as a whole. The economic progress of the South has been disjointed. The list of achievements includes the ability of OPEC to raise the oil revenues of its members, the signing of the three Lome conventions by 64 African, Caribbean, and Pacific states and the rise of the Newly Industrialized Countries of East Asia.[74] But the collective institutional framework of the South has not contributed to, or been strengthened by, these developments; instead, some of these regional successes have lessened the relevance and solidarity of the larger Third World platforms.

The post–Cold War South faces simultaneous pressures for rebellion and adaptation within the established international system. The experience of the past decades has shown the futility of the South's confrontational approach vis-à-vis the North and induced a greater degree of pragmatism on its part in global negotiations. The major institutions of the Third World, their unity and credibility diminished, have accordingly adopted a more moderate attitude in pressing for the reform of the global economic and security order. But since the leading formal institutions like the NAM and the Group of 77 appear to be in a state of terminal decline, they are being replaced by more informal and ad hoc coalitions (as evident in the recent UN meetings on the environment and human rights) in articulating and advancing the South's interests in global North–South negotiations. Regional organizations can also play a useful role in accommodating the growing diversity of the South while projecting a basic and common outlook on political and distributive issues.

A tale of many worlds: the regionalization of conflict and order

Structural realist thinking holds that any significant change in the global distribution of power has uniform effects on the entire international system. Thus, the shift from bipolarity to multipolarity will be destabilizing for the entire international system. The preoccupation with "structure" allows little room for considering regional variations in the pattern of conflict in the international system. In this view, domestic and regional sources of disorder do not matter very much. In seemingly accepting structural realism as a valid theoretical lens for analysing Third World security and viewing the post–Cold War international order in terms of two very broad categories – a stable core and an unstable periphery – Goldgeiger and McFaul also acknowledge no variations in regional security relations within the Third World.

But there are good reasons to be skeptical of such a homogenous view of the periphery. Two are especially important. First, the major sources of conflict in the Third World are often unrelated to the global distribution of power and are therefore unaffected by changes in the latter. Several studies have established that the primary threats to stability of Third World states are internal and regional in nature, including problems of weak national integration, economic underdevelopment, and regime insecurity.[75] During the Cold War, domestic and regional disorder in the Third World enjoyed a great deal of autonomy from external factors, including the bipolar system structure and the attendant superpower rivalry.[76] There is little reason to believe that things will be much different in the post–Cold War era. As Fred Halliday argues: "since the causes of third world upheaval [were] to a considerable extent independent of Soviet–US rivalry they will continue irrespective of relations between Washington and Moscow."[77]

Secondly, the period since the 1970s has seen the emergence of significant regional differentiation in the economic conditions of states within the Third World. The affluence of OPEC members and the rise of newly industrializing countries contrast sharply with the worsening poverty and underdevelopment of Africa and

South Asia. John Ravenhill has proposed a greater differentiation among Third World economies.[78] Differing levels of economic development within the Third World call for a more differentiated view of its security predicament. Although rapid economic growth (especially if it is not accompanied by an equitable distribution of wealth) may pose threats to the stability of Third World regimes (including demands for greater power-sharing), it also addresses the root causes of conflict in the Third World in the post-colonial era. According to Rosenbaum and Tyler, "It is . . . generally understood within the Third World that economic development can contribute to national security; an economically weak nation can be exploited or defeated more easily by foreign powers and may be exposed periodically to the violent wrath of dissatisfied citizens."[79] Accordingly, the security outlook for the Third World's economic achievers will be more positive than that of those left behind. Growing disparities between Third World regions in the economic sphere introduce a new variable that challenges the conception of Third World as a homogenous entity in the security sphere.

An analysis of emerging regional security systems in the Third World points to a range of possibilities. At least three deserve notice.

Pluralistic security communities

Karl Deutsch defined a security community as a group of states which have attained "a sense of community, accompanied by formal or informal institutions or practices, sufficiently strong and widespread to assure peaceful change among members of a group with 'reasonable' certainty over a 'long' period of time."[80] In a security community, "War among the prospective partners comes to be considered as illegitimate," and "serious preparations for it no longer command popular support."[81] Security communities may be amalgamated where its constituent units – states – lose their sovereignty or pluralistic, in which states remain formally sovereign, but develop a common "we feeling." Security communities are characterized by a high degree of mutual responsiveness. In such communities states will exhibit a preference for common security doctrines over balance-of-power approaches. Arms races either disappear or are muted to the point of irrelevance. Inter-state relations are governed by well-defined norms. Institutional mechanisms for conflict resolution are both available and accepted. States within such communities develop substantial functional cooperation, including regional economic interdependence and integration. This, in turn, further reduces the likelihood of war within the community. The dynamics of such communities are best understood by using a liberal theoretical perspective.

Until now, all cases of pluralistic security communities identified by IR theorists have been drawn from the developed world. But in the Third World, at least two regions have developed attributes which closely parallel those of a security community. In Southeast Asia, the members of the Association of Southeast Asian Nations (ASEAN) have not fought a war since the grouping's formation in 1967. ASEAN members have developed an elaborate set of norms, institutions and practices for pacific settlement of disputes. The feeling of "community" is also particularly strong in ASEAN, as revealed in frequent references to the "ASEAN spirit" or "ASEAN way" of inter-state behaviour. While ASEAN members do not share a common commitment to liberal-democracy (but a common opposition to communism and acceptance of the "soft authoritarianism" was an early catalyst of ASEAN solidarity), growing economic interdependence has served to cement the desire for war-avoidance. ASEAN's record in ensuring regional peace has been so successful that it has attracted considerable support from the world's major powers in developing a larger regional security system for the entire Asia Pacific region based on the ASEAN model.

The picture is somewhat less rosy in Latin America, but here too the only serious case of inter-state conflict since the Falklands War between Britain and Argentina was the brief war between Peru and Ecuador. Moreover, unlike ASEAN, the emergence of a Latin American security community is strengthened by a shared commitment to democracy and economic interdependence among the vast majority of states. Latin America is today the most democratic continent outside of Europe, and it has seen the emergence of two new trade groupings – the Mercosur group including Argentina, Brazil, Paraguay and Uruguay, created in 1991, and the Group of Three including Mexico, Venezuela and Colombia, established in 1994.[82] Moreover, the success of the Central American-initiated Contadora and Esquipulus processes in ending the bloody civil and inter-state conflicts involving Nicaragua and El Salvador, challenges the view that Third World regional groupings are incapable of effective conflict resolution. The efforts by the Latin American regional grouping, OAS, to strengthen its peace-keeping, conflict resolution and human rights mechanisms are hopeful steps in the further consolidation of the emerging democratic security community in Latin America.

Internationalized rivalries

Internationalized rivalries display characteristics that are exactly the opposite of pluralistic security communities. Some analysts have called them "enduring rivalries."[83] Here, regional security relations are highly unstable. The probability of inter-state war remains very strong. States seek security through balancing behaviour, rather than through common and cooperative security mechanism. Such strategy heightens the security dilemma, producing destabilizing arms races, and, in many cases, a proliferation of weapons of mass destruction. Since most Third Word states are not self-reliant in military power, those facing serious external threats are driven to seek security by forging alliances with outside Great Powers. In such a situation, regional mechanisms for conflict management are either non-existent or tend to be extremely weak and ineffective. These sort of regional security systems are best understood from a realist theoretical perspective.

There are several examples of such rivalries in the Third World today, with the three most important being the Middle East, South Asia and Northeast Asia. All these regions share at least four common features: (1) a high-intensity conflict situation, derived from historical, social-political, religious and ideological factors;

(2) an arms race, featuring both conventional arms and weapons of mass destruction; (3) weak regional mechanisms for conflict resolution; and (4) a high degree of dependence on external security guarantees. Although regional in scope, these conflicts attract the world's attention because of the high probability of armed conflict, the likely use of weapons of mass destruction, and the external military alliances of the regional actors. Despite the geopolitical retrenchment of the major powers from the Third World in the post–Cold War era, these areas remain within their sphere of "vital interest." Security alliances involving the regional actors and external great powers ensure that any outbreak of military conflict will invite great power involvement and intervention.

Localized anarchies

Somewhere in-between pluralistic security communities and internationalized rivalries are states and societies plagued by a great deal of internal instability and chaos. These regions are largely inhabited by "weak" states, with very low levels of socio-political cohesion. The writ of the central government does not extend to all parts of what it claims to be its national territory. Governments lack legitimacy and the contest for political power is not regulated through durable and commonly accepted institutional mechanisms. The capacity of the states to address socio-economic grievances is extremely limited. The nation-state is in a state of steady decline, overwhelmed by a crisis of governability. Conflicts tend to derive not so much from inter-state animosity or external intervention, but from essentially local factors such as poverty, overpopulation, refugee migrations, crime, resource scarcity and environmental degradation. Moreover, these conflicts do not attract a great deal of external geopolitical (as opposed to humanitarian) attention and involvement, as they usually fall outside the sphere of "vital interest" of the world's great powers. Great powers are likely to be quite selective in choosing their areas of engagement. In these marginal areas of the Third World, bloody conflicts are likely to go unnoticed by the international community (as happened in Liberia in 1990–1992 and initially in Somalia in 1991 and Rwanda in 1994).

Africa is a microcosm of such localized anarchies in the post–Cold War era. Robert D. Kaplan has called West Africa "the symbol of worldwide demographic, environmental, and societal stress, in which criminal anarchy emerges as the real 'strategic' danger."[84] While his predictions about the "coming anarchy" are supposed to apply to other parts of the world, it is certainly more true of Africa (and to a lesser extent, of Southern Asia) than Latin America or Eastern Asia. Localized anarchy has been a hallmark of the recent history of much of the African continent. Between 1990 and mid-1992, as many as 11 African leaders[85] including the governments in Ethiopia, Liberia, Chad and Somalia were overthrown. Beyond regime insecurity, localized anarchies in Africa approximate what Homer-Dixon identifies as "simple scarcity conflicts" (conflict over natural resources such as river, water, fish, and agriculturally productive land), "relative deprivation conflicts" (the impact of environmental degradation in limiting growth and thereby causing popular discontent and conflict), and "group-identity conflicts" (the problems of social assimilation of the migrant population) in the host countries.[86]

The categories outlined above are not exhaustive, nor are they clearly demarcable. It is entirely possible that some regions will combine the attributes of more than one of the suggested categories. Moreover, these categories are not necessarily permanent. Regional situations could change over a period of time in response to new local and international developments. But they capture the major types of regional security systems most likely to obtain in the Third World in the emerging post–Cold War order. In addition, they challenge the simplistic division of the post–Cold War order into the two broad arenas of the core and the periphery.

Conclusion

The foregoing analysis leads to a number of concluding observations. The correlation between structural stability and regional order is much weaker than what structural realist theory expects us to believe. During the Cold War, a stable structure permitted a great deal of regional disorder; in the post–Cold War era, a supposedly unpredictable and uncertain structure, while contributing to greater anarchy in some areas, should not preclude the possibility of pluralistic security communities in others.

Structural realism may not be the only, or even most useful, theoretical lens to analyse and predict the prospects for Third World instability in the post-bipolar era. Liberal concepts such as security communities, democratic peace and interdependence may have considerable relevance in explaining the security predicament in the Third World.

Furthermore, there is a need to rethink the broad categories of "Third World" or "periphery" as homogenous entities. For some time, political economists have called for the disaggregation of the Third World to account for the oil-producing nations and the NICs. Now, security studies scholars should follow suit. The post–Cold War order will not be a "A Tale of Two Worlds." A more differentiated view of the periphery is called for.

This view is not only more optimistic than the structural realist thesis; it also has implications for the research agenda of international security studies. During the Cold War, the Third World security issues were largely excluded from "mainstream" theory-building (although empirical studies abounded) in security studies. Instead, security studies scholarship concentrated on the central strategic balance. Regional conflicts, with the exception of European security issues, were viewed as a relatively unimportant sideshow to the main drama of superpower rivalry. Theories and concepts of international security studies were abstracted from the Western experience with little regard for conditions obtaining in the Third World. Now, the Third World, appropriately disaggregated, should receive greater attention in the theoretical literature on security studies.

The time has come for security studies scholars to move away from an excessive focus on great power relationships as the chief determinant of international conflict and order. Realists like Waltz, who started the whole debate on the relationship between polarity and stability, pay too much attention to the structural or system-level determinants of peace and stability, and too little to regional patterns and variables. While neorealism or structural realism is useful in explaining some aspects of Third World anarchy, especially the security dynamics of internationalized rivalries, it is mistaken in ignoring the possibility of security communities. It does not offer a system-wide and comprehensive explanation of conflict and cooperation in the Third World. As the Third World becomes evermore differentiated, security studies should be more sensitive to regional variations and particularities within Third World security environment.

A postscript: trends in conflict, 1991–2004

Since the chapter was first written, a pioneering report released by the Human Security Centre at the University of British Columbia confirmed its overall assessment of the trend in Third World conflict. The report points to several significant trends in armed conflicts around the world. See Box 4.1.

BOX 4.1 TRENDS IN ARMED CONFLICTS AROUND THE WORLD

- A 40% drop in armed conflicts in the world since 1991. (This counts only conflicts with at least 25 battle-related deaths where one of the parties was a state.)
- An 80% decline in the number of genocide and "politicides"* between the high point in 1988 and 2001.
- A 70% decline in the number of international crises between 1981 and 2001.
- A 45% decrease in the number of refugees between 1992 and 2003. But the number of internally displaced persons has increased, although accurate information is hard to obtain.
- A 98% decline in the average number of battle deaths per conflict per year. In 1950, an average armed conflict killed 38,000 people. In 2002, the figure was 600.**

Source: *Human Security Report*, 2005.[87]

* The term "politicide" describes policies that seek to destroy groups because of their political beliefs rather than religion or ethnicity (the latter being captured by the term "genocide").

** Most of the battle deaths in the Cold War period were accounted for by the Korean and Vietnam wars. If these are excluded, the drop in battle deaths will be less dramatic.

The report listed several factors that would explain the downward trend in armed conflicts around the world including those identified in this chapter: growing democratization (the underlying assumption here being that democracies tend to be better at peaceful resolution of conflicts); rising economic interdependence (which increases the costs of conflict); the declining economic utility of war owing to the fact that resources can be more easily bought in the international marketplace than acquired through force; the growth in the number of international institutions that can mediate in conflicts; the impact of international norms against violence, such as human sacrifice, witch-burning, slavery, duelling, war crimes, and genocide; the end of colonialism, and the end of the Cold War. Another important reason identified by the report is the dramatic increase in UN's role in areas such as preventive diplomacy and peace-making activities, post-conflict peace-building, sanctions, the willingness by the UN Security Council to use force to enforce peace agreements, the deterrent effects of war crime trials by International Criminal Court (ICC) and other tribunals, greater resort to reconciliation and addressing the root causes of conflict. The 80 per cent decline in the most deadly civil conflicts since the early 1990s, argued the report, is due to the dramatic growth of international efforts at preventive diplomacy, peace-making and peace-building. I would add that the growing acceptance of the principle of responsibility to protect (R2P) norm, despite problems with its application, not only offsets the Cold War tendency among the superpowers to view Third World regional conflicts as "permissible" or even necessary to "let off steam," but also provides additional global (UN) and regional mechanisms and authority to act to stop lives.

The decline in armed conflicts around the world is not necessarily irreversible. Some of the factors contributing to the decline of conflicts, such as democratization and the peace operations role of the UN can suffer setbacks due to lack of support from major powers and the international community. And there remain serious possible threats to international peace and security which can cause widespread casualties, such as a conflict in the Korean peninsula, and war between China and Taiwan. Indeed, the optimism created by the first *Human Security Report* of 2005 has been offset by the data contained in the *Human Security Report* for 2009 to 2010, which found a 25 per cent increase in armed conflicts in the years from 2003 to 2008. A large percentage of these conflicts – a quarter of those that started between 2004 and 2008 – were related to "Islamist political violence." Overall, the increasing trends in conflicts during 2003 to 2008 were partly due to "minor conflicts" with few casualties. While the "war on terror" played an important part in the increasing number and deadliness of conflicts, viewed from a longer-term perspective, the level of conflict in the Islamic world is lower than two decades earlier. And in terms of casualty levels, the average annual battle-death toll per conflict was less than 1,000 in the new millennium compared to the 1950s. The report also warned of the increasing possibility of violence associated with the "Arab Spring" and its aftermath, which, although low for now, could escalate due to the ongoing strife in Syria and instability in transitional societies.[88] But overall, there is little evidence of the return to the level of Cold War era violence in the developing world, and more importantly, nor is there any systemic reason today for viewing regional conflicts in the developing world as "permissible."

Notes

1 Parts of this chapter first appeared as "Beyond Anarchy: Third World Instability and International Order after the Cold War," in *International Relations Theory and the Third World*, ed., Stephanie Neumann (New York: St Martin's Press, 1997), 159–211. This version contains an entirely new section, "A Tale of Many Worlds: The Regionalization of Conflict and Order," also written around 1997, as well as a postscript.
2 John Mearsheimer, "Back to the Future: Instability in Europe After the Cold War," *International Security* 15, no. 1 (1990): 5–55.
3 Critical responses to Mearsheimer can be found in three subsequent issues of *International Security*. Although no forceful and predictive commentary about Third World security has yet been made, Mearsheimer's thesis appears to have found an echo in a number of recent scholarly writings on the subject.
4 Jose Thiago Cintra, "Regional Conflicts: Trends in a Period of Transition," in *The Changing Strategic Landscape*, Adelphi Paper no. 237 (London: International Institute for Strategic Studies, 1989), 96–97.
5 Stanley Hoffmann, "Watch Out for a New World Disorder," *International Herald Tribune*, 26 February 1991, 6.
6 Testimony by Lieutenant General James Clapper to the Senate Armed Services Committee, 22 January 1992, in "Regional Flashpoints Potential for Military Conflict" (Washington, D.C.: United States Information Service, 24 December 1992), 6.
7 Robert Jervis, "The Future of World Politics: Will it Resemble the Past?" *International Security* 16, no. 3 (1991–1992): 39–73, 59.
8 James M. Goldgeier and Michael McFaul, "Core and Periphery in the Post-Cold War Era," *International Organization* 46, no. 2 (1992): 467–492.
9 Ibid., 470.
10 John Lewis Gaddis, "International Relations Theory and the End of the Cold War," *International Security* 17, no. 3 (1992–1993): 5–58, 30.
11 Kenneth N. Waltz, "The Stability of a Bipolar World," *Daedalus* 93, no. 3 (1964): 881–909, 882. In this article, Waltz identified four factors as the reasons for the stability of bipolar systems: absence of peripheries, the range and intensity of competition, the persistence of pressure and crisis and the preponderant power of the two leading actors.
12 Kenneth N. Waltz, *Theory of International Politics* (Reading, Mass.: Addison-Wesley, 1979), 168.
13 Waltz, *Theory of International Politics*, 171.
14 John Mearsheimer, "Why We Will Soon Miss the Cold War," in *Crosscurrents: International Relations in the Post-Cold War Era*, eds., Mark Charlton and Elizabeth Ridell-Dixon (Toronto: Nelson Canada, 1993), 16.
15 Waltz, "The Stability of a Bipolar World," 907.
16 John Lewis Gaddis, "The Long Peace: Elements of Stability in the Post-War International System," *International Security* 10, no. 4 (1986): 99–142, 103–104.
17 Robert Gilpin, *War and Change in World Politics* (Cambridge: Cambridge University Press, 1981), 92.
18 Gilpin, *War and Change in World Politics*, 91.
19 Richard N. Rosecrance, "Bipolarity, Multipolarity, and the Future," in *International Politics and Foreign Policy*, ed., James N. Rosenau (New York: The Free Press, 1969), 326–327.
20 Karl W. Deutsch and J. David Singer, "Multipolar Power Systems and International Stability," in *International Politics and Foreign Policy*, ed., James N. Rosenau (New York: The Free Press, 1969), 318.
21 Deutsch and Singer, "Multipolar Power Systems and International Stability," 320.

22 Rosecrance, "Bipolarity, Multipolarity and the Future," 328.

23 John Lewis Gaddis, "International Relations Theory and the End of the Cold War," *International Security* 17, no. 3 (1992–1993): 5–58; and Jack S. Levy, "The Causes of Wars: A Review of Theories and Evidence," in *Behaviour, Society and Nuclear War.* Volume 1, eds., Philip E. Tetlock et al. (New York: Oxford University Press, 1989), 235.

24 This applies especially to Mearsheimer, whose arguments to the effect that bipolarity is more stable are specifically derived from the European experience.

25 Gaddis, "The Long Peace: Elements of Stability in the Post-War International System,"104.

26 Waltz, *Theory of International Politics*, 172.

27 Rosecrance, "Bipolarity, Multipolarity and the Future," 327.

28 Major theoretical attempts to develop an understanding of Third World regional conflict and security issues in terms of their local, rather than systemic or structural, determinants during the Cold War period include Ayoob's work on regional security in the Third World, and Buzan's work on "regional security complexes." Contending that "issues of regional security in the developed world are defined primarily in Cold War terms (NATO versus Warsaw Pact, etc.) and are, therefore, largely indivisible from issues of systemic security," Ayoob convincingly demonstrated that "the salient regional security issues in the Third World have a life of their own independent of superpower rivalry . . ." Buzan similarly urged greater attention to the "set of security dynamics at the regional level" in order to "develop the concepts and language for systematic comparative studies, still an area of conspicuous weakness in Third World studies." His notion of "security complex," defined as "local sets of states . . . whose major security perceptions and concerns link together sufficiently closely that their national security perceptions cannot realistically be considered apart from one another," was designed to understand "how the regional level mediates the interplay between states and the international system as a whole." It should be noted, however, that while both Ayoob and Buzan called for greater attention to the regional and local sources of conflict and cooperation, Ayoob's was specifically focused on the Third World. Buzan's approach is also more structuralist, emphasizing the role of systemic determinants such as colonialism and superpower rivalry (which he called "overlays") in shaping regional security trends. This seems to undercut his earlier call for "the relative autonomy of regional security relations." See: Mohammed Ayoob, "Regional Security and the Third World," in *Regional Security in the Third World*, ed., Mohammed Ayoob (London: Croom Helm, 1986); Barry Buzan, *People, States and Fear* (Brighton, U.K.: Wheatsheaf Books, 1983), 186; and Barry Buzan, "Third World Regional Security in Structural and Historical Perspective," in *The Insecurity Dilemma: National Security of Third World States*, ed., Brian L. Job (Boulder, Colo.: Lynne Rienner, 1992), 167–189.

29 Waltz, *Theory of International Politics*, 168.

30 Francis M. Deng and I. William Zartman, "Introduction," in *Conflict Resolution in Africa*, eds., Francis M. Deng and I. William Zartman (Washington, D.C.: The Brookings Institute, 1991), 13.

31 Barry Buzan, "New Patterns of Global Security in the Twenty-First Century," *International Affairs* 67, no. 3 (1991), 431–451, 441.

32 Roberto Garcia Moritan, "The Developing World and the New World Order," *The Washington Quarterly* 15, no. 4 (1992): 149–156, 151.

33 Ted Robert Gurr, "Peoples Against States: Ethnopolitical Conflict," Presidential Address to the International Studies Association Annual Meeting, 1 April 1994, Washington, D.C., 3, 13; and Ted Robert Gurr and Barbara Harff, *Ethnic Conflict in World Politics* (Boulder, Colo.: Westview, 1994), 3–4, 13.

34 "Next Test for Eritrea," *International Herald Tribune*, 29 April 1993, 8.

35 "Another Country," *The Economist*, 24 April 1993, 20.

36 Holsti significantly adds that "there have been remarkably few militarized boundary disputes between states in the Third World. And where they have arisen, (e.g. India and China, Libya and Chad) values other than territory drove the conflicts . . . Control of

territory (excluding certain strategic areas such as the Bekka Valley) . . . is declining in importance as a major object of competitive claims and military actions . . . Protection of territory is less the main task of national security policy than is protection of the state apparatus from various domestic challenges." K. J. Holsti, "International Theory and War in the Third World," in *The InSecurity Dilemma: National Security of Third World States*, ed., Brian L. Job (Boulder, Colo.: Lynne Rienner Publishers, 1992), 55–57. As Buzan himself concedes, no direct and clear link can be established between the Cold War and adherence to norms regarding territorial status quo, such as those adopted by the Organization of African Unity relating to the inviolability of colonial boundaries. In this respect, the situation in Europe is rather different. In Europe, the Cold War did play a part in freezing the territorial status quo once they were formally or tacitly agreed upon by the superpowers prior to the unravelling of their wartime alliance. But in the Third World, the only credible attempt to devise norms regarding territorial status quo – the OAU – was an indigenous attempt, rather than superpower-influenced. Finally, the major sources of territorial disputes today are not necessarily the legacies of colonial rule, but the relatively recent Law of the Sea which has contributed to a host of maritime boundary disputes. These disputes were not caused by end of superpower rivalry, but by disagreements regarding the Law of the Sea. Thus, fears that end of bipolarity could lead to the unravelling of territorial consensus could be overstated.

37 On the contrary, SIPRI data shows that the total number of major conflicts over territorial issues in the world remain constant at 16 from 1989 to 1992. In the Third World, territorial conflicts have actually declined from 15 in 1989 to 12 in 1992, while for Europe they increased from 1 to 4. In Africa, where the vast majority of conflicts continue to be intra-state, rather than inter-state, the number of territorial conflicts has actually declined, from 3 in 1989 to 1. Ramses Amer, et al. "Major Armed Conflicts," in *SIPRI Yearbook 1993: World Armaments and Disarmament* (Oxford: Oxford University Press, 1993), 87.

38 "When Cold Warriors Quit," *The Economist*, 8 February 1992, 15; Gary Milholin and Jennifer Weeks, "Better to Block Nuclear and Chemical Weapons at the Source," *International Herald Tribune*, 29 March 1990, 6.

39 L.L.P. van de Goor, "Conflict and Development: The Causes of Conflict in Developing Countries," paper presented to the Conference on Conflict and Development: Causes, Effects and Remedies, The Netherlands Institute of International Relations, The Hague, Netherlands, 22–24 March 1994, 46.

40 Amitav Acharya, *An Arms Race in Post-Cold War Southeast Asia? Prospects for Control*, Pacific Strategic Papers no. 8 (Singapore: Institute of Southeast Asian Studies, 1994); and Desmond J. Ball, "Arms and Affluence: Military Acquisitions in the Asia-Pacific Region," *International Security* 18, no. 3 (1993–1994): 78–112.

41 Rosecrance, "Bipolarity, Multipolarity and the Future," 328.

42 On nuclear-weapon-free zones, see Amitav Acharya, *Nuclear Weapon-Free Zones in the New World Order* (Ottawa: Department of Foreign Affairs and International Trade, 1997).

43 Brad Roberts, "Human Rights and International Security," *The Washington Quarterly* 13, no. 2 (1990): 65–75, 72–73.

44 Christopher Carle, "The Third World Will Do More of Its Own Fighting," *International Herald Tribune*, 15 March 1989.

45 Cited in Paul Wolfowitz, "Regional Conflicts: New Thinking, Old Policy," *Parameters* 20, no. 1 (1990): 1–9, 2.

46 Shahram Chubin, "Third World Conflicts: Trends and Prospects," *International Social Science Journal*, no. 127 (1991), 157.

47 Yezid Sayigh, *Confronting the 1990s, Security in the Developing Countries*, Adelphi Papers no. 251 (London: International Institute for Strategic Studies, 1990), 64.

48 Lawrence Freedman argues that the US victory over Iraq would discourage Third World regional powers from mounting a frontal assault on Western interests. "The Gulf War and the New World Order," *Survival* 33, no. 3 (1991): 195–209, 203.

49 Gilpin, *War and Change in World Politics*, 91.

50 Richard Falk, "Recycling Interventionism," *Journal of Peace Research* 29, no. 2 (1992): 129–134, 133.

51 I am grateful to Sean M. Lynn Jones for raising and discussing this point.

52 Roberts, "Human Rights and International Security," 72–73.

53 Cited in Francis M. Deng, "Anatomy of Conflicts in Africa," paper presented to the Seminar on "Conflict and Development: Causes, Effects and Remedies," Netherlands Institute of International Relations, The Hague, The Netherlands, 22–24 March 1994, 7.

54 John Mueller, *Retreat from Doomsday: The Obsolescence of Major War* (New York: Basic Books, 1989), 254–256.

55 For an interesting debate on the link between war and democracy in the context of the post-Cold War era, see the response published in three subsequent issues of *International Security* to Mearsheimer's article on "Back to the Future."

56 Barry Buzan, "People, States and Fear: The National Security Problem in the Third World," in *National Security in the Third World*, eds., Edward Azar and Chung-in Moon (Aldershot, U.K.: Edward Elgar, 1988), 14–43, 32;. See also, Mohammed Ayoob, *Conflict and Intervention in the Third World*; and Ayoob, "Regional Security and the Third World."

57 "NAFTA is Not Alone," *The Economist*, 18 July 1994, 47.

58 A recent survey by *The Economist* reveals the extent of North–South economic interdependence. The Third World and the countries of the former Soviet bloc is the destination of 42% of America's 20% Western Europe's (47% if intra-European Union trade is excluded) and 48% of Japan's exports. On the import side, the magazine reports that America's imports of manufactured goods from the Third World rose from 5% of the value of its manufacturing output in 1978 to 11% in 1990. "A Survey of the Global Economy," *The Economist*, 1September 1994, 13, 16.

59 "Rich North, Hungry South," *The Economist*, 1 October 1994, 18.

60 Samuel P. Huntington, "A Clash of Civilizations?" *Foreign Affairs* 72, no. 3 (1993): 22–49.

61 On the origins and role of NAM see: Peter Lyon, *Neutralism* (Leicester, U.K.: Leicester University Press, 1963); A.W. Singham and S. Hune, *Non-Alignment in the Age of Alignments* (London: Zed Books, 1986); Peter Willetts, *The Non-Aligned Movement* (London: Frances Pinter, 1978); Satish Kumar, "Non-Alignment: International Goals and National Interests," *Asian Survey* 23, no. 4 (1983): 445–462; Fred Halliday, "The Maturing of the Non-Aligned: Perspectives from New Delhi," *Third World Affairs* (London: Third World Foundation, 1985), 37–53; Bojana Tadic, "The Movement of the Non-Aligned and Its Dilemmas Today," *Review of International Affairs* 32, no. 756 (1981): 19–24; and A.W. Singham, ed., *The Non-Aligned Movement in World Politics* (Westport, Conn.: Lawrence Hill & Co., 1978).

62 Pervaiz Iqbal Cheema, "NAM and Security," *Strategic Studies* (Islamabad) xiv, no. 3 (1991): 15.

63 Mohammed Ayoob, "The Third World in the System of States: Acute Schizophrenia or Growing Pains," *International Studies Quarterly* 33, no. 1 (1989): 67–79, 75.

64 Cheema, "NAM and Security," 18.

65 Peter Lyon, "Marginalization of the Third World," *Jerusalem Journal of International Relations* 11, no. 3 (1989): 65.

66 "Chance for NAM to Redefine Role," *Times of India*, 11 May 1992, 9.

67 "NAM Must Stay United Against Developed States," *The Straits Times*, 7 August 1992, 23; and "NAM Needed to Balance North Bloc," *The Straits Times*, 4 August 1992, 21.

68 "Jakarta Wants NAM to Focus on Pressing Economic and Human Problems," *The Straits Times*, 4 August 1992, 17.

69 "Goodbye Nehru, Hello Suharto," *The Economist*, 19 September 1992, 32.

70 "Jakarta Wants NAM to Focus on Pressing Economic and Human Problems," 17.

71 Timothy M. Shaw, "The Non-Aligned Movement and the New International Division

of Labour," in *New Perspectives in North-South Dialogue: Essays in Honour of Olof Palme*, ed., Kofi Buenor Hadjor (London: I. B. Tauris, 1988), 178.

72 On NIEO, see Ervin Laszlo et al., eds., *The Objectives of the New International Economic Order* (New York: Pergamon Press, 1978); Craig Murphy, *The Emergence of the NIEO Ideology* (Boulder, Colo.: Westview Press, 1984); Jagdish Bhagwati, "Ideology and North-South Relations," *World Development* 14, no. 6 (1986): 767–774; and Robert W. Cox, "Ideologies and the New International Economic Order: Reflections on Some Recent Literature," *International Organization* 32, no. 2 (1979): 257–302.

73 Helen O'Neill, "The North-South Dialogue and the Concept of Mini-NIEO," in *Region-to-Region Cooperation Between Developed and Developing Countries*, ed., Kimmo Kiljunen (Aldershot, U.K.: Avebury, 1990), 4.

74 Fred Halliday and Maxine Molyneux, "Olof Palme and the Legacy of Bandung," in *New Perspectives in North-South Dialogue: Essays in Honour of Olof Palme*, ed., Kofi Buenor Hadjor (London: I. B. Tauris, 1988), 158.

75 Robert Jackson and Carl G. Rosberg, "Why Africa's Weak States Persist: The Empirical and the Juridical in Statehood," *World Politics* 35, no. 1 (1982): 1–24; Mohammed Ayoob, "Security in the Third World: The Worm About to Turn," *International Affairs* 60, no. 1 (1984): 41–51; Udo Steinbach, "Sources of Third World Conflict," in *Third World Conflict and International Security*, Adelphi Papers no. 166 (London: International Institute for Strategic Studies, 1981), 21–28; Soedjatmoko, "Patterns of Armed Conflict in the Third World," *Alternatives* 10, no. 4 (1985): 477–493; Edward Azar and Chung-in Moon, "Third World National Security: Towards a New Conceptual Framework," *International Interactions* 11, no. 2 (1984): 103–135; Buzan, "People, States and Fear: The National Security Problem in the Third World," 14–43; Yezid Sayigh, "Confronting the 1990s: Security in the Developing Countries," Adelphi Papers no. 251 (London: International Institute for Strategic Studies, 1990); Mohammed Ayoob, "The Security Predicament of the Third World State," in *The (In)Security Dilemma: The National Security of Third World States*, ed., Brian Job (Boulder, Colo.: Lynne Rienner, 1992); and Steven R. David, "Explaining Third World Alignment," *World Politics* 43, no. 2 (1991): 232–256.

76 This point is made forcefully by Mohammed Ayoob who argued that ". . . most of the salient regional security issues in the Third World have a life of their own independent of superpower rivalry, although . . . the latter . . . more often than not, exacerbates regional problems. This is as true of inter-state as of intra-state disputes and conflicts." Mohammed Ayoob, "Regional Security and the Third World," in *Regional Security in the Third World*, ed., Mohammed Ayoob (London: Croom Helm, 1986), 15.

77 Fred Halliday, *Cold War, Third World: An Essay on Soviet-US Relations* (London: Hutchinson Radius, 1989), 162.

78 John Ravenhill, "The North-South Balance of Power," *International Affairs* 66, no. 4 (1990): 731–748.

79 H. John Rosenbaum and William G. Tyler, "South-South Relations: the Economic and Political Content of Interactions among Developing Countries," *International Organization* 29, no. 1 (1975): 243–274.

80 Karl W. Deutsch, "Security Communities," in *International Politics and Foreign Policy*, ed., James Rosenau (New York: Free Press, 1961), 98.

81 Ibid., 276.

82 "NAFTA is Not Alone," 47.

83 For an overview of this literature, see: Gary Goertz and Paul F. Diehl, "Enduring Rivalries: Theoretical Constructs and Empirical Patterns," *International Studies Quarterly* 37, no. 2 (1993): 147–171.

84 Robert D. Kaplan, "The Coming Anarchy," *The Atlantic Monthly* 273, no. 2 (1994): 44–76.

85 Keith Somerville, "Africa After the Cold War: Frozen Out or Frozen in Time?" paper prepared for the Workshop on Developing States and the End of the Cold War, Oxford University, 30 September–1 October 1994, 6.

86 Thomas F. Homer-Dixon, "On the Threshold: Environmental Change as Causes of Acute Conflict," *International Security* 16, no. 2 (1991): 76–116.

87 *The Human Security Report 2005: War and Peace in the 21st Century* (New York: Oxford University Press, 2005), http://www.humansecurityreport.info/index. php?option=content&task=view&id=28&Itemid=63.

88 *Human Security Report 2009–2010* (Vancouver: Simon Fraser University, Human Security Research Group, 2011), http://www.hsrgroup.org/human-security-reports/20092010/ text.aspx.

5

STATE SOVEREIGNTY AFTER 9/11: DISORGANIZED HYPOCRISY[1]

The 9/11 terrorist attacks have introduced a new complexity to the debate about sovereignty in world politics. Before 9/11, this debate revolved around two main issues. The first was the impact of globalization on the nation-state framework, including questions about whether sovereignty is being eroded by transnational economic linkages, such as trade, production networks and financial flows. The other centred on the doctrine of humanitarian intervention, and the normative question about whether the non-intervention principle should be relaxed or bypassed to allow military action against genocide or state failure.[2] The principal challengers to sovereignty in these debates were multinational corporations, "activists beyond borders" and, to a lesser extent, multilateral organizations.

While the above debates about the place of sovereignty in the emerging world order are by no means settled, they have been joined in the post-9/11 era by debates about sovereignty from a new source: the "war on terror" waged by world's most powerful state and its allies against their "severest" foe – transnational terrorist networks led by Al-Qaeda.[3] This challenge differs from the pre-9/11 (although still ongoing) challenges in two respects. First, it has returned the rationale for intervention to *national security*, rather than human security, which were central to the humanitarian intervention framework. Although one has to be mindful that terrorism is not the same as aggression, and that the source of the terrorist threat is not another state or alliance but a transnational network of non-state actors, the response of the states to terrorism has been framed overwhelmingly as a threat to state security and international order. Hence, the securitizing metaphor: the "war on terror." Second, the post-9/11 challenge to sovereignty is organized and led by a hegemonic state (although it is also backed by a number of other states allied with it) which is seeking simultaneously to safeguard and limit Westphalian sovereignty to suit its particularistic interests. Indeed, the attempt by the US to limit sovereignty is being justified in the name of protecting it, or safeguarding the system of sovereign states.

To elaborate, the war on terror and the related "limits to sovereignty" concept of the George W. Bush administration is justified as protecting "national security" from a transnational menace which challenges it by its very mode of organization and operation and its presumed political agenda, including an alleged aspiration to restore the pre-Westphalian Caliphate. But in doing so, the leading state waging this war and its supporters also exempt themselves from the norms of the Westphalian order, and approve instruments that could be profoundly subversive of that order. It is this paradoxical framing of the war on terror and its implications for the state of state sovereignty in the post-9/11 world that constitute the focus of this chapter.

A good starting point for examining the paradox of Westphalian sovereignty in the age of terror is the theoretical framing of sovereignty as "organised hypocrisy" by political scientist and senior Bush administration official Stephen Krasner.[4] The essence of this concept revolves around an apparent puzzle: "the presence of long-standing norms that are frequently violated."[5] Although previous studies of sovereignty tended to separate two categories of challenges: voluntary efforts such as the European integration process, or coercive efforts such as interventions of geopolitical or humanitarian variety, Krasner's notion attempts to place both types of challenges under the same umbrella, regarding them as manifestations of organized hypocrisy. The key aspect of organized hypocrisy is that the violators justify their acts in the name of other, alternative or higher set of norms. As Krasner writes, organized hypocrisy occurs when the rules of sovereignty are "worked around," and when "the workarounds, which have been things like claims about human rights, minority rights, religious toleration, have always evoked alternative norms."[6] Moreover, these transgressions occur without much protest: "there are very clear rules about how sovereignty works, and they were violated frequently, much more frequently than people had imagined . . . Yet people were not screaming and yelling about hypocrisy, nor were they trying to find new rules."[7]

The organized hypocrisy formulation does seem to capture some aspects of the war on terror, which includes, but is not limited to, the war in Iraq. First, as a host of observers and writers, from UN Secretary-General Kofi Annan[8] to Krasner himself (who served twice in the George W. Bush administration)[9] have noted, the US occupation of Iraq did breach Westphalian sovereignty. Anan termed the US invasion "illegal," while Krasner said rather unambiguously: "We didn't just go and say, 'We're going to reconstruct these countries and then allow them to choose their own form of government.' We said, 'We are going to transform these countries.'" This to him is "a total violation of Westphalian–Vattelian sovereignty."[10] Second, the war in Iraq was justified by the US in the name of alternative principles – i.e. human rights and international stability, two of the four alternative norms which Krasner identifies (the other two being religious toleration and minority rights) as the basis for violating sovereignty.

But I raise three objections to applying the organized hypocrisy concept to describe and analyse the state of state sovereignty in the post-9/11 era. First, the "limits to sovereignty" thesis put forward by the US and allies like UK and Australia, and related policy instruments such as pre-emption and regime change, are not so much about transgression of state sovereignty as instruments to preserve and protect a "well-ordered system of sovereign states." In other words, the question is not whether sovereignty is at stake, but whose sovereignty. Second, the war on terror, inclusive of the invasion of Iraq, has been justified for the sake of higher principles, especially the human rights of the Iraqis, but these are now understood to have been a façade to mask the geopolitical and ideological underpinnings of the invasion. The real justification is not about a "higher" principle, but the conventional requirements of "national security," and an international order conducive to the protection and promotion of the national security interests of the most powerful states. And even so, those at the forefront of the global war on terror vastly exaggerate the capacity of their adversary to subvert the Westphalian order and hence undermine their national security. The ability, or even the intention, of terror groups to inflict such damage is limited by their divergent and varied objectives, their lack of physical capacity to fundamentally disrupt international security, and the need for at least some of these groups for state-like institutions and territorial organizations to realize their professed political objectives. This, notwithstanding their actions, provoked retaliatory measures, which have strengthened the national security state domestically vis-à-vis the civil society and externally in relation to the agents of and mechanisms of globalization.

Third, while violations of sovereignty have occurred through history, and the war on terror may thus simply be seen as the most recent manifestation of what has been a long-standing and familiar story in world politics, it is simply wrong to lump all sorts of challenges to state sovereignty under the single overarching rubric of organized hypocrisy. Krasner accepts that Westphalian–Vattelian sovereignty can be compromised either coercively (such as the United States in Germany or Japan after World War II) or voluntarily (as in the European Union, and the European Human Rights regime). But violations undertaken in the name of a narrowly defined conception of national security, which is what America's Bush Doctrine is really about, do not have the same moral weight or legitimacy as collective violations of Westphalian sovereignty by the international community for the sake of preventing genocide or protecting lives. Similarly, voluntary surrenders of sovereignty by a group of states for the sake of long-term pacification and community-building, such as the EU's integration agenda, can hardly be treated in the same light as violations of others' sovereignty by a hegemon committed unilaterally in fulfillment of an imperial (neo-conservative) ideology. Humanitarian intervention, of the type outlined in the R2P report, may be considered a form of organized hypocrisy, but the norm it invokes as justification does not have the same moral equivalence as the strategic and national security justifications advanced by the US in support of pre-emption or regime change.

In other words, the rationale for violations of sovereignty and the mode of the violations differ. More importantly, these variations do matter. This leads to a fundamental problem with labeling post-9/11 sovereignty as organized hypocrisy: how "organised" is the "organised hypocrisy" in the war on terror? To qualify actions undertaken by the Bush administration such as the invasion of Iraq and the doctrine of pre-emption as "organised" would accord them a legitimacy that they simply do not enjoy. At the very least, the degree of complicity in the organization of hypocrisy varies between those who joined the coalition of the willing and those who did not. The most powerful state bears the disproportionate share of the responsibility for the organization of these particular acts of hypocrisy.

The idea that sovereignty is open to interpretation and construction, which lies at the heart of the organized hypocrisy thesis, is itself hardly new. A good deal of the constructivist literature on sovereignty grapples with this question.[11] What is distinctive about Krasner's thesis, however, is not that such interpretations and constructions occur, but that they occur without evoking much protest or challenge, (people do not scream and yell, or try to find new rules). This assertion, however, is open to serious question. US pronouncements about the limits to sovereignty after 9/11 are far from being accepted or tolerated by the majority of the international community, including many of its allies in Western Europe. And people *are trying to find new rules*, not to replace sovereignty per se as the *grundnorm* of international politics, but to reframe it as "responsibility to protect." People throughout the world, governments as well as civil society organizations, are indeed "screaming and yelling," even though this may not be reaching the ears of senior US officials. The term organized hypocrisy obscures real divisions and struggles over the meaning of sovereignty in the international community, as well as variations in the ways in which different actors or groups of states violate the norms of Westphalian sovereignty. The more appropriate term for describing the war on terror's reshaping of the concept and practice of state sovereignty is not organized hypocrisy, but *disorganized hypocrisy*. Disorganized hypocrisy occurs, first, when the leading state, backed by a small number of like-minded allies (often in disregard of their own domestic opinion), unilaterally change (or attempt to change) the rules of sovereignty (or any other meta-norm) by falsely basing the change on previous and legitimate attempts at limiting sovereignty; and, second, when such transgressions are contested by others in the international community who are themselves striving, through alternative arguments and modes of action, for a consensus on how to limit state sovereignty in a more legitimate and multilateral manner. A review of the war on terror conducted by the US attests to the relevance of my reformulation.

Selective sovereignty: the responsibility to attack

The first important question about sovereignty as organized hypocrisy in the context of the war on terror is to ascertain whether actions undertaken in the name of the war on terror constitute a violation of sovereignty and, if so, under what pretext or in the name of which other, higher principles are such violations justified. From the perspective of the US post-9/11, there is little doubt about the US argument that the war on terror constituted a turning point requiring limitations to the traditional notion of sovereignty. President Bush's speech immediately after 9/11 warned:

> . . . we will pursue nations that provide aid or safe haven to terrorism. Every nation, in every region, now has a decision to make. Either you are with us,

or you are with the terrorists. From this day forward, any nation that continues to harbor or support terrorism will be regarded by the United States as a hostile regime.[12]

This speech, presaging the US attack on the Taliban in December 2001, in retaliation against the Taliban's sheltering of Osama bin-Laden and other terrorist leaders and groups, was the basis of the administration's "limits to sovereignty" thesis put forward by Richard Haas, the director of Policy Planning in the US State Department:

> Sovereignty entails obligations. One is not to massacre your own people. Another is not to support terrorism in any way. If a government fails to meet these obligations, then it forfeits some of the normal advantages of sovereignty, including the right to be left alone inside your own territory. Other governments, including the United States, gain the right to intervene. In the case of terrorism, this can even lead to a right of preventive, or peremptory, self-defense. You essentially can act in anticipation if you have grounds to think it's a question of when, and not if, you're going to be attacked."[13]

Haas's words should not be construed as the philosophical musings of a lone administration intellectual heading the think-tank-like Policy Planning office of the State Department led by Colin Powell, whose own influence over issues related to the war on terror was eclipsed by Dick Cheney's White House or the Donald Rumsfeld's Pentagon. Indeed, more than four years after 9/11, Douglas Feith, Haas's counterpart in the Pentagon as Under Secretary of Defense for Policy, would argue in a speech before the Council on Foreign Relations (now headed by Richard Haas):

> The United States strengthens its national security when it promotes a well-ordered world of sovereign states: a world in which states respect one another's rights to choose how they want to live; a world in which states do not commit aggression and have governments that can and do control their own territory; a world in which states have governments that are responsible and obey, as it were, the rules of the road. The importance of promoting a well-ordered world of sovereign states was brought home to Americans by 9/11, when terrorists enjoying safe haven in remote Afghanistan exploited "globalization" and the free and open nature of various Western countries to attack us disastrously here at home. Sovereignty means not just a country's right to command respect for its independence, but also the duty to take responsibility for what occurs on one's territory, and, in particular, to do what it takes to prevent one's territory from being used as a base for attacks against others.[14]

Two aspects of the "limits to sovereignty" thesis stand out. The first is its conscious linking or equating of the war on terror with the earlier discourse about humanitarian intervention. And from a more long-term perspective, it adds terrorism to the list of causes, including acute human rights violations, that could justify

disregarding the Westphalian norm of non-intervention. The second is its extension of the mode of intervention from reactive to preventive. Together, they
constituted a significant broadening of the framework of intervention since the
emergence of the Westphalian order.

The invasion of Iraq, which after Afghanistan was the next stage in the war on
terror, produced an additional rationale for, and broadening of, the "limits to sovereignty" thesis. This came a year after 9/11 in the form of the National Security Strategy of the United States, otherwise known as the Bush Doctrine. John Lewis Gaddis
has described the Bush Doctrine, including its emphasis on regime change and pre-
emption, as "a grand strategy of transformation."[15] Already indicated in statements
like Haas's comments cited earlier, the Doctrine called for using force, pre-emptively
if necessary, to deal with regimes which pose a threat to US strategic interests, not
just by sponsoring or sheltering terrorists but also by acquiring or seeking to acquire
weapons of mass destruction. Post-modern terrorists, ever so elusive and willing to
commit suicide are "undeterrable non-state enemies,"[16] that is, ill-suited for deterrence and containment, which work only against a clear and identifiable adversary.[17]
"If we wait for threats to fully materialize, we will have waited too long."[18]

The resulting Bush Doctrine was not a lone American crusade. Although the
US as the world's sole superpower was at its forefront, it was also endorsed, to
varying degrees, by a number of other countries, especially Australia.[19] What are
the conditions or provocations that would justify limiting sovereignty? The war
on terror has identified several immediate and long-term reasons, ranging from
the removal of terrorist sanctuaries, to the threat posed by the weapons of mass
destruction in the hands of terrorists and their sponsoring states, and the protection
of human rights from abusive regimes who are also sponsors of terrorism and pro-
liferators of weapons of mass destruction.[20] Interestingly, the Bush administration's
promotion of democracy in the Middle East is not seen as a violation of sovereignty
because it could be undertaken without resort to force. "Respect for sovereignty"
did not "require us to ignore the depredations of tyrannical regimes," since "one
can . . . encourage countries to adopt democracy without offending the principle
of sovereignty."[21] This is notwithstanding the fact that the ideology behind the Iraq
invasion, promoted by the neo-conservatives, is not shy of sanctioning the use of
military power to realize and maintain US pre-eminence and places the promotion
of democracy as the core of the ideology.

To be sure, an expanded agenda of intervention is nothing new in world politics. The debate about humanitarian intervention has been going on for decades.
In 1992, a *New York Times* editorial noted: "In just a few years the idea has been
established that countries which fail to care decently for their citizens dilute their
claim to sovereignty and forfeit invulnerability to outside political–military intervention."[22] Some writers had taken it much further, adding ecological and proliferation issues to the agenda of intervention. Laurence Martin, then President of
the Royal Institute of International Affairs, had argued that despite the end of the
Cold War, there would "remain substantial motives for the greater powers . . . to
interest themselves in the third world," because of the dangers of proliferation of

weapons of mass destruction, migration caused by demographic pressures, and "moral concern for the welfare of fellow men." To this, he would add "the current wave of enthusiasm for democracy and the market, lest failure should engender new authoritarian and potentially aggressive tendencies."[23] Another writer has suggested "three classes of purpose warranting possible intervention":

> intervention to prevent or stop the wide-spread violation of human rights ("humanitarian intervention"); intervention to halt the imminent and continued use of weapons of mass destruction, including chemical, biological, and nuclear weapons, perhaps borne by ballistic missiles ("security intervention"); and intervention to block or contain the release of materials causing severe and wide damage to the climate, landscape, or seascape ("environmental intervention").[24]

Yet, the war on terror's challenge to sovereignty assumes a special significance that could not have been foreseen by the post–Cold War ideas about intervention. First, it links different types of reasons for intervention within its "axis of evil" formulation: bringing together sponsorship of terrorism, weapons of mass destruction and abuse of human rights as reasons for intervention. Second, this consolidated agenda for intervention is spearheaded by the world's most powerful state, thereby upsetting the balance between what Hedley Bull had called the Cold War era balance between the "interveners" and the "intervened against."[25]

Moreover, as noted, the war on terror, unlike the logic of humanitarian intervention, is not aimed at eroding (in however principled manner) the Westphalian system, but to strengthen it. Fighting terrorism through intervention is just as important to national security and the sanctity of the Westphalian order as fighting conventional aggression to preserve territorial integrity, which had historically been the most important concern for protecting the Westphalian order. This is because while the war on terror may involve some transgressions of sovereignty of states which are part of or similar to the "axis of evil" members, the threat to Westphalia posed by the US and the coalition of the willing is nothing compared to the threat to sovereignty posed by terrorist organizations and networks – at least viewed from the perspective of those waging the war on terror.

Westphalia and Caliphobia

This brings us to the next question about framing the war on terror as organized hypocrisy. This concerns the possible justification for the war on terror for the sake of a "higher principle." Given that the protection of human rights and promotion of democracy were not offered as the only or the most important justifications for the war, even by the Bush administration (it was weapons of mass destruction and alleged Iraqi support for Al-Qaeda),[26] the question of higher principles has to do with the preservation of the Westphalian system, or as administration officials would put it: "promoting a well-ordered world of sovereign states."

In redefining sovereignty in the wake of 9/11, the US initially targeted two categories of actors: failed states which offer, either deliberately or due to a lack of capacity to control their borders, sanctuary to terrorists, and regimes which export terrorism and acquire weapons of mass destruction. This basically reflected the administration's rationalization of its attacks on Afghanistan and Iraq respectively. As the insurgency in Iraq worsened, it came up with another target: this time a non-state actor, but with the aspiration to restore a pre-Westphalian state – the Caliphate.[27]

Thus, speaking at Johns Hopkins University's Paul H. Nitze School of Advanced International Studies on 5 December 2005, Defense Secretary Donald Rumsfeld warned: "Iraq would serve as the new base of a new Islamic caliphate to extend throughout the Middle East and which would threaten legitimate governments around the world . . . This is their plan. They have said so."[28] Eric Edelman, the new Under Secretary of Defense for Policy argued: "Iraq's future will either embolden terrorists and expand their reach and ability to re-establish a caliphate." General John Abizaid, the top American commander in the Middle East, warned: "They will try to re-establish a caliphate throughout the entire Muslim world." And Vice President Dick Cheney reminded: "They talk about wanting to re-establish what you could refer to as the seventh-century caliphate," to be "governed by Shariah law, the most rigid interpretation of the Koran" (Stephen Hadley, the national security adviser, has also warned of the Caliphate). Bush himself, although not using the Caliphate per se, has warned of "a totalitarian Islamic empire that reaches from Indonesia to Spain."[29]

But the US is not alone in invoking the Caliphate, nor is the Al-Qaeda seen as its only agent. Founded in 2003, the Jemmah Islamiah (also spelled as Jammah Islamiah) is not only Southeast Asia's "principal" terrorist network, it is also said to be the "regional franchise" of Al-Qaeda, with aspirations for creating a regional Islamic superstate. In 2002, CNN reported its "breathtaking" plan "to create one Islamic state from Indonesia, Malaysia, Singapore to parts of the Philippines, Thailand and Myanmar."[30] Singapore's Prime Minister Goh Chok Tong spoke before the Council on Foreign Relations to warn:

> JI's objective was to create a *Daulah Islamiyah*, an Islamic state in Southeast Asia. This was to be centred in Indonesia but would include Malaysia, Southern Thailand, Southern Philippines, and, inevitably, Singapore and Brunei . . . Their followers want to recreate the Islam of 7th Century Arabia which they regard as the golden age. Their ultimate goal is to bring about a Caliphate linking all Muslim communities.[31]

What is the evidence that terrorist organizations have embarked on such a grand design? Among other things, US officials cite a letter purportedly written by Osama bin-Laden's deputy, Aiman al-Zawahiri, to the now-deceased leader of the Iraqi insurgents, Abu Musab al-Zarqawi. Dated 9 July 2005, the letter outlines four "incremental goals" of the Iraq insurgency. The main goal during the first stage is to expel the Americans from Iraq. The second stage involves establishing an

Islamic authority or amirate and developing it "until it achieves the level of a caliphate – over as much territory as you can to spread its power in Iraq." The third stage is to see the jihad wave extended "to the secular countries neighboring Iraq," while the fourth stage is to "coincide with what came before: the clash with Israel, because Israel was established only to challenge any new Islamic entity."[32]

The JI's plans for an Islamic superstate in Southeast Asia are even more elaborate. An unprecedented insight into its ideological and organizational makeup is provided by a document, known as PUPJI or "General Guide for the Struggle of Jemmah Islamiyah."[33] Released by JI's Central Leadership Council, it may be one of the most important documents on the transnational terrorist movement's ideas and approaches to Islamic state, since there is no comparable comprehensive strategy document recovered for Al-Qaeda.

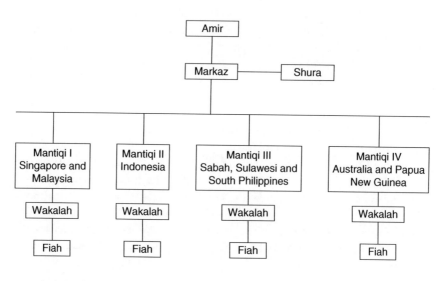

Amir: leader
Markaz: Leadership council
Shura: consultative councils
Mantiqi: geographic divisions

Mantiqi 1 and IV mainly assigned fundraising
Mantiqi II mainly assigned leadership and recruitment
Mantiqi III mainly assigned training

Waklah and Fiah: sub-groups

FIGURE 5.1   Jemaah Islamiah Structure

Source: *Transnational Terrorism: The Threat to Australia* (Canberra: Department of Foreign Affairs and Trade, 2004)

Note: Although the *mantiqis* and *wakalahs* were originally defined as districts and subdistricts, they were "actually a territorial command structure of brigades, battalions, companies, platoons, and squads."[34]

According to this document, the goal of the JI's struggle is to "restore the Islamic Caliphate and the sovereignty of the Syariah all over the world." The first part of PUPJI, "The Principles for the Methodology to Establish the Religion," which consists of principles for understanding the religion, maintains that "establishing the religion means establishing the Islamic state and subsequently the Islamic Caliphate." This implies that a national or regional Islamic state is a first step towards an Islamic Caliphate, or world state. Principle four of the first part restates the "aim in the struggle" as "to guide mankind to submission to Allah, only by the restoration of the caliphate on earth." Part III, containing the Constitution of the JI, states its objective as "to ensure that the administration of *Jamaah Islamiyah* is organized in order to establish the caliphate in accordance with the way of the Prophet, which guarantees the implementation of the *Syariah* in a comprehensive way." And Article 4 of the Constitution defines the "aim of the struggle" as "to establish the *daulah* as a step towards the restoration of the Caliphate."

Can we then take this as a manifesto for an Islamic state that would subsume Westphalian sovereignty? First, the objective of Caliphate or even the national/regional state is presented very generally and vaguely. PUPJI is basically a document about the objectives and organization of the *jama'ah* (group), not of the *daulah* (state) or *khilafah* (Caliphate). Second, while PUPJI mentions "coordination and collaboration with other Islamic states," under "Methodology to Establish the Religion," there is no explanation of how this is to be achieved. And the very fact that it envisages cooperation with other Islamic states implies it accepts a plurality of sovereign states, even if they may all be Islamic, at least in the interim, before the *Khilafah* is established. There is no sense in the PUPJI of how the move from the *daulat* to *khilafah* is to be achieved.

The JI is an offshoot of the Darul Islam (DI), a long-established Indonesian national group, whose goal was the creation of an Islamic state *within* Indonesia. It was only when this goal proved unattainable, despite the opportunity offered by the chaos accompanying the toppling of the Suharto regime in 1998, that the DI moved towards its regional aspirations. Indeed, there is growing evidence that internal disunity in JI has led its Indonesian members to revert to move away from the goal of a regional superstate and focus on creating a local Islamic state or Islamic areas within Indonesia.[35] If an Islamic movement could not achieve its goals domestically, could it be in a position to do so regionally, despite the support from Al-Qaeda, the extent of which remains disputed?

Indeed, the actual motivations and capabilities of terrorist organizations assume importance in view of the Bush administration's *Caliphobia*. Most terrorist groups aspire to a national state, not a supranational polity. They develop transnational linkages as a matter of tactics, because external aid is necessary to compensate for their own limited resources, rather than as a strategic ambition. Even the Taliban, often seen as an extreme form of an Islamic state, was more concerned with establishing its authority within the internationalized frontiers of Afghanistan vis-à-vis its main foe, the Northern Alliance, rather than sponsoring a regional or global Caliphate. As one assessment in 1999 put it, while the goal of the Taliban was to "establish an Islamic government in Afghanistan where the *shariah* law . . . will be the law of the land," it also "believes in non-interference in the affairs of other countries and similarly desire no outside interference in their countries internal affairs."[36] And it was quite willing to cooperate with the US over oil matters.[37]

The terror warriors in the Bush administration who invoke the spectre of the Caliphate exaggerate the unity of terrorist organizations in challenging the Westphalian order. "It's like saying the Christians will be united under one banner," said one critic of the Bush administration's Caliphobia, adding: "It sounds nice, but whose banner will it be?"[38]

On a theoretical level, the radical Islamic ideology supposed to motivate terrorist organizations does challenge the Westphalian conception of state sovereignty. Radical Muslim political thinkers like Maulana Maududi, Syed Qutb, Ayatollah Khomeini and Ali Shariati argued that Islam placed sovereignty in God, while the modern Western state placed it either in the state or people (popular sovereignty).[39] Their ideas also challenge the decentralized Westphalian state-system to the extent that sovereign authority is supposed to be "universal": "the Muslim community is seen as one *Ummah* (people) . . . united under one sovereign by virtue of their faith and submission to the will of God."[40]

Yet what happens when the champions of Islamic sovereignty and statehood take the reins of power either through elections or revolution? There is no single model of a contemporary Islamic state. Entities which have called themselves Islamic states have differed widely in terms of their institutional structures: Iran displays clerical supremacy over political institutions, in Saudi Arabia and Sudan rulers govern in consultation with the clerics without being subordinate, and the fusion of clerics and government was the key feature of the Taliban regime.[41] Furthermore, whether there is any such thing as an Islamic state is a matter of debate among Muslim intellectuals. Asgar Ali Engineer, a prominent Indian Muslim thinker, argues:

> The Prophet, in a way, took a revolutionary step, in dissolving tribal bonds and laying more emphasis on ideological boundaries on one hand, and territorial boundaries, on the other. However, the Prophet's aim was not to build a political community but to build a religious community instead. If Muslims evolved into a political community it was accidental rather than essential. Hence the Qur'an lays more emphasis on values, ethic and morality than on any political doctrines. . . . The political system had to evolve over a period of time and in keeping with the needs and requirements.[42]

Engineer claims that "the later emphasis on integral association between religion and politics is . . . totally absent in the Holy Qur'an."[43] Indeed, the leader of Mohammaydia, the second largest Muslim organization in the world's largest Muslim state, Indonesia, and which is more conservative than the largest organization, Nadhlatul Ulama, argues that "There is no Islamic state."[44]

What is unmistakable is the differences among various interpretations of the political aspects of Islam as they relate to the possibility, nature and objectives of an Islamic state. When it comes to state and sovereignty, Islamic ideology, like any other religious doctrine, is hardly a homogenous body of thought. There is little reason to give more credence to the Bush administration's portrayal of the Caliphate as the ultimate goal of today's terrorists than to the interpretation by scholars of Islam like Engineer regarding the apolitical nature of Islam. As M.A. Muqtedar Khan argues, "sovereignty is a complex concept and any attempt to simplify it can only cause problems."[45] While various strands of Islamic thinking may well agree that "sovereignty belongs to God," Khan argues that Islam also delegates sovereignty to "human agency."[46] If human agency matters, then the foreign policy of Islamic states and their attitude towards state sovereignty should be expected to vary from state to state, depending on the leadership and regime in power.

Moreover, there is little evidence that the Islamic world is about to be swept by the notion of the Caliphate. This would not be the first time that a pan-national ideology has challenged the Westphalian system in the Middle East. In the post-war period, the Arab state-system was imperilled by the idea of a single Arab nation-state. But despite the emotional appeal of pan-Arabism, it was the Westphalian concept which prevailed in the Arab state system.[47] The idea of the Caliphate may well suffer a similar fate especially because, while pan-Arabism was backed by state power from Nasser's Egypt, few states are backing the Caliphate idea and most seem to be fighting it as part of their campaign against terrorism. According to a poll taken by Shibley Telhami of the University of Maryland in Egypt, Saudi Arabia, Morocco, Jordan, the United Arab Emirates and Lebanon, only 6 per cent sympathized with Al Qaeda's goal of seeking an Islamic state.[48] The toppling of Westphalian sovereignty in the hands of terrorist groups, a scenario pained darkly by the Bush administration, is thus plain fear-mongering inspired by failure in Iraq.

According to the Bush administration, a terrorist victory in Iraq would spread chaos to neighbouring states, causing the death of nation-states there and thus paving the way for a Caliphate. Yet, state death is a relatively rare phenomenon in international relations.[49] Moreover, causes of state death or failure have had little to do with terrorism. The lesson of Taliban's Afghanistan is not that terrorism causes state failure, but that state weakness and failure causes and aggravates terrorism. Afghanistan was already a failed state before the terrorists took over. The reality is that few terrorist organizations have the capacity to challenge the contemporary state system, even though some may come close to achieving secession, as in Sri Lanka. As Robert Philips notes, "Terrorist acts are profoundly immoral. In addition, they are not as politically effective as their practitioners claim."[50] International norms have been, and remain robustly in favour of territorial sovereignty that lies at the heart of the Westphalian system. Indeed, the territorial integrity norm is one of the most successful legal and political norms of our time, and no combination of the world's contemporary terrorist groups is about to challenge the status quo.[51]

The war on terror has reversed popular thinking about whether globalization

undermines state sovereignty. States, which have been at the forefront of globalization have since 9/11 reasserted control over global financial flows for the sake of
cutting off the financial lifeline of terrorist organizations.[52] Transborder flows of
capital, people and goods are increasingly subject to state surveillance and control,
supported by homeland security doctrines and mechanisms and growing information and intelligence sharing among governments, joint border patrols, visa regula-
tions, and monitoring of tourism and travel.[53]

Moreover, and paradoxically for terrorist organizations, instead of helping their
cause of restoring the global Caliphate, their actions have actually strengthened the
modern national security state.[54] As Kofi Annan notes, the war on terror has helped
governments:

> to demonize political opponents, to throttle freedom of speech and the press,
> and to delegitimize legitimate political grievances. We are seeing too many
> cases where States living in tension with their neighbours make opportunistic
> use of the fight against terrorism to threaten or justify new military action on
> long-running disputes. Similarly, States fighting various forms of unrest or
> insurgency are finding it tempting to abandon the slow, difficult, but some-
> times necessary processes of political negotiation, for the deceptively easy
> option of military action."[55]

This is ironic, especially when one looks at the US portrayal of "sovereignty as
freedom." As Douglas Feith put it, "Our nation's most basic interest is to protect
the freedom of the American people – our ability to govern ourselves under the
Constitution. The sovereignty of the United States is another way of referring to
this freedom."[56] If so, then the setback for civil liberties after 9/11[57] would constitute a setback for US sovereignty, at least in the sense of popular sovereignty, even
as its government goes about defending national sovereignty and security from
transnational terrorists allegedly committed to recreating the Caliphate.

Moreover, while defending its own national sovereignty, the US not only limits
the freedom of its own citizens, but also the freedom of other nations. A case in
point is "rendition" (to the US) of "illegal enemy combatants," which after 9/11
has "expanded beyond recognition."[58] Scott Horton, in a report issued by N.Y.U.
Law School and the New York City Bar Association, estimates the number of people rendered under the program since 2001 to be a hundred and fifty. To bypass
the Geneva Conventions, the Bush administration classified detainees in the war
on terror, including those from Afghanistan, not as civilians or prisoners of war,
since both these categories would be protected by the Conventions, but as "illegal
enemy combatants."[59] In a replay of its invoking humanitarian intervention as a
justification for pre-emption without regard to the principles of multilateralism,
the administration violated well-established norms and procedures of rendition,
including the requirement for an extradition treaty and judicial proceedings in the
country where the arrests have been made, during which some evidence to support
the charge must be produced.[60]

Conclusion: post-9/11 sovereignty as disorganized hypocrisy

The attempt to link the war on terror and the regime change and democracy promotion agendas on the prior and evolving justifications for humanitarian intervention is one of the most remarkable ironies of US foreign policy after 9/11. It also concerns my third objection to the application of the organized hypocrisy formulation to the war on terror.

The most serious effort to offer a rationale for pre-emption and preventive war by linking it with the earlier justifications for humanitarian intervention can be found in a speech by Richard Haas to the International Institute for Strategic Studies on 13 September 2002. In that speech, he traced the "departure from the traditional notion of near-absolute sovereignty" in three stages. First, Rwanda triggered and Kosovo upheld the belief that "sovereignty should only provide immunity from intervention if the government upholds basic, minimum standards of domestic conduct and human rights." 9/11 was the second stage; it was not a whole new development, but merely "accelerated new thinking that had already begun about the limits of sovereignty," and "expanded the circumstances in which most countries condoned external intervention in the affairs of a state" by adding terrorism to the list of triggers. The impending action against Iraq, Haas argued, would constitute "a third adjustment" to this evolving thinking about sovereignty, whereby the classical notion of deterrence and containment had little effect in countering groups like Al-Qaeda or Saddam Hussein. Hussein, argued Haas, was "someone who has repeatedly violated his international obligations and who is doing everything in his power to develop and conceal weapons of mass destruction." In view of his "history of violence against his neighbors and his own people . . . and his aggressive pursuit of nuclear and other weapons," and in the "new international environment where terrorism and WMD are intersecting," "a strong case can be made for preventive military action."[61]

Scholars of norm diffusion would see such American framing of the war on terror in terms of an evolving debate about intervention as a form of "grafting."[62] On the one hand, the US has sought to capitalize on the humanitarianism debate which was undercutting the rationale for absolute sovereignty. Yet, by so doing, it also drew attention to the evolving criteria for such intervention which would render its attack on Iraq illegitimate. Those criteria had been offered, ironically, in a few weeks after the 9/11 attacks, in the form of the report of the International Commission for Humanitarian Intervention and State Sovereignty.[63] Among other things, the report set down specific conditions for intervention, including "right authority," "just cause," "right intention," "last resort," "proportional means" and "reasonable prospects."

A brief discussion of these criteria is in order here.[64] In defining "just cause," the Report excludes intervention to restore democracy or to stop human rights abuses that do not entail large-scale killing and ethnic cleansing, or intervention by states to protect their nationals in a foreign territory. "Right intention" is similarly limited to alleviation of acute human suffering rather than alteration of boundaries or even supporting claims of self-determination. Outright overthrow of oppressive regimes is not justified, while destroying their ability to cause harm to their own people is justified.

From this perspective, the R2P can hardly be construed as a justification for Bush's "regime change" agenda. Regime change would be a ground for intervention only if suppression of such demand by a government entails large-scale loss of life and ethnic cleansing.

In a similar vein, the "last resort" principle is a point marked by the failure of negotiations to achieve compromise due to intransigence of one or both parties, accompanied by the prospects for imminent violence. "Proportional means" implies minimalism in terms of the scale, intensity and duration of military action, all of which must be commensurate with the provocation. This entails ensuring a minimal impact on the target country's political system and strict observance of international humanitarian law. "Reasonable prospects" is defined not in terms of the defeat of a state, but of a tangible chance of success in stopping or avoiding atrocities and suffering that acted as a trigger for the intervention. Actions that stand no chance of offering protection or which could aggravate an existing crisis are to be avoided.

The R2P deemed the "right authority" criterion, key to the legitimacy of humanitarian intervention, to be important enough to deserve treatment in a separate chapter. The UN is designated as the most appropriate authority, the chief "applicator of legitimacy" in humanitarian interventions. While acknowledging its limitations and imperfections, the Report leaves "absolutely no doubt" that the Security Council remains the best place for authorizing humanitarian intervention. The task of the Report is not to seek alternatives to the Council, but to make that mechanism work better. The Report mandates Council approval in all cases of intervention, while urging it to act promptly to such requests.

While, on the one hand, the Bush administration's claim to speak on behalf of the international community is justifying its war on terror and related instruments, regime change, pre-emption, and democracy promotion in terms of "how the concept of sovereignty ha[d] evolved over the years," on the other, it paid scant attention to the fact that this evolving discourse of sovereignty included consideration of criteria that would legitimize/delegitimize intervention. As Nicholas Wheeler put it, "In seeking to frame the Bush Doctrine as a natural development of the norm of 'sovereignty as responsibility,' Haas sidestepped the crucial issue of who should decide when a state has forfeited its right to be treated as a legitimate sovereign," and "where authority should be located for deciding when a state has forfeited its right to be protected by the principle of non-intervention."[65]

The R2P was not a unilateral effort by any one state or grouping of states (such as the Third World coalition) dominated by those with a vested interested in pushing for, or arresting, the reform of the international order. Although it drew heavily from the "just war" principles, if anything, it reflected as genuine as possible an international consensus on the fate of Westphalian sovereignty. Its membership was representative of the international community in political, civilizational and developmental terms. And going by its criteria, the doctrine of asymmetrical sovereignty fell far short of the criteria for legitimacy for humanitarian intervention that was supposed to be the prior rationale for the war on terror. Moreover, given that the R2P could justify intervention, certain conditions should be met, such as preventing large-scale loss of life and ethnic cleansing, as well as undertaken through a legitimate multilateral framework, that is, only as an "extreme," "extraordinary" and "exceptional" measure. Yet, few members of the international community would agree that Iraq necessitated such a response, especially when the evidence of its weapons of mass destruction program and links with Al-Qaeda had not been conclusive.

Indeed, there is strong case to be made, as Dale T. Snauwaert has argued, that "from the perspective of the Just War tradition the [Bush] doctrine's linkage with a power-driven, hegemonic foreign policy strategy undermines the moral credibility of the doctrine, and thus the moral credibility of the United States."[66] On the Iraq war, among other commentators, Jimmy Carter has argued that "clear alternatives to war" did exist. Moreover, Carter points to the lack of legitimate authority for the war. The Security Council's authorization which forms the administration's stated legal basis of the war was meant to eliminate Iraq's weapons of mass destruction, and not "achieve regime change and to establish a Pax Americana in the region, perhaps occupying the ethnically divided country for as long as a decade. For these objectives, we do not have international authority."[67]

The disjunction between the "limits to sovereignty" thesis integral to the war on terror and the humanitarian intervention principles was highlighted by UN Secretary-General Kofi Annan, who refused to see the Bush Doctrine as an "extension" of the humanitarian intervention rationale and challenged the attempt by Messrs Haas and Feith to link the war on terror with the intervention in Kosovo. "The attacks that struck the United States on 11 September 2001," noted Annan, "shifted the global debate – and action – away from military intervention on behalf of others, to intervention in self-defence; from a Kosovo-like debate about how far – and under what conditions – the international community would act against a State perceived to be abusing its own citizens in gross and systematic ways, to considering how far – and under what conditions – individual States, alone and in concert, would act to halt terrorism and root out its cells in dozens of countries."[68]

In the chaos that the attack on Iraq generated, the recommendations and significance of the R2P report was temporarily sidelined. But it did cast a shadow over the legitimacy of the Iraq invasion.[69] And its recommendations did get a new lease of life in the report of the UN Secretary-General's High-Level Panel on Threats, Challenges and Change in 2004. The report "endorse[d] the merging norm that there is a collective international responsibility to protect, exercisable by the Security Council authorizing military intervention as a last resort, in the event of genocide and other large-scale killing, ethnic cleansing or serious violations of international humanitarian law which sovereign Governments have proved powerless or unwilling to prevent." The criteria specified by the report to justify humanitarian intervention correspond closely to the criteria found in the R2P report.[70] And this norm of humanitarian intervention was one of the few major substantive items from the High Level Panel Report (and the subsequent Report by Secretary-General Kofi Anan, "In Larger Freedom") to survive in the 2005 UN Summit in September 2005.[71]

The war on terror and the attack on Iraq have produced an extended crisis in the global multilateral order. There have been thousands of protests. Anti-Americanism throughout the world is growing. In Asia, the Bush Doctrine has caused deep uneasiness about the US power and intentions.[72] The US–Europe fracture over Iraq cannot be seen as the kind of acquiescence that is supposed to mark the consensual organization of hypocrisy in the global sovereignty regime. Even Francis Fukuyama, who proclaimed the "end of history" after the end of the Cold War, acknowledged that the US–Europe divisions raises the question "whether the West is really a coherent concept," since "an enormous gulf has opened up in American and European perceptions about the world, and the sense of shared values is increasingly frayed."[73]

Against this backdrop, to assert that the challenge posed by the war on terror to state sovereignty has not led to people "screaming and yelling," or that it has not generated efforts to find new rules (not to replace sovereignty, but to identify legitimate ways of limiting it) would be simply untrue. The rationalization offered in the name of the war on terror as an extension of the logic of humanitarian intervention is a form of organized hypocrisy, but this overlooks the fact that different forms of violation of sovereignty may have differing degrees of legitimacy. The legitimacy of humanitarian intervention cannot be equated with the legitimacy of the war on terror. Failure to distinguish principled and organized departures from Westphalian sovereignty aimed at protecting human security (as outlined in the R2P report) from unilateral breaches of sovereignty aimed at protecting national or coalitional security and fulfilling an ideology-driven foreign policy agenda is a critical flaw in Krasner's organized hypocrisy thesis. The doctrine of limited sovereignty in the war on terror is more accurately regarded as "disorganised hypocrisy," since the responsibility for this particular act of hypocrisy is not evenly distributed, and the actions of the hegemonic power-led coalition have severely undermined the multilateral system, including the unity of the so-called "West."

The term organized hypocrisy obscures real divisions and struggles over the meaning of sovereignty in the international community, as well as the variations in the ways in which different actors or groups of states violate the norms of Westphalian sovereignty. In the war on terror, it was just plain hypocrisy, rather than organized hypocrisy, that we were dealing with.

Notes

1 Originally published in *Political Studies* 55, no. 2 (2007): 274–296.
2 See for example, Raymond Vernon, *Sovereignty at Bay: The Multinational Spread of US Enterprises* (New York: Basic Books, 1971); Joseph A. Camilleri and Jim Falk, *The End of Sovereignty? The Politics of a Shrinking and Fragmenting World* (Aldershot, U.K.: Edward Elgar, 1992); Robert Keohane, "Sovereignty in International Society" in *The Global*

Transformation Reader – An Introduction to the Globalization Debate, eds., David Held and Anthony McGrew (Oxford: Blackwell Publishers, 2000); Michael Mann "Has Globalization Ended the Rise and Rise of the Nation State?" in *The Global Transformation Reader – An Introduction to the Globalization Debate*, eds., David Held and Anthony McGrew (Oxford: Blackwell Publishers, 2000); Sylvia Ostry, "Globalization and the Nation State: Erosion from Above," Timlin Lecture, University of Saskatchewan, February 1998, www.utoronto.ca/cis/ostry/docs_pdf/timlin.pdf; Linda Weiss, *The Myth of the Powerless State* (Ithaca: Cornell University Press, 1998); Margaret Keck and Kathryn Sikkink, *Activists Beyond Borders: Advocacy Networks in International Politics* (Ithaca: Cornell University Press,1998); Martha Finnemore, "Constructing Norms of Humanitarian Intervention," in *The Culture of National Security: Norms and Identity in World Politics*, ed., Peter J. Katzenstein (Ithaca: Cornell University Press, 1996), 153–185; Stanley Hoffman, "The Debate About Intervention," in Turbulent Peace: The Challenges of Managing International Conflict, eds., Fen Osler Hampson, Chester A. Crocker and Pamela Aall (Herndon, Va.: United States Institute of Peace Press, 2001); Nicholas J. Wheeler, Saving Strangers: Humanitarian Intervention in International Society (New York: Oxford University Press, 2000); Martha Finnemore, *The Purpose of Intervention* (Ithaca: Cornell University Press, 2004); and Gene M. Lyons and Michael Mastanduno, eds., *Beyond Westphalia: State Sovereignty and International Intervention* (Baltimore and London: Johns Hopkins University Press, 1995).

3 Bush Administration officials have described terrorism as the "greatest threat to peace in our time," Cited in Karen Walker, "No Apologies for U.S. WMD Policy," *Defense News*, Special Issue for the Asia Pacific Security Conference, Singapore, 22–23 February, 2004.

4 Stephen Krasner, *Sovereignty: Organized Hypocrisy* (Princeton: Princeton University Press, 1999). Krasner was not the first to note the violations of sovereignty, however. Many others who do so nonetheless argue that these violations do not constitute "obsolescence, irrelevance, or transformation." Kal J. Holsti, *Taming the Sovereigns* (Cambridge: Cambridge University Press, 2004), 140. See also F. H. Hinsley, *Sovereignty*, 2nd ed., (Cambridge: Cambridge University Press, 1986); Alan James, *Sovereign Statehood: The Basis of International Society* (London: Allen and Unwin, 1986); Robert Jackson, ed., *Sovereignty at the Millennium* (Oxford: Blackwell, 1999); and Daniel Philpott, *Revolutions in Sovereignty: How Ideas Shaped Modern International Relations* (Princeton: Princeton University Press, 2001).

5 Krasner, *Sovereignty: Organized Hypocrisy*, backcover blurb.

6 "Sovereignty," Interview with Stephen D. Krasner, by Harry Kreisler, "Conversations with History," Institute of International Studies, UC Berkeley, 31 March 2003, http://globetrotter.berkeley.edu/people3/Krasner/krasner-con3.html.

7 "Sovereignty," Interview with Stephen D. Krasner.

8 "Iraq War Illegal, Says Annan," *BBC News*, 16 September 2004, http://news.bbc.co.uk/2/hi/middle_east/3661134.stm.

9 As the head of policy planning in the State Department after having served an earlier term in the White House staff where he claims to have written a memo arguing that "sovereignty was contingent on responsibility, which has actually been achieved throughout the history of sovereignties," which "is something that we've echoed since September 11th." "Sovereignty," Interview with Stephen D. Krasner.

10 Ibid.

11 See, Nicholas Onuf, "Sovereignty: Outline of a Conceptual History," *Alternatives: Global, Local, Political* 16, no. 4 (1991): 425–446; Jens Bartelson, *A Genealogy of Sovereignty* (Cambridge: Cambridge University Press, 1995); Thomas Biersteker and Cynthia Weber, *State Sovereignty as a Social Construct* (Cambridge: Cambridge University Press, 1996); Cynthia Weber, *Simulating Sovereignty: Intervention, the State and Symbolic Exchange* (Cambridge: Cambridge University Press, 1995); and Alexander Wendt, *Social Theory of International Politics* (Cambridge: Cambridge University Press, 1999), and his various previous writings on the subject.

12 President George W. Bush, Speech before Congress, 20 September 2001, http://www. whitehouse.gov/news/releases/2001/09/20010920-8.html.

13 Nicholas Lemann, "The Next World Order," *The New Yorker*, 1 April 2002, http:// www.newyorker.com/fact/content/articles/020401fa_FACT1.

14 Douglas J. Feith, Under Secretary of Defense for Policy, Speech to the Council on Foreign Relations, 17 February 2005, U.S. Department of Defense: Office of the Assistant Secretary of Defense, Public Affairs, News Transcript, http://www.defenselink.mil/transcripts/2005/tr20050217-2127.html.

15 John Lewis Gaddis, "A Grand Strategy of Transformation," *Foreign* Policy, 1 November 2002, http://www.foreignpolicy.com/articles/2002/11/01/a_grand_strategy_of_transformation.

16 Jeffrey Record, "The Bush Doctrine and War with Iraq," *Parameters* 33, no. 1 (2003): 4–21.

17 Ibid.

18 Michael E. O'Hanlon, Susan E. Rice, James B. Steinberg, "The New National Security Strategy and Preemption," Working Paper, Brookings Institution, http://www.brookings.edu/dybdocroot/views/papers/ohanlon/20021114.pdf.

19 Amitav Acharya, "The Bush Doctrine and Asian Regional Order: the Perils and Pitfalls of Preemption," in *Confronting the Bush Doctrine: Critical Views from the Asia-Pacific*, eds., Mel Gurtov and Peter Van Ness (London: RoutledgeCurzon, 2005).

20 "The world has decided that sovereignty shouldn't protect a government perpetrating large-scale crimes against humanity within its own borders. Before us all now hangs the question of how long-standing ideas about sovereignty can be squared with the dangers of biological or nuclear weapons. Should governments with troubling records of aggression, support for terrorism, human rights abuses and the like be allowed to invoke sovereign rights to protect their development of catastrophic weapons that threaten the sovereign rights of others in the world?" Douglas J. Feith, Speech to the Council on Foreign Relations, 17 February 2005.

21 Douglas J. Feith, Speech to the Council on Foreign Relations, 17 February 2005.

22 "Hamane Intervention," *International Herald Tribune*, 27 November 1992, 6.

23 Laurence Martin, "National Security in a New World Order," *The World Today*, February 1992, 21.

24 Alan K. Henrikson, "How Can the Vision of a 'New World Order' Be Realized?," *The Fletcher Forum of World Affairs* 16, no. 1 (1992): 63–79, 70–71.

25 Bull had identified four major constraints on Western intervention in the Third World: (1) "a remarkable growth in Third World countries of the will and capacity to resist intervention"; (2) "a weakening in the Western world of the will to intervene, by comparison with earlier periods, or at least of the will to do so forcibly, directly and openly"; (3) the growing Soviet capacity to project power, which "facilitated Third World resistance to Western intervention"; and (4) "the emergence of a global equilibrium of power unfavourable to intervention" in the sense that "there has emerged a balance among the interveners which has worked to the advantage of the intervened against." Hedley Bull, "Intervention in the Third World," in *Intervention in World Politics*, ed., Hedley Bull (Oxford: Clarendon Press, 1984), 135–156.

26 For further discussion of the various justifications for the war, see Amitav Acharya, *The Age of Fear: Power Versus Principle in the War on Terror* (New Delhi, India: Rupa and Co, 2004), 172–174.

27 The Caliphate, according to a media representation, "was a period of centralized rule over much of the Muslim world in . . . the seventh and eighth centuries . . . an empire that stretched from Spain to Central Asia." Drew Brown, "Rumsfeld warns of Islamic superstate if U.S. leaves Iraq too soon," *Knight Ridder Newspapers*, 5 December 2005, http://www.realcities.com/mld/krwashington/13335698.htm.

28 News Transcript, U.S. Department of Defense, Office of the Assistant Secretary of Defense (Public Affairs), http://www.defenselink.mil/news/Dec2005/20051205_3541. html

29 All quotations in this paragraph are from Elisabeth Bumiller, "White House Letter:

Watchword of the day – Beware the caliphate," *The New York Times*, 1 December 2005.

30 "The quest for SE Asia's Islamic 'super' state," *CNN*, 20 August 2002, http://edition.cnn.com/2002/WORLD/asiapcf/southeast/07/30/seasia.state/.

31 "Beyond Madrid: Winning Against Terrorism," Speech to the Council on Foreign Relations, Washington, D.C., 6 May 2004, http://www.mfa.gov.sg/sanfrancisco/cfr-6may.html; See also: Ministry of Foreign Affairs, Singapore, "MFA Press Statement on the Request for Addition of Jemaah Islamiah to List of Terrorists Maintained by the UN," 23 October 2002.

32 Letter from al-Zawahiri to al-Zarqawi, Office of the Director of National Intelligence, ODNI News Release no. 2–05, 11 October 2005, http://www.dni.gov/release_letter_101105.html

33 *Pedoman Umum Perjuangan Al-Jama'ah Al-Islamiyyah (PUPJI, General Guide for the Struggle of Jemmah Islamiyah)*, released by the Central Leadership Council, Jemmah Islamiyah, translated by the International Center for Political Violence and Terrorism Research, Institute of Defence and Strategic Studies, Nanyang Technological University, Singapore.

34 "Jemaah Islamiyah in South East Asia: Damaged but Still Dangerous," *Asia Report N°63* (Paris: International Crisis Group, 26 August 2003).

35 Jonathan Ross-harrington, "Re-Examining Jemaah Islamiyah in the Wake of the Zawahiri Letter," *Terrorism Monitor* 3, no. 21 (3 November 2005), http://www.jamestown.org/terrorism/news/article.php; Sidney Jones, "New Developments within Jemaah Islamiyah," Singapore: Institute of Southeast Asian Studies, 5 July 2005, http://nettv.1-net.com.sg/iseas/sidney_july05/ (webcast).

36 Kamal Matinuddin, *The Taliban Phenomenon* (Oxford: Oxford University Press, 1999), 42.

37 Ahmed Rashid, *Taliban* (New Haven: Yale University Press, 2001), chs 12 and 13.

38 Brown, "Rumsfeld warns of Islamic superstate if U.S. leaves Iraq too soon."

39 M. A. Muqtedar Khan, "Sovereignty in Islam as Human Agency," *Ijtihad*, http://www.ijtihad.org/sovt.htm

40 Ibid.

41 Mohammed Haniff Hassan, "Islam and International Relations," memo, Singapore: Institute of Defence and Strategic Studies, November 2005.

42 Asghar Ali Engineer, "The Concept of Islamic State," http://www.punjabilok.com/faith/islam/islamstate.htm

43 Ibid.

44 Amien Rais, "Negara Islam Tidak Ada (There is no Islamic State)," in *Tidak Ada Negara Islam: Surat-Surat Politik*, (in Indonesian) revised edition, eds., Nurcholish Majid and Mohamad Roem (Jakarta, Indonesia: Djambartan, 2000), xxii–xxiii.

45 Khan, "Sovereignty in Islam as Human Agency."

46 Ibid.

47 Michael Barnett, "Sovereignty, Nationalism, and Regional Order in the Arab States System," *International Organization* 49, no. 3 (1995): 479–510.

48 Cited in Bumiller, "White House Letter: Watchword of the day – Beware the caliphate."

49 Stephen D. Krasner and Carlos Pascual, "Addressing State Failure," *Foreign Affairs* 84, no. 4 (2005): 153–163.

50 Robert L. Phillips, "The Roots of Terrorism," http://www.religion-online.org/showarticle.asp?title=1032.

51 Mark W. Zacher, "The Territorial Integrity Norm: International Boundaries and the Use of Force," *International Organization* 55, no. 2 (2001): 215–250.

52 Donald G. McNeil, Jr., "European Union Expands Its List of Terrorist Groups, Requiring Sanctions and Arrests," *New York Times*, 29 December 2001, B3; and Kenneth Janda, "Global Terrorism, Domestic Order, and the United States," in *Professionals for Cooperation*, volume 5, ed., Anatoly Kulik (Moscow, Russia: Russian-American Academic Exchanges Alumni Association, 2002), http://www.prof.msu.ru/publ/book5/c5_1_2.htm

53 Amitav Acharya, "State–Society Relations after September 11," in *Worlds In Collision: Terror and Future of Global Order*, eds., Ken Booth and Tim Dunne (London: Palgrave Macmillan, 2002).

54 Acharya, *Age of Fear: Power Versus Principle in the War on Terror.*

55 Kofi Annan, "University Degree Ceremony Address in Netherlands Calls For Attack on Root Causes, New Vision of International Security," Press Release, SG/SM/8518 21/11/2002, http://www.un.org/News/Press/docs/2002/SGSM8518.doc.htm

56 Douglas J. Feith, Speech to the Council on Foreign Relations, 17 February 2005.

57 Acharya, *Age of Fear;* Acharya, *"State–Society Relations."*

58 Jane Mayer, "Outsourcing Torture: The Secret History of America's 'Extraordinary Rendition' program," *The New Yorker*, 14 February 2005, http://www.newyorker.com/printables/fact/050214fa_fact6

59 Ibid.

60 Susan Mandiberg, "Domestic Criminal Law," http://www.lclark.edu/dept/collcomm/mandiberg.html

61 Richard N. Haass, "Reflections a Year After September 11," Remarks to International Institute for Strategic Studies' 2002 Annual Conference, 13 September 2002, http://www.cfr.org/publication/5098/reflections_a_year_after_september_11.html

62 Amitav Acharya, "How Ideas Spread: Whose Norms Matter? Norm Localization and Institutional Change in Asian Regionalism," *International Organization* 58, no. 2 (2004): 239–275.

63 *The Responsibility to Protect: Report of the International Commission on Intervention and State Sovereignty* (Ottawa, Canada: International Development Research Centre, December 2001). Hereafter, cited as the Report or *The Responsibility to Protect.*

64 The following discussion draws heavily from: Amitav Acharya, "Redefining the Dilemmas of Humanitarian Intervention," *Australian Journal of International Affairs* 56, no. 3 (2002): 373–382.

65 Nicholas Wheeler, "The Bush Doctrine: The Responsibilities of Sovereignty or a Revolutionary Challenge to the Principles of International Order," Social Science Research Council, November 2002, http://www.ssrc.org/programs/gsc/gsc_activities/wheeler.page.

66 Dale T. Snauwaert, "The Bush Doctrine and Just War Theory," *OJPCR: The Online Journal of Peace and Conflict Resolution* 6, no. 1 (2004): 121–135.

67 Jimmy Carter, "An Attack Not Yet Justified," *International Herald Tribune*, 10 March 2003.

68 Annan, "University Degree Ceremony Address in Netherlands Calls For Attack on Root Causes, New Vision of International Security." Annan himself was a champion of limited sovereignty. See Kofi Annan, "Two Concepts of Sovereignty," *The Economist*, 18 September 1999; and Edward Luttwak, "Kofi's Rule: Humanitarian Intervention and Neocolonialism," *The National Interest*, no. 58 (Winter 1999–2000): 57–62.

69 See also, Ramesh Thakur, "Developing Countries and the Intervention-Sovereignty Debate," in *The United Nations and Global Security*, eds., Richard M. Price and Mark W. Zacher (New York: Palgrave Macmillan, 2004), 193–208; and Ramesh Thakur, "Iraq and the Responsibility to Protect," *Behind the Headlines* 62, no. 1 (2004): 1–16.

70 *A More Secure World: Our Shared Responsibility*, Report of the Secretary-General's High-Level Panel on Threats, Challenges and Change (New York: United Nations, 2004), 66, 106. See also the subsequent Report by Secretary-General Kofi Anan: *In Larger Freedom*, http://www.un.org/largerfreedom/

71 The Resolution of the Summit stated that the world leaders "are prepared to take collective action, in a timely and decisive manner, through the Security Council, in accordance with the Charter, including Chapter VII, on a case-by-case basis and in cooperation with relevant regional organizations as appropriate, should peaceful means be inadequate and national authorities are manifestly failing to protect their populations from genocide, war crimes, ethnic cleansing and crimes against humanity."

Resolution adopted by the General Assembly, 24 October 2005, 60/1, 2005 World Summit Outcome, http://daccessdds.un.org/doc/UNDOC/GEN/N05/487/60/PDF/N0548760.pdf?OpenElement.

72 Brendan Pereira, "Mahathir makes a stinging attack on West," *The Straits Times*, 20 June 2003, 3.

73 Francis Fukuyama, "The West May Be Coming Apart," *The Straits Times*, 10 August 2002.

PART III

Institutions, autonomy and regional orders

6

MULTILATERALISM: BEYOND HEGEMONY AND WITHOUT VICTORY[1]

It is often fashionable in academic and policy debates to ask: does multilateralism have a future? A more appropriate question, in my view, would be this: which multilateralism has a future? There is little question, short of a global cataclysm, that some form of multilateralism will continue to characterize the global order. But the traditional conceptualization of multilateralism is under challenge. That concept of multilateralism privileged the state, American power, Western leadership, transnational activists and the global level of interactions. What is coming in their place is as yet indeterminate, but in this chapter, I will propose one possible direction, which I would characterize as "post-hegemonic multilateralism." In the sections that follow, I outline the dominant concept of multilateralism in the post-war period. Then I look at three principal challenges to it: namely, civil society and transnational actors, emerging powers and the relatively less noticed challenge from regionalism, both in terms of their strengths and limitations. In the final section, I discuss the cumulative impact of these challenges against the backdrop of a relatively declining US, as well as in redefining the residual elements of the multilateral order that had developed under American hegemony. While some Liberal defenders of hegemonic multilateralism believe that the old multilateralism would outlive American hegemony (partly because that hegemony will persist even in a less direct or visible form), I argue that the prospects for change are much greater, even short of a major war or hegemonic victory that has been viewed in the past as the basis for reinventing world order.

Post-hegemonic multilateralism refers to formal and informal cooperation among actors, including but not limited to states, on the basis of shared principles and non-coercive leadership at global and regional levels. The concept is similar to, but not identical with, Cox's notion of "counterhegemonic" bloc. Cox's "counterhegemonic order" is "anchored in a broader diffusion of power, in which a large number of collective forces, including states, achieve some agreement upon universal principles of an alternative order without dominance."[2]

Unlike Cox, who uses "post-hegemonic" and "counterhegemonic" interchangeably, I see the former as a distinctive category that is defined in more specific terms. The dominance under question is specifically those of the superpowers or the great powers, whose role has been privileged in traditional writings on multilateralism. Instead, leadership in post-hegemonic multilateralism is shared among great powers, middle powers and weaker states, and sometimes the latter two categories can offer leadership over the great powers. Second, the very idea of counterhegemonic[3] emphasizes resistance from below. It is through a "reinvigorated civil society" that Cox sees the prospects for a genuine reconstruction of the prevailing multilateralism and world order. Despite admitting a role for states, Cox nonetheless believes that "very little can be accomplished towards fundamental change through the state system as it now exists."[4] The "counterhegemonic" perspective probably places too much reliance on the civil society resistance in defining multilateralism.

My perspective on post-hegemonic multilateralism draws upon, but goes beyond the opposing views of Keohane and Cox. Keohane[5] believed that multilateral regimes created by the hegemonic power (the US) can survive their decline on the strength of the benefits they offer, such as reducing uncertainty, providing information and lowering transactions costs. The continuation of shared interests plus sunk costs and networks of communication created by these institutions would help their continued usefulness. Cox, on the other hand, argued that institutions that reflect the values and purpose of the hegemonic capitalist world order could be seriously challenged by resistance from below, led by a transnational civil society, whether the hegemon itself declines or not. In my formulation, a post-hegemonic multilateral order originates not just from resistance to hegemony (Cox's point of emphasis), which could be aggravated by the self-seeking and unilateral policy of the hegemonic power, but also from hegemonic decline (Keohane's point of emphasis) even when the hegemon remains committed to peaceful and cooperative conduct and hence does not provoke a lot of resistance. But hegemonic decline, when combined with other forces, including resistance from civil society, the emergence of transnational issue areas and especially state and non-state actors and regional institutions in the *non-Western* world, will much more severely challenge the purpose and governance structure of the existing multilateral institutions than *After Hegemony* suggested. While agreeing with Keohane (and Ikenberry in his *Liberal Leviathan*), one should not underestimate the continued authority and adaptability of existing state-led institutions to changing circumstances that call for a more socially inclusive and democratic multilateralism. I suggest that multilateralism may be more fundamentally challenged and reinvented "*after hegemony*" and "without victory" (a major war) due to the disillusionment on the part of the weaker or newly-empowered actors with the supposed benefits of an existing hegemonic framework compared to the costs it imposes and the vulnerabilities it induces. Even the stickiness of institutions due to their socializing functions, as stressed by constructivists, may not spare them from a fundamental restructuring over the long-term.

A post-hegemonic multilateral order may also be distinguished from a "constitutional" order, as developed by Ikenberry. For Ikenberry, a hegemonic order is built around the principle of hierarchy; states are "integrated vertically with highly defined superordinate and subordinate positions.[6] By contrast, a constitutional order is organized around "agreed-upon rules and political institutions that operate to allocate rights and limit the exercise of power."[7] But as I shall discuss later, a constitutional order is not entirely divorced from hegemonic initiative and power, but is essentially a form of hegemonic socialization. It is the hegemon that initiates and controls the multilateral institutional-binding framework, whereby its restraint is exchanged for the lesser states' respect or deference.

What are the catalysts of post-hegemonic multilateralism? Most analysts point to the changes in the distribution of power. An aspect of the change is the phenomenon of rising powers. But to present this as simply a redistribution of power is misleading, since it also entails a fundamental reshaping of ideational forces and modes and networks of socializing. Hence, unlike many recent articulations of change in the multilateral system, the catalysts for post-hegemonic multilateralism rest not only, or mainly, on the shifting distribution of power, but also on the changing aspirations for autonomy and identity, a central political norm of regional forms of multilateralism in the developing world, as well as political changes in the domestic sphere of the actors, such as democratization. Other important factors which could move a group of states to question their continued acquiescence with a hegemonic framework include the need to respond to certain types of transnational challenges such as climate change, labour migration, etc. Some such problems are often induced or aggravated by the hegemon's ideological (e.g. neo-liberal) paradigm. As a result, actors may be moved towards a new sense of multilateral purpose and identity even under the material conditions of continued hegemony. In a variety of ways, they may be prompted to redefine and broaden their multilateral space beyond what was "permitted" under a framework of hegemonic multilateralism. A post-hegemonic multilateral order is thus one in which multilateralism, employing the norms, leadership structures and decision-making procedures, developed through indigenous socialization processes, is used to pursue local priorities and identities outside the framework of the hegemonic paradigm, even as the regional actors acknowledge the salience of the latter.

The Gramscian notion of hegemony captures the hegemon's ability to maintain its authority through a mixture of coercion and consent, with consent being the more important element. By contrast, the notion of post-hegemonic multilateralism suggests that the hegemon no longer controls all the resources necessary for coercion without resorting to outright war. It faces growing normative and material (because of the situation of interdependence brought about by its self-promoted economic and security framework) constraints on its coercive power. Moreover, in a post-hegemonic multilateral order, other states and civil society groups, or some combination of them, do not necessarily consent to (consenting as understood here is a more positive, pro-active and voluntary gesture than concede), the dominant *material* position of the hegemon in the global economy and security order. But even while remaining dependent on the hegemon's material resources (market access, security umbrella, etc.), these actors no longer accept or endorse the organizing ideas and the leadership role of the hegemonic power. Instead, actors actively pursue priorities and identities as defined by local interests and conditions, with a long-term view of overcoming, or at least minimizing, hegemonic controls. The act of *conceding without consenting* and differentiating between material dependence, on the one hand, and ideational, entrepreneurial and inter-subjective (identity) autonomy, on the other, is the key element that distinguishes the notion of hegemony from that of post-hegemony.

Hegemonic multilateralism

It is useful to start with the work of John Ruggie, whose widely known and influential 1993 edited volume, *Multilateralism Matters*, embodies the dominant concept of multilateralism that obtained during the Cold War, as well as the immediate post-Cold War period. The first is the definition of the concept. In his introduction to the volume, Ruggie defines multilateralism as "coordinating relations among three or more states in accordance with certain principles."[8] With this definition, Ruggie claims to improve upon a prior formulation of the term by Keohane, who defined multilateralism as "the practice of coordinating national policies in groups of three or more states." The improvement is supposed to be in specifying a *qualitative* aspect of multilateralism; the latter is not just a matter of numbers. That qualitative aspect is normative, as captured in the phrase *certain principles*, two of which are especially important: indivisibility and diffuse reciprocity. Hence, compared to Keohane's functional definition, Ruggie's is more of a constructivist formulation, even though he was not writing within an explicitly constructive framework.

Ruggie's second, and the more important claim for the purpose of this chapter, has to with agency. Ruggie asserted that while multilateralism was not a post-war American invention, "Looking more closely at the post-World War II situation . . . it was less the fact of American *hegemony*, that accounts for the explosion of multilateral arrangements than of *American* hegemony."[9]

In making both the above points, Ruggie contrasted post-War American-inspired-and-led multilateralism with the New Economic Order of Nazi Germany. That order, though it coordinated economic relations among more than three states, would not qualify as multilateral because it was founded upon a system of bilateralist trade and clearing arrangements between Germany and foreign trading partners that made the system "inherently and fundamentally discriminatory."[10] That order functioned as a sphere of influence, lacking in openness and equal access, even though Germany did often import more from its partners than exporting to them. True multilateralism must be non-discriminatory, such as the GATT (later WTO) "most favoured nation" principle. Curiously, Ruggie does not cite the example of Japan's Greater East Asia Co-Prosperity Sphere, although it too did exhibit the qualities of a sphere of influence, even though it was presented as a collective arrangement among three or more states.

Ruggie's explication of multilateralism took the state as the primary actor. Neither in the conceptualization, nor in the case studies was there any acknowledgement of the role of the civil society or non-state actors. Their place and role in multilateralism, which would present a powerful challenge to the dominant post-war conceptualization of multilateralism found in Keohane and Ruggie, and which would soon become a major point of advance in the literature, will be discussed shortly. But Ruggie's second claim, the representation of multilateralism as a distinctively American close association between multilateralism and American hegemony, remains less contested, even by those who saw the statist concept of multilateralism as inadequate and proposed civil society multilateralism as a "counterhegemonic" solution. This leads to the question that is important to this chapter: can multilateralism be conceivable and viable without American sponsorship and leadership? My answer is that it can.

This leads to a closely related point. Ruggie does not take multilateralism to be an exclusively global phenomenon. Regional organizations can be multilateral, where they too abide by the principles (i.e. non-discrimination, indivisibility and diffuse reciprocity). This helpfully challenges a view which tends to view regionalism and multilateralism (or universalism) as mutually competitive and exclusive.[11] But it is revealing that while *Multilateralism Matters*, contained three chapters on Europe, – NATO, the European Community, and a more general chapter on multilateral security focusing on the CSCE/OSCE – as examples of such region-specific multilateralism, it leaves out all other parts of the world. This neglect is not explained, except in the case of the Asia Pacific. Here contrasting Europe's growing turn to multilateralism, including the adaptation of NATO "to the new European geopolitical realities," rather than a "return to a system of competitive bilateral alliances,"[12] with Asia Pacific region's lack of multilateralism, Ruggie states that:

> Security relations in the Asia-Pacific region make the same point in the negative. It was not possible to construct multilateral institutional frameworks there in the immediate post-war period. Today, the absence of such arrangements inhibits progressive adaptation to fundamental global shifts . . . In Asia-Pacific, there is no European Community and no NATO to have transformed the multitude of regional security dilemmas . . . Indeed, no Helsinki-like process through which to begin the minimal task of mutual confidence building . . .[13]

If as I believe, *Multilateralism Matters* can be seen as a leading example of the state-of-the art in mainstream scholarship on multilateralism in the Cold War period and the early 1990s, then such a statement is especially suggestive of its limitations of that scholarship. First, why was there no NATO in Asia Pacific? If one accepts that the United States intrinsically favoured a multilateral approach, why did it not encourage an Asia-Pacific version of NATO. Surely, the absence of US interest in creating a NATO in Asia would challenge the close association between multilateralism and US hegemony that Ruggie posits. Some answer this puzzle by pointing out that the power asymmetries between the US and its putative multilateral partners were so large that a multilateral approach would have amounted to free riding on the part of the allies, without significantly adding to the US strategic capacity to meet the Soviet and Chinese threats there.[14] Challenging this "power gap" explanation, Hemmer and Katzenstein offer a constructivist explanation, which locates the reason for "why there was no NATO in Asia" in an "identity-gap." In their view, multilateralism requires a measure of collective identification among partners. While post-war US strategic planners could identify with their European partners as equal and trustworthy, they saw the prospective multilateral Asia Pacific partners as inferior, hence unworthy of collective identification to build a multilateral framework. In reality, evidence suggests that while both views have merit, a third view that deserves attention is that the United States under the Eisenhower administration *wanted, but could not get*, a viable multilateral security framework because of normative opposition from a group of nationalist leaders in Asia, who saw an unequal alliance with the US as an unacceptable form of neocolonial dominance.[15]

To sum up, the state-of-the art work on multilateralism had three key features (1) it ignored the role of non-state actors, (2) it was Americanocentric, and (3) it was Eurocentric. I call this literature "hegemonic multilateralism." To anyone familiar with the literature on multilateralism and regionalism, this is hardly surprising.[16] It is against this backdrop that one might take note of the challenges and shifts in the conceptualization of multilateralism in the past 20 years.

But before one studies these challenges, it is important to take note of an important attempt from within the liberal school to redefine multilateralism in terms of its purpose, if not agency. This came from John Ikenberry's *After Victory*. Here Ikenberry offered a powerful corrective to *Multilateralism Matters*. Like the latter, Ikenberry believes that multilateralism goes hand in hand with American hegemony, as a way of legitimacy. But while *Multilateralism Matters* described *how* the US had pursued multilateralism as the new global hegemon, in *After Victory*, Ikenberry offers an explanation of *why* the US pursued multilateralism. Multilateralism represents a measure of self-restraint, or "institutional self-binding," which generates trust, respect and legitimacy for preponderant US power.

With less emphasis on crude material power, and more on institutions and institutional-binding, Ikenberry argues that a multilateral framework, featuring strategic restraint on the part of the hegemon and institutional bargaining in which the hegemon self-binds in return for loyalty and compliance from weaker and subordinate actors, provides the best framework or durable stability. In such a constitutional order, "power is tamed by making it less consequential."[17] Why does the hegemon resort to such constitutionalism and strategic restraint? The short answer is to "to get the willing participation of and compliance of other states." Because it "has an interest in conserving its power"[18] by offering "to limit its own autonomy and ability to exercise power arbitrarily," the leading state gains recognition and legitimacy.[19]

Despite its attempt to move away from hegemonic framework, the focus is still on the role of the dominant power. Socialization in international relations requires a hegemon. It is the victorious hegemon that crafts the institutional framework in which it can self-bind, and the weaker states merely "accept the deal."[20] The main motivation for weaker states in accepting the hegemon's offer of a constitutional order is that it helps to mitigate their fear of domination or abandonment.[21] Weak states accept constitutional orders if there are credible commitments from the hegemon to refrain from exploitation and domination. The motivations and actions of the leading state in self-binding are "broadly realist" and instrumentalist, i.e. "to preserve and extend its power position into the future." As such, "it is willing to give up some 'returns' on its power in the short run in favor of a great longer-run return on its power."[22]

By focusing on hegemonic initiative, i.e. by looking at the development of constitutional orders from the vantage-point of the hegemon, Ikenberry's model provides a limited range of ways of interaction from which one could derive generalizations about the relationship between power and socialisation, the weak powers accept the hegemon's offer of a constitutional order if there is a credible offer of restraint, and if they are sufficiently motivated by the potential gains such as amelioration of their fear of abandonment and domination; or the weak powers may decide to pursue alternative strategies, such as balancing/bandwagoning. What if the hegemon is not willing to accept self-restraint because it is a strategic predator? Ikenberry's model ignores the possibility that institutions that are created by hegemonic power, even if they are not primarily motivated by a desire to secure their objectives through non-coercive means ("strategic restraint"), may not still be viewed in a benign light by weaker states, whether or not such institutions are threat-oriented (such as NATO or SEATO). Without the support of weaker states, such multilateral institutions would lack legitimacy, and this in itself could become a weapon in the hands of the weaker states with which they could counter institutional designs based on the superior material resources of a great power.

Such a metanarrative of multilateralism leaves out cases in which institutions are created and maintained by weaker states in an effort to manage their relationship, including binding stronger powers on their own terms (OAS and ASEAN). There is no accounting for regional norms that may militate against any form of binding of outside powers. Moreover, because of differing local conditions, material and normative, weaker states may develop alternative institutions that are suited to their own specific goals. Such institutions may not include stronger powers, especially if the objective is management of internal security or development (comprehensive security). Will the stronger powers join if invited? The answer is that materially stronger powers, frustrated by their inability to secure legitimacy for institutions proposed by themselves, may well accept institutional designs that are proposed and developed by weaker states if they serve their common goals. In some cases, stronger powers may accept such institutions even when they may initiate institutional designs that constrain the hegemon.

What happens if the hegemon is defeated in limited wars? Its global hegemony continues, but its local hegemony is undermined, along with the credibility of its commitment. This is not a hypothetical situation, as anyone who has followed the Asian security situation after the Vietnam War should know. So what sort of institutional binding takes place "after defeat," as opposed to "after victory"? Such situations lie outside of Ikenberry's model, but they do provide significant opportunities and incentives for institution-building, especially for weaker states. One of the possibilities in this situation is not "binding" but extrication. Weaker states may develop institutions that seek to keep out all non-local powers – great or middle, hegemon or simply another strong power. ASEAN did this after the Vietnam War. Ikenberry's model does not take into consideration aspirations for regional autonomy. Just as hegemons have the choice of isolation, weaker states can move toward collective autonomy, including through regional institutions.

Multilateralism: old and "new"

The first major challenge to the hegemonic conceptualization of multilateralism came in the post-Cold War period and was especially catalyzed by the concept of "new multilateralism," which evolved through the work of Robert Cox and the *Multilateralism and the United Nations System*.[23] As O'Brien, Goetz, Scholte, and Williams point out, the "new multilateralism" concept made a number of claims: new multilateralism differs from existing notions of multilateralism in three different respects. The first is that it is evolving, rather than a finished product. Second, that it is a bottom–up phenomenon, rather than state-centric; the role of states has to be seen in conjunction with that of social forces, especially civil society groups. The third aspect of "new multilateralism" is its "post-hegemonic organizing," to wit:

> A hegemonic approach to multilateralism takes a dominant set of assumptions about social life and then attempts to universalise the principles through expanding key institutions. For example, hegemonic assumptions might include the primacy of the free markets in the allocation of resources or the naturalness of patriarchal social relations. A post-hegemonic approach to multilateralism must begin with far more modest assumptions. It acknowledges the differences in assumptions about the social world and attempts to find common ground for cooperation. In the place of universalistic principles of neoclassical economics, one is aware of alternative methods of social organizing and cultural diversity.[24]

The hallmark of new multilateralism was not just the embracing of a dynamic and broad scope of multilateralism, but the strong focus of the idea on protest and resistance. This view is especially associated with Cox, but was embraced to different degrees by others in the new multilateralism literature. Hence, as noted and discussed earlier, instead of calling it "post-hegemonic," I would term it as "counter-hegemonic." But here too "new multilateralism" did leave some uncertainties and controversies. Some of these controversies are associated with the concept of a global civil society,[25] the main platform for resistance to the hegemonic world order. Given the diversity of its constituents in terms of locations, issue areas, strategies of mobilization and normative orientations, it is difficult to convince skeptics why the global civil society is any more a coherent and meaningful term than the term "international system" or "International community" that underpins traditional multilateralism. A more appropriate term is transnational civil society which operates across borders, but not necessarily on a global scale. But even then controversies persist over "who elected the NGOs" or the legitimacy of social movements "to substitute for the state."[26] Moreover, given that the leadership and discursive agenda of this new multilateralism was largely centred in the West, new multilateralism was especially susceptible to a "moral cosmopolitanism" bias, which privileged the role of transnational moral agents at the expense of regional or local actors, especially in the non-Western world. For example, the literature on transnational advocacy of human rights, especially the Boomerang model, privileged the role of transnational actors and "paid far less attention to the local embodiments of human rights norms in the developing world."[27] Although in the Boomerang model local groups initiate "the process, their location, obscure language, and marginality have limited scholarly inquiry."[28] Yet, the agency of local civil society groups is critical: "Transnational NGOs and networks can monitor, inform, and advocate all they want, but without serious investments of time and effort by local human rights champions, nothing much will change on the ground."[29]

The new multilateralism concept, however, was somewhat overtaken by two new developments in global affairs. First, for no fault of its own, it was to remain at least for a while more of an aspiration than a reality, because of the appearance of the unipolar moment, and its most extreme manifestation – the unilateral turn of George W. Bush's foreign and security policy, leading to the invasion of Iraq. This led to considerable soul searching and concern about the future of multilateralism as a whole, that is, not just of "new multilateralism" as evident from a volume titled: *Multilateralism Under Challenge?* Although the Bush challenge to multilateralism would be explained by some liberals as the result of a short-term hijacking of US foreign policy by a small power elite, the neocons, rather than as a fundamental deviation from the American commitment to multilateralism, the Iraq invasion did raise the question of whether there was anything really natural or structural about the association of American power and purpose with multilateralism, as one might derive from the conceptual framework of *Multilateralism Matters*. Indeed, some would question the very assumption that power (hence hegemony) matters as much in multilateralism as had been claimed by previous scholars. As the editors of *Multilateralism Under Challenge* (summarizing the chapter by Guzzini) put it, ". . . whilst today many observers suggest that pre-eminent U.S. power is enabling – or perhaps motivating – the country to ignore or undermine [multilateral] institutions, in the past theorists of international relations argued on the contrary that *declining* power resulted in declining support for multilateral institutions and regimes.[30] This supported a fundamental element of new multilateralism, but it did render it more aspirational than might have been the case.

A second aspect of the new multilateralism concept is that while it highlighted resistance mainly through the global society (this being especially true of Cox's formulation) to the Americanocentric concept of hegemonic multilateralism, it was not clear on the role of regional and emerging powers in resisting the prevailing hegemonic multilateralism. This is presumably because the category "emerging powers" did not exist by then. This, after all, was before Goldman Sachs coined the term BRICs. These two developments are closely linked. It was the "rise of the rest" and the end of the unipolar moment that necessitate a rethink at multilateralism. A third issue with the new multilateralism concept was the role of ideational forces, including norms. To be sure, it not only questioned the role of the hegemon's material power, but also, in a truly Gramscian sense, as might be expected from Cox, the hegemon's ideology and social purpose. But what was not clear was the extent to which "normative multilateralism" can be a substitute for multilateralism anchored on material powers or resistance to it, even if it challenges the hegemon's ideology. Also, given that both in the past and even in the post–Cold War period the most globally prominent norms including the emerging norm of Responsibility to Protect (R2P) were the handiwork of Western, if not American power, what might be the role of non-Western states in norm creation? Were they to be regarded as passive recipients of Western norms or active agents of norm creation and propagation?

Multilateralism and the emerging powers

This leads us to a second challenge to hegemonic multilateralism, and a consequent shift in the conceptualization of multilateralism, which occurred in the 2000s and which has to do with the "emerging powers." Here, the shift is not in relation to issue areas (although the G-20, a group which epitomizes the role of emerging powers in multilateralism, has helped to put more focus on financial multilateralism than before), but actors. The concept of emerging powers is hardly coherent or uncontested, but generally refers to the BRICS, the members of the G-20 and other clubs such as IBSA, BRISCAM, etc. And this is a special category of actors. First, the emerging powers discourse has highlighted the functional inadequacies and legitimacy deficits of the existing multilateral system. Second, it has led to demand for and, in at least one instance, the creation of a new multilateral institution (or at least a group, since it is yet to be fully institutionalized). Both are important.

One of the key problems of the earlier multilateralism literature was that it paid much more attention to the role of institutions as the arbiter legitimacy of state action than to the legitimacy of the institutions themselves. The debate over the Iraq war was not about the legitimacy of existing multilateralism, but the legitimacy of action by the US sans multilateralism – the UN's authorization of the use of force. But the emerging powers discourse highlights the issue of the legitimacy within the existing multilateral structure. Here, the issue of legitimacy hinges on improving the representation and decision-making authority of the emerging powers through reform of the UN Security Council, or the voting and leadership structures of the IMF, World Bank, etc. As such, the emerging powers phenomenon challenges not only American, but Western dominance over the traditional post-War multilateralism.

The G-20 has emerged as the key site for attempts to redefine and relegitimize multilateralism today. But questions cloud the legitimacy of the G-20 itself. The G-20's membership criteria remain shrouded in controversy, over the overrepresentation of Europe and non-inclusion of important players in the developing world, such as Egypt and Nigeria. This is especially important if the G-20 is to go beyond its initial role in stabilizing the world financial system, where it has proven its worth, and take on a political and security role, as some proponents advocate.

As the most visible institution of the emerging powers, the G-20 is supposed to represent, as Andrew Cooper put it, "universalistic values": "favoring equity and justice for the less powerful and seeking curtailment of unilateral or plurilateral or coalitional activity by the most powerful."[31] Yet, it is not clear whether the G-20 really embodies these new principles that could be the basis for a post-hegemonic multilateralism. Many of the emerging power members of the G-20 remain beholden to old Westphalian principles of sovereignty, resource mercantilism, and resistant to emerging principles such as the R2P.

A novelty of the G-20 is that its membership is supposed to bridge the traditional North–South divide. Yet, there is the question whether the G-20 itself is representative of the developing world, or the catalysts of a new fault line between the "poor South" and the "power South." Unless and until these issues are addressed, the potential of the emerging powers in general and the G-20 in particular as the catalyst for a post-hegemonic multilateralism will remain unfulfilled.

Yet, at the end of the day, while the influence of the emerging powers may have been exaggerated, it will redefine the existing multilateral framework that has characterized the post-war world order. It is inconceivable that the ongoing redistribution of power will not be accompanied by some form of redistribution of ideas and reshaping of leadership. I would concede, however, that the emerging powers may not be the most powerful source of redefining the existing order. They cannot successfully challenge that order without help from other sites of resistance to that order. One such site is regionalism, itself a changing phenomenon, to which I turn now.

Regionalism and post-hegemonic multilateralism

A third challenge to the dominant post-war conceptualization of multilateralism is but an old challenge; it concerns the relationship between regionalism and multilateralism. If multilateralism is a matter of both interactions and principles, whose interactions and principles might they be? As noted, the literature on multilateralism no longer views it as antithetical to regionalism, but complimentary. At least some forms of regional interactions can be multilateral if they embrace "certain principles." But need they exclusively be American-led global and European-based regional interactions and principles?

The key principle of multilateralism is inclusiveness (which correlates with the notion of indivisibility in Ruggie's 1993 definition).[32] If so, then privileging NATO and the European Union and neglecting regional multilateralism in other parts of the world, a hallmark of hegemonic multilateralism, makes little sense. First, was NATO ever a truly multilateral organization? NATO is based on the principle of collective defence (security against an outside threat), rather than collective security (security against an inside threat) formula, a fact that earlier writers on collective security had correctly recognized,[33] but which Ruggie and others in the post-Cold War had conveniently ignored.[34] One of the foremost writers on collective security, Inis Claude, reminds us that "the label [collective security] has frequently been attached to NATO and other alliances, despite the fact that collective security was originally proposed as a substitute for the alliance system, a way of managing international relations that was deemed incompatible with, antithetical to, and infinitely more promising than the old system that featured competitive alliances."[35] While NATO operates on the basis of indivisibility, that principle is applied only to its members. Despite its post-Cold War expansion of membership and roles, it is not *inclusive* enough to qualify the true meaning of multilateralism, even for the whole of the European region. On the contrary, the continued existence and expansion of NATO might have undermined other, more inclusive security frameworks such as the OSCE

On the other hand, a whole host of regional organizations have been more inclusive and non-discriminatory. With limited exceptions, OAS in the case of Cuba, Africa in the case of South Africa under the apartheid regime, and the Arab League in the case of Israel have been fairly inclusive. In Asia, cited by Ruggie as an antithesis of multilateralism both in the Cold War, they would include ASEAN (in existence since 1967) and "ASEAN-led" regional institutions, which emerged after the end of the Cold War. Asia also defied Ruggie's prognosis in *Multilateralism Matters*, with the creation in 1994 of the ASEAN Regional Forum (ARF), which had been widely called a *multilateral* institution from its inception.[36] The underlying security formula of the ARF and many other regional groups (including the OSCE) is common or cooperative security – different from collective security or collective defence because it does not rely on "security against" an adversary (whether an inside or outside) but "security with" it. As such, common/cooperative security frameworks do not rely on deterrence or military force, but on confidence-building measures, which can be military and political–diplomatic, material as well as normative. Why should this form of cooperation not be recognized as "multilateral"?

A related question is: If multilateralism is to be defined qualitatively as being based on certain principles, should these principles be limited to quintessential liberal principles such as diffuse reciprocity and indivisibility (in the sense of collective security)? Is multilateralism compatible with other norms and principles? What about principles such as non-intervention and equality of states, and, more recently, human security,[37] which militate against the organization of multilateralism on the basis of hierarchy and hegemony? Liberal theorists often assume a close nexus between multilateralism and liberal democracy; hence, it is seen as a distinctive aspect of the leadership of liberal world powers. Yet, this linkage is questionable, as we have seen security communities emerging out of interactions among non-democratic states,[38] and we have seen that some democratic states, at least on some occasions (as the US under George

Bush Jr.) can be anti-multilateral, while authoritarian regimes can be pro-multilateral (Singapore in relation to the global trade regime and the UN). If we define multilateralism as a normative order with a plurality of principles, then the limitations of its Americancentric definition would become clearer. Regional organizations in the Americas, Africa, Asia and the Middle East have pursued inclusiveness. Most have championed other principles such as anti-colonialism, anti-racism, and more controversially, the norms of non-intervention and equality of states.[39] This redefinition of multilateralism has been more commonplace in the literature on regionalism, especially in what has become known as "new regionalism." Here, there is a greater recognition of the diversity of actors, principles and modalities, thereby redressing some of the Eurocentrism of that literature.[40]

Not all forms of regionalism are post-hegemonic. There is a distinct possibility of regionalism emerging within the sphere of influence of a great power or a regionally dominant power. In fact, such forms of regionalism within a great power orbit had been advocated as the solution to the problem of world order by Winston Churchill, Walter Lipmann, and George Liska, among others. Today, some forms of regionalism in West Africa, Southern Africa, Russia and its immediate vicinity, South Asia and the Persian Gulf, are already dominated or risk being dominated by such regional powers. But this type of regional order is likely to turn out to be exclusive and discriminatory, the very opposite of the principles that underpins a genuine multilateral order. Absent such multilateral principles, regional bodies cannot be regarded as multilateral. Asian regional institutions, anchored on ASEAN, are more in tune with post-hegemonic regionalism. Such a role for regionalism and regions is integral to "multilateralism 2.0":

> . . . in multilateralism 2.0, there are players other than sovereign states that play a role and some of these players challenge the notion of sovereignty. Regions are one such type of actor. Conceived by states, other players can have statehood properties and as such aim to be actors in the multilateral system. Regional organizations especially are willing and able to play such a role. But sub-national regions as well increasingly have multilateral ambitions as demonstrated by their efforts towards para-diplomacy. As a result 'international relations' is becoming much more than just inter-state relations. Regions are claiming their place as well. This has major consequences for how international relations develop and become institutionalized, as well as for how international relations ought to be studied.[41]

In the world of emerging powers, regionalism can be a powerful basis for multilateralism. Wedded to the old and new legitimizing multilateral principles of inclusiveness, tolerance of diversity and human security, it can be a powerful new basis for the requirements of legitimacy to have a strong regional basis. While regionalism by itself is not sufficient to fulfill the demand and necessity for multilateralism, it can play an important bridging role between the emerging powers and the multilateral requirements of global governance. Many global issues of today have strong regional roots. Yet not all aspiring global powers who want to reinvent the existing multilateral system are capable of exercising regional leadership. While some emerging powers like Japan after World War II, or Indonesia in ASEAN, take an accommodationist and communitarian approach towards their neighbours, others are known for pursuing a domineering attitude towards their neighbours. Still others fall somewhere in-between. Many emerging powers are embroiled in conflicts within their own neighbourhoods, which undercuts their regional legitimacy. Without regional legitimation, the emerging powers will get bogged down in their own neighborhood problems, and thus undermine their capacity for global leadership. On the other hand, regional legitimation and effective regional leadership will not only free them from such neighbourhood security dilemmas, but also help them prepare better for a global governance role.

Conclusion: multilateralism under the invisible imperium?

While the three challenges to hegemonic multilateralism focusing on the role of the civil society, emerging powers, and regionalism, assumed continued US primacy, the discussion has now shifted to the future of multilateralism in the post–unipolar era, when American power may actually be suffering relative decline. Some hope[42] that the waning of US hegemony is not necessarily a setback for multilateralism because the rules and institutions established by the US have staying power, and even the capacity to co-opt the emerging powers since they could not have emerged without exploiting the benefits of the US–led multilateral order ("Liberal hegemonic order"). In his *Liberal Leviathan*, an elegant variation of the old Hegemonic Stability theory, Ikenberry offers a vision of what I call an *invisible imperium*.[43]

This is a narrative of American Power, essentially what Ikenberry calls the story of "a liberal hegemonic order and the acquiescence and support of other states."[44] This order is known by a variety of names: "liberal hegemonic order,"[45] "American-led liberal world order,"[46] "American-led liberal hegemony,"[47] "free world, the American system, the West, the Atlantic world, Pax Democratica, Pax Americana, the Philadelphia system."[48] I would call it the American World Order. After sketching the origins and evolution of this order, Ikenberry says that this order is now being undermined by three forces: rise of unipolarity, eroded norms of state sovereignty and shifting sources of violence.[49] He describes these challenges as "a crisis of authority."[50] The first of these three may be passé – unipolarity is itself eroding rapidly, but the challenge today is multilpolarity, including emerging powers, perhaps an even more powerful challenge to the liberal world order.[51]

Perhaps the most controversial claim about this order is that despite the crisis it faces, it remains durable.[52] No alternatives – or serious prospect for transformation – have emerged. On the contrary, "the rise of non-Western powers and the growth of economic and security interdependence are creating new constituencies and pressures for liberal international order."[53] The liberal hegemonic order is evolving and needs to change. There are multiple pathways for it to change, but "there are also constituencies that support a continued – if renegotiated – American hegemonic role."[54]

All in all, this selective but hopeful account of the American World Order ignores a good deal of contestation over the world order that even predates the Bush Jr. administration. Ikenberry claims that "The British and American-led liberal orders have been built in critical respects around consent."[55] Two things about this claim are not convincing. The first is that while Ikenberry believes that the contestations about the liberal hegemonic world order are coming about only recently because of the three challenges, I argue that they have always been contested, from both within and outside of that order. In drawing attention to the shifting sources of violence that Ikenberry refers to include privatization of war or the rise of informal violence.[56] This is a reference to the war on terror. But clearly, there have been other redefinitions of security, including human security and climate change that he does not refer to. Also missing from the account is any sense of the North–South divide, and its impact on the past or the emerging world order. And there have been plenty of contestations both within the liberal order – i.e. within the "West" (for example over the Arab-Israeli conflict and the invasion of Iraq) – and more strikingly between the proponents of the American-led order (one of whose names is "the West") and those who have not found it attractive or just, including many from the non-West. The picture of world order is not just of consent but also of contestation and coercion.

While Ikenberry concludes by acknowledging that the American-led liberal order is at least facing a crisis and would require adjustments and undergoing alterations, he does not outline any particular pathway to transformation (the third part of his subtitle). The challenges identified by Ikenberry as crises of American authority, namely the rise of unipolarity, eroded norms of state sovereignty and shifting sources of violence, are not the only challenges to America-led multilateralism. The challenges I have described, i.e. civil society resistance, emerging powers and regionalism, also pose challenges to America-led multilateralism. Ikenberry dismisses the second of these, saying that they would be co-opted. Some of them perhaps, individually. But collectively? Most likely no, especially when combined with the other challenges. Moreover, these three forces – namely, the role of civil society, the emerging powers and regionalism – were suppressed by US dominance. At least they have not had an easy relationship with US hegemony. The US attitude towards each of these elements has not been especially accommodating to them. The US has either opposed or been selective in its support for these elements. The relationship between the US-led multilateralism, especially economic multilateralism (IMF, World Bank, GATT/WTO), and the global civil society has been a hostile one. The US has also been selective in its support for regional multilateralism: supporting it in Europe but not in Asia. In the case of emerging powers, the US has encouraged India's emergence as a world power, while resisting China's to some extent. The US opposes the induction of values other than its own as the basis of refining old multilateralism and creating new multilateral institutions. The decline of the US hegemony could mean redefinition of existing multilateral institutions, encouragement of new forms of multilateralism, including regional multilateralism, and new coalitions of transnational and local actors. It will accentuate the three challenges to hegemonic multilateralism discussed above. While none of these challenges could individually suffice to unseat hegemonic multilateralism, together they could facilitate the transition to a post-hegemonic multilateralism.

Notes

1 A shorter version of this chapter appears as "Post-Hegemonic Multilateralism," in Thomas G. Weiss and Rorden Wilkinson, ed., *International Organization and Global Governance* (New York: Routledge, 2013).
2 Robert W. Cox, "Multilateralism and World Order," *Review of International Studies* 18, no. 2 (1992): 161–180, 180.
3 Robert W. Cox, ed., *The New Realism: Perspectives on Multilateralism and World Order* (New York: St. Martin's Press, 1997).
4 Robert W. Cox, "Civil Society at the Turn of the Millennium: Prospects for an Alternative World Order," *Review of International Studies* 25, no. 1 (1999): 3–28, 27–28.
5 Robert O. Keohane, *After Hegemony: Cooperation and Discord in the World Political Economy* (Princeton: Princeton University Press, 1984).
6 G. John Ikenberry, *After Victory: Institutions, Strategic Restraint, and the Rebuilding of Order after Major Wars* (Princeton: Princeton University Press, 2000), 26.
7 Ikenberry, *After Victory: Institutions, Strategic Restraint, and the Rebuilding of Order after Major Wars*, 29.
8 John Gerard Ruggie, ed., *Multilateralism Matters: The Theory and Praxis of an Institutional Form* (New York: Columbia University Press, 1993), 8.
9 Ibid.
10 Ibid., 9.
11 This tendency is more common now in the literature of international political economy than in security, see: Jagdish Bhagwati, "Regionalism versus Multilateralism," *The World Economy* 15, no. 5 (1992): 535–556. For an overview of the early post-war debate which pitted regionalism against universalism – hence multilateralism, see Francis Wilcox, "Regionalism and the United Nations", *International Organization* 19 (1965): 789–811.
12 Ruggie, *Multilateralism Matters: The Theory and Praxis of an Institutional Form*, 3, 4.
13 Ibid., 4.
14 Donald Crone, "Does Hegemony Matter? The Reorganization of the Pacific Political Economy," *World Politics* 45, no. 4 (1993): 501–525.
15 Amitav Acharya, *Constructing a Security Community in Southeast Asia: ASEAN and the Problem of Regional Order*, 2nd edition (London: Routledge, 2009).
16 In the introductory chapter entitled "Theory of World Politics" in his 1989 book, *International Institutions and State Power*, Robert Keohane confessed that: "An unfortunate limitation of this chapter is that its scope is restricted to work published in English, principally in the United States. I recognize that this reflects the Americanocentrism of scholarship in the United States, and I regret it. But I am not sufficiently well-read in works published elsewhere to comment intelligently on them." Robert Keohane, "Theory of World Politics: Structural Realism and Beyond," in *International Institutions and State Power Essays in International Relations Theory*, ed., Robert O. Keohane (Boulder, Colo.: Westview Press, 1989), 67.
17 Ikenberry, *After Victory: Institutions, Strategic Restraint, and the Rebuilding of Order after Major Wars* (29).
18 Ibid., 53.
19 Ibid., 51.
20 Ibid., 56.
21 Ibid., 51.

22 Ibid., 53.

23 Cox, "Multilateralism and World Order"; Robert W. Cox, ed., *The New Realism: Perspectives on Multilateralism and World Order* (New York: St. Martin's Press, 1997); Michael G. Schechter, ed., *Future Multilateralism: The Political and Social Framework* (London: Palgrave Macmillan, 1999).

24 Robert O'Brien, Anne Marie Goetz, Jan Aart Scholte, and Marc Williams, *Contesting Global Governance: Multilateral Economic Institutions and Global Social Movements* (Cambridge: Cambridge University Press, 2000).

25 Ronnie D. Lipschutz, "Power, Politics and the Global Civil Society," *Millennium: Journal of International Studies* 33, no. 3 (2005): 747–769.

26 O'Brien, Goetz, Scholte, and Williams, *Contesting Global Governance: Multilateral Economic Institutions and Global Social Movements.*

27 James Ron, "Legitimate or Alien? Human Rights Organizations in the Developing World," paper circulated at the Workshops on Religion and Human Rights Pragmatism: Promoting Rights across Cultures, Columbia University, New York, 24 September 2011.

28 Ibid.

29 Ibid.

30 Edward Newman, John Tirman, and Ramesh Thakur, eds., *Multilateralism Under Challenge? Power, International Order, and Structural Change* (New York: United Nations University Press, 2006), 8.

31 Andrew Cooper, "Labels Matter: Interpreting Rising States through Acronyms," in *Rising States, Rising Institutions* eds., Alan S. Alexandroff and Andrew F. Cooper (Waterloo, Ontario, Canada and Washington D.C: The Center for International Governance Innovation and Brookings Institution, 2010), 71.

32 Indeed in another essay, Ruggie offered the following definition of multilateralism: "In its pure form, a multilateral order embodies rules of conduct that are commonly applicable to countries, as opposed to discriminating among them, based on situational exigencies and particularistic preferences . . . The [multilateral] principle in economic relations prescribes an international economic order in which exclusive blocs of differential treatment of trading partners and currencies are forbidden, and in which point-of-entry barriers to transactions are minimized." John Gerrard Ruggie, "Third Try at World Order: America and Multilateralism after the Cold War," *Political Science Quarterly* 109, no. 4 (1994): 556–557.

33 Arnold Wolfers, "Collective Defense versus Collective Security," in *Discord and Collaboration*, ed., Arnold Wolfers (Baltimore: Johns Hopkins University Press, 1962), 181–204.

34 This point was forcefully raised by Mearsheimer in his debate with institutionalists over his "False Promise of International Institutions." Replying to his critics, which included such institutionalists as Ruggie, Keohane and Lisa Martin, Mearsheimer argued "the responses by Ruggie and by Keohane and Martin suggest that a crucial change may be occurring in their thinking about institutions. They make frequent reference to NATO in their responses, which implies that alliances are now a central element in institutionalist theory. Thus, the fact that NATO helped deter the Soviet threat is invoked as evidence that institutions cause peace. However, NATO's success in the Cold War cannot be cited as support for institutionalist theory, because deterrence has virtually nothing to do with the long-standing claims of institutionalist theory." While I disagree with Mearsheimer's overall dismissal of the value of institutions, I agree with him on this point, which is consistent with the classical distinction between collective security and collective defence. John J. Mearsheimer, "A Realist Reply," *International Security* 20, no. 1 (1995), 82–93.

35 Inis L. Claude, "Collective Security after the Cold War," in *Collective Security in Europe and Asia*, ed., Gary L. Guertner (Carlisle Barracks, Pa.: Strategic Studies Institute, US Army War College, 1992), 7–28, http://www.dtic.mil/dtic/tr/fulltext/u2/a249705.pdf, 8. See also Wolfers, "Collective Defense versus Collective Security."

36 Gary J. Smith, *Multilateralism and Regional Security in Asia: The ASEAN Regional Forum*

(ARF) and APEC's Geopolitical Value, Working Paper no. 97-2 (Cambridge, Mass.: Weatherhead Center for International Affairs, Harvard University, 1997; and Amitav Acharya, *Constructing a Security Community in Southeast Asia: ASEAN and the Problem of Regional Order*, 2nd edition (London: Routledge, 2009).

37 Amitav Acharya, "Human Security: East versus West," *International Journal* 56, no. 3 (2001): 442–460.

38 Amitav Acharya, "Collective Identity and Conflict Management in Southeast Asia," in *Security Communities*, eds., Emanuel Adler and Michael Barnett (Cambridge: Cambridge University Press, 1998), 198–227.

39 Amitav Acharya and Alastair Iain Johnston, eds., *Crafting Cooperation: Regional International Institutions in Comparative Perspective* (Cambridge: Cambridge University Press, 2007).

40 Björn Hettne, András Inotai and Osvaldo Sunkel, *Globalism and the New Regionalism* (Basingstoke, U.K.: Palgrave Macmillan 1999).

41 Luk Van Langenhove, "Multilateralism 2.0: The transformation of international relations," United Nations University, 31 May 2011, http://unu.edu/publications/articles/multilateralism-2-0-the-transformation-of-international-relations.html.

42 Keohane, *After Hegemony: Cooperation and Discord in the World Political Economy*; Robert O. Keohane, "Hegemony and After: Knowns and Unknowns in the Debate Over Decline," *Foreign Affairs*, July/August 2012.

43 John Ikenberry, *Liberal Leviathan: The Origins, Crisis, and Transformation of the American World Order* (Princeton: Princeton University Press, 2011).

44 Ibid., 224.

45 Ibid., xi, 224.

46 Ibid., xii.

47 Ibid., 224.

48 Ibid., 35.

49 Ibid., xiii.

50 Ibid., xii.

51 The book feels more like a critique of the Bush Jr. presidency than a long-term analysis of the changing world order as the subtitle suggests.

52 Ikenberry, *Liberal Leviathan: The Origins, Crisis, and Transformation of the American World Order*, 6.

53 Ibid., 6.

54 Ibid., 9.

55 Ibid., 15.

56 Ibid., 251.

7

THE CONTESTED REGIONAL ARCHITECTURE OF WORLD POLITICS[1]

For a long time, the study of regions and regional orders occupied a small, if not insignificant, place in IR theory and scholarship. Now two books have appeared that claim that regions are *central* to our understanding of world politics.[2] Not only have regions become "substantially more important" sites of conflict and cooperation than in the past,[3] they have also acquired "substantial" autonomy from the system-level interactions of the global powers.[4] While globalization has been the buzzword of IR scholars in describing the emerging world order, at most it co-exists with "regionalization,"[5] so much so that "it is now possible to begin more systematically to conceptualize *a global world order of strong regions*"[6] or "*a world of regions.*"[7]

Not all IR scholars may be persuaded by such claims. This reviewer agrees that the study of regional orders, including how regions are constructed and organized, the cultural, political, economic and strategic interactions that occur both within and between them, and the interrelationship between these interactions and the international system at large, are vital to our understanding of how the world works. The two books under review offer conceptual tools and insights to understand these dynamics that ought to be compulsory reading for all scholars of IR. But it disagrees over a central question: *what* makes regions go around? In other words, who determines their shape and role as building blocs of international order?

The two volumes seem to answer this question from their title pages. Regions are defined by powers of various kinds: the sole superpower and its imperium, great powers including "core states" who serve the power and purpose of the imperium, and to a lesser extent, regional powers.[8] This review chapter advances an alternative view, which has received considerably less attention in the literature on regions and regional orders. Power matters, but local responses to power may matter even more in the construction of regional orders. How do regions resist and/or socialize powers is at least as important a part of the story as how powers create and manage regions. Regions are constructed more from within than from without.

This is the central argument of this review chapter. After examining the empirical and theoretical contributions of the two volumes, which are considerable, the final section of this chapter discusses the variety of ways in which regions respond to powers, both at state and societal levels. Overall, the chapter calls for balancing the top-down and power-centric analytical prism found in the two books with an agency-oriented perspective that acknowledges local resistance to, and socialization of, powerful actors and attests to the endogenous construction of regions.

Empirical and theoretical contributions: how power shapes regions

Structuring regions

In *Regions and Powers* (hereafter referred to as *R&P*), the regional structure of international security is shaped by $1+4+x$ distribution of power. At the top is the United States, followed by EU-Europe, Japan, China and Russia, then the rest. This structure is divided into three types of regional spaces. The first is "overlay," where a region is shaped by outside forces (such as the colonialism and superpower rivalry during the Cold War). Such regional spaces have more or less disappeared since the end of the Cold War. The second type is called "unstructured regions." Here regional interactions are not sufficient to generate a discernable structure of interdependence. It may be the residual space left by all the other security complexes (e.g. South Pacific).[9] The third and most important (as well as the most common) are called "regional security complexes" (RSCs), which "refers to the level where states or other units link together sufficiently closely that their securities cannot be considered separate from each other."[10]

There are eleven RSCs in the world, divided into three main categories on the basis of the number of great powers located in them. Three of them are called *centred* (North America, the CIS, and EU-Europe). These are created either by a global level power or some collective institution that allows the RSC to act collectively at the global level. One is a *great power complex* (East Asia), so called because of the presence of more than one global level power. The remaining seven are *standard* (South America, South Asia, Middle East, Horn of Africa, West Africa, Central Africa and Southern Africa). They are characterized by the absence of any global level power in the complex, thereby allowing local polarity to be defined exclusively by regional powers.[11] In sum, power is the central variable in differentiating regions conceptualized as security complexes. One great power makes a *centred* RSC, more than one makes for a *great power* RSC, and having no great power leads to a *standard* RSC, although the last category may have regional-level powers.

In Katzenstein's world of regions, as articulated in his *A World of Regions* (hereafter referred to as *AWR*), only one power really matters. This is the US, which maintains a global presence and whose power and preferences are critical to the shape and functioning of all regions. But a crucial role in this hegemonic order is played by the "core states" of Germany and Japan. These states provide "steady support for American purpose and power while also playing an important role in the region's affairs."[12] *AWR* is thus founded on a dual hierarchy, between the US imperium and the "core" states (Germany in Europe and Japan in Asia), and between the latter and others in their respective regions.

If "regions" in *R&P* are internally interdependent but mutually exclusive security complexes, in *AWR* they are conceptualized as distinctively institutionalized but "porous" spaces hierarchically linked with the core states under an overarching US imperium. Regions are made porous by globalization and internationalization. Globalization is driven by technology, non-territorial actors and processes, such as multilateral corporations and non-governmental organizations, while internationalization is about territorially based exchanges, where national sovereignty is "bargained away," rather than transcended. Since no region is immune to these two processes, there can be no exclusionary and autarchic blocs in Katzenstein's world of regions.

Unlike *R&P*'s global focus, *AWR* concentrates on comparing Europe and Asia. It regards them to be the two most important sites of geopolitical and economic interactions today. Both regions are affected by globalization and internationalization. Hence both are considerably porous. But their regional institutions differ in three ways. European regionalism is more "formal and political" and relies more on "state bargains and legal norms." Asia's is "informal and economic" and relies more heavily on "market transactions and ethnic or national capitalism."[13] A second difference concerns the role of core states: Germany and Japan. Germany is more committed to multilateral action within Europe so much so that its national identity has become Europeanized. By contrast, Japan retains a strong sense of national identity and remains wedded to bilateral over multilateral arrangements.[14] Finally, European and Asian regionalisms differ in terms of their attitudes towards sovereignty. "Europe's regionalism is more transparent and intrusive than Asia's," while "[a]bsent in Asia are the pooling of sovereignty and far-reaching multilateral arrangements that typify Europe's security order."[15]

An important puzzle addressed by *AWR* concerns the question of why Europe developed multilateralism well before Asia did.[16] Here too the role of the United States assumes critical importance, although it was not America's physical power, but its sense of collective identity. In the immediate post-war period, American policy-makers viewed their potential European allies as "relatively equal members of a shared community." By contrast, the potential Asian allies of the US were seen as "an alien and . . . inferior community."[17] The greater sense of a transatlantic community compared to a transpacific one explains why Europe rather than Asia was seen by the US as a more desirable arena for its multilateral engagement.

But *AWR*'s ideational but Americanocentric explanation of why there was no "NATO in Asia"[18] ignores a fundamental difference between Asian and European regionalisms. The emergence of European regionalism consummated the declining legitimacy of nationalism – blamed for two world wars – while in Asia, regionalism was founded on nationalist cross-currents. Unlike in Europe, nationalism and regionalism enjoyed a symbiotic relationship in post-war Asia. Indeed, Japan's approach to security as well as economic regionalism, opting for a "network" style rather than a EC-style formal institutionalist approach, was partly due to its fear of stoking Asian nationalist (anti-Japanese) sentiments that would have accompanied any effort to develop a formal regional group under Japan's leadership. One consequence of *AWR's* "core state" model is the limited attention it gives to the Association of Southeast Asian Nations (ASEAN), which successfully used regionalism in the service of nationalism and sovereignty, and which has been the central institutional building bloc of Asian regionalism. In this important sense, the trajectory of Asian regionalism and its core feature (i.e. it would be led by ASEAN, rather than the US or Asia's major powers), was neither Japan's nor America's choice.

(Re)conceptualizing regions

The two books reflect and advance recent shifts in the literature on how regions are to be conceptualized.[19] As Mansfield and Milner note, regions are increasingly viewed in non-geographic terms. Physical proximity and shared cultural, linguistic, political or economic ties are no longer considered to be a sufficient condition for regionness.[20] Behavioural approaches which employed inductive, quantitative methods to delineate regions[21] have also lost their appeal. The new emphasis is on the social construction of regions. Adler and Crawford argue that regions are not to be conceptualized "in terms of geographic contiguity, but rather in terms of purposeful social, political, cultural, and economic interaction among states which often (but not always) inhabit the same geographical space."[22] Moreover, there has been an increasing tendency to view regions in ideational terms. Regions could express collective identities − self-generated and recognized as such by outsiders.[23] Regionness could also be a function of regionalist ideas and discourses, and the prominence of regions may well depend as much on "representation" as on "reality."[24]

Both books profess a constructivist understanding of regions. *R&P* holds that regional security complexes "are socially constructed by their members, whether consciously or (more often) unconsciously."[25] For *A&R*, "Regions are not simply physical constants," but "express changing human practices."[26] But both reject the view that regions can be simply a product of shared imagination of "imagined communities." Neither book considers social construction to be adequate. It has to be combined with materialist determinants. In *R&P*, the materialist element includes the neorealist-favoured notions of bounded territoriality and distribution of power. This is blended with securitization theory, which focuses on political "speech acts" with which a "security issue is posited (by a securitizing actor) as a threat to the survival of some referent object (e.g. nation, state, the liberal international economic order, the rain forests) claimed to have a right to survive."[27] The book argues for combining neorealist, globalist and regionalist perspectives in understanding post-Cold War global or regional security orders.[28] *AWR* finds the boundaries between materialism/rationalism and constructivism to be thin, and extols "the value of relying on multiple explanatory frameworks" that are "formulated on pragmatic assumptions."[29] It uses "analytic eclecticism," a perspective that draws upon geopolitical, behavioural and constructivist understanding of regions. Instead of testing "the relative explanatory power" of realism ("the material capabilities of the US and the core states"), liberalism ("the relative efficiency of institutional forms built around the core states") and constructivism ("collective identities in European and Asian affairs"), it pulls "selectively from all three in the effort to establish the interconnections between the various processes."[30]

The syncretism of the two volumes extends to the relationship between disciplinary approaches and Area Studies. *R&P* laments the tendency among area specialists to focus on the cultural uniqueness of their respective regions and reject comparative studies. By contrast, IR theories aspire to a global reach and systematizing capability, which neglect the regional level. The RSC theory (RSCT) is supposed to provide a way out of this by sharply distinguishing between the regional and the global levels, while at the same time focusing on "self-defining regional dynamics" (requiring Area Studies knowledge) in a world-wide setting of mutually exclusive regions (requiring the help of theory).[31] *AWR* acknowledges that "exclusive specialization in a particular area . . . misses the connections between developments in different parts of the world." But Area Studies is crucial for analyzing transnational relations. It offers "contingent generalizations that go beyond specific locales" and thus compensates for the "superficial and speculative" connections that strictly disciplinary perspectives make "to the variegated experiences of various parts of the world."[32]

The conceptualization of regional dynamics found in the two volumes is not without problems. The Waeverian constructivist facade of *R&P* sits uneasily atop its Buzantine neo-realist foundation. Geography and geopolitics still rule. Although regions change,[33] they cannot change too much. It would be extremely rare for a RSC to travel the distance from being anarchic (conflict formation) to become a security community.[34] What then are we to make of the transformations in EU-Europe, and to a lesser extent in Southeast Asia and the Southern Cone? Norms have no place in RSCT. The role of regional institutions as agents of transformation gets limited attention. As such, the line between RSCT and neorealism becomes blurred. *R&P* even offers to make RSC Theory (RSCT) the "fourth tier" of neo-realism, provided the latter can "accept the importance of the regional level and its distinct shaping effects."[35]

By giving more play to the role of identity, *AWR* raises possibilities for deeper regional transformation. National and regional identities, the product of historical memory, cultural flows and political action by elites, are not constant, but subject to reinterpretation and alteration.[36] When a regional identity emerges, it need not replace national, sub-national, and local identities. The two can co-exist, and may even complement one another. Hence, it is possible for former enemies to become friends, and for security communities to replace historical patterns of anarchy and disorder.

But *AWR* 's analytic eclecticism, which allows it to discuss the role of US power as well as its sense of collective identity, gives little space to ideational variables, which speak essentially to local agency. These include the anti-colonial ideologies of regional groups in the developing world, regionalist ideas (e.g. pan-Arabism, pan-Africanism, pan-Americanism) and personalities (e.g. Monnet in Europe, Nehru and Sukarno in Asia, Bolivar in Latin America, Nasser in Egypt, and Nkrumah in Africa).

Another gap in the conceptualization of the regional architecture of world politics common to both books may be noted. Both extensively discuss the vertical relations of regions, i.e. between regional and global powers, but there is not enough on the horizontal relationship between regions. To identify and compare regions is not necessarily to study their interrelationship. Neither volume tells us much about inter-regional flows (especially important given *AWR*'s insistence that regions are not autarchic blocs), as well as their relationship of emulation and learning, including the demonstration effects of one type of regionalism on another.[37] Yet the question of emulation becomes more important with the growing attention to the global diffusion of the norms and practices of the European Union.[38]

Ordering regions

A *central* and complex question for those theorizing about the regional architecture of world politics is how regions produce order. As Alagappa notes, while order is a "slippery" concept in international relations, and can be used in "multiple ways," policy-makers and academics use the term as though its meaning were self-evident. Very few define the concept or even clarify how it is used."[39] Neither book rises to the occasion.

International relations scholars have used the concept of order (international and regional) in two main ways. The first refers to it "as a description of a particular status quo."[40] Here, order means an existing distribution of power or institutional arrangement, irrespective of its consequences for peace or conflict. The second usage has more normative content; it refers to increased stability and predictability, if not peace per se. Hedley Bull defined international order as "a pattern of activity that sustains the elementary or primary goals of the society of states, or international society."[41] He identified the goals towards which the pattern of activity is geared: preservation of the state system, maintaining the sovereignty or independence of states, relative peace or absence of war as normal conditions among states, limitation of violence, keeping of promises and protection of property rights.[42] Bull's conception of international order informs the concept of order at the regional level. Thus, Morgan defines regional order as "dominant patterns of security management within security complexes."[43] Alagappa stresses "rule governed interaction," that is, "whether interstate interactions conform to accepted rules."[44]

Both books seem to use regional order in its descriptive sense as a particular type of arrangement. In *R&P*, we do not get a generic definition of regional order, but only identification of possible types of regional orders: collective security, alliance, concert, regime, and security community, as well as hierarchical orders built around great powers.[45, 46] But how do different types of RSCs (standard, centred, Great Power, etc.) that the book spends so much time explicating correlate with these specific types of orders? *R&P* offers an elaborate schema for identifying security complexes, but as Lake and Morgan point out, "Regional security complexes . . . are distinct from regional orders. The existence of security externalities linking states together does not itself define the way in which those states seek to manage their security relations."[47] Regional order cannot be conflated with the structural and institutional forms of regions. Is there a causal relationship between a particular type of RSC and a particular type of regional order? There is a hint that institutionally centered RSCs are likely to produce security communities.[48] What sort of security order would a great power RSC or a standard RSC produce? South America is a standard RSC and a security community. Southeast Asia is a standard RSC, but it is only a security regime. East Asia is a centred (through a great power) RSC and a security regime. In other words, the structural schema proposed by *R&P* is not very helpful in telling us what type of security order will emerge from different types of RSCs. To understand how RSCs produce regional order, therefore, we need to know how and why actors within a RSC go for a certain approach to conflict management. It cannot simply be inferred from the descriptive features of a RSC.

Here, Katzenstein's institutionalist approach is more helpful. While regions should not be conflated with regional institutions, the existence, design and performance of regional institutions can tell us much about the conditions and prospects of regional order, including protection of sovereignty, prospects for conflict management and rule-governed behaviour among states. Institutions in this sense reflect as well as shape the state of regional peace and stability. But uncertainty exists in *AWR* about how different institutional forms relate to regional order. Since *AWR* establishes clearly that European regionalism is more institutionalized and less sovereignty-bound than Asia's, does it then mean that Europe has more regional order? The book could, but chooses not to, make such a claim, mindful of Katzenstein's own earlier warning that in comparing the two regionalisms it would be "a great mistake to compare European 'success' with Asian 'failure'. Such a Eurocentric view invites the unwarranted assumption that the European experience sets the standard by which Asian regionalism should be measured."[49]

Nonetheless, more attention to variations among regional institutions and the implications of these variations for conflict management could be a productive avenue for further research on regional orders. For example, a recently completed comparative study of regional institutions looks not only at why regional institutions differ in terms of their design, but also how these differences correlate with their effectiveness, including their role in ensuring regional order (peace and stability).[50] One of the findings of the project is that if effectiveness is measured in terms of the ability of a regional institution to achieve its "set goals," then regional institutions with less formal and binding rules have helped to preserve the state system and maintain the independence of states – the key "set goal" of all regional institutions in the Third World. This supports Katzenstein's view that one should not think of EU-style supranationalism as the only model of success that other regional institutions ought to emulate. Another finding of the project, however, is that the distribution of power is not a key factor in the effectiveness of regional institutions in promoting peace and order. Regional institutions created by great powers or regional powers are not necessarily more effective in limiting violence and generating rule-governed interactions than those created by small or weak states.[51]

This leads to the main question raised in the introduction, which has to do with the relationship between regions and power, the possibility of regions without hegemonic construction, and regional orders where local responses to powerful actors play a defining role.

The missing picture: how regions shape power

Regions and hegemony

The idea of a regionalized world order suggests not only that regions are becoming more important sites of international interactions, but also that they enjoy relative autonomy from system-level forces. While both books accept that regions are to a large extent social constructs, their answers to the question "who constructs regions" reflect a great power bias, especially with Buzan and Waever's (*B&W*) 1+4+x matrix and *AWR*'s focus on the American imperium. How can regions have autonomy if great powers and the sole superpower play such a dominant role in shaping them?

R&P argues that regional dynamics need not follow global power interactions. But is this disjuncture simply a product of great power design, indifference, overstretch or domestic isolationism? Or is it shaped by the normative preferences, if not the physical resistance of the regional actors? *R&P* allows that the US "can remove itself (or be removed)" from Europe, East Asia and South America.[52] But this tantalizing prospect, notwithstanding who or what can remove the US from the regional worlds, is unfortunately not explored further.

In *AWR*, it is the "U.S. policy [that has] has made regionalism a central feature of world politics."[53] Even globalization and internationalization, central processes that make regions porous, often work "in accordance with the power and purpose of the American imperium."[54] Yet, this overstates the role of the US as a consistent promoter of regionalism and regional institutions around the world. The continental organizations of the post-war era, the League of Arab States and the Organization of African Unity (now African Union), were not a product of US policy, but expressions of local nationalisms (e.g. pan-Arabism, pan-Africanism) with a general anti-Western, if not specifically anti-US, bias. And some parts of the world have developed regionalism in opposition to US preferences. In Southeast Asia, ASEAN was formed and emerged as an indigenous alternative to the Southeast Asian Treaty Organization (SEATO), a regional alliance sponsored by the US.[55] Another recent example would be the idea of security multilateralism in Asia, represented by the ASEAN Regional Forum (ARF), an idea which Bush Sr. administration had opposed as a "solution in search of a problem."[56]

What about the influence of regions on the US? Is that another measure of regional autonomy? For *AWR*, "the American imperium shapes and is shaped by porous regions."[57] It puts forward a "two-way Americanization" thesis, which holds that while America changes others, "others change America, at home and abroad."[58] But does America really learn from others, as should be the case with any genuine "two-way" influence and feedback situation?

For *AWR*, changing US public attitudes towards security, including the general public support for pre-emption (at least before and during the early stages of the war against Iraq) evident in America's response to the 9/11 attacks, is an example of "two-way Americanization." This shows that just as the US can and does shape regional orders around the world, "that world has the capacity to react, often with a complex mixture of admiration and resentment and occasionally with violent fury – thus remaking America."[59] To this writer, however, anti-Americanism fuelled by the resentment of US dominance that might have contributed to the 9/11 attacks is not "feedback," but "blowback." The Bush Jr. administration's reaction to that resentment through a nationalistic, unilateralist and assertive foreign policy and security approach can hardly be construed as a case of America learning from others, or adapting the ways of others. *AWR* does not deal with the variety of ways in which the role of the US might be challenged from within regions, including Asia and Europe.

Emphasis on the role of great powers in the creation of regional orders is not unusual in the IR literature. Indeed, the latter often privileges the influence of such powers.[60] Mearsheimer sees a natural and inevitable tendency among great powers towards coercive regional domination.[61] Cooper and Taylor hold that great powers shape regional institutions in a way that gives weaker states little choice but to join, even when not joining may be preferable.[62] Grieco's argument that great powers may actually undermine the regional integration efforts of weaker states, rather than use them as a means of legitimation, also suggests that power matters much in shaping regional order.[63] Even liberal–constructivist perspectives acknowledge the hegemonic construction of regions. Ikenberry posits that hegemonic states may develop consensual and benign international orders with weaker states, with a view to legitimize the power differential.[64] His notion of "self-binding" suggests, however, that it is the hegemonic actor, rather than the weaker states, that shapes and tailors the terms of cooperation, although this could coincide with the interests of the weaker states.

Power matters in the construction of regional orders, but local responses to power may be more important. As Mittleman and Falk note: "Just as regionalism functions as a hegemonic strategy for the United States, it may also provide space for a variety of counter-hegemonic projects."[65] Acharya and Hettne discuss regionalisms by weaker states aimed at challenging the dominance of great powers, and/or socializing them through norm-setting.[66] Further research into and discussion of how regions respond to powerful actors, both within and outside, is crucial to establishing their relative autonomy and hence to any theoretical claim about the regional reordering of world politics.

In the following sections, I highlight six types of regional responses to power (not mutually exclusive) which shape regional order by influencing the role of outside and regional powers (Figure 7.1, illustrated with examples from Asia).

Regions and autonomy

Boxes 3 and 4 in Figure 7.1 may overlap, as minor states/powers may adopt exclusion and binding strategies directed simultaneously at both extra-regional and regional powers.

Overlap between Boxes 1 and 2 is possible where a regional power develops a sphere of influence directed not just at extra-regional powers, but also a regional power rival.

The first type of response (Box 1) may be led by a great power located within the region. One possibility here is normative dissent, if not outright physical challenge, by the "core states" – Germany in Europe and Japan in Asia – that currently serve the interests of the US imperium.[67] As American soft power dissipates, normative dissonance between the core states and the US has grown. If unchecked, it could possibly lead to the former's defection, or at least abandonment of some of their functions as core states. Europe's opposition to the US invasion of Iraq was led

	Responses initiated by regional powers	Responses initiated by minor states/powers in the region	Societal responses
Extra-regional power, targeted	1. Normative dissent (e.g. Opposition to US diplomacy) New spheres of influence (e.g. Sino-centric Asian order)	3. Resistance (e.g. Opposition to SEATO)* Exclusion (e.g. ASEAN's ZOPFAN)** Socialization/Binding (China and the US in ARF)***	5. Anti-globalization/Anti-Americanism
Regional power, targeted	2. Regional rivalry between emerging regional power vs. US-backed existing regional power (e.g. Sino-Japanese rivalry)	4. Resistance (e.g. Opposition to Chinese sphere of influence) Exclusion (e.g. ASEAN's ZOPFAN) Socialization/Binding (e.g. China and Japan in ARF)	6. Challenging legitimacy (e.g. Anti-Japanese and anti-Chinese protests and riots)

* South East Asia Treaty Organization
** Zone of Peace, Freedom and Neutrality
*** ASEAN Regional Forum

FIGURE 7.1 Regional responses to powers

not only by France, but also by Germany. In East Asia's case, Japan remains within the US security orbit. But it has shown a willingness to organize its own economic region, especially during the aftermath of the Asian financial crisis in 1997 when it proposed an Asian Monetary System to counter the US-dominated IMF.[68]

Another type of challenge to the American imperium could be a sphere of influence by an organized great power located within the region (Box 1, second row). Such regional spheres of influence can be either benign/open or coercive/closed. Kupchan envisages the possibility of "benign regional unipolarity," which would presumably remain open to rival great powers.[69] In Asia, Kang foresees a stable Sino-centric regional order that revives the tradition of economic exchange and geopolitical practices of the old tributary system (although it is not clear whether such an order will be open to non-Asian powers such as the US, which did not exist during the tributary system).[70] On the other hand, some analysts have described China's relationship with the region, especially Southeast Asia, as a "centre-periphery" relationship, or a Chinese Monroe Doctrine that might challenge and isolate US power.[71] Richard Armitage, Deputy Secretary of State under the first Bush Jr. administration, has described East Asian regionalism as a "thinly-veiled way to make the point that the US is not totally welcomed in Asia . . . It seems that China is quite willing to be involved in fora that do not include the US."[72]

The primacy of the American imperium may also be challenged indirectly by intra-regional rivalries, in which an emerging regional power challenges the influence of the "core state" serving US power and purpose (Box 2). Contemporary Sino-Japanese rivalry illustrates this possibility for Asia. This leads to a larger point in contemporary Asia – a vital arena of the emerging regional architecture of world politics, the sudden slippage of US power, the rise of China, Japan, and India, and the growing interdependence and interaction among Asian countries – may redefine regional order in ways not anticipated by the two books.

For example, India's rising power and growing interaction with East Asia may call into question not only *AWR*'s scant attention to India as a force in *East Asian* regional order, but also *R&P*'s designation of India as a regional, rather than a global-level power (hence the designation of South Asia as a *standard*, rather than *Great Power* security complex), and the separation of the South Asian security complex from the East Asia one. As regards the role of China, while it is far from imposing a "Monroe Doctrine" in Southeast Asia, Beijing is already challenging Japanese influence there through its growing economic and political clout, as well as diplomatic "charm offensive."

Katzenstein discusses the role of *overseas* Chinese networks, but the emerging pattern of Asian regionalism could be based on China's *own* economic linkages and influence as it reshapes the Asian division of labour. Already it is China, rather than Japan, which is the largest single trading partner of Asian states.[73] Regional production networks in East Asia are increasingly China-oriented as the result of foreign enterprises using China as an assembly platform for components of finished products. The emerging China–ASEAN free trade area (FTA) covers a total population of some 1.7 billion people and a combined GDP of about US$2 trillion. For China, while ASEAN's market of more than 500 million people and rich natural resources are important considerations behind its drive for an FTA with ASEAN, trade liberalization also offers potential political benefits. China can exploit it to replace Japan as the primary driving force for economic growth and integration. Indeed, China's likely political gains from its proposed FTA with ASEAN might have prompted Japan to propose its own trade initiative in the region. China's interest in an FTA with ASEAN is also challenging to the US, and puts paid to any remaining hope of Washington promoting free trade through the Asia-Pacific Economic Cooperation (APEC).

Against this backdrop, *AWR* goes a bit too far in affirming the relative importance of Japan over China in shaping Asian regional order.[74] The focus on Japan as the architect of Asian regionalism had more validity for the 1970s to 1990s period. But the rise of China and India is likely to spur new and different types of regionalisms in Asia, ones less closely wedded to US power and purpose. Asian regional order will be shaped less by Japan acting as a core state within the American imperium and more by a fluid and complex pattern of regional interactions featuring the consolidation of China's ties with selected states in its periphery on the one hand, and an informal coalition of Japan, Australia, India and the US on the other.[75]

The dilution of American hegemony and Japan's role as its main agent may be accentuated by changes occurring to the "San Francisco system" of US bilateral alliances, the main basis of its strategic pre-eminence in Asia which also cushioned Japan's role in Asian regionalism. A variety of factors – the rise of complex transnational threats which cannot be handled through exclusionary alliances (not the least because they require the cooperation of China), the emergence of cooperative security ("security with" as opposed to "security against") norms through regional institutions like the ARF, the emergence of India and Singapore as de facto US allies outside of the San Francisco system, and domestic popular discomfort in allied nations such as South Korea and the Philippines with US military presence – challenges the traditional integrity and importance of the San Francisco system, with the US–Japan security alliance as its cornerstone.[76]

Another type of regional state-based responses to power would feature attempts by a region's "minor" states to resist, exclude or socialize/bind stronger powers. Such strategies may be applied to either outside (Box 3) or regional powers (Box 4), or both at the same time.

Resistance: the minor states of the region may offer direct physical resistance to outside or regional powers (or both) themselves. The resistance of Frontlines States of Africa to the apartheid regime, the Arab League's disjointed but durable resistance to America-backed Israel, the Gulf Cooperation Council's (GCC) security measures against Iran and Iraq, and ASEAN's resistance to Soviet-backed Vietnam's attempt at sub-regional dominance are examples of intra-regional resistance.[77] Regional resistance to power may also be normative. In Asia, intrusive US policies have been challenged by states which remain deeply wedded to Westephalian sovereignty. In the case of Europe, Francis Fukuyama, who proclaimed "the end of history" after the Cold War was over, now doubts "whether the West is really a coherent concept," since "an enormous gulf has opened up in

American and European perceptions about the world, and the sense of shared values is increasingly frayed."[78] The EU challenges the American imperium in various ways: first, through normative dissent (at least over multilateralism, even if one does not accept Kagan's more dramatic characterization of these differences);[79] second, by increasingly self-organizing its own defence so as to lessen, if not eliminate, security dependence on the United States; and third, by providing an alternative source of peace operations (peacekeeping, humanitarian intervention and nation-building) in out-of-area locations (Aceh, Bosnia, Kosovo, etc.). Similar resistance to the US could emerge in Asia as the region begins to self-organize its political and economic space and develop regional peace operations mechanisms and capabilities.

Exclusion: regional coalitions of weaker states or minor powers may act cooperatively to reduce the scope for intrusion by stronger powers in their region's affairs. This has been an important common feature of many regional organizations in the Third World that have resisted or attempted to regulate outside power intervention in their regions through norms of non-intervention and proposals for zones of peace and neutrality.[80] Examples include the idea of the Indian Ocean as a Zone of Peace and ASEAN's Zone of Peace, Freedom and Neutrality (ZOPFAN, proposed in the 1970s with a view to keep Southeast Asia "free from any form or manner of interference by outside Powers"). Another category of examples would be several established or proposed regional nuclear-weapon-free zones in the South Pacific, Southeast Asia (negotiated but not ratified by the nuclear powers) and the Persian Gulf (proposed but not negotiated, the targets being Iran and Israel).[81] Although the success of such initiatives in excluding outside powers has been limited, they do create pressures for restraint on the part of the latter, sometimes with voluntary initiatives so as to reduce provocations to the regional states.

Binding: a relatively more successful approach is the attempts by the less powerful states of a region to pursue socialization/binding strategies directed at both outside and regional powers. Ayoob suggests that success in regional order-building depends on "a consensus regarding the role of the pivotal power within the regional grouping, a consensus shared by the pivotal power itself."[82] This consensus characterizes Indonesia's role in ASEAN and Saudi Arabia's within the GCC, but not India's in South Asia. The future of regional order of East Asia may well depend on such a consensus regarding the role of China. Regional institutions are an important means in the hands of weaker and smaller regional powers to *socialize* and constrain stronger powers. Latin American regionalism in the early twentieth century offers a good example of such binding, when the US accepted the non-intervention principle, thereby ending the Monroe Doctrine in exchange for the participation by Latin American states of the US-led regional security order – the Inter-American System.[83] In more recent times, the power of the US over its regional neighbours (both North America and South America) has been reduced as the result of growing institutional enmeshment.[84] In Asia, the creation of the ARF was an initiative of the weaker states of the region and was intended to engage and socialize both the US and China into a system of regional order and thereby dampen their mutual rivalry.[85]

Regional response to power can also be found at the societal level directed at both the global hegemon (Box 5) and great/regional powers (Box 6). *AWR*'s discussion of Americanization and anti-Americanism in Europe and Asia generated by the invasion of Iraq and the war on terror is a welcome departure from *R&P*'s plainly state-centric perspective. For *AWR*, however, globalization and internationalization provide "both a common foil of anti-Americanism and a common experience of Americanization."[86] Yet, society-level anti-Americanism is a much more enduring phenomenon, precisely because much of it is rooted in the perceived inequities and injustices of globalization that are structurally linked to the US imperium.[87] Anti-Americanism may bring together a broad range of social forces challenging internationalization and globalization (and hence the American imperium) and networking, among whom constitutes an alternative form of regionalism. This is a hallmark of "new regionalism." Hettne notes: "Whereas the old [regionalism] was concerned with relations between nation-states, the new [regionalism] formed part of a global structural transformation in which also a variety of non-state actors were operating at several levels of the global system."[88]

As with the global hegemon, regional powers (or aspiring ones) can be targets of society-level resistance (Box 6), which may be even more influential in shaping the prospects for regional order. *AWR*, which discusses anti-Americanism extensively and fully accounts for the integrative role of Japanese capital (as well as the legitimizing influence of Japanese cultural products and cultural diplomacy) and the key place of overseas Chinese production networks in Asian regional order, offers surprisingly little discussion of anti-Japanese and anti-Chinese protests in the region. Societal resistance to regional powers could be inspired by local resentment against their economic and political dominance. It could also represent a reaction led by civil society actors against globalization (and its regional variant, regionalization), especially if the regional powers, like the US itself, are seen as fuelling the inequities and injustices of globalization.

There are two main kinds of societal resistance to regional powers. Just as some forms of societal anti-Americanism are sanctioned by the regional powers (such as China sanctioning and/or tolerating anti-American demonstrations), societal resistance to regional powers could be instigated (often quietly) by a rival regional state (some of the recent anti-Japanese demonstrations in China may fall into this category). Another kind of resistance represents grassroots sentiments mobilized by non-governmental organizations and nationalist pressure groups. Examples in East Asia would include past anti-Indian riots in Burma, anti-Japanese riots in Indonesia under Suharto, recent anti-Chinese riots in Malaysia and Indonesia and rising anti-Japanese sentiments and demonstrations in Korea and China. The role of ethnic minorities in regional relations and the problem of anti-ethnic riots did form part of the agenda of early Asian regionalist efforts, such as the Asian Relations Conference of 1947, and affects the prospects for regional community-building in East Asia today.[89]

The main rationale for studying regional responses to power is to compensate for the top-down view of power-constructed regions that the two volumes under review present. Such a perspective also gives short shrift to regionalist ideas and discourses. But these play a central role in the endogenous construction of regions. As Iver Neumann puts it, the conceptualization of regions must pay attention to its nature as a "cognitive construct shared by persons in the region themselves."[90] Despite mentioning discourses about national identity in India and European Identity,[91] *R&P* dismisses "local discourses about regionalism"[92] in the making of regional orders. This undercuts its claim that regions are socially constructed through securitization and desecuritization processes. After all, local discourses about regionalism may contain "speech acts" central to securitization theory. *AWR* speaks of regional identity in terms of history, culture and institutionalization, but discounts their creation as "ideological constructs."[93] Nonetheless regionalist ideas and discourses are an important part of region-building. To quote Alexander Murphy, "As social constructions, regions are necessarily ideological and no explanation of their individuality or character can be complete without explicit consideration of the types of ideas that are developed and sustained in connection with the regionalization process."[94] While an "ideas all the down" approach to regional definition may not be called for, regionalist ideas do determine who is included and excluded from regions and explain why membership of regional institutions may not coincide with the recognized geographic boundaries of regions. In other words, regions, like nation-states, are to some extent imagined communities.[95] They can be constructed through both discourses and socialization processes.

Conclusion

The two volumes have presented us with a range of new and challenging ideas about how to conceptualize and study the emerging regional architecture of world politics. As such, they made a substantial contribution that no student of regional order can afford to miss. But further work is needed to develop a more complete understanding of regional orders. This chapter has focused on one key area for further research: the relationship between regions and powerful actors from outside and within. This involves identifying the conditions that lead regions to challenge external influence and theorizing about the different forms such resistance can take, both at state and societal levels. One should also pay attention to how regions socialize powerful actors on their own terms, rather than simply playing to the hegemon's tune. Study of these dynamics is ultimately crucial to understanding the endogenous construction of regions. Other areas of further research include the relationship between regional structures/institutions and regional order. Scholars of regional order should also pay more attention to inter-regional (region-to-region, as opposed to just global-to-regional) dynamics. Both of these are neglected in the two books under review, yet they play an important role in determining whether regions truly matter in world politics.

Finally, in contributing to a theory of regional orders, the two books have much to learn from each other. The statist and materialist orientation of RSCT (*R&P*) can benefit from the close attention to society, culture and identity found in *AWR*. *R&P*'s emphasis on securitization can be usefully complemented by *AWR*'s attention to socialization. A theory of regional order should combine the former's elaborate structural schema with the latter's attention to process politics. *AWR*'s stress on the dynamic long-term variables of regional orders such as globalization, internationalization and economic interdependence can enrich security complex theory, which needs to pay more attention to the economics–security nexus. In a similar vein, *AWR*'s framework can usefully borrow from the rich descriptions and conceptualization of different types of regional structures so that it can look beyond a world of regions that is constituted mainly by core states serving US power and purpose.

Notes

1 Originally published as "The Emerging Regional Architecture of World Politics: A Review Essay," *World Politics* 59, no. 4 (July 2007): 629–652.
2 Barry Buzan and Ole Waever, *Regions and Powers: The Structure of International Security* (Cambridge: Cambridge University Press, 2003; Peter J. Katzenstein, *A World of Regions: Asia and Europe in the American Imperium* (Ithaca: Cornell University Press, 2005).
3 Buzan and Waever, *Regions and Powers*, 10; Katzenstein, *A World of Regions*, 24. Another important work that makes a similar claim is David A. Lake and Patrick M. Morgan, "The New Regionalism in Security Affairs," in *Regional Orders: Building Security in a New World*, eds., D. Lake and P. Morgan (University Park: Pennsylvania State University Press, 1997), 7.
4 Buzan and Waever, *Regions and Powers*, 4.
5 Katzenstein, *A World of Regions*, 21, 41–2.
6 Buzan and Waever, *Regions and Powers*, 20 (emphasis added).
7 Despite agreement on these basic points, the two books differ in significant ways. *Regions and Powers* covers all the major regions of the world, while *A World of Regions* focuses on Europe and Asia, with a concluding chapter that discusses how its framework applies to other regions – South Asia, Middle East, Latin America and Africa. The thematic scope of *A World of Regions* is wider, incorporating the economics-security nexus and the role of culture and identity in shaping regional interactions. *Regions and Powers* concentrates on security dynamics.
8 Katzenstein uses the terms "imperium" (i.e. the combination of America's territorial and nonterritorial power) and "core states" (Japan and Germany); while Buzan and Waever stick to more traditional categories such as superpower, great power and regional power.
9 I disagree with the characterization of the South Pacific as an "unstructured region." It has a fairly active regional institution, the South Pacific Forum, and the relatively small size of most of its member states creates a shared vulnerability and engenders a sense of security interdependence.
10 Buzan and Waever, *Regions and Powers: The Structure of International Security*, 43. The notion of regional security complex has evolved since Buzan first proposed it in 1983. Then, RSCs designated only areas of intense rivalry (e.g. India–Pakistan; Arab–Israel, North and South Korea), ignoring regions where the main pattern of relationship is cooperative. Barry Buzan, "A Framework for Regional Security Analysis," in *South Asian Insecurity and the Great Powers*, eds., Barry Buzan and Gowher Rizvi (London: Croom Helm, 1986), 8. In the new formulation, they may vary from anarchy ("conflict formations") to "security communities," where war has been rendered unthinkable.
11 There are other types of complexes. *Supercomplexes* are a number of RSCs bound together by one or more great powers who generate "relatively high and consistent levels of interregional security dynamics." *Subcomplexes* are similar to RSCs, but are firmly embedded within a larger RSC. *Precomplexes* are potential RSCs, or RSCs in the

making, but where bilateral relationships have not yet reached the level of interdependence to qualify as a full-fledged RSC. *Protocomplexes* occur when the degree of security inter-dependence within a region is sufficient to differentiate it from its neighbours, but the overall regional security dynamics remains thinner and weaker than a fully fledged RSC. (Buzan and Waever, *Regions and Powers: The Structure of International Security*, 490–492) Finally, a 'mini-complex' is a RSC in small-scale, composed at least partly of substate actors.

12 Katzenstein, *A World of Regions*, 237.
13 Katzenstein, *A World of Regions*, 27, 219.
14 Katzenstein, *A World of Regions*, 36.
15 Katzenstein, *A World of Regions*, 219, 125.
16 Katzenstein, *A World of Regions*, 50–60.
17 Christopher Hemmer and Peter J. Katzenstein, "Why Is There No NATO in Asia: Collective Identity, Regionalism, and the Origins of Multilateralism," *International Organization* 56, no. 3 (2002), 575–607, 575.
18 Beyond the US role, *AWR* identifies state power, regime type and state structures as the factors that make Asian regionalism different from Europe's. Katzenstein, *A World of Regions: Asia and Europe in the American Imperium*, 220. European regionalism is a regionalism of relatively equal neighbours, of similar regime types and of states with well-functioning bureaucracies. Intra-Asian relations are more hierarchical, Asian political regimes differ widely and Asian states are "non-Weberian" in the sense that "rule by law" rather than "rule of law" prevails.
19 On the various ways of defining regions, see: Louis J. Cantori and Steven L. Spiegel, eds., *The International Politics of Regions: A Comparative Approach* (Englewood Cliffs, N.J.: Prentice Hall, 1970); William R. Thompson, "The Regional Subsystem: A Conceptual Explication and a Propositional Inventory," *International Studies Quarterly* 17, no. 1 (1973): 89–117; Andrew Hurrell, "Regionalism in Theoretical Perspective," in *Regionalism in World Politics*, eds., Louise Fawcett and Andrew Hurrell (Oxford: Oxford University Press, 1996); Iver Neumann, "A Region-Building Approach to Northern Europe," *Review of International Studies* 20, no. 1 (1994): 53–74; Kanishka Jayasurya, "Singapore: The Politics of Regional Definition," *The Pacific Review* 7, no. 4 (1994): 411–20; Mitchell Bernard, "Regions in the Global Political Economy: Beyond the Local-Global Divide in the Formation of the Eastern Asian Region," *New Political Economy* 1, no. 3 (1996): 335–353; Hari Singh, "Hegemonic Construction of Regions: Southeast Asia as a Case Study," in *The State and Identity Construction in International Relations*, ed., Sarah Owen (London: Macmillan, 1999); Amitav Acharya, *The Quest for Identity: International Relations of Southeast Asia* (Singapore: Oxford University Press, 2000); Alexander Murphy, "Regions as Social Constructs: The Gap Between Theory and Practice," *Progress in Human Geography* 15, no. 1 (1991): 23–35; and Raimo Varynen, "Regionalism: Old and New," *International Studies Review* 5, no. 1 (2003): 25–51.
20 Charles Pentland, "The Regionalization of World Politics: Concepts and Evidence," *International Journal* 30, no. 4 (1974–1975), 589–627.
21 Pentland, "The Regionalization of World Politics: Concepts and Evidence," 615; On the behavioural perspective on regions, see: Bruce Russett, *International Regions and the International System: A Study in Political Ecology* (Chicago: Rand McNally, 1967); and Bruce Russett, "Delineating International Regions," in *Quantitative International Politics: Insights and Evidence*, ed., Joel David Singer (New York: Free Press, 1968), 317–352.
22 Emanuel Adler and Beverly Crawford, "Constructing a Mediterranean Region: A Cultural Approach," Paper Presented at the Conference on "The Convergence of Civilizations? Constructing a Mediterranean Region," Lisbon, Portugal, 6–9 June 2002, 3.
23 Ole Weaver, "Culture and Identity in the Baltic Sea Region," in Pertti Joenniemi, ed., *Cooperation in the Baltic Sea Region* (London: Taylor and Francis, 1993).
24 See Arif Dirlik, "The Asia-Pacific Region: Reality and Representation in the Invention of the Regional Structure," *Journal of World History* 3, no. 1 (1992), 55–79.
25 Buzan and Waever, 48.

26 Katzenstein, 12.

27 Buzan and Waever, 71.

28 Buzan and Waever, 13.

29 Peter J. Katzenstein and Rudra Sil, "Rethinking Asian Security: A Case for Analytical Eclecticism," in *Rethinking Security in East Asia: Identity, Power and Efficiency*, eds., J. J. Suh, Peter J. Katzenstein, and Allen Carlson (Stanford: Stanford University Press, 2004), 5.

30 Katzenstein, *A World of Regions*, 39.

31 Buzan and Waever, *Regions and Powers*, 468.

32 Katzenstein, *A World of Regions*, x–xi.

33 Security complexes may merge to become "supercomplexes" or may split. They may become conflict prone or peaceful through "securitization and desecuritization." Securitization involves taking extraordinary measures to address challenges that have been labelled/constructed as existential threats to a state or other international actors (including regions). Buzan and Waever, *Regions and Powers*, 71. Desecuritization refers to the reverse process whereby issues already labelled as such are taken out of the emergency mode and put back into normal political sphere. Buzan and Waever, *Regions and Powers*, 71.

34 Buzan and Waever, *Regions and Powers*, 480.

35 Buzan and Waever, *Regions and Powers*, 481–482.

36 Katzenstein, *A World of Regions*, 76, 81.

37 *R&P* discusses material security linkages between the neighbouring RSCs, such as South, Southeast and Northeast Asia, Middle East and Africa, North and South America, and the links between Russia and Europe and Asia. Buzan and Waever, *Regions and Powers*, Ch. 6 and 258–260, 333–337, 429–433.

38 Amitav Acharya, "How Ideas Spread: Whose Norms Matter? Norm Localization and Institutional Change in Asian Regionalism," *International Organization* 58, no. 2 (2004): 239–275.

39 Muthiah Alagappa, "The Study of International Order," in *Asian Security Order: Instrumental and Normative Features*, ed., Muthiah Alagappa (Stanford: Stanford University Press, 2003), 34. For a discussion of regional orders produced by internationalist coalitions, see Etel Solingen, *Regional Orders at Century's Dawn: Global and Domestic Influences on Grand Strategy* (Princeton: Princeton University Press, 1998).

40 Mohammed Ayoob, "Regional Security and the Third World," in *Regional Security in the Third World*, ed., M. Ayoob (London: Croom Helm, 1986), 4.

41 Hedley Bull, *The Anarchical Society*, 2nd edn. (Basingstoke: Macmillan, 1999), 8.

42 Ibid., 16–19.

43 Morgan, "Regional Security Complexes and Regional Orders," in *Regional Orders: Building Security in a New World*, eds., D. Lake and P. Morgan (University Park: Pennsylvania State University Press, 1997), 32.

44 Alagappa, "The Study of International Order," 39.

45 Buzan and Waever, *Regions and Powers*, 474–475.

46 Of these, the definitions of three types of regional security orders are noteworthy. *Conflict formation:* "a pattern of security interdependence shaped by fear of war and expectations of the use of violence in political relations"; *Security regime:* "a pattern of security interdependence still shaped by fear of war and expectations of the use of violence in political relations, but where those fears are restrained by agreed set of rules and expectations that those rules will be observed." *Security community:* "a pattern of security interdependence in which the units do not expect or prepare for the use of force in their political relations with each other." Buzan and Waever, *Regions and Powers*, 489, 491.

47 David A. Lake and Patrick M. Morgan, "The New Regionalism in Security Affairs," 12.

48 Buzan and Waever, *Regions and Powers*, 65.

49 Peter J. Katzenstein, "Introduction: Asian Regionalism in Comparative Perspective," in *Network Power: Japan and Asia*, eds., Peter J. Katzenstein and Takashi Shiraishi (Ithaca: Cornell University Press, 1997), 3.

50 Amitav Acharya and Alastair Iain Johnston, eds., *Crafting Cooperation: Regional International Institutions in Comparative Perspective* (Cambridge: Cambridge University Press, 2007). This study is different from the Rational Design of International Institutions (RDII) project, which addressed why and how international institutions differ (in terms of their membership rules, scope of issues, centralization of tasks, rules for controlling the institution, and flexibility of arrangements), but bracketed considerations of their effectiveness. Barbara Koremenos, Charles Lipson and Duncan Snidal, eds., *The Rational Design of International Institutions* (Cambridge: Cambridge University Press, 2004); John S. Duffield, "The Limits of 'Rational Design'," *International Organization* 57 no. 2 (2003): 411–430. The RDII project did not study regional institutions. The Acharya-Johnston project looks at both material and ideational aspects of design variations among regional institutions and then studies the impact of these features on the effectiveness of institutions.

51 Amitav Acharya and Alastair Iain Johnston, "Conclusion: Institutional Features, Cooperation Effects, and the Agenda for Further Research on Comparative Regionalism," in *Crafting Cooperation: Regional International Institutions in Comparative Perspective*, eds., Amitav Acharya and Alastair Iain Johnston (Cambridge: Cambridge University Press, 2007).

52 Buzan and Waever, *Regions and Powers*, 456.

53 Katzenstein, *A World of Regions*, 24.

54 Katzenstein, *A World of Regions*, 13.

55 Amitav Acharya, "Why Is There No NATO in Asia? The Normative Origins of Asian Multilateralism," Working Paper, no. 05-05 (Cambridge, MA: Harvard University, The Weatherhead Center for International Affairs, July 2005).

56 Amitav Acharya, *Constructing a Security Community in Southeast Asia: ASEAN and the Problem of Regional Order* (London: Routldge, 2001), 182.

57 Katzenstein, *A World of Regions*, 179.

58 Katzenstein, *A World of Regions*, 198.

59 Katzenstein, *A World of Regions*, 206.

60 Singh, "Hegemonic Construction of Regions: Southeast Asia as a Case Study."

61 John Mearsheimer, *The Tragedy of Great Power Politics* (New York: W.W. Norton, 2001), 41.

62 Scott Cooper and Brock Taylor, "Power and Regionalism: Explaining Regional Cooperation in the Persian Gulf," in *Comparative Regional Integration: Theoretical Perspectives*, ed., Finn Laursen (U.K.: Ashgate. 2003), 105–6; and Lloyd Grubber, *Ruling the World: Power Politics and the Rise of Supranational Institutions* (Princeton: Princeton University Press, 2000).

63 Joseph M. Grieco, "Realism and Regionalism: American Power and German and Japanese Institutional Strategies During and After the Cold War," in *Unipolar Politics*, eds., Ethan B. Kapstein and Michael Mastanduno (New York: Columbia University Press, 1999).

64 G. John Ikenberry, *After Victory: Institutions, Strategic Restraint, and the Rebuilding of Order after Major Wars* (Princeton: Princeton University Press, 2000).

65 James Mittleman and Richard Falk, "Global Hegemony and Regionalism," in *Regionalism in the Post-Cold War World*, ed., Stephen C. Calleya (U.K.: Ashgate, 2000), 19.

66 Amitav Acharya, "Regional Military-Security Cooperation in the Third World: A Conceptual and Comparative Study of the Association of Southeast Asian Nations," *Journal of Peace Research* 29, no. 1 (1992): 7–21; Bjorn Hettne, "The New Regionalism: Implications for Development and Peace," in *The New Regionalism: Implications for Global Development and International Security*, eds., Bjorn Hettne and Andras Inotai (Finland: UNU World Institute for Development Economics Research, 1994).

67 Christopher Layne, "The Unipolar Illusion: Why New Great Powers Will Rise," *International Security* 17, no. 4 (1993): 5–51. Layne does not discuss ideational and normative challenges. The durability of unipolarity is asserted in William Wohlforth, "The Stability of a Unipolar World," *International Security* 24, no. 1 (1999): 5–41.

68 The effort failed due to US opposition, but has not faded away. For possible areas of Japanese challenge to the US, see: Robert Gilpin, "Sources of American-Japanese Economic Conflict," in *International Relations Theory and the Asia Pacific*, eds., G. John Ikenberry and Michael Mastanduno (New York: Columbia University Press, 2003).

69 Charles Kupchan, "After Pax Americana: Benign Power, Regional Integration, and the Sources of Stable Multipolarity," *International Security* 23 no. 2 (1998): 40–79. By contrast, Wohlforth dismisses such regional unipolarities because all potential challengers to US have great power neighbours which could turn into natural allies of the US or balance each other. Wohlforth, "The Stability of a Unipolar World."

70 David Kang, "Getting Asia Wrong: The Need for New Analytical Frameworks," *International Security* 27, no. 4 (2003): 57–85. For a contrarian view, see, Amitav Acharya, "Will Asia's Past Be Its Future?" *International Security* 28, no. 3 (2003–2004): 149–164.

71 S.D. Muni, *China's Strategic Engagement with the New ASEAN*, IDSS Monographs, no. 2 (Singapore: Institute of Defence and Strategic Studies, 2002), 21,132; "Economic Juggernaut: China is Passing US as Asian Power," *New York Times*, 29 June 29 2002, cited in, Friedrich Wu, et. al., "Foreign Direct Investments to China and Southeast Asia: Has ASEAN Been Losing Out," *Economic Survey of Singapore* (Third Quarter 2002), http://unpan1.un.org/intradoc/groups/public/documents/APCITY/UNPAN010347.pdf, 96; Robert A. Manning, "The Monroe Doctrine, Chinese Style," *Los Angeles Times*, 16 August 1998, 2. Ernst Bower, the then president of the US-ASEAN Business Council, said in 2003: "I do feel the Chinese Monroe Doctrine is being built here in the region. As the Chinese get their act together and play on the world stage, this region is the first of a series of concentric circles," cited in Jane Perlez, "The Charm From Beijing," *New York Times*, 9 October 2003, http://taiwansecurity.org/NYT/2003/NYT-100903.htm.

72 Quoted in Bernard Gordon, "The FTA Fetish", *Wall Street Journal*, 17 November 2005, A.16.

73 John Ravenhill, "In Search of an East Asian Region: Beyond Network Power," in Vinod K. Aggarwal and Min Gyo Koo, eds., "Roundtable: Peter J. Katzenstein's Contributions to the Study of East Asian Regionalism," *Journal of East Asian Studies* 7 no. 3 (2007): 359–412.

74 Katzenstein, *A World of Regions*, 91–92.

75 Japan is vulnerable to China's challenge not just materially, but as Katzenstein himself notes, ideationally. After all, it was China which had the central role in the historical identity of East Asia. And "Japan's inability to recognize its militarist past reinforces political suspicion throughout Asia, and its atypical national security policy has had remarkably little influence in reshaping Asia's regional security order." Katzenstein, 140.

76 Amitav Acharya and William T. Tow, "Obstinate or Obsolete: The US Alliance Structure in the Asia Pacific," Manuscript, Department of International Relations, Research School of Pacific and Asian Studies, Australian National University, August 2006.

77 Mahnaz Z. Ispahani, "Alone Together: Regional Security Arrangements in Southern Africa and the Arabian Gulf," *International Security* 8, no. 4 (1984): 152–175.

78 Francis Fukuyama, "The West May Be Coming Apart," *The Straits Times*, 10 August 2002.

79 Kagan asserts that compared to Americans, Europeans are "more tolerant of failure, more patient when solutions don't come quickly." They eschew "finality" in international affairs, prefer "negotiation, diplomacy, and persuasion," and emphasize "process over result." Many of these observations are true of Asian regionalism as well. Robert Kagan, "Power and Weakness," *Policy Review*, no. 113 (2002): 3–28.

80 Amitav Acharya, "Regionalism and the Emerging World Order: Sovereignty, Autonomy, Identity," in *New Regionalisms in the Global Political Economy*, eds., Shaun Breslin (London and New York: Routledge, 2002), 20–32; Arie M. Kacowicz, *Zones of Peace in the Third World: South America and West Africa in Comparative Perspective* (Albany: State University of New York Press, 1998).

81 B. Vivekanandan, "The Indian Ocean as a Zone of Peace: Problems and Prospects," *Asian Survey* 21 no. 12 (1981): 1237–1249; "Zone of Peace, Freedom and Neutrality Declaration, Malaysia, 27 November 1971," http://www.aseansec.org/1215.htm; Heiner Hanggi, *ASEAN and the ZOPFAN Concept* (Singapore: Institute of Southeast Asian Studies, 1991); Amitav Acharya and Sola Ogunbanwo, "The Nuclear Weapon-Free Zones in South-East Asia and Africa," *SIPRI Yearbook 1998* (Oxford: Oxford University Press, 1998); *Nuclear Weapon-free Zones: Advantages, Shortcomings and Prospects* (Paris, France : Le Centre Thucydide, 2005), http://www.afri-ct.org/article.php3?id_article=1636.

82 Mohammed Ayoob, "The Primacy of the Political: South Asian Regional Cooperation (SARC) in Comparative Perspective," *Asian Survey* 25, no. 4 (1985), 444; Mohammed Ayoob, "From Regional System to Regional Society: Exploring Key Variables in the Construction of Regional Order," *Australian Journal of International Affairs* 53, no. 3 (1999): 247–260.

83 J. Lloyd Mecham, *The United States and Inter-American Security 1889–1960* (Austin: University of Texas Press, 1962).

84 Hurrell, "Regionalism in Theoretical Perspective," 143.

85 Michael Leifer, *The ASEAN Regional Forum*, Adelphi Paper, no. 302, London: International Institute for Strategic Studies, 1996.

86 Katzenstein, *A World of Regions*, 86.

87 Mark Beeson, "Resisting hegemony: The sources and limits of anti-Americanism in Southeast Asia," Paper for the workshop on *Globalisation, Conflict and Political Regimes in East and Southeast Asia*, Fremantle, Australia, 15–16 August 2003, http://eprint.uq.edu.au/archive/00000623/01/mb-cgpr-03.pdf.

88 Bjorn Hettne, "The New Regionalism and the Return of the Political," paper presented at the XIII Nordic Political Science Association Meeting, Aalborg, Denmark, 15–17 August 2002, 2.

89 Peter Symonds, "Behind Indonesia's anti-Chinese riots," 14 February 1998, http://www.wsws.org/news/1998/feb1998/indones.shtml; Leo Suryadinata, "Anti-Chinese riots in Indonesia Perennial problem but major disaster unlikely," *The Straits Times*, 25 February 1998, 36, http://www.hartford-hwp.com/archives/54b/066.html; Bhubhindar Singh, "ASEAN's Perceptions of Japan: Change and Continuity," *Asian Survey* 42 no. 2 (2002): 276–296; and Aron Patrick, "Origins of the April 2005 Anti-Japanese Protests in the People's Republic of China," Working Paper, Lexington: University of Kentucky, Patterson School of Diplomacy, January 2007, http://www.aronpatrick.com/essays/PATRICK2005AntiJapaneseProtests.pdf. Anti-Chinese riots in Malaysia and Indonesia are directed against the ethnic Chinese community, rather than China itself. But they do have an undercurrent of resentment against the Chinese state. This was stronger in the past, when the local Chinese were known as "overseas Chinese" potential fifth columnists. While most have become local citizens, there is still a possibility that the rise of China will lead to ethnic riots in which local Chinese are victimized in states where the majority ethnic group blames China's economic and security policies for damaging its economic well-being.

90 Neumann, "A Region-Building Approach to Northern Europe," 57.

91 Buzan and Waever, *Regions and Powers*, 122–123, 361–364.

92 Buzan and Waever, *Regions and Powers*, 481.

93 Katzenstein, *A World of Regions*, 12.

94 Murphy, "Regions as Social Constructs: The Gap Between Theory and Practice," 30.

95 Acharya, *The Quest for Identity: International Relations of Southeast Asia*. See also Adler's notion of 'cognitive' regions in Emanuel Adler, "Imagined (Security) Communities: Cognitive Regions in International Relations," *Millennium: Journal of International Studies* 26, no. 2 (1997): 249–277.

PART IV

Ideas, agency and normative cultures

8

HOW IDEAS SPREAD: WHOSE NORMS MATTER? NORM LOCALIZATION AND INSTITUTIONAL CHANGE IN ASIAN REGIONALISM[1]

> In considering the imprint of cultural contacts, and the undoubted fact that ideas are imported along with goods, there is a need to develop a more supple language of causal connection than source and imitation, original and copy. The transfer of cultural forms produces a redistribution of imaginative energies, alters in some way a pre-existent field of force. The result is usually not so much an utterly new product as the development or evolution of a familiar matrix.
>
> *Stanley O'Connor*[2]

Why do some transnational ideas and norms find greater acceptance in a particular locale than others? This is an important question for international relations (IR) scholars, who are challenged by Risse, Ropp and Sikkink to pay more attention to "the causal mechanisms and processes by which . . . ideas spread."[3] A "second wave" of norm scholarship is responding to this challenge by focusing on how domestic political structures and agents condition normative change. As such, it compliments the earlier literature focusing on transnational agents and processes shaping norm diffusion at the level of the international system.[4]

In this chapter, I extend this line of investigation in two ways: first, by proposing a framework for investigating norm diffusion that stresses the agency role of norm-takers through a dynamic congruence-building process called localization, and secondly by using this framework to study how transnational norms have shaped regional institutions in Southeast Asia and the role of Asian regional institutions and processes (specifically the Association of Southeast Asian Nations (ASEAN)) in transnational norm diffusion. Empirically, the chapter focuses on how transnational ideas and norms produced institutional change (as the dependent variable of norm diffusion) in ASEAN, the oldest regional political organization in Asia.[5] In the 1990s, ASEAN faced two sets of proposals that would significantly redefine its agenda and reshape its institutional machinery. The first, emerging in the early 1990s, was for a multilateral security institution for the Asia Pacific on the basis of the "common security" norm. Originating in Cold War Europe, this norm had been reframed in Asia Pacific discourses as "cooperative security." The second proposal, in the late 1990s, sought to develop ASEAN's role in addressing transnational problems that would require it to go beyond its traditional adherence to the norm of non-interference in the internal affairs of its members. This effort had its normative roots in the post-Cold War notion of humanitarian intervention, albeit reframed in the regional context as "constructive intervention" and "flexible engagement."

After a period of contestation, the first proposal led ASEAN to formalize intra-mural security dialogues, adopt a more inclusive posture towards outside powers' role in regional order, and anchor a new security institution for the wider Asia Pacific region. In contrast, the attempt to dilute the non-interference norm on the basis of the flexible engagement idea failed, producing only some weak policy instruments.

Why this variation? Central to the norm dynamic I present is the contestation between emerging transnational norms and pre-existing regional normative and social orders. But unlike other scholars who have addressed the question of resistance and agency of local actors (which in most cases are domestic, rather than regional or regional organizational), I place particular emphasis on a dynamic process called localization. Instead of just assessing the existential fit between domestic and outside identity norms and institutions, and explaining strictly dichotomous outcomes of acceptance or rejection, localization describes a complex process and outcome by which norm-takers build congruence between transnational norms (including norms previously institutionalized in a region) and local beliefs and practices.[6] In this process, foreign norms, which may not initially cohere with the latter, are incorporated into it. The success of norm diffusion strategies and processes depends on the extent to which they provide opportunities for localization.

The chapter's focus on ASEAN and Asian regionalism is important. Founded in 1967, ASEAN was arguably the most successful regional institution outside Europe during the Cold War period.[7] As Miles Kahler writes, "Given the short and less-than-useful lives of many regional organizations in the developing world, ASEAN is unusual, not only for its longevity, but also for its flexibility in serving the purposes of its members."[8] Asia is the only region where a new macro-regional security institution had emerged after the end of the Cold War. Based on the ASEAN model, this regionalism is regarded as a distinctive form of regional institutionalization compared to Europe.[9] Yet, ASEAN and its role in the creation of Asia Pacific regionalism in general remains neglected in IR theory and the study of norm diffusion.

It is also necessary to stress at the outset that this chapter investigates norm diffusion, rather than norm displacement. Constructivist norm scholars have often sought out cases involving fundamental normative change, thereby avoiding "the dog who didn't bark."[10] But I accept Ted Hopf's view that constructivism should be "agnostic about change in world politics . . . What [it] does offer is an account of how and where change may occur."[11] Studies of norm dynamics should account for a range of responses to new norms – from constitutive compliance to outright rejection, and evolutionary and path-dependent forms of acceptance which fall in between. The latter may be more common forms of norm diffusion in world politics, but have received less attention in constructivist writings.

Two perspectives on norm diffusion

The first wave scholarship on normative change speaks to a moral cosmopolitanism. It has three main features. First, the norms that are being propagated are "cosmopolitan," or "universal" norms, i.e. the campaign against land mines, ban on chemical weapons, protection of whales, struggle against racism, intervention against genocide, and promotion of human rights, etc.[12] Second, the key actors who spread these norms are transnational agents, be they individual "moral entrepreneurs" or social movements.[13] Third, despite recognizing the role of persuasion in norm diffusion, this literature focuses heavily on what Ethan Nadelmann has called "moral proselytism," which is concerned with conversion rather than contestation (although the latter is acknowledged),[14] and regards resistance to cosmopolitan norms as illegitimate or immoral.

The moral cosmopolitanism perspective has contributed to two unfortunate tendencies. First, by assigning causal primacy to "international prescriptions," it ignores the expansive appeal of "norms that are deeply rooted in other types of social entities – regional, national, and subnational groups."[15] Moreover, it sets up an implicit dichotomy between good global/universal norms and bad regional/local norms.[16] For moral cosmopolitans, norms making a universalistic claim about what is good are considered more desirable and more likely to prevail than norms that are localized or particularistic.[17]

Second, moral cosmopolitans view norm diffusion as *teaching* by transnational agents, thereby downplaying the agency role of local actors.[18] This perspective captures a significant, but small part of norm dynamics in world politics focusing on principled ideas, which establish a fundamental distinction between what is good and what is evil. But norm diffusion in world politics involves other kinds of ideas as well. For example, what have been called "prescriptive norms" combine moral principles with considerations of efficiency and utility.[19] In such cases, norm dynamics would be shaped by different conditions and processes, with greater scope for the agency role (voluntary initiative and selection) of norm-takers.

A second perspective on norm diffusion looks beyond international prescriptions and stresses the role of domestic political, organizational, and cultural variables in conditioning the reception of new global norms.[20] Its notion of "congruence" describes the fit between *international* norms and *domestic* norms, rather than "the degree of fit between two, competing international norms" (which is also a concern for the moral cosmopolitanists).[21] A key example is Legro's notion of "organizational culture," which acts "as a heuristic filter for perceptions and calculation" employed by actors in responding to outside norms.[22] Another is Checkel's notion of "cultural match," which describes "a situation where the prescriptions embodied in an international norm are convergent with domestic norms, as reflected in discourse, the legal system (constitutions, judicial codes, laws), and bureaucratic agencies (organizational ethos and administrative agencies)."[23] Norm diffusion is "more rapid when . . . a systemic norm . . . resonates with historically constructed domestic norms."[24]

While capturing the role of "local agents" in norm diffusion, these perspectives, which remain confined to the domestic arena (as opposed to a regional context involving two or more states which is the focus of this chapter), can be unduly static in describing an existential match – how "historically constructed domestic identity norms create barriers to agent learning from systemic norms"[25] – rather than a dynamic process of *matchmaking*. They conform to the general thrust of institutionalist approaches, which "have been better at explaining what is not possible in a given institutional context than what is."[26]

Two other concepts – framing and grafting – offer a more dynamic view of congruence. Framing is necessary because "the linkages between existing norms and emergent norms are not often obvious and must be actively constructed by proponents of new norms."[27] Through framing, norm advocates highlight and "create" issues "by using language that names, interprets, and dramatizes them."[28] Audie Klotz's study of the anti-apartheid campaign shows the critical role of the framing of the global norm of racial equality and the global anti-apartheid campaign in the context of the prevailing civil rights discourse in the US. Framing can thus make a global norm appear local.[29]

"Grafting" (or "incremental norm transplantation" to use Theo Farrell's phrase, to be distinguished from "radical transplantation" or "norm displacement"[30]) is a tactic employed by norm entrepreneurs to institutionalize a new norm by associating it with a pre-existing norm in the same issue area, which makes a similar prohibition or injunction. Richard Price has shown how the campaign to develop a norm against chemical weapons was helped by invoking the prior norm against poison.[31] But grafting and framing are largely acts of reinterpretation or representation rather than reconstruction. More importantly, neither is necessarily a local act. Outsiders usually perform them.[32] Moreover, there is no sense of whether, to what extent, and how the pre-existing norm helps to *redefine* the emerging norm at least in the local context, or at the receiving end.

Localization goes further. It may start with a reinterpretation and re-representation of the outside norm, including framing and grafting, but may extend into more complex processes of reconstitution to make an outside norm congruent with a pre-existing local normative order. It is also a process in which the role of local actors is more crucial than that of outside actors. Instead of treating framing, grafting and other adaptive processes as distinct and unrelated phenomena, I use localization to bring them together under a single conceptual framework and stress the agency role of local actors in performing them.

The dynamics of norm localization

In developing the concept of localization, I draw upon Southeast Asian historiographical concepts which claim that Southeast Asian societies were not passive recipients of foreign (Indian and Chinese) cultural and political ideas, but active borrowers and localizers.[33] Localization describes a process of idea transmission in which Southeast Asians borrowed foreign ideas about authority and legitimacy, and fitted them into indigenous traditions and practices. Ideas that could be constructed to fit indigenous traditions were better received than those that did not have such potential.

In the following sections, I draw from this literature to develop the idea of localization in three important areas: what is localization, why does localization take place and under what conditions is it likely to occur, and what kind of change does it produce?

What is localization?

To localize something is to "invest [it] with the characteristics of a particular place."[34] I define localization as the active construction (through discourse, framing, grafting, and cultural selection) of foreign ideas by local actors, which results in the former developing significant congruence with local beliefs and practices. O.W. Wolters, a leading proponent of localization in Southeast Asian studies, calls this a "local statement . . . into which foreign elements have retreated."[35]

The concept of localization extrapolated from Southeast Asian historiography offers three important ideas about how and why ideas travel and produce change across cultures and regions.[36] The first is "the idea of the local initiative," associated with the Dutch economic historian Jacob Van Leur, who contended that Indian ideas came into Southeast Asia neither through conquest (the thesis that Indian had conquered large parts of Southeast Asia), nor through commerce (that Indian religious and political ideas were introduced by early traders from the subcontinent), but through indigenous initiative and adaptation.[37] Southeast Asian rulers sought out Indian ideas that they found to be instrumental in boosting their legitimacy and enhancing their political and religious and moral authority. The implications of "local initiative" for the modern constructivist concept of norm entrepreneur will be discussed shortly.

A second insight of the Southeast Asian literature concerns the idea-recipient's adjustments to the formal shape or content (or both) of foreign ideas to make it more congruent with the recipient's own prior beliefs and practices. This might start with an act of cultural selection: borrowing only those ideas which are, or can be made, congruent with local beliefs and which may enhance the prestige of the borrower. As Osborne puts it, "Southeast Asians borrowed only those Indian and Chinese cultural traits that complemented and could be adapted to the indigenous system."[38] This was followed by adjustments to foreign ideas to find a better fit with existing local beliefs and practices.[39] The foreign idea was thus "pruned."

Such adjustments were motivated by two main realities. First, the idea-recipient's chief goal was to strengthen, not replace existing institutions such as kingship, with the infusion of new pathways of legitimation. Hence, wholesale borrowing of foreign ideas that might supplant existing institutions could not be undertaken. Second, cultural predilections, and deeply ingrained beliefs in the importance of existing institutions sanctified by popular beliefs (such as myth of origin) and nurtured through rituals and practices, could not be easily sacrificed without incurring social and political costs. Thus, there could be "rational" exclusion of certain elements of new ideas that might harm the existing social order or increase the risk of social and political instability. In the next section, I will discuss the implications of these considerations in explaining the motivation of norm diffusion.

A third relevant insight of the localization idea in Southeast Asian historiography concerns its effect. Far from extinguishing local beliefs and practices, foreign ideas may help to enhance the profile and prestige of local actors and beliefs. Wolters claims that while borrowing Hindu ideas about legitimacy and authority, Southeast Asian rulers did not abandon their prior political beliefs and practices. Instead, the latter were "amplified," meaning that "ancient and persisting indigenous beliefs [were brought] into sharper focus."[40] The latter included prior local beliefs about the individual strength of the ruler (the "man of prowess") and his innate spiritual energy ("soul stuff"). Similarly, Thomas Kirsch's analysis of the evolution of Thai religion suggests that the advent of Indian Buddhism did not lead the Thais to abandon their existing practice of worshipping local spirits. Rather, Thai shrines placed Buddhist deities alongside local spirits. This transformed the status of both religions simultaneously, giving a local frame to Indian Buddhism ("parochialization") and a universal frame to Thai animism ("universalization"). This contributed to a greater civilizational complexity in Thai religion and society.[41]

Why localize?

Why do norm-takers want to localize international norms and what are the conditions that may affect the likelihood of localization due to their actions? One may start to address this question by looking at several generic forces which create the demand for new norms in the first place. First, a major security or economic crisis (war or depression) can lead to norm borrowing by calling into question "existing rules of the game."[42] Another catalyst is systemic change, such as shifts in the distribution of power or the great powers' interests and interactions.[43] The end of the Cold War brought to the fore a set of European norms about security cooperation, which in turn attracted the attention of regional actors outside of Europe.[44] A third catalyst could be domestic political changes in the norm-taker.[45] For example, newly democratic regimes may seek to import ideas about human rights promotion and assistance as the basis of their own foreign policy because such ideas would legitimize their new identity. Finally, international or regional demonstration effect could prompt norm borrowing through emulation, imitation, and contagion, etc.[46]

The key question for this chapter, of course, is why the demand for new norms leads to their *localization*, in which some key characteristics of the pre-existing normative order are retained, rather than displaced wholesale. From a rationalist perspective, localization is simply easier, especially when prior norms are embedded in *strong local institutions*. Institutionalist scholars hold that it is "easier to maintain and adapt existing institutions than to create new ones."[47] But existing institutions might have been discredited to the extent that local actors may seek to replace them with new ones. As Keck and Sikkink's study of the anti-foot binding campaign in China at the turn of the nineteenth century and the anti-circumcision campaign in Kenya in the 1930s show, norm displacement occurs when a foreign norm seeks to replace a local norm whose moral claim or functional adequacy has already been challenged from within, but fails when it competes with a strong identity norm.[48] But if norm-takers believe that their existing beliefs and approaches are not harmful, but merely inadequate (i.e. not geared towards addressing newer challenges) and therefore have to be broadened and strengthened with the infusion of new ideas, then localization is more likely than displacement.

But localization is not simply a pragmatic response to the demand for new norms. The prospects for localization also depends on their positive impact on the legitimacy and authority of key norm-takers, the strength of prior local norms, the credibility and prestige of local agents, indigenous cultural traits and traditions, and the scope for grafting and pruning presented by foreign norms.

First, localization is likely if the norm-takers' come to believe that new outside norms – which may be initially feared and resisted simply because of their alien quality – could be used to enhance the legitimacy and authority of their extant institutions and practices, *but without fundamentally altering their existing social identity.* Cortell and Davis show that actors borrow international rules to "justify their own actions and call into question the legitimacy of others."[49] But while strengthening the norm-taker's hand, these rules may not extinguish its identity. In Southeast Asian historiography, Indian ideas came to be accepted once the rulers realized that could help to enhance their authority by associating the kingship with the notion of a universal sovereign found in Hindu religious–political traditions (absent in local theology). But the borrowing could be done in a manner in which even after Hindu ideas amplified their status and authority, indigenous identities such as a belief in the ruler's innate spiritual energy ("soul stuff") were not fundamentally altered, but "remained dominant."[50]

A second factor favouring localization is the strength of prior local norms. Some local norms are foundational to a group. They may derive from deeply ingrained cultural beliefs and practices or from international legal norms which had, at an earlier stage, been borrowed and enshrined in the constitutional documents of a group. In either case they have already become integral to the local group's identity in the sense that "they constitute actor identities and interests and not simply regulate behavior."[51] The stronger the local norms, the greater the likelihood that new foreign norms will be localized rather than accepted wholesale.

A third condition favouring localization is the availability of credible local actors ("insider proponents") with sufficient discursive influence to match or outperform outside norm entrepreneurs operating at the global level. The credibility of local agents depends on their social context and standing. Local norm entrepreneurs are likely to be more credible if they are seen by their target audience as upholders of local values and identity and not simply "agents" of outside forces or actors, as well as whether they are part of a local epistemic community which could claim a record of success in prior normative debates.

The standard constructivist definition of norm entrepreneur often privileges "transnational moral entrepreneurs." It defines their task as being to: "mobilize popular opinion and political support both within their host country and abroad," "stimulate and assist in the creation of likeminded organizations *in other countries*" (emphasis added), and "play a significant role in elevating their objectives beyond its identification with the national interests of their government."[52] Much of their effort is "directed toward persuading foreign audiences, especially foreign elites."[53] The localization perspective calls for a shift in the understanding of norm entrepreneurship from "outsider proponents" committed to a transnational or universal moral agenda to "insider proponents." These actors can be individuals, regionally based epistemic communities, or non-governmental organizations, whose primary commitment is to localize a normative order and whose main task is to legitimize and enhance that order by building congruence with outside ideas.[54]

While the initiative to spread transnational norms can be undertaken either by local or foreign entrepreneurs, diffusion strategies that accommodate local sensitivity are more likely to succeed than those which seek to supplant the latter. Hence, outsider proponents are more likely to advance their cause if they act through local agents, rather than going independently at it. An example of the insider proponent's role can be found in Geoffrey Wiseman's analysis of the diffusion of the non-provocative defence norm to the Soviet Union. Wiseman shows how local supporters of this norm within the Soviet defence community facilitated its acceptance "by resurrecting a defensive 'tradition' in Soviet history," thereby reassuring "domestic critics that they were operating historically within the Soviet paradigm and to avoid the impression that they were simply borrowing Western ideas."[55]

Fourth, localization is facilitated by the norm-takers' sense of identity, especially if they possess a well-developed sense of being unique in terms of their values and interactions. For example, Desmond Ball has identified the existence of such a sense of uniqueness affecting regional interactions.[56] The "ASEAN Way" is regarded as a unique set of norms and practices shaping regional cooperation in Southeast Asia.[57] Such actors are unlikely to adopt a foreign norm wholesale and are likely to have developed a habit of localizing foreign ideas. Scholars of Southeast Asia have spoken of a deeply ingrained habit in Southeast Asian societies, which "adapted . . . foreign ideas to suit their own needs and values."[58] In his study of Indonesian politics, Benedict Anderson mentions the "whole trend to absorb and transform the Western concepts of modern politics within Indonesian–Javanese mental structures."[59] Similarly, looking at modern political institutions in Southeast Asia, McCloud concludes that: "At national and popular levels, Western political and social institutions have been rejected, not out of hand, and categorically, but with the qualification – as old as the region itself – that externally derived concepts and institutions will be blended with the indigenous (much of which was also previously imported) and fitted to local sensibilities and needs."[60]

Although the chapter presents localization as a dynamic process, the existential compatibility between foreign and local norms must not be ignored as another catalyst. The prior existence of a local norm in similar issue areas as that of a new external norm and which makes similar behavioural claims makes it easier for local actors to introduce the latter. Moreover, the external norm must lend itself to some pruning, or adjustments to make it compatible with local beliefs and practices, without compromising its core attributes. Hence, the relative scope for grafting and pruning presented by a new foreign norm contributes to the norm-taker's interest to localize and is critical to its success.

Drawing upon the immediate discussion of the motivating forces of and conditions favoring localization and the previous discussion of the three aspects of localization in Southeast Asian historiography, Table 8.1 outlines a trajectory of localization, specifying the conditions for progress.

TABLE 8.1 The trajectory of localization and conditions for progress

Prelocalization (Resistance and Contestation)	Local actors may resist to new external norms because of doubts about their utility and applicability and fears that they might undermine existing beliefs and practices. The contestation may lead to localization if some local actors begin to view the external norms as having a potential to contribute to the legitimacy and efficacy of extant institutions without undermining them significantly.
	Condition 1: Some aspects of the existing normative order remains strong and legitimate, although other aspects may already be discredited from within or found inadequate to meet new and unforeseen challenges.
Local initiative (Entrepreneurship and Framing)	Local actors borrow and frame external norms in ways that establishes their value to the local audience.
	Condition 2: There must be willing and credible local actors (insider proponents). The tendency to localize is especially salient if local agents are not seen as "stooges" of outside forces and if their local audience has developed a reputation for being unique.
Adaptation (Grafting and Pruning)	External norms may be reconstructed to fit with local beliefs and practices even as the latter may be adjusted in accordance with the former norm. To find this common ground, local actors may redefine the external norm, linking it with specific extant local norms and practices and pruning it, selecting those elements which fit the pre-existing normative structure and rejecting those which do not.
	Condition 3: There must be some scope for grafting between the external norm and some aspects of an existing norm hierarchy. Borrowing supplements, rather than supplants an existing norm hierarchy.
Amplification and "Universalization"	New instruments and practices are developed from the syncretic normative framework in which local influences remain highly visible.
	Condition 4: Borrowing and modification should offer scope for some elements of an existing norm hierarchy to receive wider external recognition through its association with the foreign norm.

What kind of change?

Localization does fundamentally alter the interests and identities of norm-takers. In some respects, localization is similar to behaviour that scholars have described as *adaptation*.[61] But adaptation is a generic term that can subsume all kinds of behaviours and outcomes. Localization has more specific features. As Wolters points out, "adaptation shriek[s] the crucial question of where, how and why foreign elements began to fit into a local culture" and obscures "the initiative of local elements responsible for the process and the end product."[62] In localization, the initiative to seek change normally belongs to the local agent. Moreover, while adaptation may involve an "endless elaboration of new local-foreign cultural 'wholes,'" in localization, the "local beliefs . . . were always responsible for the initial form the new 'wholes' took."[63]

Moreover, in Southeast Asian historiography, localization is conceived as a long-term and evolutionary assimilation of foreign ideas, while some forms of adaptation in the rationalist IR literature are seen as "short run policy of accommodation."[64] Thus, while adaptation may be tactical and to some extent forced on the target audience, localization is voluntary and the resulting change likely to be more enduring.

Localization is different from norm displacement. It does not extinguish the cognitive prior of the norm-takers, but leads to its mutual inflection with external norms. In constructivist perspectives on socialization, norm diffusion is viewed as the result of adaptive behaviour in which local practices are made consistent with an external idea. Localization, by contrast, describes a process in which external ideas are adapted to meet local practices.[65] Here, the existing normative order and an external norm "mutually constitute" one another in a given local setting, but the resulting recipient behaviour can be understood more in terms of the former than the latter, although it can only be fully understood in terms of both.

Localization is progressive, not regressive or static. It reshapes both existing beliefs and practices and foreign ideas in their local context. It is an evolutionary or "everyday" form of progressive norm diffusion. Wolters and Kirsch use the Parsonian term "upgrading" to describe the political and civilizational advancement of Southeast Asian societies from the infusion of foreign ideas,[66] while Bosch describes the outcome of localization as a situation in which "the foreign culture gradually blend[s] with the ancient native one so as to form a novel, harmonious entity, giving both eventually to a higher type of civilization than that of the native community in its original state."[67]

In Southeast Asian historiography, localization of Indian ideas produced two kinds of change: expansion of a ruler's authority to new functional and geographic areas and the creation of new institutions and regulatory mechanisms which in turn legitimized and operationalized such expansion.[68] But as Paul Wheatley points out, the changes to the region's symbolic and organizational features produced by Indian ideas are best seen as "merely redefinitions of indigenous institutions."[69] Modern political science will find it hard to translate this into usable dependent variables. This chapter's focus on a regional organization allows us to conceptualize and represent localization as a form of institutional change induced by transnational norms, with a view to enhance its authority and legitimacy.

Drawing upon the institutionalist literature, I focus on two generic types of institutional change: (1) task and membership expansion (broadening of functional scope[70] and expansion of membership[71]), and (2) changes in the means through which these new tasks are pursued, including, but not limited to, creation of new policy instruments,[72] procedural changes[73] (such as modification of decision-making procedures from consensus to majority voting), legalization,[74] and the creation of new institutions.[75]

Localization is indicated when an extant institution responds to a foreign idea by functional and/or geographic extension, and creates new workable policy instruments to pursue its new tasks/goals without supplanting its original goals and *institutional* structures (defined as "organizational characteristics of groups and . . . the rules and norms that guide the relationships between actors."[76] Parallels can be drawn between what Wheatley calls "mere redefinitions of indigenous institutions" and historical institutionalism's notion of "path dependence" (the claim that the design of new institutions are shaped by pre-existing choices),[77] and Aggarwal's notion of "nested institutions."[78]

Figure 8.1 illustrates three main forms of local responses to transntional norms. In localization, institutional outcomes such as task expansion and procedural innovation result from the displacement of the target norm. But the overall norm hierarchy and the institutional model remain unaltered. This means a locally modified foreign norm can enter the norm hierarchy of an extant institution without necessarily taking precedence over its other prior norms.

But over the long-term, localization may produce an incremental shift towards fundamental change or norm displacement. After local actors have developed greater familiarity and experience with the new ideas, functions and instruments, resistance to new norms may weaken, opening the door to fundamental changes to the norm hierarchy. This comes at the very long end of localization, which occurs and defines normative interactions in the interim. Localization provides an initial response to new norms pending norm displacement, which may or may not occur. But at least localization gives such change *a decent chance*.

In the following sections, I compare two proposals about reshaping ASEAN in the 1990s to explain an important puzzle: why proposals underpinned by a reframed global norm (humanitarian intervention) that was more convergent with the policies of powerful actors, and was conceived as an answer to the severe economic crisis facing the region, fared poorly with ASEAN compared to proposals underpinned by a reframed European norm (common security), which had been rejected by the powerful actors (especially the US). The answer, I argue, lies in the relative scope of localization for the two norms. Drawing upon a range of secondary and primary sources, I employ a process-tracing approach to illustrate how the process of localization shaped the progress of the outside norm at different junctures and look for evidence of localization in terms of the dependent variable of institutional change discussed above.

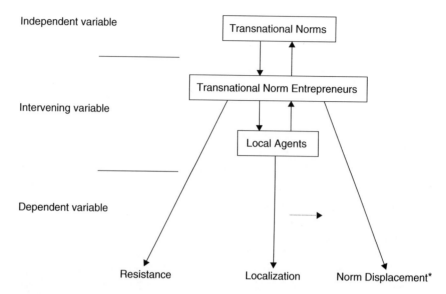

FIGURE 8.1 Local responses to transnational norms

Notes

Resistance: no new tasks and instruments are created, and the target norm** and the institutional model remain largely intact. Too much and sustained resistance leads to failure of norm transmission.

Localization: new tasks and new instruments are created, and the target norm is displaced or significantly modified. The norm hierarchy*** remains unaltered. The original institution remains in place, although there could be "new" institutions mimicking the existing norm hierarchy and institutional design/model.

Norm Displacement: new tasks and instruments are created, the target norm is displaced and the norm hierarchy altered. A new institution (without much similarity with the previous one) appears or the old institution is significantly modified.

* a rarer occurrence.

** *Target* norm refers to the specific prior norm that entrepreneurs, both outsider and insider, want to dilute or displace.

*** Norm hierarchy[79] refers to the salience of the target norm in relation to other core norms of the institution.

Case studies

Case 1: ASEAN and cooperative security

Towards the end of the Cold War (1986–1990), leaders from the Soviet Union, Canada and Australia, advanced proposals toward multilateral security cooperation in the Asia Pacific. These proposals shared two common features.[80] First, they were influenced by the European idea of common security. Second, they called for an institution closely modelled after the Conference on Security and Cooperation in Europe (later the OSCE).[81]

The common security idea was articulated in the 1982 report of the Independent Commission on Disarmament and Security Issues, chaired by the late Swedish Prime Minister Olof Palme.[82] Although not directly espoused by the CSCE, the latter did represent, in Asian policy circles at least, the closest institutionalization of the common security norm.[83] The norm has four key features: (1) rejection of adversarial or balance-of-power approaches to security; (2) rejection of unilateralism and preference for an "inclusive" approach to security through multilateral security measures to manage the security dilemma; (3) emphasis on reassurance through confidence-building measures (CBMs), arms control, multilateral cooperation and the enhancement of the collective security functions of the United Nations;[84] and (4) establishing a link between domestic and regional/international security.[85]

Proposals for common security approaches in the Asia Pacific date back to 1986, when the Soviet leader, Mikhail Gorbachev, proposed a "Pacific Ocean conference along the Helsinki [CSCE] conference" to be attended by all countries "gravitating" towards the Pacific Ocean to discuss peace and security in the region.[86] The next such proposal came from the Canadian External Affairs Minister Joe Clark, who envisaged a "Pacific adaptation" of the CSCE.[87] Australia's Foreign Minister Gareth Evans added to the momentum by finding it "not unreasonable to expect that new Europe-style patterns of cooperation between old adversaries will find their echo in this part of the world."[88] Asserting that "what Asia needs is a Europe-style CSCA" [Conference on Security and Cooperation in Asia], Evans envisaged "a future Asian security architecture involving a wholly new institutional process that might be capable of evolving, in Asia just as in Europe, as a framework for addressing and resolving security problems."[89]

Although these proposals called for an Asia Pacific institution and were not specifically directed at ASEAN, the latter, as the most successful Asian grouping, became an important site for debating them. In its initial reaction, ASEAN feared that these proposals could undermine its existing norms and practices. At stake were three key practices. One was its avoidance of military-security cooperation. This itself was due to fear of provoking its Cold War adversaries, Vietnam and China, which had denounced ASEAN as a new front for the now-defunct American-backed Southeast Asian Treaty Organization. ASEAN also felt that attention to military security issues would be divisive and undermine economic and political cooperation.

A second ASEAN norm at risk was the Zone of Peace, Freedom and Neutrality (ZOPFAN) framework. Articulated in 1972, ZOPFAN called upon major powers to refrain from interfering in the internal affairs of ASEAN members and in regional affairs. ZOPFAN was thus an "exclusionary" framework. A common security institution, in contrast, would bring together ASEAN and the so-called outside powers within a single security framework, allowing them a legitimate role in regional security. ZOPFAN had remained an official goal of ASEAN, although ASEAN members were already divided over it. Singapore and Thailand favoured closer defence links with, rather than the exclusion of, the US. ZOPFAN's post-Cold War relevance had also been questioned.[90]

A third ASEAN tradition at stake was the "ASEAN Way," a short-hand for organizational minimalism and preference for informal non-legalistic approaches to cooperation.[91] Challenging this tradition were common security mechanisms, especially the CBM and arms control regime in the Helsinki and Vienna Documents of the CSCE, which imposed formal, reciprocal and binding obligations, and allowed intrusive verification.

ASEAN's discomfort with the Soviet, Canadian and Australian proposals was aggravated by the fact that they all came from "outsider proponents." Accepting them could lead ASEAN to "lose its identity."[92] Senior ASEAN figures also argued that the common security norm and the CSCE model were uniquely suited to "European" conditions. Capturing this sentiment, Ali Alatas, the Indonesian Foreign Minister and a key leader of ASEAN, argued: "You cannot just take European institutions and plant them in Asia because the two situations are totally different."[93] "Unlike in the European situation," Alatas held, "there has been no commonly perceived, single security threat in the Asia-Pacific region, but rather a multiplicity of security concerns." To this, he added the "wide diversity of cultures, socio-political systems and levels of economic development" among regional countries and their consequent lack of "a distinct sense of a community" as obstacles to a CSCE-type structure in the Asia Pacific.[94]

It was "sensitivity" to such ASEAN's reaction that led Australian Foreign Minister Evans to modify his proposal.[95] Dropping the CSCE analogy, Evans recognized ASEAN's "past success as a prelude to the future," thereby endorsing the ASEAN model as the basis of further regional security cooperation.[96] In exchanges and dialogues hosted by a regional think-tank network, the ASEAN Institutes of Strategic and International Studies (ASEAN-ISIS),[97] the common security norm was reframed as "cooperative security."[98] The latter retained two key elements of the original common security idea: the principle of "inclusiveness" and the rejection of deterrence-based security systems, but rejected the legalistic measures of security cooperation found in the CSCE process.

Though formally established in 1988, ASEAN-ISIS had been in existence as an informal network for over a decade, organizing "Second Track" meetings that brought together Asian and Western scholars and policy-makers interested in multilateral security. A 1991 ASEAN-ISIS document, "A Time for Initiative," urged dialogues and measures that would result in a multilateral security institution.[99] ASEAN-ISIS thus made proposals from outsiders appear as a local initiative.

Its push for cooperative security was due to a realization that the end of the Cold War and the settlement of the Cambodia conflict (which had hitherto preoccupied ASEAN and contributed to its success) required ASEAN to develop a new focus.[100] Helping to create a cooperative security institution promised a new and enhanced role for ASEAN in the Asia Pacific region.[101] Underlying this aspiration was a measure of self-confidence that ASEAN itself represented a proven model of regional security cooperation. Later, Indonesia's Alatas would acknowledge: "There was a feeling . . . that we had something to offer, not in terms of European-style structures, but in terms of a forum . . . proposals for security cooperation in Asia by Russia, Canada, and Australia were seen by us as outsiders, with good intentions, telling us what to do. So we told them: Why don't you learn from what we have achieved, how we did it."[102]

An equally important factor behind ASEAN's more receptive attitude towards cooperative security was its recognition of some important common ground between this norm and the existing ASEAN principles and processes. The rejection of deterrence fitted well into ASEAN's existing policy of not organizing itself into a regional collective defence system. And the idea that security should be pursued multilaterally resonated well with Indonesia's prior effort to develop a shared understanding of security in ASEAN through a doctrine of regional resilience.[103]

At its Singapore summit in January 1992, ASEAN agreed to "use established fora to promote external security dialogues on enhancing security as well as intra-ASEAN dialogues on ASEAN security cooperation.[104] As a follow-up, ASEAN-ISIS meetings contributed to an official Japanese initiative for a new regional security institution based on the ASEAN model. In 1993, the Japanese Foreign Minister, Taro Nakayama, proposed that an existing ASEAN mechanism, the ASEAN Post-Ministerial Conferences, be turned into the foundation of a new security organization for the Asia Pacific.[105] The resulting institution, the ASEAN Regional Forum (a proposal to call it Asian Regional Forum was rejected), came into life comprising the ASEAN members, China, Japan, Russia, the US, Australia, Canada and South Korea (India and others joined later).[106]

As the first Asia Pacific institution dedicated to security issues, the ARF represents a significant expansion of ASEAN's security agenda. It is the most inclusive regional institution: counting among its members all the major powers (including the EU) of the contemporary international system. Its creation marked a significant break with ASEAN's ZOPFAN norm.[107] ASEAN was to occupy "the driver's seat" and "dominate and set the pace" of the ARF.[108] At its very first meeting in 1994 in Bangkok, the ARF endorsed ASEAN's own Treaty of Amity and Cooperation, stressing non-interference, "as a code of conduct governing relations between states and a unique diplomatic instrument for regional confidence-building, preventive diplomacy and political and security cooperation."[109] As such, ASEAN's basic norm hierarchy (with non-interference at the top) remained unchanged, while the ZOPFAN idea was displaced with a cooperative security approach.

The ARF's policy instruments have been characterized as "evolutionary developments from extant regional structures rather than the importation of Western modalities or the creation of new structures."[110] Unlike the OSCE's intrusive and constraining CBMs backed by an inspection regime, the ARF's CBM agenda remains "ASEAN-like" in being non-intrusive and non-legalistic, providing for *voluntary* compliance. A Concept Paper in 1995 envisaged three stages of security cooperation: confidence-building, preventive diplomacy and "elaboration of approaches to conflicts" – the latter being modified from the notion of "conflict-resolution" that was deemed to be too "Western" and intrusive.[111] The ARF imitates ASEAN's organizational minimalism. Its main institutional structure consists of an annual Foreign Ministers' conclave, a Senior Officials Meeting, and no

ARF secretariat. ASEAN's centrality is further evident in the fact that ARF annual sessions are held in ASEAN countries only.

To sum up, the cooperative security norm contributed to two institutional outcomes: new tasks (security cooperation) for an existing regional institution (ASEAN) that displaced a long-standing norm (ZOPFAN), and the creation of a "derived" institution, the ARF, closely modelled on ASEAN. For the first time in history, Southeast Asia and the Asia Pacific acquired a permanent regional security institution.

The diffusion of the cooperative security norm was also indicated by the participation of China and the US in the ARF. Neither was at first supportive of multilateral security. China saw in it the danger that its neighbours could "gang up" against its territorial claims in the region. But its attitude changed in the mid-1990s. To quote a Chinese analyst, China was "learning a new form of cooperation, not across a line [in an] adversarial style, but [in a] cooperative style." This, he added, would change Chinese strategic behaviour in the long-term. Chinese policy-makers consistently stressed cooperative security as a more preferable approach to regional order than balance of power approaches.[112]

During initial debates about cooperative security, Richard Solomon, Assistant Secretary of State for East Asian and Pacific Affairs in the senior Bush Administration, argued that the region's problems could not be solved "by working through a large, unwieldy, and ill-defined region-wide collective security forum."[113] The Bush administration feared that an Asian multilateral institution would undermine America's bilateral security alliances in the region.[114] But the US position changed as ASEAN began to localize the common security idea. Secretary of State James Baker conceded that while America's bilateral ties would remain the most important element of its security strategy in the region, "multilateral actions may . . . supplement these bilateral ties."[115] President Clinton, who made Japan and Korea his first overseas destinations as President, stated in Korea in July 1993 that "new regional dialogues on the full range of our *common security* challenges" (emphasis added) would be one of the priorities for his administration's security strategy for the Asia Pacific region.[116] Six years later, Ralph Boyce, Deputy Assistant Secretary of State for East Asian and Pacific Affairs, defended the cooperative security institution: "nay-sayers expected ASEAN Regional Forum to be short-lived, but it has confounded these pessimists by not only surviving, but also thriving."[117]

Case 2: ASEAN and flexible engagement (1998–2000)

The establishment of the ARF in 1994 boosted ASEAN's international prestige. But the glory was short-lived. ASEAN suffered a major setback in the wake of the Asian economic crisis beginning in mid-1997. The crisis revealed the vulnerability of ASEAN to global economic trends. Its failure to respond to the crisis with a united front drew considerable criticism. A key fallout was proposals for reforming ASEAN to make it more responsive to transnational challenges. Leading the reformist camp was Surin Pitsuwan who became the foreign minister of a new Thai government in 1997. At a time when ASEAN's critics were blaming the currency crisis on its lack of a financial surveillance system,[118] Surin targeted ASEAN's "cherished principle of non-intervention . . . to allow it to play a constructive role in preventing or resolving domestic issues with regional implications."[119] According to an official Thai document:

> All the ASEAN members have the responsibility of upholding the principle of non-interference in the domestic affairs of one another. But this commitment cannot and should not be absolute. It must be subjected to reality tests and accordingly it must be **flexible**. The reality is that, as the region becomes more inter-dependent, the dividing line between domestic affairs on the one hand an external or trans-national issues on the other is less clear. Many "domestic" affairs have obvious external or trans-national dimensions, adversely affecting neighbors, the region and the region's relations with others. In such cases, the affected countries should be able to express their opinions and concerns in an open, frank and constructive manner, which is not, and should not be, considered "interference" in fellow-members' domestic affairs" (Emphasis added).[120]

Surin's idea, known as "Flexible Engagement," became a focal point of debate in Southeast Asian regionalism during the 1998–2000 period. Although ostensibly geared to an economic crisis, Surin's real aim was to promote greater political openness and transparency in ASEAN, both at the domestic and regional levels. Among the ideational underpinnings of flexible engagement were emerging post-Westphalian concepts of collective action, including the norm of humanitarian intervention and the advocacy of human rights and democratization by the West.[121]

In Southeast Asia, the human intervention norm had attracted no insider advocacy, only suspicion and rejection. Malaysia's foreign minister Syed Hamid Albar found it "disquieting."[122] He urged the region "to be wary all the time of new concepts and new philosophies that will compromise sovereignty in the name of humanitarian intervention."[123] Its clash with existing ASEAN's policy frameworks was most evident in the case of the Burmese military regime. Western governments – the US, Canada, Australia and the European Union, pushed for sanctions against Burma, with the EU threatening to block economic cooperation with ASEAN if it offered membership to Burma. Southeast Asian NGOs such as Forum Asia and Alternative ASEAN, backed by Western donor agencies, demanded a more interventionist posture towards Burma. In contrast, ASEAN pursued a policy of "constructive engagement" towards the regime, displaying greater deference to its non-interference norm than to the promotion of human rights and democracy.

Neither had the norm received backing from the local epistemic community. ASEAN-ISIS was too divided over this norm to play an advocacy role. Support for a diluted form of regional intervention came only from two individual leaders. The first, Anwar Ibrahim, then Deputy Prime Minister of Malaysia, proposed the idea of "constructive intervention" as a compromise between human intervention and "constructive engagement." In July 1997, he urged ASEAN to assist its weaker members in avoiding internal collapse.[124] But unlike the standard formulation of human intervention, his policy implied supportive assistance, rather than coercive interference.[125] Constructive intervention would take the form of (1) direct assistance to firm up electoral processes, (2) an increased commitment to legal and administrative reforms, (3) the development of human capital, and (4) the general strengthening of civil society and the rule of law in the target country.[126]

Thanks to opposition from fellow ASEAN members, Anwar's proposal was never officially tabled. Against this backdrop, Surin, who was clearly influenced by Anwar's idea,[127] felt the need to reframe and "prune" the idea further to make it more palatable to his ASEAN colleagues. He made no mention of coercive interference or sanction-based regional interactions. Flexible engagement was invoked at a time when "ASEAN needed to put its house in order,"[128] and build "more solid ground for regional action."[129] Surin stressed the potential utility of flexible engagement in making ASEAN more transparent and interdependent, which might make it more effective in addressing a range of current transnational issues, including financial crises as well as challenges related to "drugs, environment, migrants."[130]

Though diluted, flexible engagement, nonetheless, was the most significant challenge to ASEAN's non-interference norm. Regional crisis and domestic change were important catalysts behind Surin's initiative. Surin viewed the former as "a clear and present danger" to ASEAN.[131] His new Thai government was keen to prove its democratic credentials to the international community by distancing itself from ASEAN's non-interference-based support for Burma's repressive regime, and its lack of transparency and accountability.[132]

But Surin's intrusive regionalism was not backed by any prior regional tradition. ASEAN was founded as a grouping of illiberal regimes with no record in promoting human rights and democratic governance. The anti-apartheid movement in South Africa had succeeded partly because campaigners could link their struggle with the prior norm against racism. The campaign by human rights activists against Burma failed because advocacy of human rights and democratic governance had no place in ASEAN, which did not even specify a democratic political system as a criterion for membership.

Moreover, while ASEAN's ZOPFAN norm had already been discredited internally, non-interference was still enjoying a robust legitimacy. As Singapore's Foreign Minister S. Jayakumar put it, "ASEAN countries' consistent adherence to this principle of non-interference" had been "the key reason why no military conflict ha[d] broken out between any two members countries since the founding of ASEAN."[133]

Surin's critics within ASEAN argued that ASEAN's existing mechanisms and processes were adequate for dealing with the new challenges. Malaysia's Foreign Minister Badawi claimed that ASEAN members had always cooperated in solving mutual problems, which sometimes required commenting on each other's affairs, but they had done so "quietly, befitting a community of friends bonded in cooperation and ever mindful of the fact that fractious relations undermine the capacity of ASEAN to work together on issues critical to our collective well-being."[134]

Flexible engagement offered no opportunity for enhancing ASEAN's appeal within the larger Asia Pacific community. Instead, ASEAN members feared that such a policy would provoke vigorous Chinese opposition and undermine the ARF, the very brainchild of ASEAN. Indeed, the very survival of ASEAN would be at risk. Leading the opposition from founding members Indonesia, Malaysia and Singapore, Singapore's Jayakumar argued that abandoning non-interference would be "the surest and quickest way to ruin . . . ASEAN."[135]

Success in localization depends on the insider proponent being seen as upholders of local values and identity. But both Anwar and Surin were seen by their ASEAN peers as "agents" of the West, promoting the latter's agenda of human rights promotion and democratic assistance. Though local in persona, they were insufficiently local in their inspiration and motivation.

Flexible engagement failed to produce any meaningful institutional change in ASEAN.[136] At the annual ASEAN Foreign Minister's Meeting held in Manila in July 1998, Surin dropped the term.[137] ASEAN nominally adopted a new policy of "enhanced interaction" (although this was not reflected in any official statement) as a framework to deal with transnational issues.[138] Surin would later claim some successes of flexible engagement, including a brief discussion of Burma's internal affairs at an official ASEAN meeting in Singapore in 2000. This he saw as the "first ever talking about issues of internal nature in ASEAN."[139] But to consider this to be a true agenda expansion would be misleading, as ASEAN continues to avoid any discussion of, or approaches to, the protection of human rights or the provision of democratic assistance to fellow member states. Even the more modest proposals mooted by Anwar Ibrahim's constructive intervention idea, such as electoral assistance or promotion of civil society, have remained outside of official ASEAN policy. In short, ASEAN has not departed from its non-interference doctrine in any significant way.[140] Its reluctance and inability to send an intervention force to the East Timor in 1999, despite pleas from the Indonesian President, further attests to the continued salience of non-interference.

ASEAN did create two new policy instruments as part of its "enhanced interaction" agenda. The first was an ASEAN Surveillance Process (ASP) created in 1998 to monitor regional economic developments, provide early warning of macroeconomic instability and encourage collective action to prevent an economic crisis.[141] The second was a ministerial "Troika" to support regional political and security crisis prevention.[142] However, the ASP is officially described as "informal, simple and based on peer review process."[143] The Troika remains a paper instrument, and is specifically asked to "refrain from addressing issues that constitute the internal affairs of ASEAN member countries."[144]

Comparison

The localization of cooperative security had three main effects on ASEAN: (1) its acceptance of security dialogues and cooperation as a formal task for ASEAN itself; (2) the displacement of the inward-looking ZOPFAN norm in favour of a more

inclusive approach, which allowed ASEAN to play the role of midwife to the birth
of a new Asia-wide security institution; and (3) the adoption by the new security institution (ARF) of new policy instruments, including CBMs, based on the
ASEAN model. It is fair to say that the target norm of ZOPFAN was not just modified, but displaced. In contrast, the flexible engagement proposal underpinned by
the human intervention norm did not produce any meaningful institutional change
in ASEAN. ASEAN continues to exclude human rights and democratic assistance
tasks and the target norm, non-interference, remains firmly in place. While some
new policy instruments were created, these remain weak and limited.

The variation can be explained in terms of the localization framework. Both
norms challenged cognitive priors in ASEAN: advocates of cooperative security
targeted the ZOPFAN concept and those of flexible engagement targeted its non-
interference doctrine. But non-interference was still enjoying a robust legitimacy,
while the ZOPFAN idea had already been discredited from within ASEAN itself.
The cooperative security norm had displaced the target norm of ZOPFAN but did
not override the doctrine of non-interference in ASEAN, which remained at the
top of ASEAN's norm hierarchy. When non-interference itself became the target
norm, as in the case of flexible engagement, norm diffusion failed.

Both norms had insider proponents, but in the case of cooperative security, it
was a transnational network: ASEAN-ISIS. The insider proponents in the second
case were two individuals, Malaysia's Ibrahim and Thailand's Pitsuwan. This was
clearly a factor explaining the variation between the two cases.

The cooperative security norm could be grafted more easily onto ASEAN
thanks to the existence of two prior *receptive* norms (one which rejected a balance
of power approach to regional security involving multilateral military pacts and the
other being the Indonesian concept of regional resilience) in the ASEAN framework. There were no such norms to host flexible engagement.

Finally, cooperative security offered greater scope for enhancing ASEAN's prestige. It enabled ASEAN to acquire a broader regional relevance and role. Flexible
engagement had no such appeal. Instead, it threatened to undermine both ASEAN
and the ARF.

Alternative explanations

Can the variation be better explained by alternative explanations? To seek explanations at the systemic level by linking the prospects for norm diffusion to the impact
of the end of the Cold War on the global normative environment – as would be
consistent with a structural constructivist framework – would not suffice. The end
of the Cold War certainly helped the diffusion of the cooperative security norm by
highlighting the contribution of the OSCE in easing East–West tensions, thereby
creating an "imitation effect" of the norm. This inspired Western norm entrepreneurs like Canada, which was part of OSCE and its CBM regime to advocate
similar efforts in Asia. Moreover, the end of the Cold War created the need for a
new Asian security order in light of the retrenchment of the US and Soviet military

presence in the region. But the end of the Cold War had a similar impact on the other norm. Both common security and humanitarian intervention were rendered more prominent after the end of the Cold War, the former because of the success of the OSCE and the latter because of the West's new security agenda focusing on democratic "enlargement" and the crisis in the Balkans. Hence, the end of the Cold War itself cannot explain the pattern of norm diffusion in Southeast Asia, or why cooperative security was relatively more successful than humanitarian intervention.

There are three other possible explanations to be considered: realist, functionalist and domestic politics. A realist perspective would explain the pattern of norm diffusion in terms of the distribution of power at the global and regional level. A popular strand of realist thinking sees the engagement of the US in the regional balance of power as the primary determinant of Asian security order and a basic motivating factor behind the security policies of many Asian states. Hence, the acceptance of any new norm to reorganize ASEAN should have depended primarily on US attitude and preferences, or by the regional actors' calculation of the impact of the new norm in keeping the US engaged in the region. Going by this logic, cooperative security, which was initially feared and opposed by the US, should have been rejected, while the flexible engagement, which conformed more to the style of regional interactions preferred by the US and the EU, relatively more powerful actors in strategic and economic sense respectively (the EU had threatened sanctions against ASEAN), should have been accepted. But the outcome of normative contestation in Asia, as discussed in the case studies, was exactly in the opposite direction – a damning indication of the limitations of the realist framework.

The US, as discussed earlier, had rejected cooperative security, at least initially. Hence, if US power is what decisively shapes Asian security order, the initiative by the normally pro-US ASEAN members to create a new regional security institution should not have been successful. Some realists have tried to move around this anomaly by arguing that the ARF was possible because ASEAN members saw it as a way of maintaining a balance of power in the Pacific by ensuring the continued engagement of the US in the post-Cold War period, when there were concerns regarding a possible US military withdrawal from the region and when China's power was rising. Hence, Michael Leifer's assertion that: "the ARF was primarily the product of a post-Cold War concern . . . about how to cope institutionally with America's apparent strategic retreat from East Asia."[145]

But this perspective suffers from major gaps. First, the goal of keeping the US strategically engaged in the region through the ARF was true only of Singapore and Thailand, but not shared by Indonesia or Malaysia. Second, if the real aim was to ensure a stable regional balance of power, then this could have been more effectively addressed by offering the US bases in order to offset the loss of its bases in the Philippines. Indeed, this is precisely what Singapore had done in 1990; it offered access to its air and naval facilities to the US Pacific forces. But Singapore's move was not matched by other ASEAN countries, and Malaysia was highly critical of

Singapore's move.[146] Third, this perspective does not explain the nature and design of the institution that emerged, which was based closely on the ASEAN model, rather than being a military alliance involving the US. In fact, the Chinese acceptance of the ARF was strongly influenced by the very fact that the ARF would not undertake defence cooperation and would not accord a privileged role to the US.[147] This puts to serious question the realist claim that ASEAN's acceptance of cooperative security was mainly aimed at maintaining a post-Cold War regional balance of power, led by the US. The US itself came to accept the ARF, but only after, and not before, ASEAN had reconstructed the cooperative security norm. And this move by ASEAN was not due to US pressure, but because of ASEAN's own urge to find congruence between its existing model of regionalism and the cooperative security norm as proposed by Canada and Australia.

What about power distribution at the intra-regional level? If this was crucial, the diffusion of cooperative security should have depended on the attitude of the more powerful East Asian and ASEAN states, such as China, Japan, or Indonesia. But as the empirical discussion shows, China was initially reluctant to accept cooperative security and came around only after ASEAN had assumed leadership of the institution-building process and reconstructed the norm. Japan's role in pushing for cooperative security was also ambivalent. Sections in the Japanese policy establishment were clearly worried that such an institution would undermine the rationale for the US–Japan defence alliance, the cornerstone of Japanese security policy. Despite an occasional initiative, Japan clearly deferred to the role of ASEAN and, as has been suggested, borrowed from ASEAN-ISIS's ideas about institutionalizing cooperative security. Within ASEAN itself, the pattern of power distribution is not overly hierarchal. No ASEAN country, including Indonesia, was in a power position to impose its preferred norm over the others. Hence, no serious link can be established between the acceptance of the cooperative security norm and intra-regional power differentials in Southeast Asia or East Asia.

Functionalist perspectives see Asian regional institutionalization primarily as a response to growing intra-regional interdependence.[148] Such perspectives would lead us to expect ASEAN's acceptance of flexible engagement, which was aimed at helping ASEAN to "put its house in order,"[149] and create a "more solid ground for regional action"[150] in responding to common economic and security challenges stemming from growing intra-regional interdependence. Had regional actors been motivated primarily by interdependence concerns, then ASEAN should have seen flexible engagement as a timely response, especially after Surin had reframed it away from purely moral politics, and stressed crisis-management and efficacy gains for ASEAN from such a policy shift. But the norm remained under-institutionalized because it conflicted with the deeply ingrained non-interference policy of ASEAN, the opportunities for localizing the norm through grafting were limited, and it did not offer any real prospects for extending and enhancing the ASEAN model. Surin's colleagues largely ignored his plea that the gains of immediately accepting such a policy framework would outweigh the costs of diluting the pre-existing local identity norms of ASEAN.

Domestic politics (regime security concerns) may better explain why the flexible engagement concept found lesser acceptance than the cooperative security norm. Those who backed a more interventionist ASEAN – Anwar, Surin, and Foreign Minister Domingo Siazon of the Philippines – were representing its more democratic polities, while the opponents of the norm, such as Vietnam, Burma and Indonesia, presided over illiberal regimes. A flexible engagement policy, given its roots in humanitarian intervention, would have undercut their legitimacy. This consideration overrode whatever utility they could perceive from Surin's idea of making ASEAN more effective. Cooperative security did not pose a similar threat to these regimes because it had no CSCE-like "human dimension" calling on the member states to offer greater protection for human rights.

But this strengthens, not weakens, my central argument that ASEAN's regional cognitive priors mattered in explaining its divergent responses to cooperative security and flexible engagement. This is because the authoritarian domestic politics in ASEAN were already incorporated into ASEAN's normative prior. The non-interference norm in ASEAN was to a large extent geared towards authoritarian regime maintenance.[151] If domestic political structures could solely determine the responses of ASEAN members to flexible engagement, then Thailand (and to a lesser extent the Philippines) should have broken ranks with ASEAN after their reformist agenda was rejected. But loyalty to ASEAN prevailed over domestic preferences. Both Thailand and the Philippines stuck with the ASEAN consensus favouring non-interference even though their preference, based on domestic politics, went against this outcome.

Realist, functionalist and domestic politics explanations thus by themselves fail to explain ASEAN's contrasting response to two new transnational norms. A more credible explanation must consider the role of ideational forces and the conditions for their localization. And what matters here is not how the prescriptive ideas backed by outside advocates converted the norm-takers, but how the cognitive priors of the norm-takers influenced the reshaping and reception of foreign norms. This was not a static fit, but a dynamic act of congruence-building through framing, grafting, localization and legitimation in which the local actors themselves played the central role.

This perspective also explains a key puzzle of Asian regionalism: why it remains "under-institutionalized"[152] despite shifts in the underlying material conditions and bargaining contexts, such as the intra-regional balance of power and economic interdependence. The path dependency created by localization tells us much about the absence of "European style" regional institutions in Asia despite recent efforts at strengthening and legalizing their institutional framework to cope with new pressures.

Conclusion

Norm diffusion in world politics is produced and directed not just by transnational agents acting out a universal moral script, while local actors remain passive targets and learners. It is also promoted by local agents who actively borrow and modify transnational norms in accordance with their pre-constructed normative beliefs and practices. Until now, agency oriented explanations of norm diffusion tended to be static and failed to explore how existing norms helped to redefine a transnational norm in the local context. This chapter has offered a dynamic theory of localization in which norm-takers perform acts of selection, borrowing, modification in accordance with a pre-existing normative framework to build congruence between that and emerging global norms. This framework is then tested in studying ASEAN's response to two major security norms of the post-Cold War era – i.e. common security and humanitarian intervention. Out the these two norms, the former found greater acceptance than the latter because it fitted more into the conditions that facilitate localization, such as the positive impact of the norm on the legitimacy and authority of key norm-takers, the strength of prior norms, the credibility and prestige of local agents, indigenous cultural traits and traditions, and the scope for grafting and pruning presented by foreign norms.

This framework of localization proposed in this chapter is helpful in understanding why any given region may accept a particular norm while rejecting another, as well as why variation between regions is undergoing normative change. It also offers an alternative to explanations of norm diffusion and institutional change that focus on powerful states or the material interests of actors derived from functional interdependence. In so doing, this chapter advances the cause of generalizing and theory-building from the milieu and behaviour of norm-recipients, especially non-Western actors who have been sidelined in the literature on norm diffusion.

While this chapter's empirical focus is Southeast Asia, comparative work could be undertaken using this framework to investigate how these and other norms spread through the international system, from the global to the local and from region to region. For example, the spread of norms about human rights and democracy can be seen in terms of a localization dynamic in which prior and historically legitimate local normative frameworks play an important role in producing variations in their acceptance and institutionalization at different locations.[153] Comparative research involving Asia and other regions could further enhance our understanding of how localization takes place under different social and normative environments, help to identify and explain conditions that enable the local agents' private and public ideas to shape the process of norm diffusion, and the different types of localization which might result from these processes.

The recent institution-building dynamics in Southeast Asia also suggests that shifts in the global normative environment alone do not produce normative and institutional change at the regional level at the expense of pre-existing normative frameworks and social arrangements. One implication is that it would be unrealistic for advocates of regionalism in Asia to expect that these institutions will any time soon develop the legalistic attributes of European regionalism, the source of much theorizing about regional institutions. The localization dynamics highlighted in this chapter should also serve as a note of caution to those expecting ideas and institution-building models that are successful in one part of the world to be replicated elsewhere. This does not mean institution-building in Asia or elsewhere is doomed to failure. What it suggests, however, is that in Asia as elsewhere in the developing world, institutional change brought about by norm diffusion is likely to follow a progressive and evolutionary trajectory through the localization of international multilateral concepts, without overwhelming regional identity norms and processes.

Notes

1 First appeared as "How Ideas Spread: Whose Norms Matter? Norm Localization and Institutional Change in Asian Regionalism," *International Organization* 58, no. 2 (Spring 2004): 239–275.

2 Standly J. O'Connor, "Introduction," In *The Archaeology of Peninsular Siam*, ed., Stanley J. O'Connor (Bangkok: The Siam Society, 1986), 1–10, 7.

3 Thomas Risse, Stephen C. Ropp, and Kathryn Sikkink, eds., *The Power of Human Rights: International Norms and Domestic Change* (Cambridge: Cambridge University Press, 1999), 4.

4 Cortell and Davis call the domestic agency and process literature as the "second wave" scholarship on norm diffusion. The "first wave" focused on the level of the international system, leading examples being Martha Finnemore, "International Organizations as Teachers of Norms: The United Nations Educational, Scientific, and Cultural Organization and Science Policy," *International Organization* 47, no. 4 (1993): 565–597; and Martha Finnemore and Kathryn Sikkink, "International Norm Dynamics and Political Change," in *Exploration and Contestation in the Study of World Politics*, eds., Peter Katzenstein, Robert Keohane and Stephen Krasner (Cambridge, MA: MIT Press, 1999), 247–277. On the second wave, see especially Jeffrey Checkel, "Norms, Institutions, and European National Identity," ARENA Working Papers, 6/98, Copenhagen, Denmark: Advanced Research on the Europeanization of the Nation-State, University of Oslo, 1998; Jeffrey Checkel, "Why Comply? Social Learning and European Identity Change," *International Organization* 55, no. 3 (2001): 553–588; Amy Gurowitz, "Mobilizing International Norms: Domestic Actors, Immigrants, and the Japanese State," *World Politics* 51, no. 3 (1999): 413–445; and Theo Farrell, "Transnational Norms and Military Development: Constructing Ireland's Professional Army," *European Journal of International Relations* 7, no. 1 (2001): 63–102; although Audie Klotz, *Norms in International Relations: The Struggle Against Apartheid* (Ithaca: Cornell University Press, 1995); Andrew P. Cortell and James W. Davis, "How Do International Institutions Matter? The Domestic Impact of International Rules and Norms," *International Studies Quarterly* 40, no. 4 (1996): 451–478; and Jeffrey W. Legro, "Which Norms Matter?" *International Organization* 51, no. 1 (1997): 31–64 also offered powerful domestic level explanations. For a comprehensive review of the second wave literature, see Andrew P. Cortell and James W. Davis, "Understanding the Domestic Impact of International Norms: A Research Agenda," *International Studies Review* 2, no. 1 (2000): 65–87.

5 In this chapter, I use ideas and norms interchangeably, recognizing that ideas can be held privately, and may or may not have behavioural implications, while norms are always collective and behavioural. Goldstein 1993.

6 "Norm-maker" and "norm-taker" are from Checkel, "Norms Institutions and European National Identity," 2.

7 ASEAN's founding members, Indonesia, Malaysia, Thailand, Philippines and Singapore, were joined by Brunei (1984), Vietnam (1995), Laos and Burma (1997) and Cambodia (1999).

8 Miles Kahler, "Institution-Building in the Pacific," in *Pacific Cooperation: Building Economic and Security Regimes in the Asia-Pacific Region*, eds., Andrew Mack and John Ravenhill (Leonards, Australia: Allen & Unwin), 16–39, 22. See also Miles Kahler, "Legalization as Strategy: The Asia-Pacific Case," *International Organization* 54, no. 3 (2000): 549–571, 551.

9 Peter Katzenstein, "Introduction: Asian Regionalism in Comparative Perspective," in *Network Power: Japan and Asia*, ed., Peter Katzenstein and Takashi Shiraishi (Ithaca, N.Y.: Cornell University Press, 1997), 1–44.

10 Jeffrey Checkel, "The Constructivist Turn in International Relations Theory (A Review Essay)," *World Politics* 50, no. 2 (1998): 324–348, 339.

11 Ted Hopf, "The Promise of Constructivism in International Relations Theory," *International Security* 23, no. 1 (1998): 171–200, 180.

12 For examples, see Kathryn Sikkink, "Human Rights, Principled Issue Networks and Sovereignty in Latin America," *International Organization* 47, no. 3 (1993): 411–441; M. J. Peterson, "Whales, Cetologists, Environmentalists and the International Management of Whaling," *International Organization* 46, no. 1 (1992): 147–186; Karen Litfin, *Ozone Discourses: Science and Politics in Global Environmental Cooperation* (New York: Columbia University Press, 1994; Audie Klotz, *Norms in International Relations: The Struggle Against Apartheid* (Ithaca: Cornell University Press, 1995); and Audie Klotz, "Norms Reconstituting Interests: Global Racial Equality and the U.S. Sanctions Against South Africa," *International Organization* 49, no. 3 (1995): 451–478.

13 See Ethan Nadelmann, "Global Prohibition Regimes: The Evolution of Norms in International Society," *International Organization* 44, no. 4 (1990): 479–524, 483; Risse, Ropp, and Sikkink, *The Power of Human Rights: International Norms and Domestic Change;* and Margaret Keck and Kathryn Sikkink. *Activists Beyond Borders: Advocacy Networks in International Politics* (Ithaca: Cornell University Press, 1998).

14 Finnemore and Sikkink, "International Norm Dynamics and Political Change," 257.

15 Legro, "Which Norms Matter?" 32.

16 Checkel, "Norms Institutions and European National Identity."

17 See Martha Finnemore, "Norms, Culture and World Politics: Insights from Sociology's Institutionalism," *International Organization* 50, no. 2 (1996): 325–347; and Finnemore and Sikkink, "International Norm Dynamics and Political Change," 267.

18 See Finnemore, "International Organizations as Teachers of Norms: The United Nations Educational, Scientific, and Cultural Organization and Science Policy"; Michael N. Barnett and Martha Finnemore, "The Politics, Power, and Pathologies of International Organization," *International Organization* 53, no. 4 (1999): 699–732.

19 On the distinction between regulative, constitutive and prescriptive norms, see Finnemore and Sikkink, "International Norm Dynamics and Political Change," 251.

20 See Thomas Risse-Kappen, "Ideas Do Not Flow Freely: Transnational Coalitions, Domestic Structures, and the End of the Cold War," *International Organization* 48, no. 2 (1994): 185–214; Cortell and Davis, "How Do International Institutions Matter? The Domestic Impact of International Rules and Norms"; Legro, "Which Norms Matter?" Checkel "Norms Institutions and European National Identity"; and Checkel, "Why Comply? Social Learning and European Identity Change."

21 See Richard Price, "Reversing the Gun Sights: Transnational Civil Society Targets Land Mines," *International Organization* 52, no. 3 (1998): 613–644; Ann Florini, "The Evolution of International Norms," *International Studies Quarterly* 40, no. 3 (1996): 363–389.

22 Legro "Which Norms Matter?" 33, 36.

23 Checkel, "Norms Institutions and European National Identity," 4.

24 Checkel, "Norms Institutions and European National Identity," 6.

25 Checkel, "Norms Institutions and European National Identity." Legro's more recent work proposes a more dynamic effect of ideational structures stemming from the undesirable consequences of existing ideas and the availability of viable replacement ideas. See Jeffrey W. Legro, "Whence American Internationalism," *International Organization* 54, no. 2 (2000): 253–289.

26 G. John. Ikenberry, "Conclusion: An Institutional Approach to American Foreign Policy," in *The State and American Foreign Economic Policy*, eds., G. John Ikenberry, David A. Lake, and Michael Mastanduno (Ithaca, N.Y.: Cornell University Press, 1988), 219–243, 242.

27 Finnemore and Sikkink, "International Norm Dynamics and Political Change," 268.
28 Finnemore and Sikkink, "International Norm Dynamics and Political Change," 268.
29 Klotz, *Norms in International Relations: The Struggle Against Apartheid.*
30 Farrell, "Transnational Norms and Military Development: Constructing Ireland's Professional Army."
31 Richard Price, *The Chemical Weapons Taboo,*(Ithaca: Cornell University Press, 1997).
32 See for example the idea of norm transplantation by Farrell "Transnational Norms and Military Development: Constructing Ireland's Professional Army."
33 See O. W. Wolters, *History, Culture and Region in Southeast Asian Perspectives* (Ithaca: Cornell University Southeast Asian Studies Program, 1999; and, Singapore: Institute of Southeast Asian Studies, 1982). For a summary of the literature, see I. W. Mabbett, "The 'Indianization' of Southeast Asia: Reflections on the Prehistoric Sources," *Journal of Southeast Asian Studies* 8, no. 1 (1977): 1–14; and I. W. Mabbett, "The 'Indianization' of Southeast Asia: Reflections on the Historical Sources," *Journal of Southeast Asian Studies* 8, no. 2 (1977): 143–161.
34 J.B. Sykes, ed., *The Concise Oxford Dictionary of Current English: Based on the Oxford English Dictionary and Its Supplements,* 6th edition (Oxford, U.K.: Clarendon Press, 1976), 638.
35 Wolters, *History, Culture and Region in Southeast Asian Perspectives,* 57.
36 While Wolters developed his concept of localization to study the diffusion of Indian and Chinese ideas into classical Southeast Asia, the discourse on localization in Southeast Asian social science literature extends well into the contemporary period. On the localization of Chinese ideas in Southeast Asia, see Wolters, *History, Culture and Region in Southeast Asian Perspectives,* 46–47; Milton Osborne, *Southeast Asia: An Introductory History* (Sydney, Boston : George Allen & Unwin, 1979), 13–14. On the Southeast Asian characteristics of Islamic ideas see: Bennedict Anderson, *Language and Power: Exploring Political Cultures in Indonesia* (Ithaca: Cornell University Press, 1990), 68.
37 Southeast Asian rulers, in an "attempt at legitimizing their interest . . . and organizing and domesticating their states and subjects . . . called Indian civilization to the east . . ." Jacob C. Van Leur, "On Early Asian Trade," in *Indonesian Trade and Society: Essays in Asian Social and Economic History* (The Hague, Netherlands: W.van Hoeve Ltd, 1955), 98. See also Mabbett, "The 'Indianization' of Southeast Asia: Reflections on the Historical Sources," 143–144. The earlier explanations focusing on conquest and commerce are also known as: (1) the *ksatriya* (Sanskrit for warrior) theory – which saw the transmission of Indian ideas as the result of direct Indian conquest and colonization of large parts of Southeast Asia; and (2) the *vaisya* (merchant) theory – which emphasized the role of Indian traders with their extensive commercial interactions with Southeast Asia, who brought with them not just goods, but also Indian cultural artifacts and political ideas. Van Leur's thesis has since been challenged by others for having over-emphasized local initiative, but it marked a decisive turning point towards an "autonomous" historiography of Southeast Asia.
38 Donald G. McCloud, *Southeast Asia: Tradition and Modernity in the Contemporary World* (Boulder, Colo.: Westview Press, 1995), 69.
39 An important example of existing tradition can be found in M.B. Hooker's analysis of how Indian legal–moral frameworks were adjusted to fit indigenous beliefs and practices in Indonesia. M. B. Hooker, *A Concise Legal History of South-East Asia* (Oxford: Clarendon Press, 1978), 35–36. While localization modifies the foreign idea at the receiving end, it does not necessarily produce a feedback on outside norm entrepreneur's own preferences and identity. In other words, localization need not be a two-way process. But the content of the foreign norm does change in the context of the recipient's milieu; *the persuader's ideas are reformulated in the local context.*
40 Wolters, *History, Culture and Region in Southeast Asian Perspectives,* 9.
41 Thomas A. Kirsch, "Complexity in the Thai Religious System," *Journal of Asian Studies* 36, no. 2 (1977): 241–266, 263.
42 Ikenberry, "Conclusion: An Institutional Approach to American Foreign Policy," 234.

43 Klotz, *Norms in International Relations: The Struggle Against Apartheid*, 23.

44 Joachim Krause, *The OSCE and Cooperative Security in Europe: Lessons for Asia*, IDSS Monograph no. 6 (Singapore: Institute of Defence and Strategic Studies, 2003).

45 Cortell and Davis, "Understanding the Domestic Impact of International Norms: A Research Agenda."

46 Finnemore and Sikkink, "International Norm Dynamics and Political Change," 262.

47 Joseph S. Nye and Robert Keohane. "The United States and International Institutions in Europe after the Cold War," in *After the Cold War: International Institutions and State Strategies in Europe, 1989–1991*, eds., Robert O. Keohane, Joseph S. Nye, and Stanley Hoffman (Cambridge: Harvard University Press, 1993), 104–126, 19. See also Vinod Aggarwal, "Analyzing Institutional Transformation in the Asia-Pacific," in *Asia-Pacific Crossroads: Regime Creation and the Future of APEC*, eds., Vinod K. Aggarwal and Charles E. Morrison (London: Macmillan Press Ltd., 1998), 23–61, 53.

48 According to their study, the anti-foot binding campaign succeeded because it added moral force to the Chinese national reform movement that was already seeking improvements in women's status as a "necessary part of their program for national self-strengthening." But attempts to ban female circumcision in Kenya failed because it conflicted with the existing nationalist agenda that saw female circumcision as integral to local culture and identity. Keck and Sikkink, *Activists Beyond Borders: Advocacy Networks in International Politics*, 63.

49 Cortell and Davis, "How Do International Institutions Matter? The Domestic Impact of International Rules and Norms," 453.

50 Wolters, *History, Culture and Region in Southeast Asian Perspectives*, 102.

51 See Checkel, "The Constructivist Turn in International Relations Theory (A Review Essay)," 325, 328.

52 Nadelmann, "Global Prohibition Regimes: The Evolution of Norms in International Society," 482.

53 Nadelmann, "Global Prohibition Regimes: The Evolution of Norms in International Society," 482.

54 Such local and insider proponents are usually located physically within the region and can be either from the government, or part of the wider local policy-making elite with reasonably direct access to policymakers, or part of an active civil society group. The theory of entrepreneurship acknowledges that there has been inadequate attention to the "adaptive role of entrepreneurs as they adjust to their environment" and "to their learning experience." Some of this learning experience may relate to the attitude of consumers, or norm-takers. David Deakins, *Entrepreneurship and Small Firms*, 2nd edn., (London: McGraw-Hill Publishing Company, 1999), 23. See also Peter F. Drucker, *Innovation and Entrepreneurship: Practice and Principles* (London: Heinemann, 1999); John G. Burch, *Entrepreneurship* (Toronto, Canada: John Wiley and Sons, 1986).

55 Geoffrey Wiseman, *Non-Provocative Defence: Ideas and Practices in International Security* (London: Palgrave, 2002), 104.

56 The principal dimensions of Asian strategic culture, Ball argues, "includes styles of policy making which feature informality of structures and modalities, form and process as much as substance and outcome, consensus rather than majority rule, and pragmatism rather than idealism." Desmond Ball, "Strategic Culture in the Asia-Pacific Region," *Security Studies* 3, no. 1 (1993): 44–74, 46.

57 See Tobias Ingo Nischalke, "Insights from ASEAN's Foreign Policy Co-Operation: The 'ASEAN Way,' a Real Spirit or a Phantom?" *Contemporary Southeast Asia* 22, no. 1 (2000): 89–112; Jürgen Haacke, *ASEAN's Diplomatic and Security Culture* (London: RoutledgeCurzon, 2003).

58 Osborne, *Southeast Asia: An Introductory History*, 5–6.

59 Describing this dynamics of ideational contestation involving ideas such as democracy and socialism, Anderson writes: "In any such cross-cultural confrontation, the inevitable thrust is to 'appropriate' the foreign concept and try to anchor it safely to given or traditional ways of thinking and modes of behaviour. Depending on the conceptions

of the elite and its determination, either the imported ideas and modalities or the traditional ones assume general ascendancy: in most large and non-communist societies it is almost invariable that at least in the short run, the traditional modalities tend to prevail." Bennedict Anderson, "The Languages of Indonesian Politics," *Indonesia* no. 1 (1966): 89–116, 113.

60 McCloud, *Southeast Asia: Tradition and Modernity in the Contemporary World*, 338.

61 Alastair Iain Johnston, "Learning Versus Adaptation: Explaining Change in Chinese Arms Control Policy in the 1980s and 1990s," *The China Journal* no. 35 (1996): 27–61.

62 Wolters, *History, Culture and Region in Southeast Asian Perspectives,* 56.

63 Wolters, *History, Culture and Region in Southeast Asian Perspectives,* 56.

64 Johnston, "Learning Versus Adaptation: Explaining Change in Chinese Arms Control Policy in the 1980s and 1990s," 8.

65 I am grateful to an anonymous referee for *International Organization* for suggesting this formulation to distinguish adaptation from localization.

66 Talcott Parsons, *Societies: Evolutionary and Comparative Perspectives* (Englewood Cliffs, N.J.: Prentice Hall, 1966).

67 F. D. K. Bosch, *Selected Studies in Indonesian Archaeology* (The Hague, Netherlands: Martinus Nijhoff, 1961), 3.

68 Wolters found the chief effect of localization being in the extension of the authority and legitimacy of the native chiefs (the "man of prowess") from the cultural and religious to the political domain. Wolters, *History, Culture and Region in Southeast Asian Perspectives,* 52. Van Leur described the effects of localization as being the "legitimation of dynastic interests and the domestication of subjects, and . . . the organization of the ruler's territory into a state." Van Leur, *Indonesian Trade and Society: Essays in Asian Social and Economic History,* 104.

69 Paul Wheatley, "Presidential Address: India Beyond the Ganges – Desultory Reflections on the Origins of Civilization in Southeast Asia," *Journal of Asian Studies* 42, no. 1 (1982): 13–28, 27.

70 Aggarwal, "Analyzing Institutional Transformation in the Asia-Pacific," 32, 60; and Robert O. Keohane, Joseph S. Nye, and Stanley Hoffman (eds). *After the Cold War: International Institutions and State Strategies in Europe, 1989–1991* (Cambridge: Harvard University Press, 1993), 386.

71 Frank Schimmelfennig, "The Community Trap: Liberal Norms, Rhetorical Action, and the Eastern Enlargement of the European Union," *International Organization* 55, no. 1 (2001): 47–80.

72 See for example, Peter Haas's study of the Mediterranean clean up Peter Haas, *Saving the Mediterranean: The Politics of International Environmental Protection* (New York: Columbia University Press, 1990).

73 Finnemore and Sikkink, "International Norm Dynamics and Political Change," 265.

74 Judith Goldstein, Miles Kahler, Robert O. Keohane and Anne-Marie Slaughter, "Introduction: Legalization and World Politics," *International Organization* 54, no. 3 (2000): 385–399.

75 Aggarwal, "Analyzing Institutional Transformation in the Asia-Pacific," 42, 44.

76 Ikenberry, "Conclusion: An Institutional Approach to American Foreign Policy," 223.

77 Peter Hall, Peter A., and Rosemary C. R. Taylor, "Political Science and the Three New Institutionalisms," in *Institutions and Social Order*, eds., Karol Soltan, Eric M. Uslaner, and Virginia Haufler (Ann Arbor: University of Michigan Press, 1998), 15–43, 19.

78 Aggarwal argues that institutional change can lead either to modifying existing institutions and creating new ones. If new ones are created, then they could take two forms: nested institutions and parallel institutions. Aggarwal, "Analyzing Institutional Transformation in the Asia-Pacific," 42, 44. The former can be a form of localization. I prefer the term "derived" institutions to "nested" institutions.

79 Farrell, "Transnational Norms and Military Development: Constructing Ireland's Professional Army," 81.

80 Joe Clark, "Canada and Asia Pacific in the 1990s," Speech presented to the Victoria Chamber of Commerce, Victoria, British Columbia, Canada, 17 July 1990; Joe Clark, "Speech at the Foreign Correspondents' Club of Japan," Tokyo, Japan, 24 July 1990; Gareth Evans, "ASEAN's past success a prelude to the future," Reproduced in Australian Department of Foreign Affairs and Trade's *The Monthly Record, July 1990* (Canberra, Australia: Department of Foreign Affairs and Trade, Australia, 1990); and Gareth Evans and Bruce Grant. 1995. *Australia's Foreign Relations: In the World of the 1990s.* 2nd edition (Carlton, Australia: Melbourne University Press, 1995).

81 There is considerable literature attesting to how the European common security norm affected security debates in Asia. See David B. Dewitt, "Common, Comprehensive and Cooperative Security," *Pacific Review* 7, no. 1 (1994): 1–15; Geoffrey Wiseman, "Common Security in the Asia-Pacific Region," *The Pacific Review* 5, no. 1 (1992): 42–59; and Kevin Clements, "Common Security in the Asia-Pacific: Problems and Prospects," *Alternatives* 14, no. 1 (1989): 49–76.

82 Palme Commission, *The Report of the Independent Commission on Disarmament and Security Issues under the Chairmanship of Olof Palme, Common Security* (New York: Simon & Schuster, 1982).

83 Common security was not formally a CSCE norm, although that is how it is widely perceived in Asian debates.

84 The CBM regime of the CSCE included the presence of observers from both sides at large military exercises, increased transparency and information sharing. On the CSCE's CBM agenda, See Krause, *The OSCE and Cooperative Security in Europe: Lessons for Asia.*

85 The CSCE successfully incorporated human rights issues into the regional confidence-building agenda, thereby setting norms that would regulate the internal as well as external political behaviour of states. Philip Zelkow, "The New Concert of Europe," *Survival* 34, no. 2 (1992): 12–30, 26.

86 Ramesh Thakur and Carlyle A. Thayer, *The Soviet Union as an Asian Pacific Power: Implications of Gorbachev's 1986 Vladivostok Initiative* (Boulder, Colo.: Westview Press, 1987).

87 Clark, "Canada and Asia Pacific in the 1990s"; Joe Clark, "Speech delivered at the Indonesia-Canada Business Council and the Canada Business Association," Jakarta, Indonesia, 26 July 1990.

88 *International Herald Tribune*, 27 July 1990.

89 Cited in ibid. Evans was clearly inspired by the Palme Commission Report and by the Common Security idea. Author's interview with Jeff Wiseman, Evan's Private Secretary, 24 March 2002.

90 For details, see Amitav Acharya, *Constructing a Security Community in Southeast Asia: ASEAN and the Problem of Regional Order* (London, and New York: Routledge, 2001).

91 Acharya, *Constructing a Security Community in Southeast Asia: ASEAN and the Problem of Regional Order.*

92 Excerpts from Lee Kuan Yew's interview with *The Australian*, published in *The Straits Times*, 16 September 1988.

93 Author's interview with Ali Alatas, Kuala Lumpur, Malaysia, 4 June 2002.

94 Ali Alatas, "The Emerging Security Architecture in East Asia and the Pacific – An ASEAN Perspective," Lecture presented to the National University of Singapore Society, Singapore, 1992.

95 Author's Interview with Jeff Wiseman, Evans' Private Secretary, 24 March 2002.

96 Australian Department of Foreign Affairs and Trade. *The Monthly Record*, July 1990 (Canberra, Australia: Department of Foreign Affairs and Trade, Australia, 1990), 430; cited in David Capie and Paul Evans, *The Vocabulary of Asia Pacific Security: A Selected Lexicon* (Singapore: Institute of Southeast Asian Studies, 2001).

97 The ASEAN-ISIS brought together think-tanks from Indonesia, Malaysia, Singapore, the Philippines and Thailand with the goal being to "encourage cooperation and coordination of activities among policy-oriented ASEAN scholars and analysts, and to promote policy-oriented studies of, and exchanges of information and viewpoints on, various strategic and international issues affecting Southeast Asia and ASEAN's peace, security and well-being." ASEAN-ISIS, "A Time for Initiative," *ASEAN-ISIS Monitor* no. 1 (1991): 1–3, 1.

98 See Dewitt, "Common, Comprehensive and Cooperative Security," for a good account of this reframing.

99 ASEAN-ISIS 1991, "A Time for Initiative," 2–3; Lau Teik Soon. *Towards a Regional Security Conference: Role of the Non-Government Organizations*, Working Papers 1 (Singapore: Department of Political Science, National University of Singapore, 1991); and Datuk Seri Najib Tun Razak, "Regional Security: Towards Cooperative Security and Regional Stability," speech delivered at the Chief of the General Staff Conference, Darwin, Australia, 9 April 1992.

100 Author's interview with Jusuf Wanandi, Centre for Strategic and International Studies and a founding leader of ASEAN-ISIS, 4 June 2002.

101 Yang Razali Kassim, "Minister: Asean will always have driver's seat in forum," *Business Times*, 25 July 1994, 3.

102 Author's interview with Ali Alatas, 4 June 2002.

103 Dewitt, "Common, Comprehensive and Cooperative Security," 1994. In the 1970s, Indonesia organized a series of seminars to disseminate the concept of national and regional "resilience," which created the basis for a multilateral security approach. Author's Interview with Kwa Chong Guan, Council Member of the Singapore Institute of International Affairs, 21 May 2003.

104 The Association of Southeast Asian Nations, "Singapore Declaration of 1992, ASEAN Heads of Government Meeting," Press Release, Singapore, 27–28 January 1992, 2.

105 This initiative drew upon recent ASEAN-ISIS proposals, with Yokio Satoh, who headed the policy-planning bureau of the Japanese Foreign Ministry, providing the link. Author's interview with Yukio Satoh, Singapore, 1 June 2002.

106 Acharya, *Constructing a Security Community in Southeast Asia: ASEAN and the Problem of Regional Order.*

107 Michael Leifer, *The ASEAN Regional Forum*. Adelphi Paper 302 (London: International Institute for Strategic Studies, 1996).

108 Yang Razali Kassim, "Minister: Asean will always have driver's seat in forum," *Business Times*, 25 July 1994, 3.

109 "Chairman's Statement: The First Meeting of the ASEAN Regional Forum (ARF), Bangkok, 25 July 1994, 2.

110 Desmond Ball, "A Critical Review of Multilateral Security Cooperation in the Asia-Pacific Region," unpublished paper, Canberra, Australia: Australian National University, 1997, 16–17.

111 The Association of Southeast Asian Nations, *The ASEAN Regional Forum: A Concept Paper* (Jakarta: ASEAN Secretariat, 1995), Annex A and B, 8–11.

112 Author's Interviews at Ministry of Foreign Affairs, Beijing; China Institute of International Studies (CIIS); China Institute of Contemporary International Relations (CICIR); China Centre for International Studies (CCIS); Institute of Asia Pacific Studies, Chinese Academy of Social Sciences (CAAS); Institute for Strategic Studies, National Defense University, The People's Liberation Army. Alastair Iain Johnston suggests that the ARF and multilateral dialogues have reduced the probability of Chinese use of force in the South China Sea. Alastair Iain Johnston, "Is China a Status Quo Power?" *International Security* 27, no. 4 (2003): 5–56.

113 Richard H. Solomon, "A New Era in US Relations with Asia," Statement given by the Assistant Secretary of State for East Asian and Pacific Affairs, 17 May 1991, reproduced in *American Foreign Policy: Current Documents 1991* (Washington DC: Department of State, 1994): 653–663.

114 For initial US reservations about multilateralism, see Richard H. Solomon, "A New Era in US Relations with Asia," Statement given by the Assistant Secretary of State for East Asian and Pacific Affairs, 17 May 1991, reproduced in *American Foreign Policy: Current Documents 1991* (Washington DC: Department of State, 1994): 653–663; James Lilley, Assistant Secretary of Defense in the Bush administration in "No need for East Asian Security Grouping: Lilley," Central News Agency, 1 March 1993, available from Lexis-Nexis; and Robert Zoellick, "US Engagement with Asia," in *United States Foreign Policy: Current Documents 1991* (Washington, DC: Department of State, 1994), 669–672, 670.

115 James A. Baker III, "The US and Japan: Global Partners in a Pacific Community," *Japan Review of International Affairs* Special Issue (1992): 3–15.

116 Bill Clinton, "Fundamentals of Security for a New Pacific Community," Speech addressed to the National Assembly of the Republic of Korea, Seoul, Korea, 10 July 1993, published in *US Department of State Dispatch* 4, no. 29 (1993): 1–2.

117 Ralph Boyce, "Moving from Confidence-Building to Preventive Diplomacy: The Possibilities," paper presented to the 13th Asia-Pacific Roundtable, Kuala Lumpur, Malaysia, 30 May–2 June 1999, 1.

118 "The Limits of Politeness," *The Economist*, 28 February 1998, 43.

119 "Surin Pushes 'Peer Pressure'," *The Bangkok Post*, 13 June 1998, 5.

120 Ministry of Foreign Affairs, Thailand, *Thailand's Non-Paper on The Flexible Engagement Approach*, no. 743/2541 (Bangkok, Thailand: Ministry of Foreign Affairs, Thailand, 1998).

121 Several discussions by the author with Surin Pitsuwan attest to this influence. Surin became a member of the Commission on Human Security and an adviser to the International Commission on State Sovereignty and Humanitarian Intervention, which was tasked to improve the legitimacy and effectiveness of humanitarian intervention. Author's interview with Surin Pitsuwan, Singapore 2, 7 September 2001. Author's interview with Surin Pitsuwan, Bangkok, 10 May 2002.

122 Datuk Seri Syed. Albar, "The Malaysia Human Rights Commission: Aim and Objective," speech given at Bar Council Auditorium, Kuala Lumpur, Malaysia, 28 October 1999.

123 "Malaysia opposes UN probe of East Timor atrocities," *Agence France Presse*, 7 October 1999.

124 Amitav Acharya, *Sovereignty, Non-Intervention, and Regionalism*. CANCAPS Paper 15 (Toronto, Canada: Canadian Consortium on Asia Pacific Security (CANCAPS), York University, 1997). The paper was presented at a workshop organized by Anwar's think-tank, Institute of Policy Studies.

125 "ASEAN Turns to 'Constructive Intervention'." *Asian Wall Street Journal*, 30 September 1997, 10. Author's interview with Adnan Abdul Rahman, policy advisor to Anwar Ibrahim, Bangkok, 23 August 1997.

126 Anwar Ibrahim, *Newsweek*, 21 July 1997, 13.

127 When Surin first presented his ideas, he used the term "Constructive Intervention." But Thai Foreign ministry officials felt this sounded "too radical" and coined the less intrusive term "flexible engagement." Capie and Evans, *The Vocabulary of Asia Pacific Security: A Selected Lexicon*.

128 Author's interview with Surin Pitsuwan, Bangkok, 30 January 2001.

129 Domingo Siazon Jr., "Winning the Challenges of the 21st Century," Address of the Chairman of the 31st ASEAN Ministerial Meeting, Manila, Philippines, 24 July 1998.

130 "Thailand Calls for 'Flexible Engagement' in ASEAN," *Kyodo News Service*, 26 June 1998; and Surin Pitsuwan, "Currency in Turmoil in Southeast Asia: The Strategic Impact," speech delivered at the 12th Asia Pacific Roundtable, Kuala Lumpur, Malaysia, June 1998.

131 Ministry of Foreign Affairs, Thailand, *Thailand's Non-Paper on The Flexible Engagement Approach*.

132 Surin Pitsuwan, "Opening Statement by H.E. Surin Pitsuwan, Minister of Foreign

Affairs of Thailand,"at the 31st ASEAN Ministerial Meeting, Manila, Philippines, 24 July 1998.

133 *The Straits Times*, 23 July 1998, 30.

134 Abdullah Badawi, "Opening Statement of the 31st ASEAN Ministerial Meeting," Manila, Philippines, 24 July 1998.

135 *The Straits Times*, 23 July 1998, 30.

136 *The Straits Times* (Internet Edition), 27 June 1998; *The Straits Times*, 25 July 1998, 23.

137 Surin Pitsuwan, "The Role of Human Rights in Thailand's Foreign Policy Statement," presented at the Seminar on Promotion and Protection of Human Rights by Human Rights Commissions, organized by the Friedrich Ebert Stiftung, 2 October 1998.

138 *Asia Pulse*, 27 July 1998; Author's interview with Surin Pitsuwan, Bangkok, 10 May 2002; Author's interview with Ali Alatas, 4 June 2002; and Author's interview with Termsak Chalermpalanupap, Special Assistant to the Secretary General, ASEAN, Bangkok, January 16, 2001.

139 Author's interview with Surin Pitsuwan, Bangkok, 10 May 2002.

140 John Funston, "ASEAN: Out of Its Depth?" *Contemporary Southeast Asia* 20, no. 1 (1998): 22–37; Nischalke, "Insights from ASEAN's Foreign Policy Co-Operation: The 'ASEAN Way,' a Real Spirit or a Phantom?"; Haacke, *ASEAN's Diplomatic and Security Culture*. At the end of the ASEAN Ministerial Meeting in Manila on 25 July 1998, which saw the most intense debate over whether ASEAN should shift from non-interference to "flexible engagement," Singapore's S. Jayakumar, the incoming Chair-man of ASEAN's Standing Committee, flatly noted: This meeting had "began amidst some confusion and speculation as to whether there would be changes to ASEAN's fundamental principles. These controversies have been laid to rest . . . The basic prin-ciples of non-intervention and decision making by consensus would remain the cor-nerstones of ASEAN." S. Jayakumar, "Closing Statement at the Thirty-First ASEAN Ministerial Meeting," Manila, Philippines, 25 July 1998, http://www.asean.org/com-munities/asean-political-security-community/item/closing-statement-of-he-prof-s-jayakumar-minister-for-foreign-affairs-at-the-thirty-first-asean-ministerial-meeting-manila-25-july-1998.

141 Author's interview with Termsak Chalermpalanupap, Special Assistant to the Secretary General, ASEAN, Bangkok, 16 January 2001.

142 Author's interview with Termsak Chalermpalanupap, Special Assistant to the Secretary General, ASEAN, Bangkok, 16 January 2001; and The Association of Southeast Asian Nations, *The ASEAN Troika: Concept Paper*, adopted at the 33rd AMM, Bangkok, Thailand, 24–25 July 2000, www.aseansec.org.

143 The Association of Southeast Asian Nations, *Terms of Understanding on the Establish-ment of the ASEAN Surveillance Process*, adopted by ASEAN Finance Ministers, Wash-ington, D.C., 4 October 1998, http://cil.nus.edu.sg/rp/pdf/1998%Terms%20of%20Understanding%20on%20the%20Establishment%20of%20the%20ASEAN%20Surveillance%20Process-pdf.pdf.

144 ASEAN, *The ASEAN Troika: Concept Paper*.

145 Michael Leifer, "Regional Solutions to Regional Problems?" in *Towards Recovery in Pacific Asia*, eds., Gerald Segal and David S. G. Goodman (New York: Routledge, 1999), 108–118, 116. See also Paul Dibb, *Towards a New Balance of Power in Asia*, Adelphi Paper 295 (London: International Institute for Strategic Studies, 1995), 38.

146 On intra-ASEAN differences over the US military presence, see Acharya, *Constructing a Security Community in Southeast Asia: ASEAN and the Problem of Regional Order*.

147 Author's Interview with Chinese Foreign Ministry Officials, Beijing, February 1999.

148 A key proponent of this view, Peter Drysdale, contends that the "main impetus" for Asia-Pacific regionalism "derives directly from the forces of East Asia industrializa-tion. It is to preserve the conditions needed to sustain the positive trend of rapid eco-nomic growth and the market-driven integration of Asia Pacific economies which derives from that growth." Peter Drysdale, "The APEC Initiative: Maintaining the Momentum in Manila," *Asia-Pacific Magazine* no. 2 (1996): 44–46, 44; see also Peter

Drysdale, *International Economic Pluralism: Economic Policy in East Asia and the Pacific* (Sydney, Australia: Allen and Unwin, 1988); and Wendy Dobson and Lee Tsao Yuan, "APEC: Cooperation Amidst Diversity," *ASEAN Economic Bulletin* 10, no. 3 (1994): 231–244.

149 Author's Interview with Surin Pitsuwan, Bangkok, 30 January 2001.

150 Siazon, "Winning the Challenges of the 21st Century."

151 This is true of most Third World regions. See Christopher Clapham, "Sovereignty and the Third World State," in *Sovereignty at the Millennium*, ed., Robert Jackson (Oxford: Blackwell, 1999), 100–115.

152 Katzenstein, "Introduction: Asian Regionalism in Comparative Perspective."

153 Ignatieff's work on human rights notes the dangers of "overestimating [the West's] moral prestige" and ignoring the Third World's capacity for resistance. Michael Ignatieff, *The Warrior's Honour: Ethnic War and Modern Conscience* (Toronto, Canada: Penguin Books, 1998), 44. Appadurai's anthropological perspective illuminates three related processes of ideational change as a subset of cultural globalization: how local communities are 'inflected' by global ideas, how global ideas are indigenized and the resulting local forms are subsequently 'repatriated' back to the outside world, and how local forms (such as Hinduism) are globalized. Note the similarities between this and the concept of localization in Southeast Asian studies. Arjun Appadurai, *Modernity at Large: Cultural Dimensions of Globalization* (Minneapolis: University of Minnesota Press, 1996).

9

NORM SUBSIDIARITY AND REGIONAL ORDERS: SOVEREIGNTY, REGIONALISM AND RULE-MAKING IN THE THIRD WORLD[1]

The study of norms occupies an important place in the recent literature on international relations (IR).[2] While norm scholars have highlighted a variety of actors, processes and outcomes concerning norm creation and diffusion in world politics, the latter has not received adequate attention in the literature on the international relations of the Third World. Constructivism, the principal theoretical perspective on norms, initially paid little attention to variations between global and regional norms, and especially to the "ideational role of non-Western regional institutions."[3] While there are now a growing number of country-and-region-specific studies (especially of Western Europe) of norms,[4] few offer a general framework for the Third World or a comparative framework for Third World regions. As a result, the question whether normative action and rule-making takes on a specific quality in Third World states remains under-theorized. Thus the questions: Why and how do Third World states and regions create new rules of the game to regulate relationships among them and with the outside world?

In this chapter, I examine the case of Southeast Asian Treaty Organization (SEATO) to address this question. A key puzzle of Asia's security order is the virtual absence of a multilateral defence organization. Unlike Europe's, Asia's Cold War security architecture was built primarily around bilateral alliances, principally involving the US. SEATO, created in 1954, was the only exception to this. But this alliance, widely regarded as ineffectual and moribund from inception, disappeared well before the end of the Cold War. The fate of SEATO as an American and British-sponsored collective defence organization is certainly of interest to students of Asian security. But it also offers important insights into international norm dynamics. It opens the door not only to an investigation of why variations occur in norm diffusion, but also to an understanding of the response of Third World states to existing global norms, and their role in the creation and diffusion of new norms.

Drawing upon the SEATO experience, I develop and test a new conceptual tool to study norm dynamics in the Third World: *norm subsidiarity*. I begin with a discussion of the definition, motivations and effects of norm subsidiarity. Then, I look at the de-legitimation and undermining of SEATO through normative action by a group of Third World leaders of Asia, led by India's Jawaharlal Nehru. Next, I offer examples from Latin America, the Middle East and Africa to highlight the practice of norm subsidiarity in the Third World. Finally, I draw some implications of this chapter for the study of IR theory.

Theorizing norm subsidiarity

Definition

I define norm[5] subsidiarity as a "process whereby local actors create rules with a view to preserve their autonomy from dominance, neglect, violation, or abuse by more powerful central actors." The concept derives from the general notion of subsidiarity, which refers to "a principle of locating governance at the lowest possible level – that closest to the individuals and groups affected by the rules and decisions adopted and enforced."[6] At its essence, subsidiarity "encourages and authorizes [local] autonomy."[7] The origins of the concept can be traced to Pius XI's papal encyclicals of 1931.[8] In IR, the principle, if not the concept per se, featured in the debate between universalism and regionalism at the time of the drafting of the United Nations Charter at San Francisco in 1945.[9] Subsidiarity is also a principle of the European Union.[10] With the dramatic expansion of US peace operations in the post-Cold War period, subsidiarity has been invoked as a principle around which a division of labour can be constructed between an overstretched UN Security Council and regional organizations.[11]

Slaughter proposes subsidiarity and proportionality as "vertical norms" of contemporary world order, "dictated by considerations of practicability rather than a preordained distribution of power," alongside the "horizontal norms of global deliberative equality, legitimate difference, and positive comity."[12] Others see subsidiarity as a fundamentally normative obligation (rather than as a matter of practicality alone); for example, as an element of "panarchy," i.e. "rule of all by all for all."[13]

The concept of norm subsidiarity is very different from "norm localization." The latter may usefully serve as a point of reference for identifying and distinguishing the essential aspects of the former. Localization is "active construction (through discourse, framing, grafting, and cultural selection) of foreign ideas by local actors, which results in the latter developing significant congruence with local beliefs and practices."[14] Although both concepts stress the primacy of local agency, there are five key differences:

- Localization is *inward-looking*. It involves making foreign ideas and norms consistent with a *local* cognitive prior.[15] Subsidiarity is *outward-looking*. Its main focus is on relations between local actors and external powers in terms of the former's fear of domination by the latter.[16]

- In localization, local actors are *always* norm-takers. In contrast, in subsidiary, local actors can be norm rejecters and/or norm makers.
- In localization, foreign norms are *imported* for *local usage only*.[17] In subsidiarity, local actors may *export* or *"universalize"* locally constructed norms.[18] (Compare Figures 9.1 and 9.2). This may involve using locally constructed norms to support or amplify existing global norms against the parochial ideas of powerful actors.
- In localization, local agents redefine foreign norms which they take as generally *good* and *desirable*, but not fully consistent with their existing cognitive prior (hence the need for their redefinition). In subsidiarity, local agents *reject* outside ideas (of powerful central actors, but not universal principles) which they do not view as worthy of selection, borrowing and adoption in any form.
- Hence, localization is generic to all actors, big or small, powerful or weak. Subsidiarity is specific to peripheral (smaller and/or weaker) actors, because by definition it's their autonomy which is more likely to be challenged. As one writer puts it, "norm localization, or the process of adapting global norms to local ideas, identities, and practices, happens in almost all instances where global norms need to be justified to domestic audiences."[19] Localization "occurs any time a global norm intersects with local/regional ideas/identities/practices." It does not "require either a sense of exclusion or a perception of big power hypocrisy,"[20] or perception of "dominance, neglect, violation, or abuse." The latter are the triggers of norm subsidiarity, and they are more likely to be found among smaller, weaker and peripheral actors.[21]

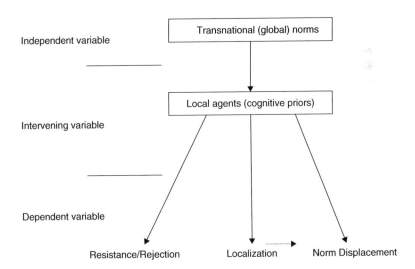

FIGURE 9.1   Localization

Source: Acharya, "How Ideas Spread."

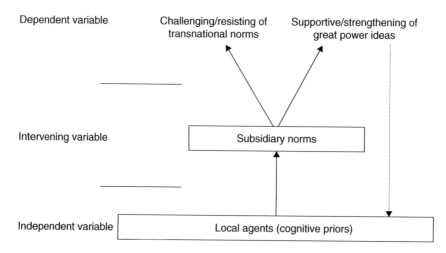

FIGURE 9.2 Subsidiarity

Note: The lower and middle layers do not necessarily comprise a single or coherent set of norms, but rather distinctive, similar, overlapping and mutually reinforcing subsidiary norms developed by different regions. Subsidiary norms may be seen as mediating/intervening between global and local norms.

Actors and motivations

This leads to a crucial question: which actors engage in norm subsidiarity, and why do they do it? As hinted, *I use norm subsidiarity to designate and conceptualize norm construction by Third World states*. It might be argued that the concept is applicable to the normative behaviour of all weak states, including those in the West (such as the Scandinavian countries), and not just the Third World. But I justify limiting the concept to the Third World for several reasons.

By "Third World," I mean states in Asia, Africa, Latin American and the Caribbean, which were either full colonies or semi-colonies (e.g. Thailand) of Western powers.[22] At their origin as independent states, these countries shared a set of conditions, namely a similar security predicament (where domestic and regime security concerns are more salient than external "national" security concerns[23]), anticolonial foreign policy outlook, relative economic underdevelopment, and membership in the Non-Aligned Movement and G-77. These features of the Third World continue to have an important bearing on their foreign policy and security behaviour despite the end of the Cold War and growing economic and political development. More important, they are not found in the Western countries which are deemed to be "weak."

The term Third World is not identical with the term "weak states" or "weak powers." Weak states display low internal socio-political cohesion and what Ayoob calls "unconditional regime legitimacy," while weak powers are states which have low level of material (military and economic power).[24] The weak countries of

Europe are not weak in terms of internal socio-political cohesion and regime legitimacy, but only in terms of independent material and military power. Third World countries, on the other hand, tend to be weak both as states as well as powers, especially the former (there are strong military powers in the Third World, like India). Because of this crucial difference in predicament, their normative behaviour tends to be different from the weak states of the Third World.

Why do Third World states engage in norm subsidiarity? I begin with the observation, following Hedley Bull and other "English School" scholars, that the post-war international system is essentially the European states system writ large.[25] It is the global extension of a European order that once specified rules of inclusion and exclusion on the basis of a "standards of civilizations" criteria, whereby only states which would meet certain conditions, e.g. ability to provide domestic law and order, administrative integrity, protection of rights of foreign citizens, and the fulfillment of contracts, could be regarded as members of international society and therefore worthy of enjoying its norms such as non-intervention and equality of states.[26] Only a handful of the non-Western societies, notably Japan, were accorded a place in the system; all colonies were excluded. Hence, it is not surprising that after gaining independence, and sometimes before it, Third World states and their leaders would question, and wherever possible reject, the norms of an international order that harked back to the era of European dominance, and seek to replace or modify them with those which were consistent with their interests and identities. In this sense, Third World states extended what Bull termed as their "revolt against the West" to the normative domain.[27] Ayoob has introduced an important variation to this argument by contending that Third World countries suffer from an "acute schizophrenia"; they have simultaneously rebelled against and adapted to the norms of the international system inherited from the colonial powers.[28] But even in their adaptive role, there is a tendency among Third World societies to question existing international norms and develop new ones, including what I call subsidiary norms that redefine the meaning and scope of the preexisting European-derived global norms to reflect Third World conditions.

Opposition to great power-sponsored collective defence pacts was part of the normative predisposition of Third World states. Rupert Emerson noted "a widespread sentiment" among societies in Asia and Africa that associated membership in collective defence pacts with "return . . . to colonial rule."[29] Cecil Crab notes that for Third World states, the offer of "protection" by super-power-led collective defence pacts was akin to "a condition of colonialism or dependency."[30]

Against this backdrop, Third World states developed subsidiary norms for two main reasons. The first was to challenge their *exclusion* or marginalization from global norm-making processes. Institutions dominated by great powers do not always reflect the ideas, interests and identities of weaker states. In such cases, norm subsidiarity is a response by the latter to the "tyranny" of higher-level institutions (formal or informal, including multilateral organizations or great power security management regimes)[31] in global governance. During the drafting of the UN's charter, newly independent states argued against investing the sole authority for handling peace and security issues in the UN Security Council and demanded "regional solution to regional problems."[32] The latter was justified because regional actors were better informed about local problems and hence would be better able to devise solutions to them than distant global bodies.[33] Subsequently, new nations like Ceylon looked to regionalism because their UN membership was yet to be assured. Norm subsidiarity was thus a means toward regional autonomy, a condition in which intra-regional "actions and responses predominate over external influences,"[34] and which allows regional groups to "keep outsiders from defining the issues that constitute the local agenda."[35]

Second, Third World states resorted to norm subsidiary when confronted with great power *hypocrisy*. This occurs when they see the violation of their cherished global norms by powerful actors and when higher level institutions tasked with their defence seem unwilling or incapable of preventing their violation. A key principle here is non-intervention in the international affairs of states. As Krasner's "organized hypocrisy" formulation holds, this and related norms of sovereignty are frequently violated, even as they remain formally at the core of the Westphalian international order.[36] Such hypocrisy is often a trigger for subsidiary norms in the Third World. These subsidiary norms would limit the scope for great power caprice or unilateralism at least in the regional context. Again although ". . . when confronted with big power violations of global norms, *all* smaller, less powerful actors may perceive hypocrisy, post-colonial actors might be especially sensitive to norms that are selectively applied/implemented."[37] During the Cold War, the global superpower competition and interventionism and the consequent paralysis of the UN created a demand for subsidiary norms of non-intervention in different regions. While such regional norms did not always turn out to be effective, they at least enjoyed a greater legitimacy in the Third World than the managerial rules of great powers (like those of the Monroe Doctrine or the Brezhnev Doctrine).

Although weak Western counties have reasons to be worried about great power hypocrisy, in general, they are generally satisfied with the system status quo. As noted, Third World countries are more rebellious and feel more marginalized from global rule making because they entered an international system that was European-created and dominated. While things may be changing now, this was the case in the formative years of post-World War II international order, which is the historical and empirical focus of this chapter. Countries like Nehru's India, Sukarno's Indonesia, Nasser's Egypt and Mao's China were largely dissatisfied with the system status quo. Hence, they had a greater imperative for developing subsidiary norms in keeping with the motivations of norm subsidiarity I have outlined. In other words, system-dissatisfied weak states/powers tend to be more prone to norm subsidiarity than system-satisfied weak states/powers. While weak Western countries or Middle Powers may develop norms of their own, these norms are not motivated by an acute sense of marginalization or a security predicament where internal security concerns trump external ones.

Effects

A final point concerns the effects of subsidiary norms. Subsidiary norms constitute an ideational structure that determines the legitimacy of a "higher level" authority, including ideas and institutions propagated and controlled by hegemonic or great powers, such as collective defence systems that offer protection to weaker states. Keohane draws attention to the importance of analysing the "legitimacy of hegemonic regimes."[38] Chayes and Chayes maintain that international institutions derive their legitimacy from "the degree of international consensus" and "participation."[39] And Ikenberry and Kupchan argue that the legitimacy of great power-led international institutions depends on the "common acceptance of a consensual normative order that binds ruler and ruled."[40] Since great powers are normally expected to possess the resources to offer sufficient material incentives (including security protection and economic aid) to lure weak states into their ambit, their failure to attract the desired level of weak state representation in institutions created by them would indicate non-material variables at work, including normative forces. Constructivists have pointed to the effects of norms in legitimation and de-legitimation of specific types of behaviour, including power politics.[41] Subsidiary norms developed by regional actors could thus determine whether a "consensual normative order" binding the ruler and the ruled within hegemonic or great power-led institutions would be possible. A good indicator of normative consensus in hegemonic or great power-led institutions would be the willing participation of the "ruled" in the "ruler's" scheme. When the latter fails to obtain such participation, despite its expressed wishes, the outcome is a legitimacy deficit capable of crippling its institutional framework. Hence, the legitimacy deficit of great power-led institutions is a function of regional or sub-systemic legitimating structures, which may be put in place through the creation of subsidiary norms.

Against this backdrop, this chapter identifies two main effects of norm subsidiarity (Figure 9.2).[42] The first may be called the *challenging/resisting effect*. Through subsidiary norms, local actors offer normative resistance to central actors, including great powers and institutions controlled by them. At the same time, local actors claim the right to formulate rules and deal with their own issues without intervention by any higher authority. The latter are entitled to perform "only those tasks which cannot be performed at a more immediate or local level."[43] The second effect of norm subsidiarity is support by local actors for existing common global norms (consistent with "rules of all by all for all") which are vital to preserving their autonomy. Some of these common global rules of the contemporary international system that are invoked and supported by weaker states include sovereignty, territorial integrity, independence and self-determination, equality of states, racial equality, non-intervention, and (after the 1945 San Francisco Conference) the principle of regional autonomy or "regional solutions to regional problems."[44] This may be called the *supportive/strengthening effect* of subsidiarity. Here, local agents create norms by invoking and supporting a *global* normative prior to secure their autonomy and resist powerful actors. The two effects of norm subsidiarity may proceed simultaneously, with local actors offering resistance to great power-controlled ideas and institutions while invoking existing global norms.

In the following section, I trace a subsidiary norm dynamic in post-war Southeast Asia, which crippled SEATO.

The fate of collective defence in post-war Asia

Why SEATO?

Why study SEATO and the period of the mid-1950s? SEATO was not the first collective defence pact to be created after World War II. That distinction belonged to NATO, established in 1949. But SEATO, created by an agreement among the US, UK, Australia, New Zealand, Pakistan, Philippines and Thailand in Manila on 8 September 1954, arguably constituted the most important post-war US effort to organize a multilateral collective defence organization in the entire Third World.

SEATO had a greater importance than the contemporaneous Baghdad Pact, or what eventually became the Central Treaty Organization (CENTO). The Baghdad Pact was signed on 24 February 1955, five and half months after the Manila Pact. It was originally a bilateral affair, between Turkey and Iraq, to which UK and Pakistan acceded later. By contrast, SEATO was multilateral from the outset, therefore of greater significance as a test of *collective defence*. Moreover, the US did not join CENTO, even though it clearly lent strong support to it. SEATO was explicitly American in conception and ownership. During the mid-1950s, the US considered Asia (including Southeast Asia) to be a more important strategic theatre than the Middle East. As Dulles would put it, it was in "Asia that Russian imperialism finds its most powerful expression."[45] At the time of SEATO's creation, Asia had already become the theatre of the first major outright war of the post-Second World War II period – the Korean War, which was also the first hot war between the US and communist forces. Moreover, Southeast Asia itself (the regional definition of which at the time included India),[46] presented itself as a highly unstable subregion, especially with the French defeat in Indo-China, which greatly alarmed the US. The Middle East was yet to be that crucial; the formation of SEATO occurred well before the 1967 Arab–Israeli War or the 1973 Arab oil embargo, which would render the Middle East a theatre of greater strategic significance to the US.

SEATO's main purpose was to counter communist advance, whether a direct attack or subversion, and to prevent what the Eisenhower administration would describe as the "domino effect" of the fall of South Vietnam to communists. SEATO did not have NATO's integrated military command, nor did it enjoy a US security commitment that would be invoked automatically in punishing aggression against any member state. On the other hand, SEATO was a unique alliance in the sense that it offered to guarantee the security of not just its members, but also that of the states which were not formally part of it, namely South Vietnam, Cambodia and Laos.

The period of the mid-1950s was also a crucial period for the foreign policy development of Third World states. Earlier on, in the late 1940s and early 50s,

Asian states like India and Indonesia were more concerned with advancing decolonisation than developing rules of conduct in international affairs, including norms concerning the legitimacy of alliances and power politics. Hence, the first major conference of post-War Asia, the Asian Relations Conference organised by India and attended by Nationalist China, did not discuss issues like non-intervention – a key Westphalian norm. But by the time of the Bandung Conference, issues of intervention and non-intervention were salient. This was thanks to the escalation of superpower rivalry in the Korean War and the onset of what would be the long Vietnam War. Whereas some opposition to superpower-led collective defence pacts in Asia predated SEATO, as a by-product of anti-colonial sentiments, the association and invoking of the non-intervention norm by Third World states to de-legitimize collective defence was more evident in the mid-1950s, partly due to the emergence of pacts like SEATO and CENTO. Finally, opposition to earlier American ideas about collective defence in Asia were muted because those proposals were just that: proposals. This was clearly not the case with SEATO.

The Bandung Conference, held during 18–24 April 1955, also makes the mid-1950s a significant period in the development of Third World international relations. It was the first international gathering of the newly independent countries of Asia and Africa. It was the first international meeting in which Communist China participated without the presence of the Soviet Union. It was the first appearance in the world stage of Egypt's newly anointed leader, Gamel Abdel Nasser, who left the conference a changed man. And it crucially influenced the foreign policy of Ghana's pan-Africanist leader, Kwame Nkrumah. Bandung was also the decisive normative beginning of the Non-Aligned Movement. The organization of the conference reflected powerful forces at work: decolonization, the outbreak of the Cold War, the escalation of the Indo-China conflict, and the leadership ambitions of new states such as India, Indonesia, Egypt and Communist China. In essence then, Bandung captured many of the basic forces and divisions that shaped the post-war international order.

Origins

The proposal for SEATO, a brainchild of US Secretary of State John Foster Dulles, constituted a reversal of previous US policy in Asia. For example, a State Department Policy Planning Staff paper in March 1949 had argued that the US should avoid setting up an "area organization" in the Pacific and focus on "joint or parallel action" until there was "a pragmatic and desirable basis for intimate association" for a "formal organization." In the meantime, the US "should encourage the Indians, Filipinos and other Asian states to take the public lead in political matters," while its own "role should be the offering of discreet support and guidance."[47] Later, when the Truman administration was presented with the idea of a collective defence system for the Pacific, proposed by Elpidio Quirino of the Philippines, and backed by its other Cold War allies such as Syngman Rhee of South Korea and Chiang Kai Shek of the Republic of China, it rejected this idea, a wise move given the controversial standing of these Asian leaders, both within their own countries and regionally. The Truman administration subsequently did consider a multilateral security arrangement to accompany the US–Japan defence treaty, but this idea was opposed by Dulles himself (who was appointed by Truman to oversee the negotiations on the US–Japan treaty) and abandoned once the treaty was successfully concluded.

Yet, the Eisenhower administration, spurred by Chinese revolution and the Korean War, and its own understanding of and approach to world affairs, took the opposite course, insisting on a formal collective defence organization for Southeast Asia. Influenced by the Korean War and the gains made by North Vietnamese communists, Dulles changed his position on collective defence.[48] Now installed as Secretary of State, he saw collective defence as a means of preventing a possible Chinese takeover of the region. In a discussion with Congressional leaders in May 1954, he contended that "if the communists gained Indochina and nothing was done about it, it was only a question of time until all of Southeast Asia falls along with Indonesia, thus imperiling our Western island of defense."[49] A month and half later, he was even more apocalyptic in discussing Indo-China with Eisenhower: "I expressed the thought that it might well be that the situation in Indochina itself would soon have deteriorated to a point where nothing effectual can be done to stop the tide of Chinese communists over-running Southeast Asia except perhaps diversionary activities along the China coast, which would be conducted primarily by the Nationalist forces, but would require sea and air support from the United States."[50]

Initial planning for a collective defence system for Southeast Asia began with the French defeat at Dien Bien Phu in January 1954. Following the event, the US significantly escalated its support for French forces in Indo-China. At the same time, a US National Security Council decision memo, NSC-5405, dated 16 January 1954, contained a reference to a coordinated regional defence system to counter any further communist expansion without directly committing American forces.[51] The US move towards a collective defence pact gathered pace during and immediately after the Geneva Conference on Indo-China held between 8 May and 21 July 1954.[52] On 24 July 1954, the NSC met and argued that such a pact would give the president discretion to attack China before a war declaration and get international support. By mid-August, NSC had developed NSC-5429, which viewed the Geneva accords as a victory for the communists, and believed that the US needed to create a Southeast Asian pact to offset the damage to Western interests. It presented two plans: Alternative A called for immediate retaliation against China in the case of any aggression in "Free" Southeast Asia, while Alternative B asked for a commitment from each member to act to meet the common danger according to their own constitutional requirements. But in either case, NSC-5429 stipulated that the US would retain "its freedom to attack its enemies as it chose, including, if necessary, with the use of nuclear weapons."[53]

Although Britain differed from the US regarding the organization and membership of SEATO, it too had come to accept the need for SEATO. Its view was that: ". . . the danger of a third world war is most grave when there is a situation of weakness, not when there is one of strength. In Europe, the existence of N.A.T.O. has created a clearly defined line that the communists have respected because it is strongly defended. It is in the absence of any such line in Asia which creates the risk of war, as exemplified in Indochina."[54]

Resistance

As the plan for collective defence in Southeast Asia intensified, the prime ministers of five Asian countries, i.e. India, Pakistan, Burma, Indonesia and Ceylon, met in Colombo in April 1954 under the informal banner of Colombo Powers (after the convener of this group: Ceylon).[55] As the first countries in Asia (along with the Philippines) to emerge from colonial rule, theirs was an important voice expressing emerging regionalist ideas in Asia. These ideas in turn were heavily inspired by nationalism and anti-colonialism. It entailed a desire for enhancing Asian representation in global councils and securing autonomy from great power meddling in regional affairs. Faced with the Cold War-induced paralysis of the UN and the growing US, Soviet and Chinese involvement in Indo-China, one of the first demands of the Colombo Powers was to call for "a solemn agreement of non-intervention" by all the great powers "to refrain from giving aid to the combatants or intervening in Indo-China with troops or war material."[56] The powers also became the focal point for contestation over the issue of regional collective defence.

This contestation was evident during the Geneva Conference. The fact that American planning for SEATO had proceeded while talks were still going on in Geneva was a sore point for the Colombo Powers. Although the US would not sign the final Geneva declaration which divided Vietnam at the 17th parallel so as not to recognize the legitimacy of PRC, it issued a separate protocol accepting agreements and undertaking not to violate them. One provision of the Geneva Accords (the 5th Accord) was that neither section of Vietnam could "constitute part of any military alliance." The accord also stipulated that Cambodia and Laos could not "join in any agreement with other States if this agreement includes the obligation to participate in a military alliance not in accordance with the principles of the Charter of the United Nations."[57] Although the Indochinese countries would not be formally included in SEATO and the latter was considered by the US to be fully consistent with the UN Charter, the Colombo Powers (with the exception of Pakistan which joined SEATO) thought the very idea of a regional collective defence pact under the US violated the spirit if not the letter of the language of the Geneva Agreement. As Nehru would remark later, SEATO represented "quite a new conception" because unlike NATO, "members of this organization are not only responsible for their own defense but also for that of areas they may designate outside of it if they so agree, this would mean creating a new form of spheres of influence." Nehru contrasted collective defence with the Geneva Agreement, which he had endorsed "because of its clause that no outside interference will be allowed in Indo-China."[58] The Indonesian position would be similar; SEATO's offer of protection even to non-members "contravened the principle of international law forbidding armed interference by foreign powers in the internal affairs of a nation" and "brought the Cold War to the South East Asian region."[59]

At this point, the British Government as well as some senior US officials recognized the importance of securing the participation of the Colombo Powers as a prerequisite for the proposed alliance's success. British Foreign Secretary Anthony Eden told Dulles that he "should avoid taking any action which might lead the Governments represented at Colombo to come out publicly against our security proposals."[60] In his view, without such countries, "the pact would simply be a white man's pact imposed from the outside and robbed of popular support."[61] He urged the US that "strong efforts to secure the participation of the Colombo Powers in the collective security arrangement, or at least their acquiescence in its formation, should be made prior to the negotiation of the treaty."[62]

There were similar voices within the US. Defense Secretary Charles Wilson believed that "without the Colombo Powers we wouldn't have much in Southeast Asia." A State Department official urged giving "real consideration to the British position—that is, that we should go slowly in forming such an organization [SEATO] in order to give ourselves time to persuade Burma, Pakistan, Ceylon, Indonesia and India to join in or, at least, to look with favor upon it."[63] Even Dulles and Eisenhower recognized the need for Indian participation, despite Dulles' personal dislike for Nehru. The US ambassador to India, George V. Allen, was summoned to the White House in May 1954 to be told of "the extreme importance they attached to carrying Indian and Asian opinion" on the matter of SEATO (this language is from a British memo based on conversation with Allen). Dulles would even maintain that: "nothing will suit the Americans better than that the Indians should not only share but actually take the initiative. Could they not organize a scheme of collective defense among South East Asian countries with the United States and United Kingdom standing behind in support?"[64] This shows that the US keenly wished for Indian participation in the SEATO (as well as that of the other Colombo Powers), rather than simply not caring about it. The fact that it failed to do get their participation attests to the role normative opposition to collective defence from Nehru and the Colombo Powers (save Pakistan) played in de-legitimizing SEATO.

At American urging, Britain took the lead in persuading the Colombo Powers to join the proposed collective defence organization, whose treaty was planned to be signed at a Conference in Manila in September 1954. On 30 July 1954, British Foreign Secretary Anthony Eden wrote to Nehru (as well as other Colombo Powers) asking them whether they would "find an invitation to be represented at the proposed meeting [Manila Conference] . . . acceptable."[65] Dulles had asked the British not to formally *invite* the Colombo Powers to the Manila Conference unless they had indicated prior willingness to accept the invitation.[66] Nehru's reply was unambiguous; to him the proposed organization:

> would be an organic military arrangement the participants in which are some
> states in the area and a larger number outside [the] area who seek to align

themselves with one another for the avowed purpose of safeguarding peace and promoting the stability of the participating countries or of the area as a whole against other countries and peoples in the area . . . It is therefore far from being a collective peace system; it is rather a military alliance. This may possibly result in the formation of a counter-military alliance . . . You have referred to the role of the Asian powers in the defence of South East Asia and mentioned its vital importance. Yet the majority of Asian countries [and the] overwhelming majority of Asian peoples will not be participants in the organization. Some it may be anticipated would even be strongly opposed to it, thus rendering South East Asia a potentially explosive theater of the Cold War.[67]

Nehru played a central role in organizing resistance to SEATO. A key figure behind early Asian regionalism, he played a central role in post-war Asian regional conferences, including the Asian Relations Conference, New Delhi, 1947, the Conference on Indonesia, New Delhi, 1949, and later the Bandung Asia–Africa Conference, 1955. Even before becoming India's Prime Minister in 1947, Nehru had criticized collective defence pacts under great powers as "a continuation of power politics on a vaster scale."[68] His opposition to collective defence invoked the principles of sovereignty, particularly the equality of states and non-intervention. It was also shaped by his involvement in India's nationalist struggle and the influence of the Gandhian doctrine of non-violence. Hence, it was of "[l]ittle surprise that he reacted viscerally to geopoliticians" like Dulles.[69]

But Nehru was not alone. Burma turned down the invitation to attend the Manila conference out of concerns about compromising its sovereignty and inviting great power intervention. As the Burmese Prime Minister U Nu put it, "an alliance with a big power immediately means domination by that power. It means the loss of independence."[70] The Indonesian government argued that a collective defence arrangement in the region would undermine its "independent foreign policy."[71] The Ceylonese Prime Minister John Kotelawala did not want his country to give the "appearance of being committed to either side" in the Cold War.[72] His opposition to SEATO reflected "the general feeling that . . . a united voice of Asia [should be] . . . heard in the councils of a world whose destinies had hitherto tended to be controlled almost entirely from another direction."[73] As such, "What was wrong about SEATO was that the opinion of Free Asia had not been sought in regard to the troubles in Vietnam and Korea . . . The Colombo Conference [of April–May 1954] was going to demonstrate to the world that the people of Asia knew what was good for them."[74] In summary, exclusion from decisions about forming such a pact, the perceived hypocrisy of SEATO's great power proponents, who while professing the principle of non-intervention were using the pact as a tool of their intervention in the region (specifically in the Indo-China conflict), and the consequent loss of autonomy of regional actors, shaped the rejection of SEATO by the four Colombo Powers.

Effects

Although the Southeast Asia Collective Defense Treaty was formally signed on 8 September 1954, normative opposition from the four Colombo Powers would not disappear. In fact, it might have intensified, especially at the Bandung Conference in April 1955.[75] Aside from highlighting great power hypocrisy and the limitations of the UN, the Bandung Conference became an arena for contesting the legitimacy of collective defence as represented by SEATO and CENTO.[76]

At Bandung, Nehru portrayed NATO as "one of the most powerful protectors of colonialism,"[77] (presumably because Portugal was seeking support from NATO colleagues to hold on to Goa). He presented collective defence pacts as a threat to the sovereignty and dignity of postcolonial states, finding it "intolerable . . . that the great countries of Asia and Africa should come out of bondage into freedom only to degrade themselves or humiliate themselves" by joining such pacts.[78]

On the other side, supporters of collective defence, notably Pakistan, Turkey and the Philippines, argued that SEATO, the first pact to be geared towards subversion (rather than just overt military attack), was necessary against the threat of communism – the main security challenge facing them. Philippines' lead delegate Carlos Romulo pointed out that the communists were routinely violating their own professed doctrine of non-intervention.[79] Pakistan's Prime Minister, Mohammed Ali, took Nehru's attack on collective defence pacts as an affront to Pakistan's own sovereignty. Later, however, Thailand and Philippines and even Pakistan would change their position about SEATO's political worth.

Why? It was because, as will be discussed shortly, the logic of norm subsidiarity would also influence them. Subsidiarity is triggered by the exclusion of regional actors from global rule-making and the perceived hypocrisy of great powers in defending agreed principles. At Bandung, both the motivating forces were clearly at work. The sense of exclusion from global norm-making processes was especially felt. At the San Francisco Conference that drafted the UN Charter, Asia had been barely represented; the only countries being India (still a British colony) and the Republic of China.[80] Western dominance of the UN became a sore point with Asian nationalists, especially after the Netherlands tried to enlist the UN's help to support its return to Indonesia. Even by 1955, more than half of the participants in the Bandung Conference, including sponsor Ceylon, were not yet even members of the UN.

Moreover, Bandung participants also perceived hypocrisy on the part of great powers in upholding the non-intervention norm and saw the UN as being incapable of preventing its violation by the great powers. The UN was seen as being ineffective in dealing with superpower interventionism in Indo-China. The UN's failure to deal with West Irian was resolutely criticized at Bandung. As Ceylon's Prime Minister John Kotelawala lamented:

> It is not the United Nations which has preserved the uneasy peace of the last decade. In all the major issues of world politics, such as the Korean and

Indo-Chinese disputes, negotiations for settlement had to be carried on out-side the framework of the United Nations . . . what we of Asia and Africa can appropriately demand, is that the United Nations Organization should be so reconstituted as to become a fully representative organ of the people's of the world, in which all nations can meet in free and equal terms.[81]

The final communiqué issued by the Bandung Conference adopted ten princi-ples as a normative charter for the newly independent states of Asia and Africa. One of the principles recognized the right of every nation to collective defence, but another stipulated the "abstention from the use of arrangements of collective defense to serve the particular interests of any of the big powers." This formulation would underpin the normative de-legitimation of collective defence in post-war Asia.

As noted, the effect of norm subsidiarity may be judged from the extent to which it resists and erodes the legitimacy enjoyed by norms and institutions created by great powers. And this legitimacy rested not just on the material variables, like military or economic aid to allies, but more crucially on issues of representation and participation. The Bandung Conference not only put paid to any US and Brit-ish hopes for drawing new members to SEATO,[82] it also aggravated anti-SEATO sentiments in two key Southeast Asian members: Thailand and the Philippines. Despite having embraced SEATO membership, these two countries had already "resented not being taken into the confidence of their Western partners" – US, UK, France, Australia and New Zealand – especially when the latter began discus-sions on a regional collective defence pact in 1954.[83] This sense of exclusion was aggravated by the growing perception of the "un-Asianness" of SEATO created at Bandung. In the Philippines, it strengthened domestic elements, which advo-cated an Asian identity for the country by moving away from too close a security relationship with the US. Emanuel Palaez, a Philippine Senator and member of its delegation to Bandung, felt a "sense of pride" after listening to Indonesian Presi-dent Sukarno's opening speech. Sukarno to him was a "fellow Asian . . . a voice of Asia, to which we Filipinos belong."[84] After Bandung, Thailand signalled a more accommodating attitude towards China, which led a US State Department memo to remark that Bangkok seemed to be "reverting to their historic policy of having at least a toe in either camp."[85] Later, a former Thai Secretary-General of SEATO echoed Nehru's normative argument against SEATO. He noted: "When member-ship is disparate and composed of great and small nations, the latter having to rely heavily on the former, the organization is bound to be at the mercy of the whip and whim of the larger nations." As regards the reason for SEATO's demise, he would stress its failure "to gather new members" and the "ironical" fact that "it was Thailand and the Philippines whose security SEATO was principally conceived to ensure, who asked . . . for its gradual phasing out . . ."[86] In short, the exclusion of the Philippines and Thailand from earlier Anglo-American deliberations over col-lective defence, the subsequent failure of Western powers to secure wider Asian participation in the alliance, and the evident conflict between the sense of Asian identity fostered by Bandung and the nature of SEATO as an outsiders' project, weakened the alliance from its very inception, and strengthened its alternative: a subsidiary norm against collective defence pacts.

Alternative explanations

Against this normative explanation of why SEATO failed, let me offer three alternative explanations, one each from functionalist, realist and constructivist (a different one from mine) perspectives (see Figure 9.3). Functionalists have argued that America's "half-hearted commitment" was what really doomed SEATO.[87] The US commitment to SEATO was based not on the NATO formula of automatic and immediate collective action against aggression, but mimicked the Monroe Doctrine, which only asked for consultations among the allies. Any collective action would be subject to the constitutional processes of each member. But Dulles insisted that the SEATO formula was "as effective as that we used in" NATO. This type of formula was necessary to preclude Congressional objections, which felt that the NATO formula allowed the President too much power over war-making at the expense of the Congress (such objections had almost wrecked Senate ratification of NATO, which Dulles did not want to see repeated).[88] And while SEATO did not have a permanent military command, neither did ANZUS (Australia, New Zealand and US), a far more successful military alliance than SEATO, suggesting that a unified command is not a prerequisite for the political success of an alliance. Moreover, as described earlier, under the SEATO formula the US retained the option of a direct attack on China, including limited nuclear strikes, which would be more credible than defending against such an attack militarily.

A realist explanation of why Asia did not develop a viable post-war multilateral security organization attributes it to America's "extreme hegemony," or the huge *power gap* between America and its Asian allies. Since the Asians had too little to offer either individually or collectively to a multilateral security grouping, Washington saw no point in a regional security organization.[89] A constructivist explanation blames *identity dissonance*. The US recognized a greater sense of a transatlantic community than a transpacific one; hence Europe rather than Asia was seen as a more desirable arena for multilateral engagement.[90] But both these perspectives are top-down. They stress why the US *did not want a* multilateral defence organization in Asia, rather than *why Asian actors did not themselves want it*. They give no consideration to the norms developed by Asians themselves. I have shown that the US and allies did seek a multilateral defence organization, but simply could not get what they wanted due to strong normative opposition *from within Asia*, which limited Asian participation and representation in SEATO, thus undercutting its legitimacy and viability.

Another alternative explanation for SEATO's failure is intra-regional rivalry such as that between India and Pakistan. But this does not explain why three other Colombo Powers, namely Indonesia and Ceylon and Burma, refused to join SEATO, even though they had no conflicts with the three who did, namely

	Material	Ideational
Dominant Power	Power gap	Identity dissonance
Local Actors	Intra-regional disputes	Norm subsidiarity

FIGURE 9.3   Alternative explanations[91]

Thailand, the Philippines and Pakistan. Multilateral alliances between a hegemonic power and weaker states are possible despite quarrels among the latter because a hegemonic power usually possesses the resources to goad quarrelling partners into a system of collective defence, as the US was able to do in relation to Greece and Turkey in NATO.

In considering normative versus rationalist/materialist explanations of why SEATO failed, I should stress that this chapter deals with what might be considered, following Katzenstein, a "hard case" for normative explanations.[92] The failure of alliances usually favours established realist and functional explanations in the field of national security. But I have demonstrated that a normative explanation of why SEATO failed is possible and this should encourage generalizations about norm subsidiarity that are applicable to other Third World regions.

Long-term consequences

The norm against regional collective defence shaped Asian regionalism that emerged from the Bandung Conference. Indeed, what was originally an injunction against "the use of arrangements of collective defence to serve the particular interests of any of the big powers," expanded into a more general norm against regional collective defence, even when not sponsored by the great powers because of the fear that such defence arrangements might be seen as a SEATO through the backdoor. Thus, the founding documents of ASEAN, created in 1967, avoided any mention of collective defence so as not to "lend credence to charges that [ASEAN] was a substitute for the ill-fated South-East Asia Treaty Organization in the making."[93] ASEAN members consistently rejected any defence role for the grouping, despite the Vietnamese invasion of Cambodia and the Soviet naval expansion in the Pacific in the 1980s. And ASEAN would become the driver of subsequent regional institutions in Asia, especially the ASEAN Regional Forum (ARF), created in 1994. The ARF, the first Asia-wide regional organization devoted to security issues, has purposely avoided any collective defence role. The agenda of ARF consists of three stages: confidence-building, preventive diplomacy and conflict-resolution. Its primary goal is to induce defence transparency among its member states, not collective defence against common threats.[94] Some writers suggest that the rise of China might create the possibility of an Asian NATO,[95] but this seems highly unlikely.

To conclude the implications of the above for Asian security regionalism, the concept of norm subsidiarity offers a better explanation for the absence of a collective defence organization in Asia than rationalist or other constructivist explanations. Why did Asian actors engage in such norm subsidiarity? The generic factor, deriving from the norm localization perspective, was the desire of local actors to fit the more abstractly defined universal norms to local context and beliefs. But more relevant were the specific factors applicable mainly to Third World states, including their exclusion from global norm-making processes and their resistance to the hypocrisy of powerful actors in selectively applying global rules of sovereignty. During the post-war period, many Asian nationalist leaders, with little say or representation in the global decision making bodies, perceived the two superpowers as violators of the norm of non-intervention, especially through their rivalry over Indo-China. Yet, the UN seemed to be too paralyzed by the Cold War to address their security concerns. Hence, developing a local norm against collective defence pacts was seen as necessary in not only countering superpower interventionism, but also compensating for the deficiencies of the UN. Moreover, while non-intervention was supposedly a "universal" norm, in reality, its European application had not been unexceptional, allowing intervention to maintain the balance of power. Yet, in post-war Asia, local conditions, especially the new-found interdependence of Asian states which had to be safeguarded, and the ideas of nationalist leaders such as Nehru or Aung San rejecting great power spheres of influence, provided the basis for reformulating the norm of non-intervention with a view to de-legitimize great power-led military pacts.

Norm subsidiarity in the Third World

The concept of norm subsidiarity can be used to study norm creation and diffusion in other regions. Here, I am not so much interested in causal inferences about norm subsidiarity, but in making a bounded generalization that is applicable to other cases under similar conditions. This means that under similar circumstances, norm subsidiarity will develop in other parts of the world.[96] In this section, I show examples of norm subsidiarity in regions which share similar historical (colonial/semi-colonial status), political (weak socio-political cohesion and regime insecurity) and strategic (marginalization through great power dominance and hypocrisy) conditions. Thus, Latin America, Middle East and Africa developed subsidiary norms, whereby they have sought to develop local rules to challenge great powers dominance and hypocrisy and secure regional autonomy. In so doing, they also supported existing global norms such as territorial integrity, self-determination, non-intervention, racial equality, and regional autonomy.

Latin American countries, the first to obtain independence from colonial rule, have been "international rule innovators."[97] A key source of regional norms, Bolivarianism, was explicitly geared towards regional autonomy; it "derived from the external threat posed by Europe's powers to the nascent South American states."[98] Although Bolivar's dream of a Latin American political union never materialized,

Latin American regional interactions became the springboard of "ideas that rejected imperialism, . . . defended sovereignty, self-determination, and nonintervention, and encouraged Latin American coordination and cooperation."[99]

One of the most prominent Latin American subsidiary norms is the doctrine of *uti possidetis juris*, or honouring inherited boundaries, after the break-up of the Spanish Empire. This norm, which respected the Spanish Empire's administrative boundaries, became "a framework of domestic and international legitimacy in the otherwise bloody passage from the Empire to its successor American states."[100] This norm clearly supported and contributed to the global territorial integrity norm, or what Brownlie calls the "creation and transfer of territorial sovereignty."[101] Another subsidiary norm of Latin America is "absolute nonintervention in the hemispheric community," both as an abstract principle and as a means to challenge US hegemony in the region (embodied in the "Monroe Doctrine"). Developed under the banner of pan-Americanism, this norm responded to the perceived hypocrisy of a superpower in dealing with its Southern neighbours.[102] Thus, the Calvo Doctrine (after Argentine jurist Carlos Calvo) rejected the right of intervention claimed by foreign powers (European and US) in order to protect their citizens who were resident in Latin America. Another rule, the Drago Doctrine, named after Argentine Foreign Minister Luis Drago, challenged the US and European position that they had a right to intervene to force states to honour their sovereign debts.[103] Over US opposition, Latin American congresses recognized revolutionary governments as de jure. Both Calvo and Drago doctrines constituted subsidiary norms of state sovereignty in Latin America's regional order. The Latin American advocacy led the US to abandon the Monroe Doctrine in 1933 and accept nonintervention as a basic principle in its relations with the region.

Advocacy of "regional arrangements" is yet another example of norm subsidiarity by Latin American states. Expressed during the debate over the post-war global security architecture, this was clearly in response to the potential "tyranny" of a higher-level institution, the UN. Faced with the Roosevelt administration's clear preference for a universal organization, Latin American states argued that placing the whole responsibility for international peace and security in the hands of the UN Security Council would compromise the autonomy of regional institutions such as their own inter-American system (the Organization of American States). Regional arrangements, of which the Inter-American system was the oldest and most elaborate example, not only had a better understanding of local challenges to peace and security, they might also be in a better position to provide assistance and mediation in regional conflicts than a distant UN Security Council.[104] Hence, to quote a Latin American delegate to the San Francisco Conference which drafted the UN Charter, "inserting the inter-American system into the [UN] Charter . . . was a question of safeguarding a whole tradition which was dear to our continent . . . and a very active one" and would "contribute . . . to world peace and security."[105] Thanks to Latin American advocacy, supported by Arab League member states, the Charter formally recognized the role of regional organizations as instruments of conflict control and member states were asked to "make every effort to achieve peaceful settlement of local disputes through such regional arrangements" (Article 33/1, Chapter VI and Article 52/2, Chapter VIII). This outcome, as US Senator Arthur Vandenberg put it, "infinitely strengthened the world Organization" by incorporating "these regional king-links into the global chain."[106] In other words, subsidiary norms embodied in regional conflict-control arrangements constituted "a sub-systemic structure underpinning the framework of global norms" embodied in the UN, as per Figure 9.1.

In the Middle East, norm subsidiary could be discerned from what Barnett calls the "norms of Arabism,"[107] which includes the "quest for independence, the cause of Palestine, and the search for [Arab] unity" and nonalignment.[108] These norms were both challenging/resisting great power policies and supportive/strengthening of existing global norms. The initial pan-Arabist norms, especially those associated with Egypt's Nasser, resisted the Baghdad Pact sponsored by the US. Nasser led the opposition to the Baghdad Pact as an instrument of US and British hegemony, which subverted regional aspirations and arrangements for peace and security. As noted earlier, the Pact was signed in February 1955 on the same pretext of fighting communism, as had been the case with SEATO. Prior to its signing, Nasser had been judged by the US State Department to be "friendly to West, especially to the United States." But the Department also pointed out that Nasser had become more "reserved" towards the West since the signing of the Baghdad Pact, which he "believes will damage Egypt's position of leadership among the Arab states."[109] Nehru himself had warned before the Bandung Conference that the Baghdad Pact would make an otherwise friendly Egyptian government wary of US intentions and radicalize the Middle East, while undermining indigenous efforts at regional cooperation.[110] Among other things, Nasser viewed the Baghdad Pact as severely undermining the scheme for an indigenous Arab Collective Security System, which had been mooted by Egypt. The Bandung Conference's "spirited rhetoric of anticolonialism, independence, and rejection of alliances with the West had a major influence on Nasser."[111] Within months of the Bandung Conference, Nasser would sign an arms deal with Czechoslovakia and nationalize the Suez Canal, thereby setting the path for a major confrontation with the US and the West in 1956.

In rejecting the Baghdad Pact, the Arab subsidiary norms were also supporting/strengthening the existing global norms of nationalism, self-determination, non-intervention and regional autonomy. Indeed, the Nasserite ideal of creating a single Arab nation out of existing postcolonial states gradually faded. But this only illustrates the working of the other subsidiary norms of the region, and their supporting/strengthening effect on the existing universal norms of national sovereignty.[112] Moreover, the cause of Palestine and the quest for regional autonomy, cooperation and non-alignment, continued to define the normative order of the Arab Middle East long after Nasser.

Finally, in Africa, Kwame Nkrumah of Ghana, the first sub-Saharan African country to gain independence, led the formulation of the subsidiary norms of an African regional order which would stress non-intervention by outside powers in

African affairs and the abstention of Africans in superpower-led collective defence pacts. As in the Middle East, the African norms supported the common global norms of territorial sovereignty, racial equality, liberation from colonial rule and regional cooperation. Nkrumah had been prevented by the British (Ghana was still under British dominion status) from attending the Bandung Conference, despite his keen desire to do so. But he too was deeply influenced by the Conference.[113] In April 1958, Nkrumah hosted the first Conference of Independent African States. Like the Bandung meeting, the African Conference was geared towards not only discussing ways to secure independence from colonial rule, but also developing norms of foreign policy conduct aimed at addressing "the central problem of how to secure peace" (similar to the Bandung agenda of World Peace and Cooperation). Among the principles agreed to at the African conference was Bandung's: "abstention from the use of arrangements of collective defense to serve the particular interests of any of the great powers."[114] As Nkrumah saw it, the conference was the first time that "Free Africans were actually meeting together, *in Africa,* to examine and consider African affairs." Moreover, the normative result of the Conference was "a signal departure from establish custom, a jar to the arrogant assumption of non-African nations that Africa affairs were solely the concern of states outside our continent."[115] This marked the beginning of the African subsidiary norms of regional self-reliance in regional security and economic development. Even after Nkrumah's eclipse, the African normative order would continue to reject superpower intervention, espouse regional autonomy, and develop regional institutions geared towards achieving African cooperation, if not outright political unity.[116]

As noted, norm subsidiarity may involve transregional extensions of locally developed rules. Asian norm subsidiarity clearly had a discernible effect on other Third World regions. The Non-Aligned Movement (NAM), which attracted considerable membership in Latin America, Africa and the Middle East, was a direct offshoot of the Bandung Conference.[117] A meeting of Foreign Ministers in 1961 limited membership in NAM to states that were not members of "a multilateral alliance concluded in the context of Great Power conflicts."[118] This has remained a core principle of NAM.

It might be asked whether the subsidiary norms of Latin America, Arab Middle East and Africa (or more broadly non-intervention in the Third World) can be really regarded as norms, since they have not always been upheld in practice. One might also ask whether those subsidiary norms could not be explained in terms of more straightforward instrumental political reasons such as political expediency. But *just because norms are violated from time to time by some actors does not disqualify their claim to be norms.*[119] What makes norms *norms* is that they develop "stickiness," backed by a "logic of appropriateness" to replace an initial "logic of consequences." The *uti possidetis* norm might have been initially motivated by "convenience and expediency" on the part of the newly independent Latin American states.[120] But while the norm "did not preclude the emergence of boundary disputes among the Latin American states," it was frequently applied to territorial disputes and "by recognizing the same norm . . . the parties at least managed to resolve their border disputes, in most cases, peacefully."[121] Asia has had no single instance of a collective defence pact since SEATO. The boundary maintenance regime in Africa has been remarkably resilient and successful. The quest for regional autonomy has been a persistent feature of all Third World regions, as seen from the policy and actions of their regional organizations.[122] While non-intervention (or the Latin American, Arab and African norms discussed above) has been selectively complied with, and there are double standards in norm compliance in both the West and the Third World, this does not invalidate their claim for this norm to be a *norm*.[123] Moreover, constructivists have long accepted that norm creation and compliance need not be inconsistent with self-interested (instrumental) motivations, expediency and behaviour. As Finnemore and Sikkink put it, "frequently heard arguments about whether behavior is norm-based, or interest-based miss the point that norm conformance can often be self-interested, depending on how one specifies interests and the nature of the norm."[124] Moreover, the tendency to juxtapose starkly interest-based explanations and normative explanations of behaviour has been increasingly challenged by constructivists themselves. The "rationalist–constructivist synthesis" in the international relations theory points to the possibility of both normative and instrumental calculations in norm compliance. As Zurn and Checkel point out, most behaviour can be subject to a "double interpretation": one from a rationalist/instrumental perspective and the other from a constructivist/normative (logic of appropriateness) perspective.[125] This is true of all the aforesaid norms.

Finally, although subsidiary norms may travel from one region to another due to snowballing, learning and emulation, and thereby retain a certain basic meaning across regions, the process of diffusion can also cause new variations in their understanding and application. The norm of honouring postcolonial boundaries, originally developed in Latin America, was adopted in Africa and to some extent in Asia. But its application in Latin America was much more legalized than in the other regions. Thus, to say that norm subsidiarity is a general feature of Third World regions does not mean that these norms would have exactly the same meaning in different regions. *Region specificity* is a hallmark of norm subsidiarity. The Latin Americans doctrine of non-intervention was a more *absolute* doctrine than that in European practice, where intervention could still be justified for the sake of maintaining the balance of power. Asians too zealously adopted non-intervention, but introduced another significant local variation: abstention from superpower-led military pacts. Hence while all Third World regions, including Latin America, Asia, Middle East, and Africa, developed subsidiary norms linked to non-intervention, this took different forms. In Asia, as the SEATO experience suggests, it produced a total opposition to collective security or defence pacts, but Latin Americans used it as a precondition for participating in a regional collective security system with the US as long as Washington pledged not to interfere in their internal affairs. The Arabs and Africans rejected superpower-led defence pacts much like the Asians, but they were prepared at least to try indigenous schemes for collective security and defence cooperation to an extent not found in Asia. Regional context, need and discourses determine how subsidiary norms develop in different regions.

Conclusion

The concept of subsidiarity is yet to receive the attention it deserves in the theoretical literature on IR. In this chapter, I have explored the concept's rich potential to propose and conceptualize a process of norm creation and diffusion in the Third World.[126] In the conclusion, I outline three main contributions of the norm subsidiarity concept for IR scholars.

First, studies of the normative behaviour of Third World states and their regional institutions remain scarce, especially compared with Western actors and European regional institutions. To be sure, there is much work on the foreign policy behaviour of Third World states.[127] But they rarely deal with normative or ideational variables. While studies of norm development by individual Third World states or regions are beginning to appear (as discussed in the previous section), thanks mainly to the work of different area specialists, what we do not have until now is an overarching framework that explains the dynamics of norm diffusion that is applicable across regions in the Third World. This chapter offers one such framework, which has comparative potential. Along with the idea of norm localization, norm subsidiarity opens the door to a systematic attempt to develop a theory of norm creation and diffusion in the Third World, thereby countering the Westerncentrism in the literature on the international relations of the Third World.

The second implication of this chapter concerns constructivism. Constructivism has been more interested in studying the diffusion of moral principles, such as norms against apartheid, chemical weapons, or the protection of whales, than the diffusion of norms whose moral claim is contested, such as the non-intervention norm, which has lost its appeal in the West (especially in the European Union) but remains important in most parts of the Third World.[128] By the time constructivism came into vogue, non-intervention was no longer regarded in the West as a moral principle; in fact, just the opposite was the case. For some Western constructivists, since state sovereignty (and hence non-intervention) can be "neither resilient nor moral," acknowledging its "constructed" nature is important in highlighting its decadence and obsolescence.[129] Hence, the constructivist literature has been more concerned with studying the diffusion of norms *against* non-intervention, for example, humanitarian intervention – than of the original norm itself.[130] Yet, it should not be forgotten that although non-intervention has been discredited due to its association with human rights abuses, it was once deemed to be a *moral* norm, and espoused by such nationalist and democratic leaders as Jawaharlal Nehru of India as a bulwark against neocolonialism and superpower intervention. The idea of norm subsidiarity helps in understanding the complexities and contestations that goes with norm creation in world politics.

The final contribution of norm subsidiarity concerns the *agency role* of Third World states. Most early accounts of the role of the Third World in world politics focused on its "revolt against the West,"[131] and the North–South "structural conflict."[132] As latecomers with scant material resources, and with a rebellious disposition, the Third World was cast as a spoiler of, rather than a contributor to, international order. Missing from the picture is the agency role of Third World states in constituting the world polity and managing international order. This chapter highlights a special type of agency: namely, the ideational and normative agency of Third World states in world politics. As Puchala notes: for "Third World countries, ideas and ideologies are far more important" than power or wealth because "powerlessness" and "unequal distribution of the world's wealth" are "constants." Hence, they drive world affairs."[133]

I share Ayoob's perspective on the "schizophrenia" of Third World states that have simultaneously challenged and adapted to the "system of states."[134] But this chapter also highlights the constitutive role of the Third World in global order in the normative domain. Moreover, while like Ayoob I deal with the "subaltern" strata of the world polity (without using the term), the idea of norm subsidiarity speaks to a "subaltern constructivism," rather than Ayoob's "subaltern realism."[135] Unlike Ayoob, and to a much greater extent than the English School, I stress the role of ideational forces as "weapons of the weak," available to and employed by Third World actors as constitutive instruments of the world polity.

Lacking in structural and material power, Third World states resort to ideas and norms to construct world politics. The study of SEATO from the prism of norm subsidiarity provides an important starting point for understanding this role. It deserves due attention side by side with the contribution of Western nations and the norms and institutions created and controlled by them.

Notes

1 First published as "Norm Subsidiarity and Regional Orders: Sovereignty, Regionalism and Rule Making in the Third World," *International Studies Quarterly* 55, no. 1 (2011): 95–123.
2 See, for example, Jeffrey Checkel, ed., "International Institutions and Socialization in Europe," *International Organization,* Special Issue 59, no. 4 (2005). For an overview of norm literature, see: Amitav Acharya, *Whose Ideas Matter: Agency and Power in Asian Regionalism* (Ithaca: Cornell University Press, 2009).
3 Acharya, *Whose Ideas Matter,* 24. Checkel's Europe-derived notion of "cultural match" and Acharya's Southeast Asia-derived notion of "localization" or "constitutive localization" represented two early attempts to study regional variations in norm creation and diffusion. See: Jeffrey Checkel, "Norms, Institutions, and National Identity in Contemporary Europe," *International Studies Quarterly* 43, no. 1 (1999): 83–114; Jeffrey Checkel, "Why Comply? Social Learning and European Identity Change," *International Organization* 55, no. 3 (2001): 553–588; and Amitav Acharya, "How Ideas Spread: Whose Norms Matter? Norm Localization and Institutional Change in Asian Regionalism," *International Organization* 58, no. 2 (2004): 239–275.
4 Checkel, "International Institutions and Socialization in Europe". See also, Thomas Diez, "Constructing the Self and Changing Others: Reconsidering 'Normative Power Europe,'" *Millennium: Journal of International Studies* 33, no. 3 (2005); Ian Manners, "The European Union as a Normative Power: A Response to Thomas Diez," *Millennium: Journal of International Studies* 35, no. 1 (2006); and Michelle Pace, "The Construction of EU Normative Power," *Journal of Common Market Studies* 45, no. 5 (2007). More general recent studies of norm creation and diffusion include, Arturo Santa-Cruz, "Constitutional Structures, Sovereignty, and the Emergence of Norms: The Case of International Election Monitoring," *International Organization* 59, no. 3 (2005):

663–693; Joshua William Busby, "Bono Made Jesse Helms Cry: Jubilee 2000, Debt Relief, and Moral Action in International Politics," *International Studies Quarterly* 51, no. 2 (2007): 247–275; Jelena Subotiæ, "Hijacked Justice: Domestic Appropriation of International Norms," Department of Political Science, University of Wisconsin-Madison, March 2005, http://www.du.edu/gsis/hrhw/working/2005/28-subotic-2005.pdf; and Elizabeth Bloodgood, "Information, Norms and NGO Influence In International Relations," Department of Political Science, Concordia University, January 2007, http://politicalscience.concordia.ca/faculty/discussions/documents/InformationsNorms.pdf. For region and country-specific discussions of norm creation and compliance, aside from the literature discussed later in this chapter, see: Arturo Santa-Cruz "Contested Compliance in a Liberal Normative Structure: The Western Hemisphere Idea and the Monitoring of the Mexican Elections," paper prepared for the Workshop on Contested Compliance in International Policy Coordination – Bridging Research on Norms and Policy Analysis, Portaferry, County Down, Northern Ireland, 17–18 December 2005; Jean Grugel, "Democratization and Ideational Diffusion: Europe, Mercosur and Social Citizenship," *Journal of Common Market Studies* 45, no. 1 (2007); Paul D. Williams, "From Non-intervention to Non-indifference: the Origins and Development of the African Union's Security Culture," *African Affairs* 106, no. 423 (2007): 253–279; Antoaneta Dimitrova and Mark Rhinard, "The Power of Norms in the Transposition of EU Directives," *European Integration online Papers(EIoP)* 9, no. 16 (2005), http://eiop.or.at/eiop/texte/2005-016a.htm; and Markus Kornprobst, "Argumentation and Compromise: Ireland's Selection of the Territorial Status Quo Norm," *International Organization* 61, no. 1 (2007): 69–98. Few of these studies offer a general theory of norm creation and diffusion in the Third World.

5 I use norm to mean "standard of appropriate behaviour for actors with a given identity." Martha Finnemore and Kathryn Sikkink, "International Norm Dynamics and Political Change," *International Organization* 52, no. 4 (1998), 251.

6 Anne-Marie Slaughter, *A New World Order* (Princeton: Princeton University Press, 2004).

7 Steering Committee on Local and Regional Authorities in Europe, "Definition and Limits of the Principle of Subsidiarity," Draft study (France: Council of Europe, 9 November 1993), 11.

8 Ibid. 10–11.

9 Minerva Etzioni, *The Majority of One: Towards a Theory of Regional Compatibility* (Beverly Hills, Calif.: Sage Publications, 1970); Norman J. Padelford, "Regional Organizations and the United Nations," *International Organization* 8, no. 2 (1954): 203–216; Ernst Haas, "Regionalism, Functionalism and Universal Organization," *World Politics* 8, no. 2 (1956): 238–263; Joseph S. Nye, *Peace in Parts: Integration and Conflict in Regional Organization* (Boston: Little, Brown and Company, 1971).

10 Andrew Moravcsik, *The Choice for Europe* (Ithaca: Cornell University Press, 1998), 455; "Protocol on the Application of the Principles of Subsidiarity and Proportionality," *Official Journal of the European Union* C 310/207, 16 December 2004; Gráinne De Búrca, "The Principle of Subsidiarity and the Court of Justice as an Institutional Actor," *Journal of Common Market Studies* 36 (1998): 214–235; Sean Pager, "Strictness and Subsidiarity: An Institutional Perspective on Affirmative Action at the European Court of Justice," *International & Comparative Law Review* 35 (2003); and Edward Swaine, "Subsidiarity and Self-interest: Federalism at the European Court of Justice," *Harvard International Law Journal* 4, no. 1 (2000).

11 UN Security Council Resolution 1631, SC/8526, 17 October 2005; W. Andy Knight, "Towards a Subsidiarity Model for Peacekeeping and Preventive Diplomacy: Making Chapter VIII of the UN Charter Operational," *Third World Quarterly* 17, no. 1 (1996): 31–52; David O'Brien, "The Search for Subsidiarity: the UN, African Regional Organizations and Humanitarian Action," *International Peacekeeping* 7, no. 3 (2000): 57–83; Sorpong Peou, "The Subsidiarity Model of Global Governance in the UN-ASEAN Context," *Global Governance* 4, no. 44 (1998): 439–460; and Connie Peck, "The Role

of Regional Organizations in Preventing and Resolving Conflict," in *Turbulent Peace: The Challenge of Managing International Conflict,* eds., C. Crocker, Fen Osler Hampson and Pamela Aall (Washington, D.C.: United States Institute Press, 2001). For its application to other international organizations, see: The Director-General's Programme of Work and Budget 2006–07, Supplement to (Reform proposals), C 2005/3/Sup.1, August 2005 (Rome: Food and Agriculture Organization of the United Nations, 2005), http://www.fao.org/docrep/meeting/009/j5800e/j5800e_sup1/j5800e03_sup1.htm.

12 Slaughter, *A New World Order.*

13 James P Sewell and Mark B Salter, "Panarchy and Other Norms for Global Governance: Boutros-Ghali, Rosenau and Beyond," *Global Governance* 1, no. 2 (1995): 156–169; Knight, "Towards a Subsidiarity Model for Peacekeeping and Preventive Diplomacy: Making Chapter VIII of the UN Charter Operational."

14 Acharya, "How Ideas Spread," 245.

15 O.W. Wolters, *History, Culture and Region in Southeast Asian Perspective* (Singapore: Institute of Southeast Asian Studies, 1999). Acharya, *Whose Ideas Matter,* 21. Here, cognitive prior is defined as an "existing set of ideas, belief systems, and norms, which determine and condition an individual or social group's receptivity to new norms." For the notion of cognitive prior in Europe, see: Jeffrey T. Checkel, "Going Native" In Europe? *Comparative Political Studies* 36, no. 1–2 (2003): 209–231.

16 Hiro Katsumata suggested this distinction.

17 "[L]ocalization reshapes both existing beliefs and practices and foreign ideas *in their local context.*" (emphasis added) Acharya, "How Ideas Spread," 252.

18 This difference between localization and subsidiarity roughly corresponds to Thomas Kirsch's idea of "parochialization" and "universalization". Analysing the evolution of Thai religion, Kirsch suggests that the advent of Indian Buddhism did not lead the Thais to abandon their traditional worshipping of local spirits. Instead, Buddhist deities are placed alongside local spirits. This transformed the status of both religions simultaneously giving a local frame to Indian Buddhism ("parochialization") and a universal frame to Thai animism ("universalization). Thomas A. Kirsch, "Complexity in the Thai Religious System: An Interpretation," *Journal of Asian Studies* 36, no. 2 (1977): 263.

19 I am grateful to an anonymous reviewer for ISQ for suggesting this distinction between localization and subsidiarity.

20 Ibid.

21 Subsidiarity and localization can be complimentary. Their motivators may occasionally overlap. There is no reason why actors can not engage in both types of normative behaviour. In fact, the creation of a single norm may involve both processes, whereby a global norm is redefined while a local norm is infused into a global common. Third World countries often do both. Together, they offer a comprehensive framework understanding and explaining norm dynamics and diffusion in world politics.

22 The term "Third World" is well established in IR Theory, despite controversy over the integrity and post-cold war relevance of the concept. I use Third World interchangeably with "Global South," "developing world" or "postcolonial states," bearing in mind, as Neuman observes, that while "Some analysts consider the term Third World inaccurate, . . . none other has gained general recognition or acceptance." Stephanie Neuman, "International Relations Theory and the Third World: An Oxymoron?" in *International Relations Theory and the Third World,* ed., Stephanie Neuman (New York: St. Martins Press, 1998), 18. Ayoob argues that while "there is much diversity as well as a host of intramural conflicts among this category of states . . . The Third World is in important ways a perceptual category, albeit one that is sufficiently well-grounded in political, economic, and social realities to make it a useful analytical tool in explaining state behaviour." In fact these common realities and perceptions provide important foundations for the concept of norm subsidiarity. See, Mohammed Ayoob, *The Third World Security Predicament: State Making, Regional Conflict, and the International System* (Boulder, CO: Lynne Rienner, 1995), 13.

23 Ayoob, *The Third World Security Predicament*.

24 On the difference between weak states and weak powers, see Ayoob, *The Third World Security Predicament*; Barry Buzan, *People, States, and Fear: An Agenda for International Security Studies in the Post-Cold War Era* (London: Wheatsheaf Books, 1983); Joel Migdal, *Strong Societies and Weak States: State- Society Relations and State Capabilities in the Third World* (Princeton, NJ: Princeton University, 1988).

25 Hedley Bull and Adam Watson, eds., *The Expansion of International Society* (New York: Oxford University Press, 1984).

26 Hedley Bull and Watson, "Conclusion," in *The Expansion of International Society*, eds., H. Bull and A. Watson (New York: Oxford University Press, 1984), 427.

27 Hedley Bull, "The Revolt against the West," in *The Expansion of International Society*, eds., H. Bull and A. Watson (New York: Oxford University Press, 1984), 239–254.

28 Mohammed Ayoob, "The Third World in the System of States: Acute Schizophrenia or Growing Pains?" *International Studies Quarterly* 33, no. 1 (1989): 67–79.

29 Rupert Emerson, *From Empire to Nation: The Rise of Self Assertion of Asian and African Peoples* (Cambridge: Harvard University Press, 1962), 395; Lynn H. Miller, "The Prospect for Order through Regional Security," in *Regional Politics and World Order*, eds., Richard Falk and Saul Mendlovitz (San Francisco: W. H. Freeman, 1973), 58; and Sisir Gupta, *India and Regional Integration in Asia* (Bombay: Asia Publishing House, 1964), 59.

30 Cecil Crabb, *The Elephants and the Grass: A Study of Non-Alignment* (New York: Praeger, 1967), 67.

31 On great power management as an institution of international order, see: Hedley Bull, *The Anarchical Society*, 2nd edition, (Basingstoke: Macmillan, 1975), chapter 9.

32 Etzioni, *The Majority of One: Towards a Theory of Regional Compatibility*; and Inis Claude, *Swords into Ploughshares* (New York: Random House, 1964), chapter 6.

33 Nye, *Peace in Parts: Integration and Conflict in Regional Organization*.

34 I. William Zartman, "Africa as a Subordinate State-system in International Relations," in *Regional Politics and World Order*, eds., Richard Falk and Saul Mendlovitz (San Francisco: W. H. Freeman, 1973), 386.

35 Thomas P. Thornton, *The Challenge to U.S. Policy in the Third World* (Boulder, Colo.: Pergamon Press, 1980), 25

36 Stephen D. Krasner, *Sovereignty: Organized Hypocrisy* (Princeton: Princeton University Press, 1999).

37 The quoted words are taken from the written comments of an anonymous reviewer for ISQ on an earlier draft of this chapter.

38 Robert O. Keohane, *After Hegemony: Cooperation and Discord in the World Political Economy* (Princeton: Princeton University Press, 1984), 39.

39 Abram Chayes and Antonia Chayes, *The New Sovereignty: Compliance with International Regulatory Agreements* (Cambridge: Harvard University Press, 1995), 41, 128.

40 G. John Ikenberry and Charles A. Kupchan, "Socialization and Hegemonic Power," *International Organization* 44, no. 3 (1990), 289. More fully developed in G. John Ikenberry, *After Victory: Institutions, Strategic Restraint, and the Rebuilding of Order After Major War* (Princeton: Princeton University Press, 2001).

41 Finnemore and Sikkink, "International Norm Dynamics and Political Change," 263.

42 Steering Committee on Local and Regional Authorities in Europe, "Definition and Limits of the Principle of Subsidiarity," Draft study (France: Council of Europe, 9 November 1993).

43 John Barnes et. al., *Federal Britain: No Longer Unthinkable?* (London: Centre for Policy Studies, 1998), 34; *Explanatory Memorandum on the EU Constitutional Treaty* (01/12/04), "Treaty establishing a Constitution for Europe including the Protocols and Annexes, and Final Act with Declarations," Command Paper Number: Cm 6429, Presented to Parliament: December 2004 (London: Foreign and Commonwealth Office, 2004).

44 For a comprehensive discussion of these norms, see: Bull and Watson, eds., *The Expansion of International Society*. On the emergence of the global norm of regional autonomy, see: Falk and Mendlovitz, *Regional Politics and World Order*.

45 John F. Dulles, "Security in the Pacific," Foreign Affairs 30, no. 2 (1952): 187.
46 "Southeast Asia" then included India, Pakistan and Sri Lanka (now considered to be part of "South Asia"). They, along with Indonesia and Burma were members of "The Conference of South-East Asian Prime Ministers," otherwise known as "Colombo Powers".
47 Cited in Chintamani Mahapatra, *American Role in the Origin and Growth of ASEAN* (India: ABC Publishing House, 1990), 48.
48 John K. Franklin, "The Hollow Pact: Pacific Security and the Southeast Asia Treaty Organization," Ph. D. Thesis, Texas Christian University, December 2006.
49 "Memorandum for the Secretary's File, Subject: Conference with Congressional Leaders Concerning the Crisis in Southeast Asia," Saturday, 3 April 1954 (Dulles Papers, the Library of Congress, 5 April 1954).
50 "Memorandum of Conversation with the President, May 19, 1954," (Dulles Papers, The Library of Congress).
51 *FRUS 1952–1954*, vol. 12, 362–376; and *FRUS 1952–1954*, vol. 13, 971–973.
52 *FRUS 1952–1954*, vol. 12, 514–516, 522–525.
53 Franklin, "The Hollow Pact: Pacific Security and the Southeast Asia Treaty Organization."
54 U.K. Foreign Office Southeast Asia Department Minutes, 17 August 1954, D1074/452, PRO-FO, 371-111881, TNA, PRO.
55 John Kotelawala, *The Colombo Powers* (undated manuscript found at Konperansi Asia–Afrika Museum, Bandung, Indonesia).
56 Southeast Asian Prime Ministers' Conference: Minutes of Meetings and Documents of the Conference, Colombo, April 1954 (hereafter cited as The Colombo Conference Minutes).
57 James Cable, Geneva Conference of 1954 on Indochina (London: Macmillan Press, 1986), 147.
58 The Bogor Conference Minutes, 2nd Session, 6.
59 Ali Sastroamidjojo, *Milestones on My Journey: The Memoirs of Ali Sastroamidjojo, Indonesian Patriot and Political Leader (Sources of modern Indonesian history and politics)*, (Australia: University of Queensland Press, 1979), 271.
60 Anthony Eden, *Full Circle: The Memoirs of Sir Anthony Eden* (London: Cassell and Company, 1960), 99.
61 Foreign Office to Washington, 26 May 1954, D1074/189, FO-371/111869. See also: Eden to Casey via Foreign Office, 22 May 1954, D 1074/45/G, FO 371/111863, TNA, PRO (Public Records Office).
62 "Report of the Joint U.S.-U.K. Study Group on Southeast Asia," 17 July 1954, *FRUS*, 1952–1954, vol. XVI, 1415; "Memorandum of Conference with President Eisenhower, Augusta, GA," 19 May 1954. Dulles Papers, Library of Congress; Telegram from British Embassy in Washington to the Foreign Office in London, 10 July 1954, FO/371/111868. This also means the US was informed of and accepted the British move to invite all the Colombo Powers to join SEATO.
63 "Memorandum by the Regional Planning Adviser in the Bureau of Far Eastern Affairs (Ogburn) to the Acting Assistant Secretary of States for Far Eastern Affairs (Drumright)," 23 July 1954, *FRUS*, 1952–54, Vol. XII, Part I, 664.
64 Inward Telegram to Commonwealth Relations Office, From UK High Commissioner in India, 27 May 1954, FO- 371-111863, UK National Archives.
65 FO-371-111875.
66 FO-371-111875.
67 UK Foreign Office, Inward Telegram to Commonwealth Relations Office, August 2, 1954, FO 371-11875. TNA, PRO.
68 Jawaharlal Nehru, *The Discovery of India*, 23rd Impression (New Delhi: Oxford University Press, 2003), 539.
69 Bharat Karnad, "India's Weak Geopolitics and What to Do About It," in *Future Imperilled*, ed., Bharat Karnad (India: Viking, 1994).
70 U Nu at a Speech to the National Press Club, Washington, D.C., in July 1955, cited in

James Barrington, (Foreign Secretary of Burma), "The Concept of Neutralism: What Lies Behind Burma's Foreign Policy?" in *Perspective of Burma, An Atlantic Monthly Supplement* (New York: Intercultural Publications, 1958), 29.

71 Foreign Office to Djakarta Embassy, 13 August 1954, D 1074/295, FO 371/111875, TNA, PRO.

72 U.K. High Commissioner in Ceylon to FO, 9 August 1954, D 1074/367, FO 371/111878, TNA, PRO.

73 John Kotelawala, *An Asian Prime Minister's Story* (London: George Harap, 1956), 118.

74 P.K. Balachandran,"Kotelawala placed Sri Lanka on the world map," *Daily News* (Colombo), 5 October 2006, http://www.dailynews.lk/2006/05/10/fea01.asp.

75 29 countries participated in the Bandung Conference held between 18 and 24 April 1955: Burma, Ceylon (Sri Lanka), India, Indonesia, and Pakistan, Afghanistan, Cambodia, China, Egypt, Ethiopia, the Gold Coast (Ghana), Iran, Iraq, Japan, Jordan, Laos, Lebanon, Liberia, Libya, Nepal, the Philippines, Saudi Arabia, Sudan, Syria, Thailand, Turkey, the Vietnam Democratic Republic, South Vietnam (later reunified with the Democratic Republic of Vietnam) and Yemen (Republic of Yemen).

76 Alastair Iain Johnston, "Treating International Institutions as Social Environments," *International Studies Quarterly* 45, no. 4 (2001), 487–516.

77 *Bandung Political Committee Proceedings.*

78 Nehru's Speech, *Bandung Political Committee Proceedings.*

79 Carlos P. Romulo, *The Meaning of Bandung* (Chapel Hill: The University of North Carolina Press, 1956), 91.

80 See the debates over "Regional Arrangements," Commission III (Security Council), Committee 4, *Documents of the United Nations Conference on International Organization, San Francisco, 1945,* vol. 12, (London and New York: United Nations Information Organizations, 1945), 663–844.

81 See Text of Kotelawala's speech to the opening session of the Bandung Conference, in *Asia- Africa Speaks from Bandung* (Indonesia: Ministry of Foreign Affairs Republic of Indonesia, 1955), 40.

82 "The Afro-Asian Conference," Foreign Office Research Department, 5 May 1955, 2231/368, FO 371-116986.

83 George Modelski, "The Asian States' Participation in SEATO," in *SEATO: Six Studies,* ed., George Modelski (Vancouver: University of British Columbia Publication Centre, 1962), 155–156.

84 "The Asian-African Conference," Address by Senator Emanuel Paelez to the Rotary Club of Manila, undated, 2231/379, 11 August 1955, FO 371-116986.

85 "Letter from the Acting Officer in Charge of Thai and Malayan Affairs (Foster) to Ambassador in Thailand (Peurifoy)," *FRUS*, Vol. XXII, Southeast Asia, 826.

86 Konthi Suphamongkon, "From SEATO to ASEAN," undated paper (Singapore: Institute of Southeast Asian), 32–35.

87 Leszek Buszynski, *SEATO: The Failure of an Alliance Strategy* (Singapore: Singapore University Press, 1983), 221. See also George Liska, *Nations in Alliance: The Limits of Interdependence* (Baltimore: Johns Hopkins University Press, 1968), 121.

88 "Verbatim Proceedings of the Third Plenary Session, Manila Conference," 7 September 1954, *FRUS*, 1952–1954, Vol. XII, Part I, 878–879.

89 Donald Crone, "Does Hegemony Matter? The Reorganization of the Pacific Political Economy," *World Politics* 45, no. 4 (1993): 501–525.

90 Christopher Hemmer and Peter J. Katzenstein, "Why Is There No NATO in Asia: Collective Identity, Regionalism, and the Origins of Multilateralism," *International Organization* 56, no. 3 (2002): 575–607; Peter J. Katzenstein, *A World of Regions:Asia and Europe in the American Imperium* (Ithaca: Cornell University Press, 2005).

91 There could be two other possible alternative explanations of why SEATO failed: (1) anticipated opposition from domestic audiences and (2) whether the conclusion of US–Japan alliance might have rendered SEATO unnecessary. These two could serve as alternative explanations of why SEATO failed. But both can be discounted. To be

sure, domestic opposition was a factor in the decision of Ceylon and Indonesia not to join SEATO. It was less important in the case of India and Burma. But even then, why should normative behaviour be seen as alternative to domestic explanations? There is plenty of constructivist work that suggests that states/governments borrow international norms to legitimize themselves before domestic audiences and that domestic considerations often motivate normative behaviour and norm compliance. Andrew Cortell and James Davis, "How Do International Institutions Matter? The Domestic Impact of International Rules and Norms," *International Studies Quarterly* 40, no. 4 (1996): 451–478. Moreover, domestic politics explanations can be indeterminate: The leaders of the three Asian countries which did join SEATO, namely Pakistan, Philippines and Thailand, also might have faced domestic opposition to their alignment with the US, but they still went ahead and did so. The other alternative explanation is also easily dismissed: the conclusion of the US-Japan defence treaty did not prevent Dulles' passionate advocacy of a Southeast Asian collective defence system. And in the early days of the alliance, which was geared towards both preventing Japanese remilitarization and deterring an overt Soviet communist military threat to Japan, its utility in deterring a Chinese Communist challenge through indirect subversion would be hardly apparent or demonstrated to render SEATO unnecessary.

92 Peter Katzenstein, "Introduction: Alternative Perspectives on National Security," in *The Culture of National Security: Norms and Identity in World Politics,* ed., Peter Katzenstein (New York: Columbia University Press, 1996), 11.

93 Michael Leifer, *ASEAN and the Security of South-East Asia* (London: Routledge, 1989), 28; Amitav Acharya, *A Survey of Military Cooperation in ASEAN: Bilateralism or Alliance* (Toronto: Center for International and Security Studies, York University, 1990).

94 Interview, *The Straits Times*, 30 July 1993, 34.

95 Derek Chollet, "Time for an Asian NATO?" *Foreign Policy* (Spring 2003); Sunanda K. Datta-Ray, "Signs Look Promising for Nato-like Asian Security Framework," *The Straits Times,* 22 April 2004.

96 This is an entirely defensible approach, even to the critics of the case study method. Indeed, specifying scope conditions under which certain independent variables will produce similar outcomes is the essence of the "social-scientific" study of IR. Moreover, it's useful to bear in mind that while IR scholars disagree over generalizations from single cases, generalizations from in-depth study of single cases or events, such as the collapse of the Soviet Union, and NATO expansion, are commonplace in IR literature. See Zeev Maoz, "Case Study Methodology in International Studies: From Storytelling to Hypothesis Testing," in *Evaluating Methodology in International Studies*, eds., Frank Harvey and Michael Brecher (Ann Arbor: University of Michigan Press, 2002), 161. As Flyvbjerg asserts, "One can often generalize on the basis of a single case and the case study may be central to scientific development via generalization as supplement or alternative to other methods." Bent Flyvbjerg, "Five Misunderstandings About Case-Study Research," *Qualitative Inquiry* 12, no. 2 (2006), 228.

The literature on case studies also holds that generalizations from single cases are best done with the help of the process-tracing method and alternative explanations, both of which feature in this chapter. Moreover, single cases are especially useful for rejecting established theories which claim to specify necessary and sufficient conditions. Alexander L. George and Andrew Bennett, *Case Studies and Theory Development in the Social Sciences* (Cambridge: The MIT Press, 2005), 33. In this chapter, I have used the case study of SEATO to refute the thesis that norm creation requires the initiative of central or powerful actors, or that power is a necessary or sufficient condition for norm creation, a bias in both rationalist and constructivist literature.

Finally, there are plenty of examples in the IR literature of generalizations from single cases that have been used to challenge an existing theory or build a new one. Liddle's study of Indonesia's development strategy refutes the earlier dependency theory literature regarding the lack of autonomy of Third World states. R. William Liddle, "The Relative Autonomy of the Third World Politician: Soeharto and. Indonesian

Economic Development in Comparative Perspective," *International Studies Quarterly* 35, no. 4 (1991). Wallander develops the concept of "asset specificity" to explain why NATO persists after the end of the Cold War. The Cuban Missile Crisis (a single event) and the end of the Cold War (both as a single event and as a complex set of events) have spawned a great number of theoretical generalizations about decision-making and role of ideas in international relations respectively. Celeste A. Wallander, "Institutional Assets and Adaptability: NATO After the Cold War," *International Organization* 54, no. 4 (2000): 705–735.

97 Jorge I. Dominguez, "International Cooperation in Latin America: The Design of Regional Institutions by Slow Accretion," in *Crafting Cooperation: The Design and Effects of Regional Institutions in Comparative Perspective*, eds., Amitav Acharya and Alastair Iain Johnston (Cambridge: Cambridge University Press, 2007), 126–127. Further discussion of Latin America's norms of peace and security, including *Uti Possidetis*, can be found in Arie Kacowitz, *The Impact of Norms in International Society: The Latin American Experience, 1881–2001* (Notre Dame: Notre Dame University Press, 2005).

98 Kacowitz, *The Impact of Norms in International Society: The Latin American Experience, 1881–2001*, 50.

99 Ibid.

100 Dominguez, "International Cooperation in Latin America," 90.

101 Ian Brownlie, *Principles of Public International Law*, 5th edition (Oxford: Oxford University Press, 2002), 132. On the high level of compliance with the global territorial integrity norm, see: Mark Zacher, "The Territorial Integrity Norm: International Boundaries and the Use of Force," *International Organization* 55, no. 2 (2001): 215–225.

102 Thomas Leonard, "The New Pan Americanism in U.S.-Central American Relations, 1933–1954," in *Beyond the Ideal: Pan Americanism in International Affairs*, ed., David Sheinin (Westport, Conn.: Praeger, 2000), 96; David Barton Castle, "Leo Stanton Rowe and the Meaning of Pan-Americanism," in *Beyond the Ideal: Pan Americanism in International Affairs*, ed., David Sheinin (Westport, Conn.: Praeger, 2000), 36.

103 Dominguez, "International Cooperation in Latin America," 92.

104 Francis Wilcox, "Regionalism and the United Nations," *International Organization* 19, no. 3 (1965): 789–811; Minerva Etzioni, *The Majority of One: Towards a Theory of Regional Compatibility* (Beverley Hills, CA: Sage, 1970).

105 *Documents of the United Nations Conference on International Organization (UNCIO), San Francisco, 1945*, (London and New York: United Nations Information Organizations, 1945), vol. VI, 9.

106 *UNCIO Documents*, vol. VI, 5.

107 Michael Barnett, *Dialogues in Arab Politics* (New York: Columbia University Press, 1998), 56, 106; Subsequently, Lynch uses a slightly different expression, "Arabist norms." Hinnebusch speaks of "pan-Arab norms." Mark Lynch, *State Interests and Public Spheres: The International Politics of Jordan's Identity* (New York: Columbia University Press. 1999), 34; Raymond A. Hinnebusch, *The International Politics of the Middle East* (Manchester: Manchester University Press, 2003), 64.

108 Barnett, *Dialogues in Arab Politics*, 56, 106.

109 British Embassy, Washington, to Foreign Office, London, US Department of State Intelligence Report No. 6830.3, "Developments relating to the Bandung Conference," 18 March 1955, D2231/283, FO 371/116982.

110 Jawaharlal Nehru, "India and World Affairs," in *Selected Works of Jawaharlal Nehru*, vol. 28 (India: Jawaharlal Nehru Memorial Fund, 2000), 310.

111 Barnett, *Dialogues in Arab Politics*, 299; and Eli Podeh, *The Quest for Hegemony in the Arab World: The Struggle over the Baghdad Pact* (New York: E.J. Brill, 1995).

112 Michael Barnett, "Nationalism, Sovereignty, and Regional Order in Arab Politics," *International Organization* 49, no. 3 (1995): 479–510. The defeat of Nasserism could be seen as a specific example of resistance and subsidiarity against a regional hegemon.

113 On the normative link between Bandung and African regionalist concepts, see: Colin Legum, *Bandung, Cairo and Accra* (London: The Africa Bureau, 1958); Kwame

Nkrumah, *I Speak of Freedom* (Westport, Conn.: Greenwood Press, 1961), 151–152, 219; and Bala Mohammed, *Africa and Nonalignment* (Kano, Nigeria: Triumph Publishing Co., 1978), 21, 54–55, 184.

114 John Woronoff, *Organizing African Unity* (Metuchen, N.J.: Scarecrow Press, 1970), 39.

115 Kwame Nkrumah, *Africa Must Unite* (New York: Prager, 1963), 136.

116 Robert H. Jackson and Carl G. Roseberg, "Why Africa's Weak States Persist: the Empirical and the Juridical in Statehood," *World Politics* 35, no. 1 (1982): 259–282; Jeffrey Herbst, "Crafting Regional Co-operation in Africa," in *Crafting Cooperation: The Design and Effects of Regional Institutions in Comparative Perspective*, eds., Amitav Acharya and Alastair Iain Johnston (Cambridge: Cambridge University Press, 2007).

117 George H. Jansen, *Afro-Asia and Non-Alignment* (London: Faber and Faber, 1966); A.W. Singham and Shirley Hune, *Non-Alignment in an Age of Alignments* (London: Zed Books, 1986).

118 Mohammed Ayoob, *The Third World Security Predicament*.

119 Tore Nyhamar, citing Hedley Bull, argues that the test of normative behaviour is not whether norms are complied with at the end, but whether they were a factor in the calculation of actors before acting. Tore Nyhamar, "How Do Norms Work? A Theoretical and Empirical Analysis of African International Relations," *The International Journal of Peace Studies* 5, no. 2 (2000); and Hedley Bull, *The Anarchical Society* (Basingstoke: Macmillan, 1977), 55–56.

120 A.O. Cukwurah, *The Settlement of Boundary Disputes in International Law* (Manchester: Manchester University Press, 1967), 112–113.

121 Kacowitz, *The Impact of Norms in International Society: The Latin American Experience, 1881–2001*, 60.

122 Amitav Acharya and Alastair Iain Johnston, eds., *Crafting Cooperation: The Design and Effects of Regional Institutions in Comparative Perspective* (Cambridge: Cambridge University Press, 2007).

123 Krasner notes the "presence of long-standing norms that are frequently violated." These norms include non-intervention (note that Krasner calls non-intervention a "norm") and human rights. But the catalogue of violations he compiles does not negate the fact that human rights remains a norm, arguably ever more important. The selective adherence of non-intervention by both the North and South (West and the non-West) does not invalidate its historical status as a norm, because it endures (it is "long-standing"). Krasner, *Sovereignty: Organized Hypocrisy,* back cover.

124 Martha Finnemore and Kathryn Sikkink, "International Norms and Political Change," *International Organization* 52, no. 4 (1998): 912.

125 Michael Zurn and Jeffrey Checkel, "Getting Socialized to Build Bridges: Constructivism and Rationalism, Europe and the Nation-State," *International Organization* 59, no. 4 (2005), 1057.

126 I use norm to mean "standard of appropriate behaviour for actors with a given identity." Martha Finnemore and Kathryn Sikkink, "International Norm Dynamics and Political Change," *International Organization*, 251.

127 See, for example, Bruce Moon, "The Foreign Policy of the Dependent State," *International Studies Quarterly* 27, no. 3 (1983): 315–340; Jeannie Hey, *Theories of Dependent Foreign Policy and the Case of Ecuador in the 1980s* (Athens: Ohio University Press, 1995).

128 While non-intervention is *now* under attack (I should stress that my focus on non-intervention was for the early post-World War II period), as is the whole idea of absolute sovereignty, both sovereignty and non-intervention remain very popular in the non-Western world. For example, neither India nor China has accepted the idea of "responsibility to protect" (R2P), or the humanitarian intervention principle, which stands as the most serious contemporary challenge to the doctrine of non-intervention. At the recent UN debate over R2P, Egypt on behalf of the Non-Aligned Movement noted that "mixed feelings and thoughts on implementing R2P still persist. There are

concerns about the possible abuse of R2P by expanding its application to situations that fall beyond the four areas defined in the 2005 World Summit Document, misusing it to legitimize unilateral coercive measures or intervention in the internal affairs of States." H.E. Ambassador Maged A. Abdelaziz, The Permanent Representative on behalf of the Non-Aligned Movement, "Statement," http://www.responsibilitytoprotect.org/ NAM_Egypt_ENG.pdf.

129 Thomas Biersteker and Cynthia Weber, *State Sovereignty as a Social Construct* (Cambridge: Cambridge University Press, 1996).

130 See for example, Martha Finnemore, *The Purpose of Intervention: Changing Beliefs about the Use of Force* (Ithaca: Cornell University Press, 2003).

131 Hedley Bull, "The Revolt against the West," in *The Expansion of International Society,* eds., Hedley Bull and Adam Watson (New York: Oxford University Press, 1984), 239–254.

132 Stephen D. Krasner, *Structural Conflict: The Third World Against Global Liberalism* (Berkeley: University of California Press, 1985).

133 Donald J. Puchala, "Third World Thinking and Contemporary International Relations," in *International Relations Theory and the Third World,* ed., Stephanie Neuman (London: Palgrave Macmillan, 1998), 151.

134 Mohammed Ayoob, "The Third World in the System of States: Acute Schizophrenia or Growing Pains?" *International Studies Quarterly* 33, no. 1 (1989): 67–79.

135 Mohammed Ayoob, "Subaltern Realism: International Relations Theory Meets the Third World," in *International Relations Theory and the Third World,* ed., Stephanie Neuman (London: Palgrave Macmillan, 1998), 31–49; Mohammed Ayoob, "Inequality and Theorizing in International Relations: The Case for Subaltern Realism," *International Studies Review* 4, no. 3 (2002): 27–48; Michael Barnett, "Radical Chic? Subaltern Realism: A Rejoinder," *International Studies Review* 4, no. 3 (2002): 49–62; and Ozgur Cicek, "Review of a Perspective: Subaltern Realism," *The Review of International Affairs* 3, no. 3 (2004): 495–501.

CONCLUSION: TOWARDS A GLOBAL IR? PATHWAYS AND PITFALLS

In his 1996 essay mentioned in the introduction, Ken Booth wondered counterfactually about "what . . . would the subject [of IR] look like today . . . if the subject's origins had derived from the life and work of an admirable black, feminist, medic, she-chief of the Zulus."[1] One might also ask what if the field's Western founders had at least made a serious effort to incorporate, notwithstanding its understandably Western origins (because of the timing and context), the substantial intellectual and practical traditions of the world's major civilizations, Mesopotamian, Egyptian, Persian, Arab, Chinese, Indian, Inca and Aztec. As if in response to Booth's counterfactual, William Olson and Nicholas Onuf, from the American University in Washington, D.C., wished to see a major transformation of the field. As I have noted in chapter 2, this would be the realization of "the ideal of a cosmopolitan discipline in which adepts from many cultures enrich the discourse of International Relations with all the world's ways of seeing and knowing." But they also knew better, warning that the so-called globalization of IR may well indicate "the successful diffusion of the Anglo-American cognitive style and professional stance rather than the absorption of alien modes of thought."[2]

Olson and Onuf were prescient. Their fears were not unwarranted and the challenge for the field now is how to reverse it. To some extent, the very idea of theory in IR contributes to this tendency towards ethnocentrism. Theory after all is a search for coherence; a narrower ontology obviously serves the ends of theory than a broader canvass. The search for theoretical parsimony often outweighs the quest for cosmopolitanism. To quote Onuf and Olson again, "If coherence within international relations is finally a product of Anglo-American nurturing, disciplinary and cosmopolitan ideals may never be realized."[3]

One way of going about mitigating the danger that Olson and Onuf talked about would be to present these chapters as a contribution to the development of what myself and Barry Buzan have called non-Western IR theory (as discussed in chapter 2). The NWIRT approach has four main elements which should be by now familiar to the reader of this book. First, it argues that the main current theories of IR are too deeply rooted in, and beholden to, the history, intellectual tradition and agency claims of the West to accord little more than a marginal place to those of the non-Western world. This creates a situation whereby these supposedly universal theories fail to capture and explain the key trends and puzzles of international relations in the non-Western world. Second, the NWIRT approach identifies the reasons for the underdevelopment of IRT outside of the West, including cultural, political, institutional factors when viewed against the "hegemonic" status of established IRTs. The third element of the NWIRT approach is to identify some of the possible sources of bringing the non-Western world into IRT, including but not limited to indigenous history and culture, the ideas of nationalist leaders, distinctive local and regional interaction patterns, and the writings of scholars of distinction working in or about different regions. The final element is that the new IRT cannot and need not supplant Western IRT but should aim to enrich Western IRT with the voices and experiences of the non-Western world, including their claims to agency in global and regional order. Each of these above is relevant to the discussions in this book into rethinking power, institutions and ideas in world politics.

The naming, if not the intent and substance, of the NWIRT approach has caused some controversy, especially over a challenge from those who would rather call the new project "post-Western" (with a more radical agenda to disavow the existing "Western" IR). While not dismissing "post-Western," I have come to view both as part of a broader challenge of reimagining IR as a global project. While by no means exhaustive, this book suggests several challenges that must be met and some pathways to consider more to advance the possibility of a Global IR.

The first concerns naming. I do not advocate renaming the discipline. This may be partly due to pragmatic reasons. So much has been written for so long about *International Relations* that it has now become a "heritage site" that deserves to be preserved. In a related vein, Global IR should not in any way diminish the contribution of theories and theorists which I have characterized as "mainstream" in the introduction. As I have pointed out in chapters 1 and 2, IR theory is not a monolith when it comes to acknowledging the world beyond the West. Even those that do neglect or marginalize the latter overall, they still offer plenty of insights and avenues that can, with debate and modification, be part of the foundation of a Global IR. In my view, having "global" coming before IR should suffice in underscoring the need for relaunching the field as IR 2.0.

This said, as I have indicated in the introduction and in the subsequent chapters, we should not leave the mainstream theories – realism, liberalism and constructivism – as is. So a second challenge to Global IR requires us to rethink their approach and extend themselves in several areas. I have indicated some of the areas in this book. For realism, the challenge is to look beyond the presumed causal linkage between the distribution of power and international order (as seen in the case of the polarity–stability linkage), and acknowledge that all forms of power-centric explanations of and approaches to world order risk obscuring other determinants and creating forms of dominance that are morally indefensible. For liberals, there is a similar challenge to look beyond *American hegemony* as the starting point of investigating the creation and preservation of multilateralism and regionalism and their institutional forms. Liberalism also needs to acknowledge the significant variations in cooperative behaviour (both in terms of determinants, designs and outcomes) that do exist in different local contexts, and acknowledge that no single model of integration or interactions can account for all or most of them. For constructivism, to put it in a nutshell, the same challenge of acknowledging variations, diversity and thus different forms of agency extends to the creation and diffusion of ideas and norms.

Third, and closely related to the above, having Global IR as the designation of the field does not and should not in any way diminish the importance of acknowledging regions and regional variations. On the contrary, regions and regionalism are a central theme of global IR. The core themes of this book, including the concept of NWIRT, the importance of area studies and the recasting of comparative regionalism in Part I, the relationship between polarity, stability and intervention in Part II, the role of institutions in engendering cooperation and security in Part III, and the agency question in the spread of ideas and norms in Part IV, all have regions and regionalism as the fundamental sites of investigation. Global IR is not an excuse for subsuming regional or local identities. Regions have been, and will continue to be crucial to understanding the dynamic interaction between power, institutions and ideas in world politics.

Fourth, Global IR calls for a new understanding of universality. Global IR is not "universal" IR if the latter is understood as "applying to all," or as the dismissal of diversity on the basis of national or cultural origins. This idea of the universal closely approximates what Cox calls Enlightenment universalism, in which "universal meant true for all time and space – the perspective of a homogeneous reality."[4] This approach to universality explains a good deal of the ethnocentric tendencies that undoubtedly exist in mainstream IRTs. Among the key examples would be rational choice approaches, social contract understandings of the origins of state, and some conceptions of human rights, which are essentially based on Western conceptions of property rights.[5]

The dark side of Enlightenment universality included the suppression of diversity, the marginalization of the local cultures, and the production of Western imperialism.[6] It is this conception of universality that Cox had in mind when he wrote, "active pretensions to universality are ultimately reducible to power."[7] Its effects, including the "standards of civilization" criteria, which, as discussed in chapter 1, led to the exclusion of most parts of the non-Western world from the so-called international society (Japan excepted). Yet, as noted throughout this book, the universalism of IRT in more modern times has been in many respects a false universality, in the sense that many of its assumptions and predictions have not been applicable to non-Western parts of the world, thereby challenging the claim of a homogenous reality. I accept Cox's alternative understanding of universality, which would mean "comprehending and respecting diversity in an ever-changing world."[8]

Fifth, a truly global IR cannot be based solely or mainly on cultural exceptionalism. Many non-Western contributions to politics and IR, whether in the academic or policy realm, often tend to ride on such exceptionalism. Exceptionalism is the tendency to essentialise locally shared characteristics and relationships to counter and exclude outsiders' identities and perspectives. While the greater incorporation of local, national and regional history into theoretical discourse and debate is necessary in order to deparochialize IR, one should also be aware of the possibility that this could be a mixed blessing. While broadening the historical foundation of IRT, it could also accentuate claims about exceptionalism with unfortunate consequences. Here, the discussion of the relationship between area studies and disciplinary approaches to IR, discussed in chapter 2, is useful to keep in mind.

Claims about exceptionalism are weakened not just by the cultural and political diversity *within* regions, as much as between them, but also by the shallowness of the exceptionalist constructs themselves – for example, some of the relativist views on democracy, human rights and intervention. Indeed, the whole notion of a Third World has been questioned. Exceptionalism is also a mixed blessing in a normative sense. It could shut the door to genuine ideational intercourse between the global and the regional, or between regions. Moreover, exceptionalist claims are frequently associated with the political agendas and purposes of the ruling elite and are susceptible to governmental abuse – a point convincingly made by the critics of the "Asian Values" concept, which was seen as justification for authoritarianism in Asia.

Sixth, the Global IR must recognize the limitations of theory-building that relies exclusively on the unique historical and cultural matrix and behaviour patterns of the nations and regions of the non-Western world. While it must do much more than simply view the non-Western world as a testing ground to revalidate Western-derived IRTs after a few adjustments and extensions, a key challenge for theories and theorists of global IR also lies in the need to develop concepts and approaches from non-Western contexts that are valid not only locally, but also have applicability to the wider world. Just as exceptionalism in a domestic sphere can lend justification to authoritarianism and suppression of freedom, exceptionalism in IRT could justify dominance of the big powers over the weak. One strand of Japan's pre-war, pan-Asian discourse, which was founded upon the conception of "Asia for Asians" illustrates this tendency. (The other strands of Japanese pan-Asianism were more egalitarian and anti-imperial, but the overall effect of Japanese constructions was to discredit pan-Asianism as a movement.) The same can be said of Nasser's pan-Arabism and Nkrumah's pan-Africanism. China's evoking of the tributary system as the basis of a Chinese School of IR (chapter 2) is pregnant with similar possibilities, since the pacific nature of that system remains seriously contested, and the Chinese "peaceful rise" discourse has invited growing skepticism over its assertive (some would say aggressive) policy in the South China Sea. Just as US exceptionalism, seemingly benign and popular at home, can be associated with the Monroe Doctrine and its self-serving global interventionism, Chinese exceptionalism carries the risk of introducing a new and dangerous parochialism to Asian IR discourse and practice. Hence, even as the rise of the rest leads to a greater questioning of the dominant status of existing Western IRTs, the challenge of building a genuinely global discipline is unlikely to be met by simply viewing regions as a unique theatre of IRT, where only theories derived from Arab, African and Asian history and culture need apply. This might simply mean replacing one kind of provincialism with another and generate its own biases and distortions that are as glaring as the other extreme tendency of explaining all societies and states in terms of Western IRTs. Just as the non-Western world cannot be analysed solely as an extension of the norms and institutions of European international society, regional order cannot be understood solely in terms of its own past or its geographic and cultural matrix.

International relations has a multiple and global heritage that must be acknowledged and promoted. The Global IR must be inclusive in every sense and across the traditionally understood but increasingly blurred East–West and North–South lines. It needs to be more authentically grounded in world history, rather than Western history, and embrace the ideas, institutions, intellectual perspectives and practices of non-Western states and societies.

Notes

1 Ken Booth, "75 Years On: Rewriting the Subject's Past – Reinventing its Future," in *International Theory: Positivism and Beyond*, eds., Steve Smith, Ken Booth, and Marysia Zalewski (Cambridge: Cambridge University Press, 1996).
2 William Olson and Nicholas Onuf, "The Growth of a Discipline," in *International Relations: British and American Perspectives*, ed., Steve Smith (New York: Blackwell, 1985), 18.
3 Ibid., 18.
4 Robert W. Cox, "Universality in International Studies: A Historicist Approach," in *The Essence of Millennial Reflections on International Studies: Critical Perspective*, eds., Michael Brecher and Frank P. Harvey (Ann Arbor: University of Michigan Press, 2002), 53.
5 Jack Donnelly, "The Relative Universality of Human Rights," *Human Rights Quarterly* 29, no. 2 (2007): 281–306.
6 Sankar Muthu, *Enlightenment Against Empire* (Princeton: Princeton University Press, 2003); Antony Anghie, *Imperialism, Sovereignty and the Making of International Law* (Cambridge: Cambridge University Press, 2005); Dorinda Outram, *The Enlightenment*, 2nd edition, (Cambridge: Cambridge University Press, 2005).
7 Cox, "Universality in International Studies," 50.
8 Ibid., 53.

INDEX

Note: The following abbreviations have been used – f = figure; n = note

abduction 48
Abizaid, General John 123
absolute sovereignty 29
Acharya, A. 23–4, 45, 48, 167, 251
adaptation 191f, 192
Adler, E. 162
Afghanistan 97, 123, 127
Africa 49, 52, 55, 63, 80;
   democratisation 99, 100;
   localised anarchies 106–7; norm
   subsidiarity 234, 236–7, 238
African Economic Community Treaty
   (1991) 100
African Union (AU) (formerly
   Organization of African Unity
   (OAU)) 7, 100, 112n, 166;
   regionalism 75, 76, 80
*After Hegemony: Cooperation and Discord
   in the World Political Economy*
   (Keohane) 142
After Victory (Ikenberry) 146, 147, 148
agency 4, 11–13, 18n, 55; denial of 26,
   35; multilateralism 144; non-Western
   approaches 38; norm localisation 183,
   184, 185; sovereignty 127; Third
   World 239–40; transnational civil
   society 149
Aggarwal, V.K. 193, 211n
Alagappa, M. 46, 164
Alatas, A. 196–7
Alexandrowicz, C.H. 53, 55, 71n
Ali, Mohammed 230

Al-Qaeda 116, 131; War on Terror 122,
   123, 124, 125, 127
al-Zawahiri, Aiman 123–4
Americanocentrism 9, 11, 23, 153, 154,
   155
amplification 191f
analytic eclecticism 163, 164
Anarchical Society, The (Bull) 38
anarchy 91, 95; anarchy–hierarchy
   divide 63; localised 106–7, 108
Anderson, B. 190, 210–11n
Annan, Kofi 128, 131
Anti-Americanism 132, 172
Anwar, Ibrahim 199–200, 201, 205
APEC *see* Asia Pacific Economic
   Cooperation
Appadurai, A. 216n
APT *see* Association of Southeast Asian
   Nations (ASEAN) Plus Three
Arab League 32, 75, 76
Arab Spring 109
area specialisation 4, 61–3, 163
ARF *see* Association of Southeast Asian
   Nations (ASEAN) Regional Forum
Argumentative Indian, The (Sen) 66
armed conflicts 108–10
ASEAN *see* Association of Southeast Asian
   Nations
ASEAN-ISIS *see* Association of Southeast
   Asian Nations (ASEAN) Institutes of
   Strategic and International Studies
ASEM *see* Asia–Europe Meeting

Asia 165, 166, 169, internationalised
rivalries 105–6; Cold War 217;
cooperative security 194–8,
202, 203, 204, 205; flexible
engagement 198–202, 203, 204, 205;
international relations theory and 45,
46, 49; multilateralism 152; non-
intervention 198–9, 200, 201, 204,
205, 225; norm localisation 186–8, 189,
190, 191, 192, 202–5; regionalism 64,
80, 104–5, 161–2, 215n; societal
resistance 172–3; *see also* Association
of Southeast Asian Nations (ASEAN);
Southeast Asian Treaty Organization
(SEATO)
Asian Relations Conference 225
'Asian values' 33–4, 253
Asia-Pacific Concert of Powers 30
Asia Pacific Economic Cooperation
(APEC) 79, 100, 170
Asia–Europe Meeting (ASEM) 80
ASP *see* Association of Southeast Asian
Nations (ASEAN) Surveillance Process
Association of Southeast Asian Nations
(ASEAN) 10, 11, 31, 33, 201–2,
Cold War and 202–5; cooperative
security 194–8, 215n; flexible
engagement 198–201; founding
of 233; multilateralism 152, 153;
norm localisation 183–4, 193, 213n;
pluralistic security community 104–5;
regionalism and 75, 82, 100, 162,
166, 171; *see also* Asia; Southeast Asian
Treaty Organization (SEATO)
Association of Southeast Asian Nations
(ASEAN) Institutes of Strategic
and International Studies (ASEAN-
ISIS) 196, 197, 202, 204
Association of Southeast Asian Nations
(ASEAN) Plus Three (APT) 80
Association of Southeast Asian Nations
(ASEAN) Regional Forum (ARF) 79–
80, 167, 197–8, 203, 233
Association of Southeast Asian Nations
(ASEAN) Surveillance Process
(ASP) 201
AU *see* African Union
autocentrism 25, 35
autonomy 9–11, 12, 82, 168f, 169–73
'axis of evil' 122
Ayoob, M. 30, 55, 111n, 114n, 171; norm
subsidiarity 220, 221, 240

Badawi, A. 200
Baghdad Pact (1955) 224, 236

Bajpai, K. 52
Ball, D. 190, 210n
Bandung Asia–Africa Conference
(1955) 12, 29, 236, 237; Asian
regionalism 225, 230, 231, 232, 233,
245n
Barnett, M. 236
Bhagabad Gita 58, 66
Bilgin, P. 49
binding strategies: regionalism 171
bipolarity 31; Cold War 5, 7, 9, 30,
97, 102; neorealism 95, 103, 107;
regionalism 89, 90–1, 98, 99;
stability 91, 92, 93, 94; *see also*
multipolarity; unipolarity
Blyden, Edward Wilmot 76
Bolivarianism 234–5
Boomerang model 149
Booth, K. 250
Bosch, F. D. K. 192
bounded territoriality 162, 235, 237, 238
Boyce, R. 198
British Committee on the Theory of
International Relations 51, 70n
Brownlie, I. 235
Brown, W. 46
Buddhism 4, 52, 58–61, 72n, 188
Bull, H. 7, 17n, 36, 37–8, 42n, 50; Cold
War 122; international systems 53,
69–70n, 71n, 164; intervention 134n;
non-Western approaches 55; norm
subsidiarity 221
Burma 199, 200, 201, 229
Bush Doctrine *see* National Security
Strategy of the United States
Bush, George 98
Butterfield, H. 35
Buzan, B. 3–4, 23, 39, 42n, 45, 48; non-
Western approaches 50, 251; Third
World 95, 111n; Westphalia system 53;
world politics 159, 160, 161, 174n; *see
also Regions and Powers: The Structure of
International Security*

Caliphobia 55, 122–3, 124f, 125–8, 134n
Calvo Doctrine (1868) 75, 235
Carter, Jimmy 131
CENTO *see* Central Treaty Organization
centrality of state 63
Central Treaty Organization
(CENTO) 224, 225
CEPAL *see* Comision Economica para
America Latin
Ceylon 222, 229, 230
Chan, S. 49

Chayes, A. and A. 223
Checkel, J. 185–6, 238
Cheney, Dick 123
Chenoy, A. 56
Chicago, University of 66
China 27, 28, 30, 31, 33, 37; collective
  defence and 225, 226, 232;
  globalisation 80; norm localisation 189,
  198, 201, 204, 210*n*; norm
  subsidiarity 222; regionalism 169–70,
  178*n*; strategic culture 45–6, 57;
  Westphalia system 54
Chinese School 51–2, 68*n*
Cintra, J. 89
civil society *see* transnational civil society
Clapham, C. 27
Claude, I. 152
Clinton, Bill 198
cognitive prior 242*n*
Cold War 5, 89–91, 109; Asia 29, 202–5,
  217; as bipolar system 5, 7, 9, 30, 91–2,
  102; cooperative security 194–8, 203,
  212*n*; 'domino effect' 224; great power
  leadership 30, 98; 'long peace' 8,
  30, 89; norm subsidiarity 222; third
  world and international order 91–4;
  third world in post-Cold War era 39,
  94–103, 107, 224–5; transnational
  norms 202–5; Western values 33–4
collective defence: long-term consequences
  of resistance to 233–4; perspectives on
  failure of 232, 233*f*; resistance to 227–
  9; sovereignty 229, 235
Colombo Powers 28, 227, 228, 229, 230,
  244*n*
colonialism 31, 32, 37, 38, 76, 109; *see also*
  post-colonialism
Comision Economica para America Latin
  (CEPAL) 64
'concert-based collective security
  system' 30
Conference of Independent African States
  (1958) 237
Conference on Security and Cooperation
  in Europe (CSCE) (later OSCE) 194,
  195, 196, 205, 212*n*
conflict 247; regionalism 103–7;
  decline in 108–10, 112*n*; localised
  anarchies 106–7; values and norms 33
Confucianism 46, 52, 57
congruence building 12, 13; norm
  localisation 185, 186, 190, 205, 206
constitutional order 142–3
constructivism 15, 78, 144, 251–2;
  Buddhism 60–1; collective

defence 232; English school 48;
  non-Western approaches 46–7;
  normative cultures 11, 12, 13, 14;
  norm diffusion 33, 35, 184–5, 192;
  norm subsidiarity 223, 238, 239;
  regionalism 79, 81, 162–3, 167, 217;
  'subaltern' 24, 240
Cooper, A. 151
cooperation: constructivism 47; institutions
  and 31–3; multilateralism 141;
  regionalism and 82; values and
  norms 33, 188
cooperative security 184, 206, 212*n*, 223;
  Asia 194–8, 202, 203, 204, 205
Cooper, S. 167
Cortell, A.P. 189, 207*n*
Cox, R.W. 25, 141–2, 148, 151, 252,
  253
Crab, C. 221
Crawford, B. 162
critique 52
CSCE *see* Conference on Security and
  Cooperation in Europe
Cuba 101
cultural match 185–6
Czechoslovakia 236

Dalai Lama 58–61, 72*n*
Darul Islam (DI) 125
Datong ('Universal Great Harmony') 52
Davis, J.W. 189, 207*n*
decolonisation *see* colonialism
'decompression effect' 31
Deduney, D. 54
democratisation 99–100, 107, 109, 121,
  143, 152–3; norm borrowing 188
'dependent origination' (*pratitya-
  samutpada*) 60, 61
Deutsch, K.W. 32, 92, 93, 104
'Dialogue Between Whom? The Role
  of the West/Non-West Distinction
  in Promoting Global Dialogue in IR'
  (Hutchings) 65–6
Diez, T. 77
disjuncture: integration theory and Third
  World 26, 28, 32–3, 35; Western
  dominance and regionalism 63
disorganized hypocrisy 8, 119, 129–32
dominance *see* Western dominance
Drago Doctrine (1902) 75, 235
Drysdale, P. 215*n*
Du Bois, W.E.B. 76
Dulles, John Foster 224, 225, 226, 228,
  229, 232
Dunn, K. 63

East Asia Summit (EAS) 80
economic regionalism 100–4
Economist 96, 113*n*
Edelman, Eric 123
Eden, Anthony 228
Egypt 222, 225, 236
emerging powers 9, 141, 143, 150–1, 155,
    169; *see also* great powers; powers
Emerson, R. 221
emptiness (*sunyata*) 59–60, 61
enduring rivalries *see* internationalised
    rivalries
Engineer, Asgar Ali 126, 127
English School 13, 35–9, 41*n*, 48, 50, 51;
    international systems 53, 65; norm
    subsidiarity 221
enhanced interaction 201
Enlightenment universalism 252–3
epistemology 56–61, 68*n*
Eritrea 96, 99
Ethiopia 96, 99
ethnocentrism 4, 15, 65, 250; non-
    Western approaches and 48, 52, 57;
    polarity/stability and 94
Europe 3, 7, 64, 178*n*; cooperative
    security 212*n*; integration 46;
    international systems and 35–9;
    sovereignty and 28
European Coal and Steel Community
    (ECSC) *see* European Union
European Concert 29
European integration theory 77, 84–5*n*
European Union 5, 10, 11, 32, 51,
    81; great powers and 89; imperium
    (US) 171; regionalism and 77, 78–81,
    161–2, 166, 175*n*; sovereignty 118
'European and the Universal Processes':
    regional integration 32
Evans, Garth 195, 196
exceptionalism 66, 253, 254
exclusion: regionalism 171
'Expansion of International Society, The'
    (English School) 450, 69–70*n*, 71*n*;
    Western dominance 35–9, 41*n*, 42*n*

Falk, R. 99, 167
false universalism 25–6, 65
falsification thesis (Popper) 59
Farrell, T. 186
Featherman, D. 62
Feith, Douglas 120, 131, 134*n*
Finnemore, M. 238
flexible engagement 198–202, 203, 204,
    205
Foucault, M. 61

framing 186, 191*f*, 218
Freedman, L. 112*n*
Fukuyama, F. 132, 170–1
functionalism 204, 205, 232

G-20 group 80, 150–1
G-77 group 103, 220
Gaddis, J.L. 91–2, 93, 121
GCC *see* Gulf Cooperation Council
General Guide for the Struggle of Jemmah
    Islamiyah (PUPJI) 124*f*, 125
Geneva Accords (5th Accord) 227
Geneva Conference on Indo-China
    (1954) 226, 227
Germany 144, 161
Ghana 225
Gilpin, R. 92, 99
global disorders 5–9
globalisation 78, 83, 116, 127–8,
    153–4, 159; norm localisation 216*n*;
    regionalism 161, 166, 172
Goetz, A.M. 148
Goh, Chok Tong 123
Goldgeier, J.M. 90, 96, 99, 103
Gorbachev, Mikhail 195
grafting 186, 189, 191*f*, 204, 218
Greater East Asia Co-Prosperity
    Sphere 144
great powers 7–8, 9, 26, 28, 74, 89;
    intervention 11, 13, 90, 101, 106;
    international order 38–9; localised
    anarchies 106–7; management 29–31;
    multilateralism 142, 147; non-Western
    approaches 55; norm subsidiarity 223;
    post-Cold War 98, 99; regionalism 78,
    90, 109, 153, 159–60, 167; regional
    security complexes (RSCs) 160;
    resistance to 170–1, 179*n*, 184, 191*f*,
    194*f*, 221–2; stability 93, 94; *see also*
    emerging powers; power
Grieco, J.M. 167
Grotius, H. 27, 55
Group of Three 100
Gulf Cooperation Council (GCC) 31,
    177, 178
Gupta, S. 30
Gurr, T.R. 96

Haas, Ernst 32, 77
Haas, Richard 120, 121, 129, 131
Habbermasian communicative
    dialogue 65–6
Halliday, F. 103
Hall, W.E. 28
Haluani, M. 64

Haq, Mahbub-ul 56
hegemony 9, 166–8; Asia 45; collective
    defence 232; multilateralism 9, 141,
    144–8, 151–4, 157*n*; regionalism 74,
    75, 166–8; Third World 98; Western
    dominance 24, 25–7, 36
Hettne, B. 167, 172
Higgott, R. 77
High-Level Panel on Threats, Challenges
    and Change (UN) 131–2, 136*n*
Hinduism 4, 57–8
Hoffmann, S. 2, 23, 89
Holsti, K. 96, 111–12
Homer-Dixon, T.F. 106–7
Hooker, M.B. 209
Hopf, T. 184
Horton, S. 128
hospitality, right of 31
Hui, V. 27
humanitarian intervention 8;
    constructivism 239; norm
    localisation 193, 199, 200, 202–6;
    sovereignty 116, 118, 120, 121, 122;
    war on terror 129, 130, 131, 132
Humanitarian Intervention and State
    Sovereignty, International Commission
    for 129–30
human rights 35, 121, 122, 129, 149, 200;
    cooperative security 200, 212*n*, 216*n*
Human Security Centre (University of
    British Columbia) 108–10
Human Security Report (Human Security
    Centre, University of British
    Columbia) 108–10
Hurrell, A. 39
Hussein, Saddam 129
Hutchings, Prof. K. 65–6

ICC *see* International Criminal Court
ideas 1, 11–13
ideational contestation 210–11*n*
identity (national/regional) 163–4, 173,
    190
Ignatieff, M. 216*n*
Ikenberry, J. 45, 167; hegemonic
    order 142–3; multilateralism 146, 147,
    148, 154, 155; norm subsidiarity 223
IMF *see* International Monetary Fund
imperium (US) 174*n*; European Union
    (EU) 171, 172; multilateralism 154;
    regionalism 159, 161, 166, 167, 168, 169
inclusiveness 151–2, 196
incremental norm transplantation 186
Independent Commission on Disarmament
    and Security Issues 195

India 28, 37, 52, 57, 75;
    democratisation 101, 102, 225;
    emerging power 155, 169;
    globalisation 80; norm localisation 189,
    192, 209*n*; norm subsidiarity 222
'Indianisation of Southeast Asia' 54
Indian Ocean 171
indivisibility 144, 151, 152
Indonesia 102, 190, 196, 197, 213*n*,
    222; collective defence 227, 229;
    colonialism 225
Inoguchi, T. 3
insider proponents 189
institutions 1, 9–11, 13, 14, 27, 55;
    Asia 206–7; change and 193, 211*n*;
    cooperation and 31–3; regionalism 10,
    165–6; *see also* neoliberal institutionalism
'interaction capacity' 42*n*
Inter-American Democratic Charter 80
interdependence 100, 104, 107, 109, 161,
    204
International Commission for
    Humanitarian Intervention and State
    Sovereignty 129–30
International Criminal Court (ICC) 109
internationalisation 161, 166, 172
internationalised rivalries 105–6
International Monetary Fund (IMF) 64, 97
international order 13, 25–7, 30, 39,
    164–6, 252; Third World and 91–4
international prescriptions 185
International Relations of the Asia-Pacific 45
International Relations, British Committee
    on the Theory of 51
international relations (IR) theory 2–5,
    69*n*, 250; adequacy of existing 2–5,
    45–7; generalisations 246–7*n*;
    humanising 55–6; origins 1, 16*n*;
    polarity and stability 90
international rule innovators 234
'international society' perspective
    see English School
International Studies Association 50
international systems 4, 45, 53–4;
    European-derived 35–9
intervention 5–9, 11, 13, 28, 80, 90;
    constructive 199–200, 201; sovereignty
    and 121, 122; Third World 7–8,
    134*n*
Iran 53
Iraq 8, 98, 112*n*, 117, 118;
    multilateralism 150; sovereignty 121,
    122, 123, 129, 130–1, 132
Islam 53, 109–10, 123, 124*f*, 126, 127
Islamic Ummah 57

Jackson, P.T. 56, 57, 58, 61
Jackson, R. 50
Japan 12, 31, 35, 37, 144, 161; cooperative
 security 197, 204; regionalism 162,
 169, 170, 172, 178n; standards of
 civilizations criteria 221
Jayakumar, S. 200, 201, 215n
Jemmah Islamiah 123, 124f, 125
Jervis, R. 29, 89
Jorgensen, K.E. 50

Kagan, R. 171, 178n
Kahler, M. 184
Kang, D. 27, 169
Kant, I. 31–2
Kaplan, M. 91, 106
Katzenstein, P.J. 33, 35, 62, 159, 160–2,
 174n; collective defence 233, see also
 *World of Regions: Asia and Europe in the
 American Imperium*
Keck, M. 189
Kenya 189, 210n
Keohane, R.O. 56, 72n, 142, 144, 145,
 156n; norm subsidiarity 223
Khan, M.A. Muqtedar 127
King, G. 56, 72n
Kirsch, T. 188, 192, 242n
Klotz, A. 186
Koh, Tommy 34
Kosovo 129
Kotelawala, John 229, 230–1
Krasner, S. 117, 118, 119, 132, 133n, 248n
Kupchan, C.A. and C.A. 30, 223

Lake, D. 165
Latin America 29, 49, 55, 64, 69n; norm
 subsidiarity 234–6, 237; pluralistic
 security communities 105; realism 68;
 regionalism 75, 76, 80, 235
League of Arab States 166
League of Nations 30
'leapfrogging' 80
Lebow, N. 54
Legro, J.W. 185
Leifer, M. 203
liberalism 15, 9, 10, 13, 14, 251–2;
 Africa 52–3; classical theological
 writers 61; Confucianism and 46;
 Kantian notion of pacific unions 31,
 32; multilateralism 146–7, 152–3;
 regionalism 167
Liberal Leviathan (Ikenberry) 154
'limits to sovereignty' thesis 119–20, 121,
 131
Lippmann, Walter 30

Little, R. 39, 42n, 49, 53
'long peace' 8, 30, 89

McCloud, D.G. 190
McFaul, M. 90, 96, 99, 103
Malaysia 101, 102
Mandaville, P. 49
Manning, C. 50, 69n
Mare Liberum 55
Martin, L. 121–2
Mastanduno, M. 45
Mearsheimer, J. 89, 91, 94, 110n, 111n,
 157n; regionalism 167
MERCOSUR 31, 100, 105
Middle East 55, 63, 80, 105–6, 121, 224;
 norm subsidiarity 234, 236
middle powers 37, 148, 228
Mill, John Stuart 33
mimicry 4, 45, 47–8, 55, 68n
Minorities at Risk Project 96
Mittleman, J. 167
Mohammaydia 126
Monroe Doctrine 29, 75, 235
moral cosmopolitanism 6, 35, 149, 185,
 205
Morgan, P. 164, 165
Morgenthau, H. 5, 6, 8, 18n
Moritan, R.G. 95–6
Moshirzadeh, H. 50
multilateralism 13, 141–4, 154–6, 161;
 emerging powers 150–1; hegemonic 9,
 144–8, 157n; institutions and 10, 11;
 old and 'new' 148–50; post-hegemonic
 multilateralism 9, 151–4
Multilateralism Matters (Ruggie) 9, 144–5,
 146, 149, 152, 157n
*Multilateralism Under Challenge? Power,
 International Order, and Structural Change*
 (Newman, Tirman and Thakur) 149
Multilateralism and the United Nations System
 (Cox) 148
multipolarity 5, 7, 30, 31, 154; great
 powers and 98–9; stability 90, 91,
 92, 93, 94, 95; strategic 96–7; see also
 bipolarity; unipolarity
Murphy, A. 173

Nadelmann, E. 185
NAFTA see North American Free Trade
 Agreement
Nakayama, T. 197
NAM see Non-Aligned Movement
Nasser, Gamel Abdel 225, 236
national/regional schools 50–1, 65, 70n
National Security Council (US) 226

National Security Strategy of the United
States (Bush Doctrine) 7, 8, 121, 149;
sovereignty 131, 132, 133*n*
NATO *see* North Atlantic Treaty
Organisation
Nehru, Jawaharlal 12, 30, 34, 64, 80;
collective defence 227, 228–9, 230,
231, 236; norm subsidiarity 218, 239
neo-functionalism 32, 46, 79, 81
neoliberal institutionalism 9, 10,
20*n*, 30, 55; multilateralism 143;
regionalism 78, 79; *see also* institutions
neorealism 5, 7, 8–9, 19*n*, 30, 55;
Africa 63; bipolarity/multipolarity 95,
103, 107; power 98; regionalism 162–
3; stability 91, 92; strategic
multipolarity 96, 98–9; *see also* realism
Network of Excellence on *Global
Governance, Regionalisation and
Regulation: The Role of the EU*
(GARNET) 78, 84*n*
Neumann, I. 173
New International Economic Order
(NIEO) 102
Newly Industrialized Countries of East
Asia 102
Newman, E. 149
'new regionalism' approach 5, 78–9, 84*n*,
172
New York Times 121
NIEO *see* New International Economic
Order
9/11 attacks 7–8, 116, 129–32, 167
Nkrumah, Kwame 225, 236, 237
Non-Aligned Movement (NAM) 31,
101–3, 220, 225, 237, 248–9*n*
non-intervention 55, 64, 75, 101, 116,
184; Africa 236–7; Asia 198–9,
200, 201, 204, 205, 225; collective
defence 229, 230, 235; Latin
America 238; norm subsidiarity
and 222, 238, 239, 248*n*
non-state actors 15
non-Western approaches 1, 2, 4, 18*n*,
51, 68*n*; adequacy of IRT and 44–5,
46, 48–50, 250–1, 253; bipolarity 8;
constructivism 11, 12; English
School 36; false universalism 64–
5; humanising IRT 55–6;
marginalisation 15; national/regional
schools 50–3; reciprocity 37, 38;
relative autonomy 16; sovereignty 27;
university studies 23; Westphalia
system 53–4; *see also* Third World
normative change 13, 14

normative cultures 11–13, 20*n*
norm circulation 13, 14
norm diffusion 129, 217, 238
norm displacement 192, 193, 194*f*
norm entrepreneurs 189, 190, 191*f*, 210*n*
norm localisation 14, 83, 193, 206, 207*n*,
213*n*; agency and 183, 184, 185; Asia
and 186–8, 189, 190, 191, 192, 202–5;
dynamics of 186–90, 191*t*, 192–3, 194*f*;
norm subsidiarity and 218, 219*f*, 234
norms 12, 27, 33–5, 183–5, 205–7;
Cold War 202–5; dynamics of
localisation 186–90, 191*t*, 192–3, 194*f*
norms of Arabism 236
norm subsidiarity 13, 83, 217–18, 239–40,
242*n*; actors and motivations 220–2;
definition 218, 219*f*, 220*f*; effects
of 223–4; Third World 12, 220–2,
234–9
North American Free Trade Agreement
(NAFTA) 100, 101
North Atlantic Treaty Organisation
(NATO) 145, 146, 151–2, 157*n*, 161,
224; colonialism 230
North–South divide 56, 151, 155
Nu, U. 229
Nye, J. 32
Nyhamar, T. 248*n*

OAS *see* Organization of American States
OAU *see* African Union (AU)
O'Brien, R. 148
O'Connor, S. 183
Okakura, Tenshin 76
Olson, W. 47, 250–1
1+4+x distribution of power 160, 166
ontology 56–61
Onuf, N. 47, 250–1
Organization of African Unity (OAU)
see African Union (AU)
organisational culture 185
Organization of American States
(OAS) 75, 76, 105, 235
Organization of Security and Cooperation
in Europe (OSCE) 89, 202
Organization of Unity 76
organised hypocrisy thesis 8, 117, 118,
122, 129, 132; collective defence 230,
234; norm subsidiarity 222
Osborne, M. 187
outsider proponents 190, 196
overlay 160

pacific unions 31
Pakistan 97, 230

Palaez, Emanuel 231
Panikkar, K.M. 74–5, 80
pan-regional movements 127, 164, 166, 235, 253–4; regionalism 75–6, 78
parochialism 66
Philippines 205, 231
Philips, R. 127
philosophy of science 15
Philpott, D. 27
pluralism 57, 58
pluralistic security communities 104–5, 107
polarity *see* bipolarity; multipolarity
political realism 6
Politics among Nations (Morgenthau) 5, 6
positivism 1, 3, 28, 55
post-colonialism 2, 8, 15, 16, 24, 27; Cold War 96; constructivism 47; neocolonialism 146; non-Western approaches 49, 55; regionalism 80; stability and 93; *see also* colonialism
post-hegemonic multilateralism 9, 151–4
post-hegemonic organising 148
power 25–9, 11, 45, 65, 159–60; neorealism 98; regionalism 167, 168*f,* 170–1; resistance to 10, 13, 160–4; *see also* great power
prescriptive norms 185
Price, R. 186
Puchala, D. J. 11, 240
PUPJI *see* General Guide for the Struggle of Jemmah Islamiyah

Qin, Y. 3, 52, 68*n*
Quirino, Elpidio 225

R2P *see* responsibility to protect
Rational Design of International Institutions (RDII) project 177*n*
rationalism 11, 188–9, 192, 238
Ravenhill, J. 104
realism 18–9, 14, 27, 252–3; classical theological writers 61; collective defence 232; Confucianism and 46; great power management 31, 96; idealism and 30; Latin America 68*n*; norm localisation 203, 205; Western dominance 52, 54; *see also* neorealism
'Realism and Geopolitics: World Conquest or World Association?' (Nehru) 30
reciprocity 37–8, 144, 152
reflectivism 3
regimes 78, 130
'regime of truth' 61
'regional flashpoints' 89

regional integration 32, 100, 104
regionalism 49, 10, 63–4, 94–5, 252; Asia 75, 82, 100, 162, 166, 171; autonomy and 168*f,* 169–73; bipolarity 89, 90–1, 98, 99; comparative 81, 82, 83; conflict and order 103–7; definition 83*n*; European Union 78–81; hegemony and 74, 75, 165–8; Latin America 75, 76, 80, 235; multiple and global heritage of 74–8; order and 164–6; post-hegemonic multilateralism 145, 151–4, 155; (re) conceptualising 162–4; structures 160–2; 'two-way Americanisation' 167, 172; universality 66, 76; Western/ non-Western theory and 4–5; world politics 14, 159
Regionalism and World Security (Panikkar) 74–5, 80
regionally-oriented disciplinarists 62–3
regional orders 9–11, 164–6, 176*n*
'regional policemen' 98
regional security complexes (RSCs) 160, 163, 165, 174–5*n,* 176*n*
'regional world' approach 66
Regions and Powers: The Structure of International Security (Buzan and Waever) 159, 174*n*; autonomy 168*f,* 169–173; hegemony 166–8; ordering regions 164–6; power and regions 160–2; (re) conceptualising regions 162–4
religion 57–8, 59
'rendition' 128
resistance: regional powers 170–1, 172–3, 179*n,* 184, 191*f,* 194*f*; norm subsidiarity 221–2, 223
responsibility to protect (R2P) 109, 118, 130–2, 150, 151, 248–9*n*
'revolt against the West' 55
'right intention' 129, 130
Risse, T. 183
rivalries 105–6
Roberts, B. 97–8, 99–100
Romulo, Carlos 230
Ropp, S.C. 183
Rosecrance, R.N. 92, 93, 97
Rosenbaum, H.J. 104
RSCs *see* regional security complexes
Ruggie, R.G. 9, 144–5, 146, 149, 152, 157*n*
Rumsfeld, Donald 123
Rwanda 129

San Francisco Conference (1945) 76
Sbragia, A. 88

Schmitter, Prof. P. 84–5*n*
Scholte, J.A. 148
scientific knowledge 57, 58–61, 62
SCO *see* Shanghai Cooperation
    Organization
SEATO *see* Southeast Asian Treaty
    Organization
securitisation theory 162–3, 173, 176*n*
security communities 10, 20*n*, 32, 33,
    104–5, 165
'security regimes' 29–30
selective sovereignty 7–8, 119–22
'self nature' 60, 61
Sen, A. 55, 66
Shanghai Cooperation Organization
    (SCO) 80
Shani, G. 57*n*
Shaw, T. 102
Siazon, Domingo 205
Sikh Khalsa Panth 57
Sikkink, K. 183, 189, 238
Singapore 34, 51, 203–4
Singer, J.D. 92, 93
Slaughter, A-M. 218
Snauwaert, D.T 131
Snyder, J. 2, 17*n*, 45–6, 52
social construction 52
socialisation 79, 146–7
'solidarist' approach 57
Solomon, R. 198
Sondhi, S. 46
South Africa 80
South America 165
Southeast Asia Collective Defense Treaty
    (1954) 230
Southeast Asian Treaty Organization
    (SEATO) 12, 166, 195, 217,
    224–5; effects of 230–2; long-term
    consequences of resistance to collective
    defence 233–4; origins 225–7;
    perspectives on failure of 232, 233*f*,
    245–6*n*; resistance to collective
    defence 227–9; *see also* Asia; Association
    of Southeast Asian Nations (ASEAN)
South Pacific 174*n*
sovereignty 4, 26, 27–9, 53, 116–19, 134*n*;
    collective defence 229, 235; emerging
    powers 151; integration and 81;
    limits to 119–20, 121, 131; post-9/11
    sovereignty 7–8, 129–32; regionalism 64;
    selective sovereignty 7–8, 119–22;
    Westphalia and Caliphobia 55, 122–3,
    124*f*, 125–8, 134*n*
Sovereignty: Organized Hypocrisy (Krasner) 8
Soviet Union 95, 97, 190

Spykman, Nicholas 30
stability 7, 10, 30; bipolarity and 91,
    92, 93, 94; material power 8, 13;
    polarity and 90, 103, 107, 252; Third
    World 90–1, 93, 94, 95, 99, 103
'standard of civilization' criteria 38, 53,
    70*n*, 221, 252–3
state death 127
'store consciousness' 60, 61
structural realism *see* neorealism
'subaltern constructivism' 24, 240
superpowers *see* great powers
Surin, Pitsuwan 198–9, 200, 201, 204,
    205, 214*n*
Syed Hamid Albar 199

Tadjkbhash, S. 56
Tagore, Rabindranath 76
Tainxia ('all under heaven') 52
Taliban 120, 125–6, 127
Taylor, B. 167
technocraticism 64
Telhami, S. 127
territorial integrity norm 127
Thailand 123, 195, 203, 205; norm
    subsidiarity 224, 230, 231, 233, 246*n*
Thakur, R. 149
Theory of International Politics (Waltz) 7, 19*n*
Third World 242*n*; agency 239–40;
    democratisation 99–100; great power
    intervention 7–8, 134*n*; institutions 9,
    55; international order and 91 4;
    military build-up 96–7, 98, 105;
    New World Disorder 89; norm
    subsidiarity 12, 220–2, 234–9; post-
    Cold War era 39, 94–103, 107, 224–5;
    regionalism 75, 90; sovereignty 28;
    stability-instability 90–1, 93, 94, 95, 99,
    103; trends in conflict 108–10, 111*n*;
    see also non-Western approaches
Tickner, A. 46, 49, 55
'Time for Initiative, A' (Association of
    Southeast Asian Nations (ASEAN)
    Institutes of Strategic and International
    Studies) 196
Tirman, J. 149
transactionalism 81, 84*n*
transnational area studies 62–3
transnational civil society 9;
    multilateralism 141, 142, 143, 145, 149,
    155; regionalism 172
Treaty of Amity and Cooperation
    (Association of Southeast Asian
    Nations) 197
Tyler, W.G. 104

uncertainty 94–5
unconditional regime legitimacy 220
unipolarity 7, 154, 169; *see also* bipolarity;
  multipolarity
United Nations (UN) 30, 64, 109, 150,
  195; Cold War 234; drafting of
  Charter 76–7, 218, 221–2, 227, 230,
  235–6; High-Level Panel on Threats,
  Challenges and Change 131–2, 136*n*
United Nations University (UNU) 78
United States 3, 5, 8;
  Americanocentrism 9, 11, 23, 153,
  154, 155; Anti-Americanism 132,
  172; collective defence 224, 225–6,
  232; cooperative security 198,
  203, 204; multilateralism 145–6,
  149–50; regionalism 166, 167, 170;
  sovereignty 116–17, 119–20, 128;
  'two-way Americanisation' 167, 172
universality 14, 53–4, 252–3; international
  society 70–1*n*; norm localisation 191;
  regionalism 66, 76; religion and 57–8;
  Western dominance 25–6, 32, 35, 36
University of British Columbia 108–10
University of Chicago 66
unstructured regions 160
upgrading 192
uti possidetis juris (honouring inherited
  boundaries) 235, 237, 238

Vale, P. 52, 57
values 27, 33–5, 39
Vandenberg, Senator Arthur 76–7, 236
Van Leur, J. 187, 207*n*
Verba, S. 56, 72*n*
Vietnam 101, 227

Waever, O. 49, 159, 160, 161, 174*n*; *see
  also Regions and Powers: The Structure of
  International Security*
Walt, S. 25–6, 63
Waltz, K.N. 7, 19*n*, 30, 31, 63, 110*n*;
  stability 91, 92, 93, 94, 95, 108
war: declining economic utility 109
warlordism 63
War on Terror 67–8, 9, 109, 116,
  117–18; disorganised hypocrisy
  129–32; multilateralism 155; selective
  sovereignty 119–22; Westphalia and
  Caliphobia 122–3, 124*f*, 125–8
Watson, A. 36, 38, 39, 42*n*, 50;
  international systems 53
weak states 11, 12, 100, 106, 142,

166; collective defence 232,
  233; multilateralism 147; norm
  subsidiarity 220–1, 222, 223
weapons of mass destruction 97–8, 105,
  106, 121, 122, 131
Weber, M. 57
Weiner, A. 77
Wendt, A. 54, 71*n*
Western dominance 1–2, 3, 4, 12;
  international relations theory and 23,
  24, 25–7, 39; key concepts 14–15;
  rest of the world and 47, 48–50, 54;
  universality 63
'Western values in international relations'
  (Wight) 33, 34, 35, 39
Westphalia 27, 29, 63, 122–3, 124*f*,
  125–8; emerging powers 151; norm
  subsidiarity 222; sovereignty 117,
  118, 122–3, 124*f*, 125–8, 134*n*;
  universality 53–4
Wheatley, P. 192, 193
Wheeler, N. 130
'Why is there no Non- Western
  IR Theory?' project (Buzan and
  Acharya) 23–4, 45
Wight, M. 33, 34, 35, 39
Williams, Henry Sylvester 76
Williams, M. 148
Wilson, Charles 228
Wiseman, G. 190
Wolters, O.W. 187, 188, 192, 209*n*, 211*n*
World Bank 64, 97
'worldly knowledge' 57, 61
world politics 20*n*, 45, 159–60, 173–4;
  localisation 14; (re) conceptualising
  regions 162–4; regional order 14,
  164–6; regional structures 160–2
*World of Regions: Asia and Europe in the
  American Imperium* (Katzenstein) 159,
  174*n*; autonomy 168*f*, 169–73;
  hegemony 166–8; ordering
  regions 164–6; power and
  regions 160–2; (re) conceptualising
  regions 162–4; *see also* Katzenstein, P.J.
World Systems theory 71*n*

Yogacara (philosophy) 60

Zhang, Y. 50
Zone of Peace, Freedom and Neutrality
  (ZOPFAN) 171, 195, 197, 198, 200,
  201–2
Zurn, M. 238